Educational Citizenship
and Independent Learning

Children in Charge series

Children in Charge
The Child's Right to a Fair Hearing
Edited by Mary John
ISBN 1 85302 386 X
Children in Charge 1

Children in Our Charge
The Child's Right to Resources
Edited by Mary John
ISBN 1 85302 369 8
Children in Charge 2

A Charge Against Society
The Child's Right to Protection
Edited by Mary John
ISBN 1 85302 411 2
Children in Charge 3

The Participation Rights of the Child
Rights and Responsibilities in Family and Society
Målfrid Grude Flekkøy and Natalie Hevener Kaufman
ISBN 1 85302 489 9 hb
ISBN 1 85302 490 2 pb
Children in Charge 4

Children as Citizens
Education for Participation
Edited by Cathie Holden and Nick Clough
ISBN 1 85302 566 6
Children in Charge 5

Children in Charge 6

Educational Citizenship and Independent Learning

Rhys Griffith

Jessica Kingsley Publishers
London and Philadelphia

The right of Rhys Griffith to be identified as author of this work has been asserted by him in accordance with the Copyright, Designs and Patents Act 1988.

First published in the United Kingdom in 1998 by
Jessica Kingsley Publishers Ltd
116 Pentonville Road
London N1 9JB, England
and
325 Chestnut Street
Philadelphia, PA 19106, U S A

Copyright © 1998 Rhys Griffith

Library of Congress Cataloging in Publication Data
A CIP catalogue record for this book is available from the Library of Congress

British Library Cataloguing in Publication Data
Educational citizenship and independent learning
1. Citizenship 2. Citizenship - Study and teaching
I. Title
323.6'071

ISBN 1 85302 611 5

Printed and Bound in Great Britain by
Athenaeum Press, Gateshead, Tyne & Wear

Contents

List of Figures 6

List of Tables 6

Acknowledgements 7

Definitions and Descriptions 8

Foreword 9

1. A Learning Process 13

2. Education and Citizenship 26

3. Research Method and Procedure 63

4. Dependent Learning 113

5. Independent Learning 143

6. The Classroom Application of
the Twelve Factors of Independent Learning 183

7. State Education in the UK
and Educational Citizenship 218

Appendices 241

References 275

Index 283

List of figures

3.1 Description of the research illustrating the multi-faceted and multi-perspective data collection of the non-intervention and intervention aspects of the fieldwork   64

3.2 The critical research spiral of the fieldwork   65

3.3 Data collection methods used during the circumspection stage of the intervention research (Sep 1988 – Dec 1989)   71

3.4 Data collection methods used during the pre-emption stage of the intervention research (Jan 1990 – Dec 1990)   72

3.5 Data collection methods used during the control stage of the intervention research (Jan 1991 – Sep 1992)   73

4.1 Bar graph showing the distribution of the 1500 minutes of Josie's timetabled week   118

4.2 Bar graph showing the distribution of the 1500 minutes of Emily's timetabled week   131

5.1 The interaction of pupils, groups of pupils, classes and schools during the 'Minorities' cross-curricular, cross-phase project for 9–13-year-olds (October 1989 – July 1990)   150

5.2 Interactions intended to promote collaborative groupwork, co-operative groupwork and the individual responsibility of pupils during the 'Minorities' cross-curricular, cross-phase project (October 1989 – July 1990)   151

List of tables

3.1 Methods of data collection   89

4.1 The distribution of the 1500 minutes of Josie's timetabled week   118

4.2 Pupils' contributions to whole class discussion Keystage 3   119

4.3 Contributions to whole class discussion by percentage of the class population   120

4.4 The distribution of the 1500 minutes of Emily's timetabled week   131

4.5 Pupils' contributions to whole class discussion Keystage 4   132

4.6 Contributions to whole class discussion by percentage of the class population   133

5.1 Details of schools involved in the Europeans cross-curricular independent learning project   154

5.2 Sources of data collection   181

Acknowledgements

There are many people to thank for their help in producing this book. I would like to thank colleagues I met in various institutions. Ideas were formed and much writing was done at these places or as a result of these meetings. Therefore, I am grateful to students at Leeds and Exeter universities; NATE Conference members at the universities of Southampton, York, Swansea, Manchester and Plymouth; members of the the NATE Council; the staff of the Multicultural Centre, Leicester; delegates and lecturers at Language in the National Curriculum, National Curriculum Assessment and Her Majesty's Inspectorate courses across the UK; the personnel of regional CSE, GCE and GCSE examination boards; advisers and advisory teachers from many local education authorities; representatives of national political parties. In particular, a toast to the long-term support of redoubtable allies: Big Al, Ali, Dave, Pat and Pete. No words can properly convey my debt of gratitude to the thousands of pupils, parents and teachers who were involved in the research for this book (but I try in the Foreword). Thanks to my parents: Dad, for conversations over so many years about politics and education and Mum, for putting up with them.

Definitions and descriptions

For the purposes of this book, the following phrases have the following meanings:

Global Citizenship: a construct of citizenship considered to be appropriate to the third millennium. The global citizen is not merely aware of her rights but able and desirous to act upon them. She is of an autonomous and inquiring critical disposition but her decisions and actions are tempered by an ethical concern for social justice and the dignity of humankind. She is, therefore, able, through her actions, to control and enhance 'the trajectory of the self' through life whilst contributing to the commonweal, the public welfare, with a sense of civic duty to replenish society.

Educational Citizenship: a concept of education based upon the premise that similarities between the qualities of the educated person and the global citizen indicate a symbiotic relationship between education and global citizenship. From this premise it is argued that pupils of all ages should be accorded citizens' rights throughout their education, both to prepare them for full and active democratic citizenship and to improve the educational provision of their state schooling.

Independent Learning: the pedagogical construct intended to translate a policy of educational citizenship into effective practice. Pupils have the independence to choose how they will learn and, through the development of the qualities of global citizenship, have the opportunity to learn to become independent in their making of decisions, both as pupils and as citizens.

Dependent Learning: the pedagogical construct in which pupils are dependent upon others for their learning and, through the suppression of the qualities of global citizenship, learn to become dependent upon the decisions of others, both as pupils and as citizens.

Foreword

This is a book that is critical of the present National Curriculum, arguing that its emphasis upon decontextualised 'factual' knowledge rather than socially placed learning, its attendant crude methods of assessment and its promulgated didactic pedagogy is antithetical to the development of an educated citizenry.

This book is based upon my experiences as a teacher, a citizen and an educational researcher. The text is an amalgamation of these experiences: reflections upon – and examples from – my own practice as a teacher, personal opinions about the nature of citizenship and education tested against literary sources and the presentation and discussion of findings from fieldwork research for my doctoral thesis.

My purpose in writing it is to examine the role of a state-maintained liberal educational system in preparing pupils for citizenship in a post-modern democratic society, principally the United Kingdom. In the light of the findings of a five-year fieldwork study undertaken in all the secondary schools of one local education authority, the rhetoric and the reality of empowerment, as an aim of the educational process that claims to produce the citizens of tomorrow, are questioned.

Classroom observation of the National Curriculum, as typically presented to pupils in the study LEA, indicates that its content-laden syllabi and concomitant dependence on a didactic transmission of knowledge is not effective in developing attributes of citizenship that the literature suggests will be appropriate to the next century. This conclusion is contrasted with the findings of action research in which the National Curriculum is used as a vehicle for the explicit promotion of likely attributes of active citizenship for the early part of the third millennium.

The dominant theme I pursue is that the concept of the educated person is coterminous with that of the critically reflective, morally autonomous and socially active citizen and that a child's education and her citizenship are enhanced when, as a pupil, she has the rights of a citizen. A major section of the research relied for its primary data upon the opinions of pupils of both sexes who were involved in action research projects in which they were treated as citizens. During these projects, pupils chose their own curriculum, pedagogy and partners. A primary concern of the research was to find ways in which pupils could reflect both upon their experiences and upon concepts that they may not have previously articulated, and then to voice their opinions.

Chapter One is autobiographical and tells of my own developing interest in democratic teaching and learning styles.

Chapter Two outlines various historical interpretations of the concept of citizenship. I suggest that a contemporary understanding of citizenship in the United Kingdom is confused and in a state of flux. The self-interest of government in promoting a particular view of citizenship through the state educational system is examined. A critique of present-day practices in education for citizenship in the state-maintained educational system of the UK is offered.

A construct of global citizenship that transcends traditional criteria of citizenship is advanced. I argue that the characteristics of the global citizen also typify those of the educated person. This perceived synthesis of education and citizenship is described as educational citizenship and the implementation of a programme of educational citizenship via its concomitant pedagogy, independent learning, is discussed. Classroom practices associated with liberal, progressive and libertarian philosophies of education within state schools that are likely to suppress the development of educational citizenship are identified and analysed. These practices are named as the three factors of dependent learning.

Chapter Three attempts to record the method and practice of the fieldwork research and to locate that research within the critical paradigm. An account is given of the development of clear criteria that were used to unify different aspects of the research, its attendant data-collection and their analysis. These criteria are named as the twelve factors of independent learning. Consideration is given to the appropriateness of various methods of research with the disempowered. The fieldwork, spanning five years and involving 97 educational establishments in one shire LEA, is summarised, a timetable of the research is given and the relationship between the researcher and the research partners is described. Whilst this relationship was pivotal to the success of the research programme, within the text I sometimes refer to 'my research'. This does not imply any self-aggrandisement on my part, nor should it be inferred that I am downgrading the contribution of others within the research partnership. But I was the director of the research, I was responsible for the data collection and its analysis, and the findings drawn from the data analysis are mine alone. In using the term 'my research' I am signalling that the conclusions that I reached and the comments and criticisms that I make are my personal responsibility.

Chapter Four reports the findings of non-intervention research undertaken between 1988 and 1993 in the Greenshire LEA, during which time lessons were observed in 97 primary, secondary, tertiary and special schools. The central conclusion is that the normal presentation and content of the National Curriculum is neither democratic nor educative and is regarded negatively by pupils.

Chapter Five reports the findings of intervention research undertaken between 1988 and 1992 in the Greenshire LEA, during which time independent learning projects, intended to develop the qualities of the global citizen, were observed in 58 primary and secondary schools. The central conclusion is that pupils, teachers, parents and other observers responded positively to independent learning projects, which they described as novel, enjoyable, educational and challenging.

Chapter Six considers in detail how the twelve factors of independent learning may be introduced to pupils so that a climate of educational citizenship is created and sustained within schools. Exemplar material is offered from a range of projects that encompassed the age and ability range of the National Curriculum and all its subjects.

Chapter Seven considers why the existing cultural climate in the state educational system of the United Kingdom legislates against educational citizenship whilst, at the same time, appearing to embrace it. The nature of power is a pivotal concept to this examination and the rhetoric of empowerment, as an aim of the educational process that claims to produce the citizens of tomorrow, is questioned. Distinctions are drawn between invested and divested power, and of the transfer and the transformation of power.

In short, this book seeks to explain why democracy is alien to state schools in the UK, to argue that both education and citizenship will deteriorate unless democratic principles and practices are introduced to schools and to suggest how such principles (educational citizenship) and practices (independent learning) may be introduced.

A note on literary style. The singular female pronoun and its possessive form are used throughout the text when referring to the citizen, the pupil or the teacher – for example:

> 'The global citizen is not merely aware of her rights but able and desirous to act upon them…'

> '…indoctrination can take place without the teacher being aware of it. She may not intend to indoctrinate – might very well strongly deny that she does indoctrinate – but if her method of teaching…'

I find the sight of 's/he' ugly and the use of 'his or her' or 'her or his' unrhythmic. Although this can be overcome by transposing sentences into the plural and using 'they' and 'their', a definition, such as that of the global citizen, describes a paradigm, a perfect example, that requires the use of the singular to avoid the sense of totalitarian imperative that the plural seems to imply: 'Global citizens are…'

The local education authority in which the fieldwork took place, a shire LEA in the south-west of the United Kingdom, is referred to as 'the study LEA' or 'Greenshire'. All proper nouns that refer to schools and people within the study LEA, apart from the author's name, are pseudonyms.

I record my thanks to the 7000 pupils and 250 teachers who made this book possible by welcoming me into their classrooms. They are not the focus of the negative comments that I make about contemporary education. My criticisms concern the construction and constitution of the present National Curriculum, but not those pupils, teachers and school managers upon whom a statutory curriculum has been imposed. During the five years of the research programme I never met a teacher who was not trying to do the best for her pupils. I hope that this book may play some small part in improving the working conditions of pupils and teachers. This can only happen if a realistic account is given of the actual practice in classrooms that the National Curriculum requires. Perhaps too much of the discussion about the National Curriculum has been at philosophical, theoretical and administrative levels and attention has not been given to what happens once the demands and implications of a statutory curriculum percolate into the living experience of British pupils.

Finally, may I thank the LEA in whose employ I worked. Under the present political climate, I do not believe that it would be possible to conduct the scale of research into educational citizenship that forms the basis for this book.

Rhys Griffith
October 1996

CHAPTER ONE

A Learning Process

INTRODUCTION

My own understanding of educational citizenship and independent learning developed over a period of years, and it was through a shared experience of successive approximation with pupils and colleagues that I clarified ideas. It was a pragmatic and meandering process. No doubt similar, or more direct and informed, journeys were being made by teachers of all subjects throughout the country who were generally interested in the democratisation of state schooling (educational citizenship) and particularly interested in the classroom consequences of such a change (independent learning). Thus, although such changes are neither exclusive to British schools nor to the time period that this personal account spans, it is not improbable that the following short ethnographic text reflects a wider process of educational change amongst teachers in British state schools during the last twenty years.

THE DIDACTIC AUTHORITARIAN
(SEPTEMBER 1975 – MARCH 1979)

I started teaching at Saltair Comprehensive School in Greenshire in 1975, at a time when shire secondary schools were still representative of a male-dominated society of didactic authority. For the next three years I was a pretty fair imitation of the kind of teacher that I'd had as a pupil, and the kind of teacher who appeared to command respect in schools at that time. Such teachers were invariably men, always wore ties, generally suits or a combination referred to as 'slacks and sports jacket', were strict but had a sense of humour, called pupils by their surnames and were called 'Sir' by their pupils. They maintained class discipline by psychological manipulation and physical presence, but the abuse common a decade earlier (clips around the head, pulling the hair close to ears, pinching elbows) was regarded with contempt by these teachers. They rarely raised their voices in anger and never really lost their tempers.

We were 'good' teachers, popular with parents and pupils alike. Pupils would say: 'He knows how to keep control', 'Griffy doesn't let you get away with anything', 'You can have a laugh with him, but then you've got to get on with your work', 'He gives you hell if you don't get your homework in on time',

'Even the boys don't mess around in his lessons', 'He makes you get on with it', 'He's a good laugh'.

After passing my probationary year I was promoted to second-in-department (English) at Saltair. Two-and-a-half years later I was appointed head of English in a small secondary modern school in the far west of the county, Carnmore School, taking up the post six months later in September 1979. In 1980 Carnmore had its first intake of comprehensive pupils.

In the sub-culture to which I belonged until about 1982, teachers didn't read anything on educational theory and certainly didn't go on courses – they were for 'trendies', we got on with the job – so there is no event, no person, nothing I read, not a course I went on that I could describe as a 'Pauline conversion' to educational citizenship and independent learning. But from the day of my appointment as head of English at Carnmore on 22 March 1979, just after my 28th birthday, I began to think about what I was doing in a way that I hadn't before – probably because the buck had never stopped at my desk until then.

On my return to Saltair, after my interview at Carnmore, I had nearly six months before I took up my new position as head of department – what I thought of then as *my* department. For the last few weeks of that spring term, as Saltair classes sat stolidly before me in unbidden but required silence, doing any daft exercise I put in front of them, I began to admit to myself the hitherto smothered acknowledgement of the futility of what I was doing and the sham that I was as a teacher.

For although my exam results were good (funny that, my, not the pupils' results), I didn't really believe 'my' pupils were learning anything at all about language. They were learning tricks to impress examiners but there was nothing that was going to stay with them, that was going to move them to go on, to engage with language after they'd left their last English lesson. They had virtually no choice at all in what they did. Furthermore, the concept of language in which they were being inculcated was culturally limited and socially damaging. A division was seen between language and literature, and the very notion of literature was confused and riddled with class values.

There was a curious dissonance between the department's adults-needs driven educational aims and its cultural heritage curriculum. Language seemed to have two schizophrenic functions: first, to get the pupil, as school-leaver, a job by passing exams and writing letters of application, second, and quite separately and for no given reason, to encourage the pupil, as artist, to mimic published literature by writing poems, stories and descriptions. It was a very hollow mimicry; writers aren't told when to write and what to write and then marked out of ten.

Language was all about writing. Of course pupils read things, but only to write about them afterwards, either in comprehension exercises or essays. The criteria for good writing were neatness, punctuation and spelling and, for the top sets, simile and metaphor (all year groups were taught in ability sets).

Talk was not properly acknowledged as a language skill. Non-print media, in all their forms, were regarded as anti-literature. All work was an individual response to a teacher-directed task; collaboration would have been censured as a form of cheating. Assessment and response were limited to numerical or alphabetical grades based on a national normative reference. All marking was undertaken privately by the teacher – no negotiation, no discussion, scant regard for the writer's purpose or effort. Drafting was not valued in the assessment. There was no thought of any audience other than the marker: teacher and, later, anonymous examiner.

The choice of texts – belonging exclusively to a restricted literary canon – was made solely by the teacher and further limited to titles allocated to different age and ability groups depending on what was in the stock-cupboard. Most of the novels, plays and anthologies were outdated and inappropriate; many of them were classist, sexist and racist. These texts were read aloud around the class, six books a year, one each half-term, the books distributed at the start and collected at the end of the lesson. All language work, irrespective of the different ability sets in which pupils were grouped, came from a series of books edited by a man called Mansfield: Mansfield 1 for the first year, Mansfield 2 for the second year, and so on. A chapter every fortnight. Each chapter followed the same format: an extract from some sub-Leavisite text, a comprehension exercise on the text, a stylistic exercise based on tropes within the text, grammar and spelling exercises, and a list of essay titles.

The hierarchy of power, based upon different forms of language, could clearly be seen in the different public exams that pupils took. Set 1 took GCE Language and Literature examinations. Sets 2 and 3 took CSE Language and Literature examinations. Sets 4 and 5 took CSE Language, but no literature exam. Set 6 was the 'remedial' class and its members left school at Easter without taking any exams. Therefore, half the pupils in their final school year were denied the chance to take a literature exam, even though their entire secondary English experience had been literature-based.

We weren't bad teachers, not wilfully so. We weren't lazy teachers – we worked hard to entertain malleable pupils and tried to make lessons as interesting as was possible, given the curriculum we were offering. The ethos of the department was kindly and supportive. Results were well above the national average. Relationships with pupils and parents were good. I very much admired the professionalism of my head of department. We weren't particularly old-fashioned in our pedagogical approach – at the time, virtually every English teacher in Greenshire taught in this way. (Two decades later, there are still those that do.)

Where we failed ourselves and our pupils was in our complacency. We prided ourselves as subject specialists but we did not question our view of an English curriculum or the way in which it was presented to pupils. And we certainly didn't consider that, as educators, we had any wider responsibilities or that our teaching styles might have implications upon the personal and social development of pupils. Our perspective was blinkered so that we saw only an adults-needs purpose to our work: we trained pupils to pass exams so that they could get jobs. Lip-service may have been paid to the esoteric idea that the sum of a pupil's school experiences should coalesce to form some fuller sense of education, but there would have been a sneer on those lips. It was teachers like us who hid the hidden curriculum.

The last term, the summer term, at Saltair, I abandoned Mansfield and that term's two set readers. Mostly, we read silently, individually, any book each person had brought in, including myself. We usually did that for five of the six weekly lessons and during the other one we went to the library and pupils did projects of their own choice. It wasn't always just copying chunks out of books, the idea was that each project was about something they were interested in and knew something about – football, hamsters, tractors, horses – and that they'd find out more and then write about it. Some pupils asked if they could also write stories or poems and, because I couldn't think why they shouldn't, I let them. The increase in writing began to invade the reading lessons, but as long as they were quiet I didn't mind. Some pupils came and asked me if they could do a joint project with a friend, but I normally didn't let them because I thought it would be too noisy and they wouldn't do any 'work'. Sometimes we went for walks to places that pupils wanted to take us to: beach, woods, nearby fields.

In the event it was a pleasant way to pass a term in a school in which I had enough of an orthodox reputation to deflect any criticism from staff. And in any case, I was leaving.

THE DIDACTIC ENTERTAINER (SEPTEMBER 1979 – JULY 1983)

When I started at Carnmore there was only one other full-time English teacher. Tamara was resistant to change but said, quite fairly, 'I'll try and do what you want if you make changes in your own lessons first and show me that they work'. I knew I was not going to use a set text, either language or literature, but I didn't really know what I was going to do instead. In retrospect, I don't think that I had given any real consideration to changing the curriculum or its presentation. I suppose what I intended to change was the *quality* of curriculum presentation, for I still saw the teacher as having the sole responsibility for the learning process. For a while I used an ancient Banda to duplicate worksheets, but as these worksheets contained vocabulary, punctuation and spelling exercises copied from a series of English textbooks edited by the Mansfield progenitor Ronald Rideout, there didn't seem much point. Might just as well use Ronnie himself, there were millions of copies of him in dusty cupboards in every English room.

What there also was was one of the earliest video-recorders, something about the size of a refrigerator, on a creaking trolley that could be wheeled around the school. Bolted to the top of the trolley was a huge old television with doors that locked across the screen. This was before the advent of domestic video-recorders and video-hire libraries, so pupils enjoyed a nourishing diet of Open University and Schools' programmes. But that was better – a lot better – than nothing, nothing being Ronald Rideout. Each English class was soon allocated one video lesson a week. That still left five more lessons to be filled with something interesting.

Pupils liked drama. It was 'better than schoolwork'. I decided to fill up one more of the English lessons as a drama lesson, even though there were no facilities and I had never taught drama. This left four lessons. The last term at Saltair had been enjoyed by myself and the pupils, hence a lesson for silent, personal-choice reading was introduced and also a lesson for self-chosen project work. Two lessons a week were left, on the timetable at least, to the traditional skills that governors, press, parents and indeed pupils felt were so important: spelling, punctuation and grammar.

In practice, of course, these arbitrary and artificial divisions in the curriculum merged, blended and blurred as lessons began to connect with each other, as a stimulus from the video was picked up in drama and carried into project work or became the spur for a pupil's homework, or a book that a pupil was reading and had recommended in group discussion was illuminated to the class by a video excerpt from the film of the book, or a project was started after watching a video documentary on some social issue or other.

Four other full-time members of the English department were appointed as the school expanded and new facilities and resources were gained: an English tutorial room, a drama studio, a teaching library, video and audio recorders and cameras, word-processors. Soon we were running a twice-weekly paperback bookshop, quickly boosted by a book-swap scheme. The library was open every lunchtime and after school and used by every class during lessons. A one-term's course in library retrieval skills was launched and all pupils were also enrolled at the conveniently adjacent public library and permission was gained for them to visit this library individually, or in pairs or small groups, during English lesson-time. A pupils' performing arts club presented drama, poetry, mime and debate each Friday lunchtime (a great audience for work developed in lessons) and a half-termly magazine was published and sold both in school and at the local newsagents. Pupils wrote a monthly column on school affairs for the district newspaper. A large-scale drama production took place each Christmas and other presentations were made throughout the year. We went on trips and speakers came in.

In 1982, 57 per cent of the 5th Year pupils, a secondary modern cohort, gained 'O' level equivalent passes in English, against a south-west counties' comprehensive school average of 12.8 per cent.

I have been candid about the pragmatic manner in which an off-the-shelf English curriculum was assembled, impelled by an intuitive reaction against my experience of mainstream English practice at the time. To some extent this does an injustice to the department and the four other teachers who were appointed during this period, for a strong case can be made for the diversity and flexibility of that curriculum and its relevance to new trends in English, such as media education, the use of technology, oracy and a movement away from decontextualised exercises. Certainly, a eudemonic test would have shown that the English curriculum was well received and well regarded by pupils – not altogether surprising as four of the six weekly lessons (video, drama, personal reading and personal project work) were timetabled as a response to the expressed desires of Carnmore pupils and the classroom experience of Saltair pupils. What I will not pretend is that these innovations were impelled – at least on my part – by a coherent philosophy of education.

There was no doubt that English was a popular subject and that lessons were lively, but as a department we came to recognise that the changes were cosmetic, giving an impression of newness, when, in fact, all that we had really done was to bring energy to an antiquated curriculum and its traditional presentation. From 1983, in a series of weekly departmental meetings, we began to discuss our whole concept of language development. This discussion soon broadened to an examination of our role as educators, and it was from these meetings that an embryonic philosophy of educational citizenship evolved.

THE CARER (SEPTEMBER 1983 – JULY 1986)

With growing unemployment, the utilitarian view of education as a means to a job had become untenable. The early to mid-1980s was a time when unemployment – particularly youth unemployment – was rising and initiatives such as FE vocational courses or youth training schemes had yet to provide a sanitised alternative to the dole. In the isolated, working-class, rural community of Carnmore, one of the keenest criteria of self-esteem was employment, but the traditional industries of farming, fishing and mining were all in decline and what few jobs were available tended to be gender-stereotypical. The opportunity for further education was restricted to Poltewan Technical College, a 60-mile round trip for which there was no direct public transport. For many pupils, particularly those in the last secondary modern cohort at Carnmore (1984), the only school-leaving option was 'signing on'. Those pupils who had gained five CSE Grade 1 passes and might have hoped to pursue higher education courses were faced with a different stumbling-block: the local Sixth Form College, which at the time only offered 'A' level courses, and insisted that they spent a year taking GCE 'O' levels before they could be considered for 'A' level courses. Faced with a year without economic support and studying subjects for which they had already earned an 'O' level equivalent grade, many pupils abandoned their plans for higher education and were reunited with their erstwhile classmates in the local DSS office.

Whilst we couldn't create jobs for pupils, we felt that we might be able to do something to protect or restore pupils' self-esteem. We could at least open their eyes to why there were no jobs, encourage them to take an interest in the world and their role in it, and to stand up for their rights – if only, to start with, by showing them how to fill in a claims form with defiance rather than subservience. We wanted these young people to value themselves as human beings, not to see themselves as the inadequate victims of an impenetrable system. From the comfortable vantage point of hindsight, one might say that we encouraged pupils to act upon their rights as citizens.

These vague and unstructured statements of intention (which, nevertheless, contained the seeds of what would later become the more considered principles of educational citizenship) began to permeate classroom practice. It is hard for people to value themselves when they appear to be failing, so, as a department, we began to find more sensitive forms of assessment and to 'confess the positive' as the Wesleyan phrase has it. If pupils weren't that keen on writing, we encouraged them to express themselves orally and pupils usually talked about the real world rather than the imaginary world of literature. And so, as well as our own parochial concern for the pupils, a wider element of social concern began to pervade lessons with pupils initiating discussions on various topical issues of interest to them. Impelled by the talk of the pupils, the content and structure of lessons altered. The atmosphere of lessons was changing too: more relaxed, more shared experiences, less didactic teaching. We were learning to talk with pupils, not just to them. Pupils' talk was real, flowing from a genuine need rather than as a decontextualised exercise. Pupils developed a greater sense of audience and realised that a good talker needs listening skills. As pupils became more aware of how language can be used to manipulate and control, they practised the use of the spoken word to influence others. They enjoyed using tone of voice, gesture and facial expression as an informed part of their communication, and interpreting body language.

This was a time of empowerment and transformation as pupils and teachers explored new roles and developed new forms of trust in each other. Some time later I would read a phrase that describes this process in both its most literal and more figurative senses: 'the voicing of the silenced' (Lincoln 1993, p.30). What I would add to Lincoln's comments is that the voicing of the silenced, encouraged by the divesting of power from teachers to pupils, empowered both parties – teachers and pupils expressed a new sense of purpose and confidence.

Pupils were involved in the choice of reading texts, either as individuals, small groups or whole classes, and a wider view was taken of literature so that pupils had access to the whole range of texts. Approaches to written work became more varied: collaborative writing in groups of various sizes; different ways of sharing the end products, such as performance, poster presentation, group readings; free choices of subject and genre. As much as possible, assessment took place in discussion with the pupil and self-assessment and peer-assessment were encouraged. What we were trying to enable pupils to achieve was made clear to them. We negotiated their education with them and encouraged pupils to measure and to take responsibility for their progress. We stressed as resources the pupils' own experiences, which pupils themselves often ignored or under-valued. We developed a greater involvement with the community by inviting local speakers and moving out of the classroom into the local environment. We gave greater consideration to the layout of the workplace: plants in classrooms, bean-bags in the teaching library, soft areas, reading-places, writing-places, display areas, resources, the use of other learning spaces – corridors, halls, marking-rooms, empty rooms, playing-fields, public and school libraries.

All of these changes in teaching and learning styles contributed to a *zeitgeist* of an early form of educational citizenship, characterised during lessons by a courteous relationship between pupil and teacher that encouraged the inquiring voice of the pupil to express itself and that regarded everyone involved in the learning experience as of equal status. Two notable practical effects of this classroom ethos were that pupils' work became more individualised and there was a movement away from the use of literary texts as a stimulus towards non-literary social texts such as newspapers, magazines and video-recordings – the change in philosophy towards educational citizenship was initiating a change in pedagogy towards independent learning. Lincoln's phrase is pertinent here too, for the move towards a more democratic classroom and a more pupil-centred approach to learning was also a movement away from the coded language of institutional authority (teachers' instructions, text-book, literature) towards the more familiar language modes of the pupils (negotiation, conversation, media-texts). Voicing was enabled by giving status to the metalanguage of the silenced.

THE LEARNING PARTNER (SEPTEMBER 1986 – DECEMBER 1988)

We capitalised on our growing experience of educational citizenship with the introduction of the GCSE examination in 1986, when we were able to offer a curriculum to all pupils based on their own choices. All pupils could choose to take Theatre Arts or Literature as a second GCSE examination within their GCSE English studies. All pupils could choose Media Education as a GCSE option. For their English GCSE course, pupils chose one of four modules each half-term for five terms, each module tutored by a different member of the department. (This had the effect that pupils selected their own teachers and could change them on a half-termly basis). Individual-needs pupils had the same choices as all other pupils and worked in their own chosen mainstream groups.

Each pupil was given a resource pack for every module, plus a bibliography, videography and directory of addresses and contacts, to enable individual and collaborative research and self-directed study. All teaching groups were mixed-ability. All four of the GCSE examinations (English, Literature, Media Education and Theatre Arts) were based on coursework and oral and practical assessment. There were no timed, written examinations. All GCSE assessment was undertaken within the English department, with the pupils grading their own work and then choosing a teacher with whom to negotiate a validation. Pupils were expected to complete three coursework assignments (each of about 400 words) each term – that is, one or two assignments for each module. Evidence of any other work was not required. Pupils could choose from such modules as 'Outsiders', 'Knowing Yourself', 'The Purpose of Education', 'Taking Risks', 'Heroes and Heroines', 'Prejudice', 'Relationships', 'Authority and Freedom'.

These modules were developed by teachers to meet the interests of pupils, as expressed during 'The Carer' period. In this way, the department was reacting to the educational and citizenship needs that pupils had identified for themselves, rather than predicting those needs. In effect, we were responding to the voicing of the previously silenced. As this system developed, individuals or small groups of pupils could approach a teacher of their own choice with their own suggestion for their own self-selected topic of study for a half-term's module and ask that teacher to be their 'base tutor'. Pupils checked in with their base tutor at the beginning of lessons and then went off to pursue their own learning paths for the half-term.

The GCSE module system, introduced in 1986, was notable in three significant ways in developing our understanding of educational citizenship:

1. The divesting to pupils of many of the traditional symbols of institutional power (such as choice of teacher, choice of topic of study, choice of GCSE examinations, the leading role in assessment, procedures for evaluating the quality of modules offered by teachers).

2. The impetus of social enquiry and personal engagement at the heart of the modules.

3. The consequent development of the critical faculties of pupils in researching, explaining, attacking or defending social and moral issues.

The first point is central to a policy of educational citizenship: the divesting of institutional power from the invested holders of power (teachers) to the previously disempowered (the pupils). The next two points lay down clear markers for the later development, via the theory-in-the-literature, of the qualities of the global citizen: 'autonomous and inquiring in her critical disposition' (point 3); 'but her decisions and actions tempered by an ethical concern for social justice and the dignity of humankind' (point 2).

A reading of the blurb for one half-term's modules (summer term, 1987) gives a clear idea of the combination of the questioning ('of an autonomous and inquiring critical disposition') and caring nature ('her decisions and actions tempered by an ethical concern for social justice and the dignity of humankind') of the global citizen:

> HEROES AND HEROINES: what makes a hero or a heroine? Pupils will research the attributes of historical, literary, cinematic and living heroes and heroines. How are the achievements of contemporary heroes and heroines different? How do different societies view heroic characteristics and actions? Is our identification with heroes and heroines a good thing? Do heroes and heroines offer realistic social models or are they merely escapist fantasies?

> PREJUDICE: what is prejudice? Is it innate? How does it vary between and within societies? How is it dealt with by the media and literature? Issues such as racism, sexism, handicap, age and class division will be discussed.

> RELATIONSHIPS: 'success' in life is very much determined by our ability to make relationships. This module will explore the difficulties and the joys of personal relationships. How do relationships develop, strengthen, weaken, fail? How can conflicts be resolved? Why are some people socially isolated? How do we cope with loneliness, bereavement, leaving home, old age?

> SURVIVAL: how to survive in conditions of physical and psychological hardship, such as shipwreck, 'plane crash, marooned on an island, lost in a wilderness. Drawing on fictional and factual accounts of people who have survived against the odds, pupils will work in groups to prepare for their own overnight expedition in inhospitable terrain. This expedition will be undertaken towards the end of the module.

The policy of educational citizenship that had been developing over the last three years was now accelerated:

- by allowing pupils to choose their teachers and their curriculum every half-term

- by discussing with each pupil their own assessment of their coursework and allowing every pupil to take their work to another teacher for a second opinion

- by asking pupils to complete an evaluation of the quality of the teacher's contribution to each module at the end of each half-term

- by giving pupils the responsibility for the filing and maintenance of their coursework folders and allowing them unrestricted access to these folders

- by encouraging individual and collaborative research and group discussion rather than didactic whole-class lessons

- by holding English evenings when parents, pupils and teachers got together to discuss departmental policy

- by printing a termly departmental newsletter with contributions by parents, pupils and teachers
- by starting an English outdoor education club as an expression of our commitment to taking the curriculum beyond the classroom and into the local community and environment
- by pupils, instead of teachers, writing the English contribution to their end-of-year school reports.

These changes demonstrated a real, not a rhetorical, commitment to educational citizenship and the learning partnership of pupil and teacher. My own use of the genitive case in describing school life epitomises the gradual transition from the didactic authoritarian to the learning partner. I no longer thought of my pupils, my results, my department, but of our pupils (parents' and teachers'), their results (pupils') and our department (teachers' and pupils').

None of this would have been possible without the unequivocal support of the headteacher and the eclectic brilliance of Carrie, Les, Ron and Shona, the other four members of the English department – committed, thinking teachers, ever eager to change, develop, experiment, question, argue, to take responsibility and to work collaboratively.

As teachers, we had to redefine our roles and develop new skills. The policy of classroom democracy and the content of the curriculum, as expressed in the modules, showed our commitment to a clearer – though still incomplete – concept of educational citizenship, now based upon the articulated premise that pupils should be accorded citizens' rights throughout their education and that the curriculum should be socially and ethically located in order to prepare pupils for full and active democratic citizenship. What we lacked were clear and precise ideas about the kind of pedagogy implicit to educational citizenship. What would, could and should pupils actually do in lessons? And what should teachers do to support them? What, to use a vogue phrase of the time, would constitute 'best practice'?

During these three years we began to recognise and then to refine certain aspects of learning in which pupils could be assisted or the quality of their learning experience could be improved. Among these aspects were various techniques of groupwork, pupils' time-management, the involvement of the community and the use of the environment, an expanded use of language technology and a sense of audience and presentation in different forms. As educational citizenship was evolving as a guiding spirit of the English department, so particular classroom practices were developed for the practical implementation of educational citizenship. In fuller form, these practices would later become known as the twelve factors of independent learning. Independent learning was to become the pedagogy of the philosophy of educational citizenship.

THE ADVISORY TEACHER (JANUARY 1989 – APRIL 1991)

I stayed at Carnmore for nine years and one term, until December 1988 when I was appointed as an LEA County Advisory Teacher for Secondary English on a three-year contract. In September 1989 I was offered a permanent position as one of two Senior Advisory Teachers for English (one, nominally, for the primary and one for the secondary sector).

'New teaching and learning styles' was the comet that flashed across the skies of a short-lived false dawn of educational enlightenment, the morning stars of which were the Cox Report, LINC and TVEI. I spent most of my time, by invitation from schools, alongside teachers and pupils in the classroom, either leading or supporting projects designed to implement the pedagogy of educational citizenship: independent learning.

As well as being responsible for the in-service training of the LEA's secondary English teachers, my particular job specifications, by negotiation, included responsibilities for primary liaison and for the development of cross-phase media education, information technology and cross-curricular studies. I worked across the 3 to 19 age range, spending about one-third of my time in the primary sector and two-thirds in the secondary. It was the ideal job for a practitioner-researcher interested in educational citizenship and its concomitant pedagogy, independent learning.

It was during this time that I entered my penultimate classroom incarnation. As the practices of independent learning became clearer, so I found my role changing from that of learning partner to that of facilitator. Although the title of Advisory Teacher was supposed to refer to my relationship with teachers, it unintentionally encapsulated my role as a peripatetic teacher working with pupils whose teachers were keen to explore the possibilities of educational citizenship and independent learning. Having established a learning climate of educational citizenship, as a teacher I withdrew, a little distanced from the action of the learning-place, resisting the impulse to intervene, but available to offer advice, when requested, on the techniques of independent learning.

It was also during this time that I decided to capitalise upon both my own personal interest in democratic schooling and a socially oriented curriculum, and also the professional opportunities that my job offered, and to undertake a more systematic programme of research into educational citizenship and independent learning. In April 1991 I enrolled as a part-time MPhil/PhD student at Exeter University, whilst continuing in my position as advisory teacher. In effect, my enrolment formalised the dual role of researcher and practitioner that had been developing for some time.

THE PRACTITIONER-RESEARCHER
(APRIL 1991 – SEPTEMBER 1995)

The starting point of my research was an issue of personal interest generated by what I considered to be the common sense theory of the practitioner in the field: 'Are the ends that are claimed for 5–16 education in relation to citizenship consistent with the means advocated for their development?'

The literature search of various groups of sociological, psychological and educational writers revealed interesting similarities between their views as to the epitome of the educated person and that of the active citizen. A working hypothesis was advanced, founded on the perceived symbiosis between education and citizenship. The hypothesis is that: 'Pupils need to learn *as* citizens to develop the mutual attributes of education and citizenship considered to be appropriate to the third millennium'.

After a search of the theory-in-the-literature, the research issue was focused to a research question: 'What practices within schools are likely to develop or to suppress attributes of citizenship considered to be appropriate to the third millennium?'

In essence, the search for the answer to this question is what the rest of this book is about.

CHAPTER TWO

Education and Citizenship

EDUCATION AND CITIZENSHIP IN THE PAST AND PRESENT

Images of the means and ends of education for citizenship

During the last decade (from around the time of the Educational Reform Act of 1988), two recurring and increasingly refined visual images have emerged to characterise the educational folklore of national politics, the popular media and, hence, the public consciousness, as 'good things in education'. These two images have had a powerful influence on the construction and presentation of the National Curriculum in state schools in England and Wales.

One image, which can be dubbed 'Princesses and Princes', depicts the *ends of education* and is of a small group of smiling and confident school-leavers: reflexive, adaptable, resourceful pupils about to claim their place as participants, the decision-takers and policy-makers, in the era and culture of high modernity.

Autonomous but morally aware, these young people will be the citizens of the next century. Words that might be found in the accompanying caption to this optimistic picture are: capability, empowerment, enfranchisement, social concern, co-operation, investigation, entitlement.

The second, equally recognisable – and perceived by a significant section of the public as equally positive – image, portrays the *means of education*, the ways in which pupils learn the content of the curriculum that they study. This picture, which can be titled 'Drudges and Frogs', is characterised by a nostalgic view of schooling that has more to do with the last, rather than the next, century: of neatly and uniformly dressed pupils sitting attentively in orderly rows, listening obediently to the didactic presentation of a clearly defined area of factual knowledge given by an authoritarian, albeit benign, teacher. Words and phrases that might be found in the caption to this image are: standards, rigour, discipline, healthy competition, traditions, back-to-basics, testing.

Photographic epitomes of both of these contrasting educational images, each commissioned by the UK government in 1992, can be found in the Parents' Charter (Princesses and Princes) and in the national press full-page advertisements intended to recruit DFE school inspectors (Drudges and Frogs). The underlying message of these before-and-after snapshots seems to be – to continue the analogy from children's literature, and such a transmogrification is exactly in the spirit of fairy tales – that the best life-preparation for an adult role in a culture of responsibility is for Princess Cinderella and Prince Bountiful to spend their formative years in a culture of repression and passivity.

It is the philosophical dichotomy and resulting pedagogical tension between these two popularly-held images (one of the twenty-first century, one of the nineteenth century, one of the aims of education, one of the means of achieving these aims) that is the focus of this book. What is the reality underpinning the rhetoric within a pupil's weekly timetable if the school managers wish to include photographs of both these images in their illustrated handbook to parents? How do schools resolve these two disparate views of the educational process?

This enquiry can be worded in another way, and in its second form becomes the research enquiry of this text: 'What practices within schools are likely to develop or to suppress attributes of citizenship considered to be appropriate to the third millennium?'

Interpretations of democratic citizenship

Whilst the concept of the citizen may have universality, a definition of citizenship does not, but varies according to the nature of different societies. An example across time: in a Western liberal democracy, citizenship demonstrates a compassion for the less fortunate (although the practical form that this demonstration may take differs across the political spectrum), an idea quite at odds with the élitism of Civis Romanus. An example across ideologies: in a democracy, citizenship is generally concerned with individual rights, whereas communism demands the willing subjugation of individual rights to the development of the state. Callan (1988) and White (1991) state that obedience to social rule is an important aspect of citizenship in a tradition-led society. Steutel (1991) goes further and argues that a citizen's personal well-being in an autarchic culture is promoted by the internalisation of rules. Contrastingly, Gray (1983), and Raz (1986) claim that the ability to reflect critically on the society of high modernity (what Giddens (1991) refers to as 'institutional reflexivity and the reflexive project of the self') is essential not only for personal well-being but also for the development of society.

This study is concerned with the development of citizenship in the state-maintained educational system of a late-twentieth-century Western liberal democracy, principally the United Kingdom. Even within these parameters there is no consensus on the concept of citizenship, although all the Parliamentary parties often refer to it. As Lister (1991) points out: 'The concept of active citizenship enjoys the support of central government politicians from all parties, and from Prince Charles' (p.254).

Douglas Hurd's (1987; 1988) notion of 'active citizenship' is embedded in the economic idea of the enterprise culture and the virtues of self-help. John Major's various Citizen's Charters (11 encompassing the United Kingdom, with a further 8 for England, 5 for Scotland, 5 for Wales and 11 for Northern

Ireland) are posited on the belief that the managers of public utilities and services should be accountable to a society of citizen-consumers. Paddy Ashdown (1989) attempted to balance a citizenship of entitlement and empowerment within a mixed market economy. The Labour Party is concerned with political reform and the decentralisation of power to locally constituted citizens' groups. As the name of the party suggests, the Ulster Unionists consider citizenship to be an issue of national sovereignty within the civic and political state of the constitutional monarchy of the United Kingdom, whilst the Scottish and Welsh National Parties both campaign for the political independence of the people of Scotland and Wales – Plaid Cymru emphasises sovereignty in terms of the cultural identity of the Welsh (Wigley 1995), whereas the SNP promotes Scotland as an existing multicultural civic nation. Citizenship is a republican concept and its application to a monarchy, in which people are actually subjects not citizens, is questionable. Nevertheless, the heir to the throne has promoted several of his own citizenship initiatives (Prince's Trust 1994;1995).

Although the interpretations of citizenship differ, common words and phrases occur: active, individuality, freedom, rights and responsibilities (or duties or obligations), community, participation. The idea of the citizen who participates in society by acting upon rights conferred by the state, thus having a responsibility to the state, is a common theme. David Held (1991) observes:

> From the ancient world to the present day, all forms of citizenship have had common attributes. Citizenship has meant a reciprocity of rights against, and duties towards, the community. Citizenship has entailed membership, membership of the community in which one lives one's life. And membership has invariably involved degrees of participation in the community. (p.20)

Differing definitions of citizenship can be illuminated by an examination of the different natures of the citizen's rights upon which they are predicated: national, cultural, social, economic, political, civil and ethical.

The idea of a citizen's rights being determined by the birthright of nationality is as old as the concept of citizenship itself, originating in the democratic Greek states and developing in the Roman republic. The 1789 Declaration of the Rights of Man and the Citizen excluded foreigners, and the American Bill of Rights, in Amendment 14 (1868), defines citizens as 'persons born or naturalised in the United States'. In the post-colonial United Kingdom national identity has been a significant factor in the citizenship debate, impelled by the Afro-Caribbean and Asian immigration of the 1950s–1970s and the possibility of large numbers of Hong Kong Chinese claimants to British nationality in the late 1990s. In 1981 a British Nationality Act, limiting citizenship, was passed. In the 1980s and 1990s the issue of national rights and sovereignty within the European Union has been inextricably linked, by some sections of the polity and the media, with individual rights.

Minority groups within and across national states have based their claims for free and equal citizenship upon the recognition of the rights of cultural diversity rather than national uniformity. Writers such as Margherita Rendel (1991) and Anne Phillips (1991) have addressed feminist issues, Sarah Benton (1991) and Simon Watney (1991) lesbian and gay rights, Bob Franklin (1992) and Roger Hart (1992) children's rights, and Bhikhu Parekh (1991) ethnic concerns. The concept of a multicultural Britain embraces these, and other, minorities: 'A concern with citizenship in its fullest sense is coterminous with a concern for issues posed by, for instance, trade unions, feminism, the black movements, ecology and those who have advocated the rights of vulnerable minorities like children' (Held 1991, p.20).

Some of these writers (Pateman 1988; Benton 1991; Watney 1991), seeking to redefine citizenship to give a more egalitarian role to disempowered groups, have drawn a distinction between the public nature of citizenship and the private nature of personhood. They have stressed that equal citizenship is about the freedom to practise diversity of lifestyle, protected by the individual citizen's rights to a uniformity of freedom and equality.

The democratic right-wing in Western Europe and America has tended to regard citizens' rights in political and civil terms, whereas the left has lobbied for a recognition and implementation of economic and social rights. In Reaganite USA, economic and social rights were seen 'more in the nature of aspirations and goals than "rights"' (US Department of State, Bureau of Public Affairs 1988, pp.1–2). In the UK the denial of social and economic support as a right is legitimised by the argument that rights are self-evident truths that are enforceable (civil and political) and that social and economic benefits are dependent upon resources which are not inevitably available. The labelling of a 'dependency culture' has diminished those who had regarded economic and social support as an entitlement and a reciprocity has been established between rights and duties: workfare in the USA, job-seekers' allowance in the UK. As Raymond Plant (1991) has observed of recent Conservative attitudes: 'The entitlements of citizenship have to be earned; it is not a status that confers rights to resources by itself.' (p.62).

The underlying idea of two classes of citizen (the independent, self-reliant producer of the state's wealth and the unproductive, dependent consumer of it) attacks the central principle of democratic citizenship, which is that of equality. Moreover, it offers no stability, no guarantee to a concept of statutory human rights: rights become subject to the fluctuation of property and market forces and the security of national interests.

Marxist socialists have refuted the possibility of citizenship based on freedom and equality within a capitalist property-owning society, distrusting the citizenship debate as a bourgeois placation of the proletariat. The left, however, in its drive to redistribute wealth and ownership, and to promote the social and economic rights of citizenship, has been accused of restricting the civil and political rights of the individual citizen, a neglect that has contributed to the fall of totalitarian socialism in Eastern Europe.

In the UK the legacy of Thatcherism and the failure of East and Central European socialism have contributed to both the Conservative and Labour parties redefining their standpoints. This has led to a shifting and blurring of their traditional positions on the criteria for citizens' rights. Charter 88 is a mainly socialist movement, the aim of which is to promote political and civil rights in the UK through a Bill of Rights. However, its list of 'inalienable rights' does not include any reference to social and economic entitlements such as welfare or a minimum wage. On the other hand, John Major's Citizens' Charters, whilst driven by market forces, seem to take up the advocacy of left wing Charter 88 members such as Ruskin (1991) and Plant (1991) and are obviously intended to suggest government's care and concern for a social commitment to minimum standards of welfare. The last two decades have seen major developments in the public and political perception of citizenship in the UK. The patriarchism of titled and land-owning 'grandee' Toryism has evolved through the 'Lord of the Flies' self-survivalism of the Thatcher years to the more pragmatic and less certain approach of John Major. The unapologetically socialist policies of Michael Foot have transmuted, via Neil Kinnock's stewardship of the party, into the comparatively bland liberalism of Blair's 'New' Labour. The Liberal Party enjoyed a government coalition with Labour, an opposition coalition with the SDP, and then reasserted its independence with a name change to the Liberal Democrats. With almost all of the areas in which national government could once pursue policy now limited by the effects of international economic, social and environmental constraints, and with the rise in the general standard of living having eroded the left's working-class support base during the last fifty years, there is both a restricted platform for the formulation of party policies and a narrower and more homogeneous demographic band to which those policies must appeal, particularly during a general election. The three political parties that have formed governments this century are now engaged in their own acts of redefinition and, at times, seem to have difficulty in communicating to an increasingly sceptical electorate the distinguishing features and differences between their manifestos and their various views on the nature of citizenship. On 25 January 1995, in the House of Lords, Lord Chief Justice Taylor, the senior law lord, called for a UK Bill of Rights based upon the Universal Declaration of Human Rights so that some baseline of the rights of the British citizen could be established.

It can be seen that whilst all the British political parties have a position on citizenship, each has a different position based upon different criteria. Amidst this motley, the hues continue to change as each party shifts its position. Nevertheless, preparation for citizenship, in whatever form it may take, has long been considered an important function of state education and continues to be so at the present time. Section 1 of the Education Reform Act (1988) places a statutory responsibility upon school managers to provide a broad and balanced curriculum which 'promotes the spiritual, moral, cultural, mental and physical development of pupils at school and of society; and prepares pupils for the opportunities, responsibilities and experiences of adult life' (Educational Reform Act 1988, p.1).

Citizenship as an educational aim of the state

Citizenship as an educational aim is hardly a new idea – it was central to the educational system of ancient Greece (although not all denizens were regarded as citizens). Carr (1991) regards Plato as the 'paradigmatic example of an educational philosopher who clearly recognised the reciprocal relationship between an educational philosophy and a social philosophy' (p.184). In Britain, writing in 1531, Sir Thomas Elyot (1962) saw learning as an all-embracing affair that went beyond schooling. He maintained that practical arts (what current writers sometimes refer to as 'life-skills') were as important to the wholeness of being educated as classical studies. In 1605 Francis Bacon elaborated this theme in his *Advancement of Learning*, complaining that the practical nature of education was being ignored for the theoretical: 'words and no matter' (1975, p.69). In 1778 Joseph Priestley, in *An Essay on a Course of Liberal Education for Civil and Active Life*, wrote that the purpose of 'liberal education' – as he called it – should be 'to qualify men [sic] to appear to advantage in future life' (p.9).

An examination of different state educational systems reveals a link between education and citizenship to be self-evident. The state has a vested interest in the educational process – its self-survival. Although there are exceptions (Dewey's interactionism, 'the constant reweaving of the social fabric', (1916, p.3); Habermas' emancipatory interest (1971); Freire's concept of dialogue and invasion (1976)), with varying degrees of conservatism, the principal purpose of education for citizenship has been seen as consolidating and perpetuating the prevalent state ideology rather than challenging and changing it (Peters 1979; Feinberg 1983; Gutmann 1990).

Totalitarian and democratic governments have in common the use of their national educational systems to promote the values of their society and to prepare young people for their role in it. Examples are not hard to find. Most countries in Central and Eastern Europe are now restructuring their educational systems to reflect education for democratic citizenship and are dismantling the old programmes of doctrinaire civic education. The intense and competitive nature of Japanese education reflects the societal demands on the adult citizen.

Judges' summations in various court cases in America are quite explicit in linking education and citizenship with the perpetuation of the *status quo*. In 1954 Chief Justice Earl Warren stated that 'It [education] is the very foundation of good citizenship.' (Branson 1991, p.39). Later cases, involving the rights to education of Mexican-American children, invoked Warren's ruling and elaborated upon it. 'Of particular importance is the relationship between the essential functions of instilling in our young an understanding and appreciation for the principles and operation of our governmental processes.' (San Antonio Independent School District v. Rodriguez 411 US 1 (1973), quoted by Branson 1991, p.40). 'We have recognised the public schools as the most vital civic institution for the preservation of our democratic system of government, and as the primary vehicle for transmitting the values on which our society rests.' (Plyler v. Doe 102 S. Ct. 2382 (1982), quoted by Branson 1991, p.41).

In the UK a Labour government (1976) introduced legislation for the comprehensivisation of the national school system as a plank of social democracy. An entrepreneurial Conservative government (1979–1997) legislated a series of acts to remove state schools from the collective responsibility of local government and to reconstruct them as self-financing businesses subject to market forces. In 1988 a Scottish report (Programme Directing Committee 1986) suggesting that some features of child-centred education that typified primary practice might usefully be extended into the secondary sector was rejected by Thatcher's government on the grounds that 'a society where enterprise and competition must be increasingly valued...must be a main determinant of what schools teach' (TESS 1988, p.1). Two hundred years earlier, during the US presidency of Thomas Jefferson, he, Noah Webster and Benjamin Rush had campaigned vigorously for the establishment of a national educational system dedicated to the fulfilment of republican aims: 'Determined to preserve the heritage of the revolution, to unify the nation, and to inculcate proper principles of government, they advocated a kind of republican indoctrination, hoping that the ensuing enlightenment [sic] would bring a salutary uniformity' (Tyack 1967, p.92).

It can be demonstrated that governments regard state-maintained schools as having an important role to play in preparing young people for participation in society, for citizenship, but that the nature of citizenship to be promulgated can fluctuate according to the prevalent state ideology.

A critique of some current practices in education for citizenship

The idea that life in the school community should be a preparation for life in the adult, social community is well documented. All the major government-commissioned educational reports from Hadow (1926) to Swann (1985) have supported and reinforced the idea. Thus the school community is seen as representing a microcosm of the social community. Many commentators have, therefore, suggested that education *for* citizenship should reflect the characteristics *of* citizenship and that the epithets associated with democratic forms of citizenship (activity, rights and responsibilities, individuality, community) should inform the practices of the school community. Jeremy Cunningham (1991) asserts that 'The balance of rights and responsibilities is of great importance in schools... Most important still are the opportunities for students to take responsibility.' (pp.91–93). David Shiman (1991) believes that '...active learning is the best preparation for active citizenship in a democracy.' (p.189).

Anthony Barnett (1991) reinforces the importance of the relationship between active learning and active citizenship with this rhetorical question on the teaching of citizenship: '...how are teachers supposed to do this if their pupils are to remain subjects?' (quoted in Starkey 1991, p.216). Maitland Stobbart (1991) defines the Council of Europe's position:

> Human rights should permeate the whole of school life – the ethos and organisation of the school, as well as the content of the curriculum. Schools should, therefore, show respect and consideration for all their members, encourage solidarity and promote dialogue. They should also provide young people with opportunities for meaningful participation in the running of their school community. (Quoted in Starkey 1991, p.2)

There are, broadly, two approaches to education for citizenship in the UK at this time: learning *about* citizenship and learning *in* citizenship. Education about citizenship consists of teaching pupils about the rights and duties they will later have as citizens but do not presently have as pupils. Education in citizenship is child-centred and aims to develop citizenship through the child's exploration of her own rights and responsibilities via personal actions within the school community and environment. These two approaches are not necessarily discrete: most schools display elements of both in their citizenship policies. However, in discussing them it is clearer to treat them separately.

Learning about citizenship

A common teaching strategy of the 'learning about' approach to citizenship is to utilise information packs and simulated activities such as role-play, improvisation, socio-drama and games. Patricia Dye (1991) expresses the emphatic opinion that 'No better way to help students grapple with human rights exists than to use (or create) a simulation that forces a degree of empathy from the students' (p.115). Best (1991) advocates simulations and role-playing games for teacher training in citizenship. There are many commercially available simulations, often computer-generated such as *Carrigan Street* or *Project Space* (Scetlander 1986) or *The Best Days Of Our Lives* (Davison 1987). There are also activity packs that combine suggestions for activities with information on specific issues, such as *Teaching and Learning About Human Rights* (Amnesty International 1983), *Do It Justice: Resources and Activities for Introducing Education in Human Rights* (Osler 1988), *Citizenship: Cross-curricular Theme Pack 1* (Edwards 1993) and the various broadsheets disseminated by the Centre for Citizenship Studies in Education (Fogelman 1991).

I have reservations about the use of such methods and materials (and, by implication, the whole of the education 'about' citizenship approach). To what extent can Dye's degree of empathy be *forced?* There have been questions about the authenticity of an approach that, for some, appears to suggest that citizenship and human rights are not a part of the pupil's present reality so that pupils have found difficulty in identifying with the subject matter (Stradling 1984;

Dyson 1986). Some pupils seem to have experienced a sense of impotence and rejected the responsibilities of citizenship (Duczek 1984; Lister 1990). Abdallah-Pretceille (1991) has noted the desensitising of young pupils: 're-peated appeals to their feelings merely blunt their sensitivity' (p.70). I have argued that simulations and the study of disadvantaged peoples extant from the pupils' own community, on behalf of whom no real action is required, can temporarily liberate pupils from the reality of their own prejudices into a utopian sense of civic virtue and good-will. But as such expressions are removed from the pupils' everyday actions, experiences and attitudes, they are therefore removed from any meaningful morality and so have little educational impact (Griffith 1999). McLeod (1991) states that experience in the Canadian ed-ucational system suggests that it is only when people are brought to a realisation and admission of their own bias or discrimination (in effect, when people are brought to an awareness of their duties as citizens and the rights of their fellow citizens) that progress can be made in developing 'cultural pluralism and positive human relations' (p.174).

Learning in citizenship

In the second approach, learning in citizenship, the school bestows some of the rights of the citizen upon the pupil and encourages their practical application and development: 'Basic concepts such as justice, equality, discrimination, freedom and self-determination…can best be taught to young pupils in a comprehensible way by reference to their own life experiences' (Heater 1991, p.242).

Citizenship and human rights issues are not seen as remote from the normal experience of pupils but as an integral part of their daily lives. The emphasis is upon a skills-based, rather than a knowledge-based, education for citizenship: 'The process is the important factor and the child is the beginning' (Lyseight-Jones 1991, p.83). Best (1991) states that her main objective is the 'realisation by every child or young person of his or her own responsibility for the advancement of human rights' (p.123). Micheline Rey (1991) observes that human rights are 'as relevant to our own social behaviour as they are to the behaviour of others in far away places of little concern to us' (p.135), a point also made by Shiman (1991): 'human rights problems…do not occur only "out there", in foreign lands, but have local and national dimensions as well' (p.190).

This approach, generally endorsed in theory, has been criticised in its practice. My main criticism is of its peripheral nature, peripheral both to the individual child and to the curriculum.

> It has to be made absolutely clear what the school stands for, and, for many school members, assemblies and meetings are the main channel for the reinforcement of fundamental principles…it is necessary for the human rights school to have its own statements of principle. These will not be referred to daily, and they may lie in brochures or staff handbooks or be pinned to walls for

weeks at a time, but they represent the bedrock of values on which the school
rests. (Cunningham 1991, pp.94–95)

So writes a secondary school headteacher. There is no recognition here of the
exercise of the individual pupil's rights within her lessons; citizenship is
extra-curricular: 'School councils, social committees, common room
committees, and fund-raising and charity groups can give a large number of
young people the experience of combining to achieve targets or solve problems.'
(Cunningham 1991, p.93). Roger Hart (1992) has warned of the inherent
danger in such bodies, of tokenism, which, with manipulation and decoration,
he regards as the three non-participatory rungs on his eight-rung ladder of child
participation. Well-intentioned practices, such as school assemblies, that draw
attention to the violation of human rights have been subject to criticism ('a
catalogue of wrongs does not add up to a child's comprehension of rights'
(Heater 1991, p.235)), as have pupils' involvement in charity appeals that can
over-emphasise negative images of cultural diversity (Claycomb 1989).

The apparent democratisation of a school via pupil representatives on
committees and councils can actually deny citizenship opportunities for the
majority of pupils because the rights of most pupils are exercised
representatively rather than by direct personal decision making and action
taking. I regard such practices, along with class monitors, prefects, pupil Heads
of House, Year and School, and sports team captains, as the doctrinaire
inculcation of favoured pupils into the existing hierarchy of invested power. The
devolution of certain responsibilities, such as caring for the class hamster,
watering the plants, tidying the book corner or reading to other children is, at
best, anodyne in fostering responsibility only to the point of convenience to the
institution and at worst, as reinforcing a two-tier system of citizenship where
some pupils (prefects et al.) are depicted as leaders and others as minions (tidiers
and carers). A view of society is offered in which responsibility is synonymous
with institutional authority. In such a society the few people with authority are
invested with the monopoly of civic responsibility and the majority are
effectively disempowered from individual or partisan agency. Moreover, such
duties are more often seen as rewards rather than responsibilities and, as they are
selective, they are certainly not rights. A further criticism is that because pupils'
'rights' can be withdrawn or superseded by the teachers, such practices are
themselves only simulations – pupils are exercising privileges, not rights (Jeffs
1995). Finally, as teachers and other adults manifestly enjoy different rights
than the pupils, such a system is not representative of the equal freedoms of
citizenship. Pupils actually have very few rights within the school institution. As
Giddens writes: 'Holding out the possibility of emancipation, modern
institutions at the same time create mechanisms of suppression, rather than the
actualisation of the self' (Giddens 1991, p.6).

The location of education for citizenship within the National Curriculum

Where, in schools, might the practices of education for citizenship be located? They might be found within the curriculum, or outside the curriculum but within the administration and extra-curricular activities of the school, or in both or in neither. The place of citizenship in the curriculum has given rise to vigorous debate (Fogelman 1991; Edwards and Fogelman 1993). Should it be a discrete subject, or absorbed within a faculty such as humanities, or developed as a cross-curricular theme?

Where citizenship has been regarded primarily as a course of content (education about citizenship), it has generally been deemed the responsibility of the social sciences. Where citizenship has been regarded more as a skill (education in citizenship) its curricular base has been pastoral: personal and social education, tutor periods. Although these regions seem to be its natural curricular home, few 11–16 schools in the UK offer citizenship as a discrete subject. Curriculum planners, limited by a legal obligation to the National Curriculum which requires 80–90 per cent of timetable time, have been loathe to find room for a high risk/low status subject. Where it appears by name on the timetable at all, it is likely to be as a topic or module for study within another subject or as a non-examination option in Keystage Four – a position that sends out derogatory messages about the esteem and universality of citizenship. Where citizenship has been regarded (as in the National Curriculum) as a cross-curricular theme – every teacher's responsibility – it has inevitably become no teacher's responsibility, 'a custom more honoured in the breach than in the observance' (Shakespeare c1598–1602, (1926, p.82).

Rey (1991) claims that all school subjects 'can serve as a basis for inter-cultural practices and thinking, providing an education in human rights' (p.147). However, she only offers exemplification in language, literature and history. Best (1991) suggests geography, the plastic arts, dance and music as vehicles for interculturalism. Shiman (1991) writes that 'Concepts such as justice, responsibility, conflict, equality, liberty and freedom...should be in-fused into the curriculum in a variety of content areas...' but he only specifies English, art and music (p.190). In his foreword to the National Curriculum Council publication, *Education For Citizenship* (1990b), the Chairman and Chief Executive of the NCC, Duncan Graham, states that citizenship 'can and must be taught through the subjects of the National Curriculum', yet the section on 'The Whole Curriculum' mentions only religious education and 'social sciences', neither of which are NC subjects. The Council of Europe's (1985) declaration on the teaching of human rights mentions five subjects which accord with the National Curriculum (history, geography, language and literature (English), art and music), but regards different disciplines as having separate functions: the humanities as information disseminating, the arts as 'the expression of feelings'.

The claims that citizenship, human rights and intercultural education are relevant across the whole curriculum are not reinforced by fully cross-curricular instances of practice. Moreover, the cognitive aspects tend to be apportioned to the humanities and the affective to the arts. Mathematics and science are not regarded as having a role to play. Yet no subject is value free. Religious convictions can be embedded within science teaching: Christian fundamentalism applied to the study of evolution in biology or the construction of the universe and the nature of time in physics. The Association for Curriculum Development's anti-racist mathematics campaign has shown that mathematics, far from being value-free, is a controversial area: 'Many problems involve profit, loss and interest, and therefore have an ideological bias. Even the traditional method of borrowing and paying back (for subtraction) uses terms that are mainly a reflection of mercantile capitalism' (quoted in Starkey 1991, p.220).

Whatever place citizenship finds for itself within the curriculum, the value system of the school must be in harmony with the value system of human rights if a teaching programme intended to develop citizenship is to make any relevant sense to pupils – a point clearly made by Cunningham (1991): 'the work on knowledge and skills in the classroom would be undermined if the whole institution were not committed to the meaning of human rights in its daily life' (p.103).

At the present, there are confusions about the nature of citizenship and, therefore, its purpose as an aspect of a child's education. There is no common agreement about the place of citizenship within (or without) the curriculum. Where guidelines have been offered, exemplification is often inconsistent. Different views of citizenship have led to different forms of its presentation to pupils, each of which has weaknesses.

EDUCATION AND CITIZENSHIP IN THE FUTURE

Citizenship in the third millennium: a construct of global citizenship

As the millennium approaches, both the political left and right hold not only different views of the nature of citizens' rights but also views that are in a state of flux. A model for the citizenship of the third millennium may be found beyond the mainstream of traditional adversarial politics, sectional and national interests, and socioeconomic or politico-civic bases of citizenship. Post-war writers such as Kandel (1949), McCluhan (1968) and, more recently, White (1991) and Giddens (1991, 1994) point out that a global citizenship to which we all *must belong* is being created as we reach the millennium: 'the level of time-space distanciation introduced by high modernity is so extensive that, for the first time in human history, "self" and "society" are interrelated in a global milieu' (Giddens 1991, p.32).

Giddens' duality of individuality and collectivism on a planetary basis is reflected in the growth of supranational democratic, human rights and 'green' movements:

> Green politics expresses aspirations of citizenship through its globalisation of the sense of community, combined with a new emphasis on individual responsibility. (Steward 1991, p.65)

> the critical future of the planet requires more than ever an ethic of solidarity, there is an urgent need to rebuild a sense of community. The crucial importance of duty in this context is that it implies a commitment, an obligation, for individuals themselves to solve the problems within their communities. It puts the local, and now the global, well-being at the centre of citizens' concerns, above that of self-interest. (Andrews 1991, p.215)

Organisations such as the Green Party, Amnesty International, Greenpeace, Friends of the Earth, the Centre for Global Education, and the Education in Human Rights Network are based upon the ideal of a citizenship of a global community living in its shared planetary environment. Although this informal alliance has no common manifesto, aspects of a shared agenda are discernible:

1. Global citizenship transcends the artificiality of national boundaries and regards Planet Earth as the common home of humanity.

2. Human beings are united by a common identity (even if this unity is not unanimously recognised) as the occupants of this shared planetary home and, therefore, by a universal code of citizenship which is not primarily cultural, national, political, civil, social or economic but ethical.

3. This code is based upon freedom and equality and the active participation of the individual citizen in the global community. Global citizenship offers a reconciliation between the social individuality traditionally championed by right-wing democratic politics and the opposing view expressed in the various left-wing theories of collectivism. The new dynamic suggests a universal ethical collectivism of social justice and an individual responsibility incumbent upon citizens actively to espouse moral principles in the action of their everyday lives. Personal responsibility for the consequences of one's actions is a prominent theme of global citizenship.

4. A fourth characteristic is a powerful sense of tradition that cherishes the best of what is past and wishes to preserve it for the future. This view of the living population as the executors of previous generations and the trustees for future generations leads to a longer-term assessment of the use of the world's natural resources and a questioning of the short-term economic benefits of technological and industrial development. This, in turn, leads to a drive for the

promotion of a more qualitative and less quantitative lifestyle in an attempt to limit the consumption and despoliation of environmental resources.

5. The idea of the diversity of the world's peoples living in planetary harmony has led to a rebuttal of the portrayal of humankind as a species at the apex of an evolutionary hierarchy, this position bestowing an inherent right to use the animal and mineral resources of the earth to its sole perceived benefit. Increasingly, human beings are depicted as just one part of a fragile and complexly inter-related and interdependent global, or even galactic, ecology.

Apart from their macro-scale, the ethics of global citizenship have resonances with the historical development of classical citizenship from ancient Greece via the Roman republic to mediaeval Florence:

> At the core of the republican ethos is the vision of the active citizen who makes the concerns of the whole society his or her own, for whom political involvement is a positive good rather than an occasional necessity or the preserve of a minority, because it is in this involvement that we develop a sense of ourselves and of others as sharers in a community, a common humanity.
> (Howe 1991, p.125)

Such citizenship is characterised by various kinds of freedoms that are claimed by citizens as their rights: freedom of action (of expression, of the press, of assembly, of demonstration, of employment, of travel), freedom of thought (intellect, conscience, censorship, belief) and freedom from discrimination (ethnicity, gender, language, class, religion, sexual orientation, physique).

'Freedom', writes Mulgan (1991), 'doesn't give any clues as to how to behave to others; how to share; how to think; or how to feel. It tells us nothing about judgment, about right or wrong.' (p.42). The freedom of global citizenship is not the self-centred liberty of Rousseau's *Emile* (1762), Neill's *Summerhill* (1926) or Steutel's animal freedom (1991). Concomitant with individual freedom is corporate responsibility, which manifests itself in an ethical concern for social justice. It is a concern for responsible action that, for Shotter (1984), is the essence of being human, of 'personhood'. This duality of freedom and responsibility typifies the citizens of the third millennium, Harre's 'bearers of honour and agentive power' (1983, p.271).

Harre (1983) and Shotter (1984) draw attention to the active nature of citizenship. The notion of action, of agency, can be traced back to the 1779 Declaration of the Rights of Man and The Citizen in which a right is defined by Creniere as 'the effect of an agreement through which one acts.' During the 1960s, a word was coined for the individual who strove to defend or extend the rights of the citizen: activist. (And in a popular television series of the time, recently repeated, the main character, an activist, was nicknamed 'Citizen' Smith).

Thus, global citizenship is based on rights, responsibility and action – the rights to certain freedoms, the responsibility not to abuse these rights and to act with fairness and ethical concern, or what Bruner (1990) terms open-mindedness, 'the keystone of what we call a democratic culture' (p.30). This moral pressure, of Kohlberg's (1971) 'social contract orientation', is mentioned by Rene Cassin in expressing doubt that moral authority can be solely entrusted to the legislative and judicial domain: 'Legal force of itself is only a secondary safety valve', it is the awareness of people of 'their dignity and their duties as citizens and as human beings' (quoted in Starkey 1991, p.15) that is of greatest importance.

The sense of dignity in action is underlined in the claim made by Marie (1985) that all rights are essentially derived from the notion of human dignity. Shiman (1991) argues that education for human rights should be impelled by the intention to 'encourage their [students'] *action* rooted in a humane conception of justice and human dignity' (p.189).

Global citizenship is dynamic, action underpinned with ethical imprimatur. Such citizenship is more complex than independence or autonomy. To be autonomous, it is true, one has to have the capacity for distanced reflection on society, but autonomy, as defined by Raz (1986) and Gray (1983) (and originally John Locke see Langford 1985) does not presuppose and include in its definition the second strand of global citizenship: moral or altruistic action (although White (1991) argues that it should). Harre (1983) goes so far as to argue that an autonomous action is necessarily one that violates the legal or moral code of a society. The commitment to moral action is regarded as central, as a duty of the citizen, and it is this duty that signifies and dignifies the citizen as a human being.

A picture, then, of the global citizen: not merely aware of her rights but able and desirous to act upon them; of an autonomous and inquiring critical disposition; but her decisions and actions tempered by an ethical concern for social justice and the dignity of humankind; therefore able, through her actions, to control and enhance 'the trajectory of the self' through life whilst contributing to the commonweal, the public welfare, with a sense of civic duty to replenish society.

It is this sense of citizenship that is referred to in the research enquiry: what practices within schools are likely to develop or to suppress attributes of citizenship considered to be appropriate to the third millennium?

Objections to the construct of global citizenship

There are objections to the notion of global citizenship which require examination.

Citizens must belong to an identifiable community from which they claim their rights: one cannot be a citizen of an ideal

Globalists do not accept that rights are in the gift of government (Mandela 1986; Freeman 1988; Howe 1991; Lynch 1992). Human rights exist because of the nature of humanity, not the nature of government. The identifiable community is humankind. The global community does exist and, although, as yet, it has no formal constitution, its existence can be discerned in the growth towards democratic international federalism and the (largely) peaceful popular movements that have brought an end to totalitarian empires, the inter-dependence of nation states created by macro-economics, the recognition of international responsibilities for the environment, the pluralism of national societies that engenders a sense of belonging to a wider culture and the adoption or creation of instruments such as the Universal Declaration of Human Rights (1948), the European Social Charter (1961), the African Charter on Human and Peoples' Rights (1981) and the UN Convention on the Rights of the Child (1989).

Universality and relativism are philosophically opposed concepts and cannot co-exist

Globalists such as Arblaster (1994) argue that there *are* universal ethics, although political and civil statements that attempt to enshrine them are likely to be relative to their historical and cultural period. The full articulation and application of universal ethics in a civic code is a process, not an event: 'The past and the future are in creative tension around the notion of human rights.' (Starkey 1991, p.16). For instance, the 1789 Declaration described a relative position. Today the slogan would more likely be liberty, equality (plus democracy) and solidarity (not fraternity), the document's title would be shortened to exclude 'the Man' and Sieyes (1789) would not comment: 'Not everyone is an active citizen. Women, at least in the present circumstances, foreigners and those who contribute nothing to the common weal, must not actively influence public affairs.' (p.18)

Universal declarations of human rights are not universally representative, but are Western patriarchal constructs (Schwab 1981; Pollis 1982; Donnelly 1984)

To a certain extent, this criticism is accepted. Franklin (1992) points out that the UN Convention on the Rights of the Child acknowledges no consultation with children and that, with its positive references to the role of the family, the Convention's ethos could be interpreted as supporting a patriarchal culture that diminishes the role of women and children. After nearly fifty years, some revision of the Universal Declaration of Human Rights may be necessary. For others, the Declaration is 'too powerful a statement of principles to be cast aside as an instructional framework on the strength of this sort of criticism' (Shiman

1991, p.192). Demonstrations for democracy in Eastern Europe, India, China, the Soviet Union, South Africa and South America suggest to writers such as Fukuyama (1992), Giddens (1994) and Arblaster (1994) that the principles of democratic human rights are universal:

> An optimistic view of recent developments suggests that the nemesis of Communism and the world-wide reverberations of this crash mark also the beginning of the global triumph of the democratic principle... These momentous developments could perhaps be interpreted as a global movement, or at least a drift, towards democracy, or popular election as the most stable and acceptable basis for government. And I think there is some basis for optimism...
> It may even be that the most powerful ideologically-based forms of non-democratic authoritarianism are now either dead or discredited and doomed. (Arblaster 1994, pp.52–54)

International agreements, declarations and conventions are formal rather than substantive

Possibly, but it is better to have a concept of citizenship based upon an unrealised but realisable ideal than an expedient but limited reality. Franklin (1992), writing about the UN Convention on the Rights of the Child, takes the position that statements of rights, per se, are useful but incomplete – they need to be activated by the groups they address: 'Documents should not be dismissed because their authority is symbolic rather than statutory. Acknowledging the legitimacy of a group's claim to rights is itself part of a process of empowerment; rights are levers which the empowered group must pick up and put to work' (p.105). This point is made starkly and emphatically by Freeman (1992): 'Rights are never given but are fought for' (p.70).

History suggests that global citizenship is an impossibility

Historically, it is claimed, citizenship travelled west from Athens across Europe and later to America and the southern continents via the European colonisation of Africa and Australasia, but there was no corresponding movement to the eastward. Thus the Soviet Union and China have no tradition of democracy and the rights and duties of citizenship, and would be incapable of making the transition (Kundera 1984; Vajda 1988; Szucs 1988). This view appears to be based upon the belief that different cultures have immutable indigenous psychologies. Its theory is challenged by pointing out that the evolution of democracy in the West has been turbulent and included, until relatively recently, slavery, genocide, colonial empire-building, subjugation, exploitation and internecine warfare. There is no 'democratic gene' that distinguishes some peoples from others. Moreover, at least for the present, there is democratic stability in the West and encouragement and support is forthcoming for those East and Central European nations that have rejected totalitarianism and are attempting to construct democracies: 'Democratic principles, the citizen ideal and the aspiration to a peacefully shared Europe provide more than enough common ground on which to work' (Howe 1991, p.134).

There are anomalies within the various instruments which purport to champion universal freedoms and equalities

This is undeniable. For instance, the Unesco Convention against Discrimination in Education permits single-sex and private schools. The European Convention for the Protection of Human Rights stipulates that its remit concerns only political, not social and economic, rights. The UN Convention on the Rights of the Child states that every child has the right to a state education and that attendance is mandatory – can a right be compulsory? Globalists accept that these documents are imperfect and incomplete, because a full consensual understanding of human rights is.

Despite these objections, there is a growing body of evidence that individuals in countries throughout the world are increasingly feeling a sense of communal identification and responsibility as global citizens. Examples are myriad and in all areas of human activity: from the inter-governmental policies exemplified by the Rio de Janeiro World Environmental Conference (1993) to the inter-cultural symbolism of the Star Trek movies; from the political, economic and social reality of an expanding European Union to the world-wide membership of individuals of organisations such as Amnesty and Greenpeace; from the immediacy of televisual images across the globe being shared simultaneously by citizens on every continent (whether those images be of sport (the World Cup), entertainment (the Eurovision Song Contest) or of warfare (the CNN syndicated reporting of the Gulf War)) to literature, both populist and academic, that addresses globalisation (for instance, *Is That It?*, the autobiography of Bob Geldof (1986) and *Beyond Left and Right* by Professor Anthony Giddens (1994)). What appears to connect these diverse examples is a common sense of questioning and caring – the attributes of the two-stranded definition of the global citizen as presented in this book: of an autonomous and inquiring critical disposition; but her decisions and actions tempered by an ethical concern for social justice and the dignity of humankind.

If, in the era of post-modernity, national governments continue to claim preparation for citizenship as a responsibility of a state-maintained educational system, what form of education might complement the ideals of global citizenship?

Educational citizenship: a concept of education for global citizenship

Three distinct groups of writers have consistently advocated principles and practices that help to illuminate a concept of education for global citizenship that, in this text, is referred to as educational citizenship. One group embraces those whose main interest is the advancement of rights for young people (amongst others: Franklin (1986); Freeman (1987); Hart (1992); Davie (1993); John (1993b)). A second group consists of those whose principal interest is pedagogical and whose wish is to protect and advance progressive, child-centred, experiential learning (amongst others: Weil and McGill (1989); Holt (1975); Meighan (1993); Darling (1994)), particularly at a time when there is evidence throughout Europe of a regression to subject-based teaching and the didactic transmission of knowledge (Torney-Purta and Hahn (1988)) – of which the National Curriculum is an obvious example. The concordance between these two groups is that the philosophy of citizenship proposed by the sociological writers requires the type of pedagogy promoted by the educational writers. The synthesis between education and citizenship is further strengthened by a third group of writers, who have emphasised the need in education for a moral and social context for knowledge and understanding and for autonomy of action (amongst others: Youniss (1980); Kohlberg (1985); Sharron (1987); Gilligan et al. (1988); Wilson (1991)). The development of moral autonomy is the second strand, along with a critical disposition, that distinguishes the global citizen.

The synthesis between education and citizenship

Each of these groups provides a valuable caucus of research that illuminates this study's description of the global citizen and its relationship to the educational process:

- the exercise of a critical disposition in making personal choices: 'of an autonomous and inquiring critical disposition'
- the synthesis of the cognitive and affective domains in developing moral autonomy: 'an ethical concern for social justice and the dignity of humankind'
- a pedagogy likely to stimulate both: independent learning.

Based upon the inter-related work of these three groups, a third approach to education for citizenship may be postulated. This is the radical suggestion that pupils should be accorded the rights of citizenship and educated not *in* or *about* citizenship but *as* citizens. Collectively, the literary canon of these writers suggests that the concepts of global citizenship and education contain symbiotic characteristics: the development of a critical disposition, moral autonomy, a sense of social justice, participation, responsibility. Thus it would not be possible to claim to be educated without having the qualities of citizenship, and vice versa. The relative problems of education 'in' or 'about' citizenship do not apply. Drawing on the reciprocal and synergistic relationship perceived between education and citizenship, the concern is not with the desirability or expediency of education for citizenship but with the necessity of citizenship for education.

The mutual characteristics of education and citizenship have been recognised throughout the history of educational philosophy. Although Dewey's (1916) interactionist theories contributed much to the educational debate in the first part of this century, he acknowledged that 'it was Plato who first consciously taught the world' about 'the social import' of education (p.88). Dewey himself believed in a spiral in which improvements in education 'bring about a better society, which should improve education and so on indefinitely' (p.91). One of the most influential educational philosophers in the United Kingdom in the second half of this century, R.S. Peters (1979), set out to clarify the educational aims that reflected 'the basic values distinctive of the kind of democratic society in which we live' (p.468). As we approach the end of the century, Meighan (1993) has written of 'the need to regenerate both schooling and society simultaneously' (p.10).

Autonomy

The extension of the political franchise to include young people has been addressed by Franklin (1992). His suggestions have obvious implications for schooling. He records that 'children in all societies are still denied rights to make decisions about their affairs which as adults we take for granted' (p.90). A critical area of denial is 'children's involvement in their education' and 'the right to a voice in deciding educational curriculum at school'. Franklin advocates the democratisation of schools so that pupils have influence over organisation and curriculum:

> I am convinced that the way to achieve rights for children does not lie in the adoption of any specific group of reforms, so much as acknowledging and supporting the general principle that wherever possible children should be encouraged to make decisions for themselves and act on their own behalf. (p.107)

Freeman (1987), commenting on the Gillick case, suggested that children, acknowledged in law as mature enough to make decisions about contraception, could no longer continue to be denied the right to make other important decisions central to their lives, including upon educational matters. Ronald Davie (1989), in the evidence submitted by the National Children's Bureau that contributed to the Elton Report, also advocated that pupils' opinions should influence their curriculum: 'One specific course of action which we would urge is the encouragement to schools to find ways of listening to and heeding the views of pupils in relation to school procedures, policies and curricula.' (p.98).

Roger Hart (1992) argues forcefully for education based upon participation, 'the fundamental right of citizenship'. For Hart, participation requires pupils, teachers and other adults to work together to resolve real community problems. The highest rung on his model of participation is 'child-initiated, shared decisions with adults'. The main object of this approach, which synthesises the child's education and her development as a citizen, is to develop the skills of critical reflection and the comparison of perspectives. Hart claims that the benefit is two-fold: 'to the self-realization of the child and the democratization of society'. Notwithstanding these demonstrable advantages (he cites examples of genuine participation-programmes that he has witnessed throughout the world), Hart maintains that there is no nation where the practice of democratic participation has been broadly adapted as a model for state-maintained education: 'Many western nations think of themselves as having achieved democracy fully, though they teach the principles of democracy in a pedantic way in classrooms which are themselves models of autocracy' (p.5).

John (1993a) reiterates Hart's view that conventional educational practices do little to develop a child's self-realisation. Like Hart, she also sees it as a duty of an educational system to develop in the child the shared attributes of the pupil and the citizen. For John, self-realisation, or personal autonomy, is a fundamental *educational* right. Referring specifically to the UK, she writes that children are presently being denied 'the learning experiences which are central to the development of a sense of personal autonomy and in that way are being denied their rights to education in its most significant and fundamental form.' (p.9).

Morality

The idea of the educated person as one who seeks serenity through the pursuit of knowledge and understanding is Socratic. But contemporary writers (Kolb 1984; Gilligan *et al.* 1988; Wilson 1991) have proposed that to be more than training or instruction, education must have a moral component that encourages the pupil's capacity to make value judgments upon transmitted knowledge. His work, originally with young Jewish immigrants from Morocco, led Feuerstein (Sharron 1987) to believe that children could not make the connections between the myriad of information that constitutes a body of knowledge without a value system.

In his early research into moral and social development, Piaget contended that the development of the individual 'is a continuing reconstitution of the self through relations' (Youniss 1980, p.13) and that of the two major interpersonal relationships in children's lives (with adults and with peers), relations with peers are more influential upon social maturity and moral development. The relationship between self and society as we approach the zenith (or nadir) of high modernity in the third millennium is, as Giddens (1991) has pointed out, more interwoven than ever before:

> Modern institutions differ from all preceding forms of social order in respect of their dynamism, the degree to which they undercut traditional habits and customs and their global impact. However, these are not only extensional transformations: modernity radically alters the day to day nature of our social

life and affects the most personal aspects of our experience. Modernity must be understood on an institutional level; yet the transmutations introduced by modern institutions interlace in a direct way with individual life and therefore with the self. (p.1)

Piaget distinguished between complementary and symmetrical reciprocity in relationships. Adult-child relationships were more likely to be complementary, with one person's actions determining the other's concept of self, and child-child relationships were more likely to be symmetrical, with the self and other as equals. Of the two relations, Piaget viewed symmetrical relationships, with their equality of interaction and consensus criteria, as more likely to contribute to mature views of society and moral conceptions: 'In sum, the seeds of a morality based on justice are relations with peers and bear fruit through the interactive process of cooperation, which is, in itself, open to further development' (Youniss 1980, p.16).

Piaget argued that if children were predominantly locked into relationships of complementary reciprocity – the relationships that typify schools and families – they would not develop as morally autonomous selves. Lawrence Kohlberg, who devoted his career largely to the study of moral development, advocated that school systems must develop a system of justice in which the rights of pupils were treated seriously if pupils were to develop a sense of personal morality. David Selman (1980) has tracked moral development in terms of 'perspective-taking' – the ability to 'see' another's point of view whilst simultaneously holding one's own. Bronwen Davies (1984) writes in a similar vein about the qualities required for social interaction, which she defines as the 'capacity to negotiate shared realities and ideally to understand and accept the realities of others' (p.291). Whilst the developmental theories of both Piaget and Kohlberg have been the subject of some reassessment (Kohlberg and Gilligan 1971; Davies 1984), there seems to be no dispute that a pedagogy that permits social interactions between pupils is more likely to encourage moral autonomy and that educational institutions have a responsibility in this area – that a purely academic course of study is only a partial education.

Pedagogy

The concern of the sociologists and psychologists with personal autonomy, predicated upon the agency of a critical disposition impelled by moral concern, as an attribute of the citizen and its development through active, collaborative and co-operative working on real problems in a real community, has an interface with the group of educational writers whose principal aim is to promulgate an experiential learning style, not as a utilitarian classroom technique but as the defining characteristic of education (Weil and McGill 1989). The close-knit connection between the philosophy of the sociological and psychological writers and the pedagogy of the educational writers is apparent in this quote from Boud and Pascoe, who regard learner control as the most important characteristic of experiential learning: 'Learners themselves need to have control over the experience in which they are engaged so that they can integrate it with their own mode of operation in the world and can experience the results of their own decisions' (Hopson and Scally 1981, p.162).

Proponents of experiential learning, like advocates of democratic global citizenship in schools, are keen to stress the importance of individuality, choice and control of the curriculum: 'In humanistic education, individuals are seen as having choice… If we can choose, it seems reasonable that we should have some choice about what we are going to learn and how it should be learned' (Hall and Hall 1988, p.27).

As Hart (1992) and John (1993a, b) draw attention to positive practices that develop both the education and citizenship of the pupil, so a parallel between negative educational and citizenship practices can be drawn. Rogers (1983), commenting on education in the US but presciently anticipating the UK National Curriculum, states that 'When we put together in one scheme such elements as a prescribed curriculum, similar tasks for all students, lecturing as the mode of instruction, standard tests…instructor chosen grades, then we can be almost sure that meaningful learning will be at an absolute minimum' (p.269). These are precisely the conditions most likely to suppress the development of educational citizenship.

The role that education has to play in a child's preparation for citizenship is put unequivocally by Lynch (1992): 'For educators the challenge of the 1990s is to deliver not just education for citizenship of a pluralist democracy, but education for active global democracy, founded on universal values about the nature of human beings and their social behaviour' (p.2).

Educational citizenship: a definition

The overlapping concerns of these three inter-related groups coalesce to give a picture of an educational system that would develop both the attributes of the global citizen and the educated person. A critical disposition would be developed within a moral dimension; the affective and cognitive domains would combine. The Council of Europe's Recommendation on Teaching and Learning About Human Rights in Schools (1985) concurs: 'The study of human rights in schools should lead to an understanding of, and sympathy for, the concepts of justice, equality, freedom, peace, dignity, rights and democracy. Such understanding should be both cognitive and based on experience and feelings' (3.3 of Rec (85) 7, 1985).

Kolb (1984) maintains that learning is not an isolated rational activity but an integrated function of the whole person. Other authorities reinforce the synthesis between the pupil and the citizen, between affective and cognitive development, and the holistic nature of citizenship and education:

> In teaching for the affective domain or even the cognitive domain it is not
> simply a matter of teaching 'about' human relations, human rights or human

and group identity and self-esteem, but of using teaching methods and strategies that are more appropriate, that focus on relating the cognitive and the affective, that make issues more personal, and that build upon the positive. (McLeod 1991, p.175)

if they [teachers] focus exclusively on the academic, teachers deprive students of the opportunity to affirm personal beliefs through rational, value-based action. (Shiman 1991, p.191)

Educational citizenship encapsulates the symbiosis, or even the synonymity, perceived between education and global citizenship appropriate to the third millennium, and that distinguishes it from education for, in or about citizenship, or Citizenship as a National Curriculum cross-curricular theme.

Building upon the experience in the field of the practitioner-researcher and the theory-in-the-literature, educational citizenship can be defined as: 'an education that prepares pupils for global citizenship by granting them active, democratic citizen's rights throughout their education; and that uses the curriculum as a vehicle for developing young citizen's explicit awareness of these rights and their ability to act upon them within an ethically informed critical context of distanced reflection.'

Educational citizenship inverts the traditional notion of a liberal education: that the process (the way in which pupils learn) serves its product (subject-based knowledge). In educational citizenship a subject curriculum has no intrinsic value – simply seeming to know something is not being educated as a citizen. Educational citizenship is dynamic; based upon a tenet that no knowledge is neutral, devoid of cultural meaning, it requires pupils to exercise their critical faculties to question and, perhaps, to change attitudes and behaviour. Thus it might be said that educational citizenship regards the process of learning as its product, the experience as the outcome. The philosophy of educational citizenship abuts closely to Meighan's (1995) definition of the aims of what he calls 'The Democratic View of Education': '…essentially, to produce people with the confidence and skills to manage their own lifelong learning within a democratic culture' (p.12).

The implications of educational citizenship

If the shared ground between education and global citizenship is accepted, how might this be applied to the organisation and curricula of schools?

Educational citizenship may imply a two-part practical change in the way that power is distributed, organised and controlled in some schools. The first part would require a re-evaluation of all the forces that contribute to the ethos of the school, such as dress codes, rules, access to school areas, forms of address. The organisation and ethos of the school, beyond lessontime, would depend on the promotion of the rights and responsibilities of global citizenship rather than upon the imposition of rules and sanctions to maintain order. In short, the hierarchical structure of invested institutional authority would change, with pupils being given greater control over their own education. This trans-formation of power would manifest itself in many ways, but most significantly in the altered roles of, and relationships between, the pupil and the teacher so that Piaget's symmetrical reciprocity was established.

This would lead to the second part of the two-part change that the implementation of a philosophy of educational citizenship would require: a change to an appropriate pedagogy within lessontime. The impact on learning styles would be that pupils, as citizens, would have equal rights within the school society and their learning would be typified, as is global citizenship, by responsible action. The consequent pedagogical style, which has been identified earlier as independent learning (and which is discussed in greater detail in Chapters 3–6), would simultaneously encourage pupils to learn more in a particular domain of knowledge and to develop the attributes of global citizenship. Schools would not be isolated, monolithic structures but would work in and with their local communities, giving young people the opportunity to gain first-hand experience of democracy, of co-operative working with peers, of research and interview, of encountering and working with others in society, of dealing with topical social issues, of understanding how to access and influence social structures and mechanisms to gain knowledge and of finding audiences for their opinions.

THREE FACTORS OF DEPENDENT LEARNING: OBSERVABLE PRACTICES THAT MIGHT SUPPRESS EDUCATIONAL CITIZENSHIP

Extrapolating from this study's definition of the global citizen and the con-sequent concept of educational citizenship, I will now propose that there are three key areas in which an educational system may suppress the attributes of global citizenship appropriate to the third millennium (the quotations in this paragraph are taken from the definition of the global citizen offered above):

- indoctrination: the indoctrinated pupil will not be 'of an autonomous and inquiring critical disposition'

- the social and moral isolation of the curriculum: the pupil whose curriculum is devoid of reference to the external world, and the possibilities of her part in it, is less likely to develop 'an ethical concern for social justice and the dignity of humankind'

- the denial to pupils of the opportunity to practise the rights and responsibilities of global citizenship: a pupil who is not given the opportunity to practise the exercise of her rights in realistic situations may be hampered in later acting as a global citizen 'not merely aware of her rights but able and desirous to act upon them'.

In short, such a pupil would be unlikely to be 'able, through her actions, to control and enhance "the trajectory of the self" through life whilst contributing to the commonweal, the public welfare, with a sense of civic duty to replenish society'. For the purpose of this text, the above pedagogical practices will be referred to as factors of dependent learning, where dependent learning is understood as the pedagogical construct in which pupils are dependent upon others for their learning and, through the suppression of the qualities of global citizenship, learn to become dependent upon the decisions of others, both as pupils and as citizens. The phrase 'dependency culture' was coined by the political right wing as a derogatory reference to those who exercised upon the state their social and economic rights as citizens. Within an understanding of global citizenship, the phrase would refer to those who were morally and intellectually dependent upon others and therefore unable to exercise their educational and ethical rights of critical and self-critical reflexivity, moral concern and participation.

With a pedagogy based upon the factors of dependent learning (in-doctrination, isolation and denial), the relationship between education and citizenship will not be that of educational citizenship but of inculcated dependence. The pupil, dependent upon others for all decisions made about her education, not only has no opportunity to develop the characteristics of personal autonomy, a critical disposition and a socio-moral concern but is ill-prepared for her role as a global citizen. After 15,000 hours over 11 years (5–16) of inculcated dependence, she does not cross the threshold of citizen-ship as a *tabula rasa* but as a slate upon which the characteristics of un-questioning dependence may be so deeply inscribed as to be irradicable in her future life. Such an 'education' does not just ignore the possibilities of educational citizenship, it acts directly against those possibilities. To return to the analogy used at the beginning of this chapter, the drudge and the frog only become the princess and the prince in fairy tales.

Dependent learning factor 1: indoctrination

Depending upon the degree and manner to which the responsibility for socialisation is pursued, the concept of the citizen to be developed, the values of the society to be instilled and the teaching and learning styles employed, state-maintained educational systems may be considered susceptible to the practice of indoctrination. A school regime that, by its practices or ideology, limits the future choice or range of action or thought of a citizen, beyond the limits of the citizen's natural potential, should be regarded as indoctrinatory, for reasons that I develop below. A school in which pupils are indoctrinated is not a school likely to develop the capacity for critical, personal choice that is a characteristic of global citizenship.

'Indoctrination', wrote Barrow and Woods (1982), 'is a term pregnant with emotive meaning and, for most people, it is a condemnatory term' (p.63).

Horvath (1991) makes similar comments about the pejorative connotations of indoctrination: '…no country or educator accepts the label…all political systems offer freedom and reject indoctrination in their schools…indoctrination seems to have become a philosophical four-letter word' (p.54). The public perception of indoctrination, in a liberal democracy, is unequivocally censorious. Media images abound and have the cumulative effect of creating a simplified caricature of an indoctrinated person as a brainwashed, mindless zombie – and the indoctrinator as the scheming and manipulative puppet-master serving his (invariably 'his') own evil ends. Even within the calmer and more considered world of educational philosophy, the subject of indoctrination can cause strong feelings: '…to take over [the child's] consciousness…will and reason have been put to sleep…' (Wilson 1972, pp.18 and 22). 'The indoctrinator…tries to make his pupils perpetual children' (Hare 1972, p.52). '…their critical capacities will be crippled…they often will be prisoners of rigid conventions…' (Spiecker 1991, pp.27–28). '…a more apt description of child abuse than of acceptable education' (Siegel 1991, p.37).

There is no universal definition of indoctrination. Kazepides (1991) argues that indoctrination can only be explicated in terms of religious beliefs. Spiecker (1991) believes that indoctrination can be defined as the suppression of a critical attitude. Green (1972) claims that '…when, in teaching, we are simply concerned to lead another person to a correct answer…then we are indoctrinating' (p.37).

Four criteria have consistently been advanced for indoctrination: content, aim or intention, method and style of belief. Kazepides (1991) and Spieker (1991) are firm advocates of the content criterion of indoctrination, although Kazepides makes the point that doctrines need not be easily identified to exist. White (1972) quotes an example that suggests that pupils can be indoctrinated without the doctrine being clearly articulated to them (although the teacher is clear about the doctrine he wishes to inculcate). He describes the teacher who wanted to inculcate the belief in his working-class pupils that they were fitted only to become manual workers. The teacher does this not by imposing upon his pupils an articulated doctrine of class and occupation but more insidiously by taking them to factories and other workplaces 'designed to make them feel that manual work is for them' (p.194). Both White and Spiecker claim that there is a doctrinal belief at issue because 'the teacher is trying to implant a belief of some sort or another in such a way that this is never questioned' (White 1972, p.194) or, as Spiecker puts it, 'the suppression of intellectual virtues and rational emotions relating to a belief is at issue' (Spiecker 1991, p.21).

White and Spiecker agree that doctrinal content need not be overt (to the pupils) for indoctrination to occur – that is, the pupil could be indoctrinated without being aware of the doctrine. Can the converse – that a doctrine could be inculcated without the indoctrinator being aware of it – apply? Kazepides

(1991) argues that as intention is not a primary criterion of indoctrination, indoctrination can take place unintentionally:

> Just as we can insult, embarrass, infuriate or intimidate other people without having the slightest intention of doing so, we can indoctrinate or otherwise miseducate them unintentionally. Educational and social planning that overlooks the unintended consequences of our actions, programmes, policies, institutional arrangements and so on must surely be considered narrow, unrealistic, reactionary and impoverished. It concentrates exclusively on the elusive intentions of teachers and overlooks the actual consequences of our interventions in the lives of the young. (p.8)

The insidious nature of a doctrine as 'an unfalsifiable belief' or a belief 'screened from criticism' makes it difficult to detect, to the extent that a teacher may indoctrinate, and a pupil be indoctrinated, without either being aware of the effect. Steedman's (1982) account of a small group of working-class girls suggests that young people may even indoctrinate themselves, or at least collude with their culture so that their socialisation is non-questioning. Other writers have concentrated on the immunity from criticism as a more identifiable criterion of indoctrination than doctrinal content. Siegel (1991) maintains that 'upshot' or style of belief is the only criterion for indoctrination. Thus if a belief is held non-evidentially (whether a doctrine or not), indoctrination has taken place:

> If a belief is held non-evidentially – that is, held without regard to evidence relevant to its rational assessment, and held in such a way that it is impervious to negative or contrary evidence – then the belief is an indoctrinated one, and the believer a victim of indoctrination. (p.31)

Siegel's definition also allows for the possibility that indoctrination can take place without the teacher being aware of it. She may not intend to indoctrinate – might very well strongly deny that she does indoctrinate – but if her method of teaching 'seeks routinely to impart to students beliefs without regard to their truth or justifiability, and in so doing so suppresses students' rational evaluation of said beliefs, then the "teacher" is rightly regarded as an indoctrinator, and the student is a victim of indoctrination.' (p.31). This is a theme he returns to several times: 'Thus, intention is neither necessary nor sufficient for indoctrination... Uncriticality and non-evidential beliefs, not intention, are the marks of indoctrination.' (pp.39–40).

According to Green (1972) and Siegel, if the main criterion of indoctrination is a non-evidential style of belief, no domain of knowledge – including science and mathematics – is exempt from an indoctrinatory presentation *per se*: 'There is no area of curricular concern which is not susceptible to the dangers of indoctrination; no subject in which belief cannot manifest "non-critical attitudes" or be maintained non-evidentially.' (Siegel 1991, p.38). Beehler (1985) gives an imaginary example of a teacher whom he claims is unintentionally indoctrinating because his subject and his presentation of it are so beyond the knowledge and understanding of the pupils that they can only accept and believe, therefore the teacher must be indoctrinating.

Kazepides (1991), Siegel (1991), Horvath (1991), Beehler (1985), Green (1972) and White (1972) have demonstrated that intention is not necessarily a criterion of indoctrination and that teachers can indoctrinate without being aware that they are doing so. It has also been argued that indoctrination can occur without the presence of a doctrine, or that where a doctrine is present, indoctrination may take place without the doctrine being articulated either to the indoctrinator or to those being indoctrinated.

As there can be different criteria for indoctrination, so there can also be different categories of indoctrination. Horvath (1991) distinguishes between both *de facto* and *de jure* indoctrination. Spiecker (1991) writes of indoctrination that suppresses the development of a critical disposition in young people and another form that intends to destroy a critical disposition in adults. Indications of indoctrination in state schools might be threefold: first, a form of indoctrination in which no doctrine is being inculcated but the style of teaching suppresses the development of a critical disposition so that the pupil is limited in her capacity for reflection, analysis and personal choice (cf. Siegel, Green); second, a covert form of indoctrination of a doctrine which is not acknowledged either by the teacher or the pupil, but is implanted by the teaching and learning methods employed (cf. Kazepides, Beehler); third, an overt form of indoctrination that deliberately exploits the non-critical dispositions of the 'softly' indoctrinated to inculcate a clearly articulated doctrine, perhaps under the legitimating guise of acculturation or socialisation (cf. Spiecker, White).

Any of these three practices would be detrimental to educational citizenship. One of the fundamental characteristics of the global citizen is her critical faculty, her ability to distance herself from society and reflect upon it. Thus any educational practices that suppress the development of a critical disposition will not develop the attributes of citizenship as defined in this chapter. The same would apply to practices that are covertly doctrinaire – such as differentiated expectations based on class or gender – or more clearly doctrinaire practices – such as the overtly ideological civic programmes of China and the USSR or the nationalist rituals and religious beliefs of some American states: daily allegiance to the flag, Christian fundamentalism applied to curricular study in the sciences (evolution in biology, construction of the universe and the nature of time in physics) and the humanities (interpretations of historical events, the length of geological time).

In assessing a programme of study and its related teaching and learning styles for any indoctrinatory element, the criteria of indoctrination (content, aim or intention, method and style of belief) might be used as follows. There may or may not be a content criterion; if it does exist it may not be in the narrow sense that Kazepides defines doctrine. The doctrine might be covert, so that neither teacher nor pupil are consciously aware of it, and intention will not be a criterion. The doctrine might be overt, but considered a respectable school policy of preparation for life. In this case the indoctrination will be intentional, although it is extremely unlikely that it will be acknowledged as indoctrination. A teaching or learning style that suppresses the development of a critical disposition would indicate the method criterion. Evidence of the style of belief criterion would be a pupil's inability to justify or criticise or even question a belief that she held.

If neither the indoctrinator nor the indoctrinated need be aware of the process, and the presence of a doctrine is not a necessary criterion, how, other than a non-evidential style of belief, might indoctrination manifest itself to the observer? The methods associated with indoctrination are those that offer no opportunity for the development of a critical disposition, so that beliefs can only be held non-evidentially. Of the various criteria of indoctrination, method (or teaching and learning styles, or pedagogy) is likely to be the most readily and consistently observable. Evidence of doctrines, intentions, styles of belief cannot always be seen; teaching and learning styles can. Pedagogy is capable of precipitating indoctrination, without either intention or content. The potential for pedagogical indoctrination can apply whether education is viewed as knowledge-based (a liberal philosophy of education), as by the Peters, Dearden and Hirst school of philosophy, or child-based (a progressive philosophy of education), as viewed by such practitioners and advocates as Dewey, Neill, Susan Issacs and the authors of the Plowden Report.

The development of these two distinct factions within the field of British state education, and their concomitant pedagogies, can be traced to the eighteenth century. The Earl of Shaftesbury described what would later be called progressive education, a view characterised for its concern with the purity of a child's natural self. It is '*Mind* alone which forms. All that is void of Mind is horrid: and Matter formless is *Deformity it-self*' (Shaftesbury 1978, Vol X1 p.405). Joseph Priestley (1778) believed that 'liberal education', as he called it, was characterised by offering pupils true – not dogmatic – knowledge that can be used in practical life:

> The general object of education is evidently to qualify men to appear to advantage in future life, which can only be done by communicating to them such *knowledge*, and leading them to form such *habits*, as will be the most useful to them hereafter: and in this *the whole of their future being*, to which their education can be supposed to bear any relation, is to be considered. (p.9)

So, the two opposing principles of liberal and progressive education: one of the transmission of organised knowledge, the other of natural development; one rational, the other emotional, one knowledge-centred, the other child-centred. These two very different educational philosophies developed divergent pedagogies, both imbued with the potential for pedagogical indoctrination.

The argument over method is put clearly, if rhetorically, by an early commentator:

> either to leave him [the young mind] to himself, suck in such Notions, and contact such Habits, as his circumstances, and the uncertain Accidents of Life shall throw his way; or to cultivate his Mind with Care, sow the Seeds of Knowledge and Virtue in it early, and improve his natural Talents by all the proper Arts of a liberal Education. (Fordyce 1757, p.115)

Shaftesbury (1978) had maintained that instruction was necessary, 'but only to form judgment and to exclude barbarity. The soul cannot be formed but will form itself by developing its own style.' (Vol 1 pp. 200, 222, 230). Priestley's liberal education required the imparting of certain bodies of knowledge by an authority to an acolyte, a method adopted in schools as the norm, but that was not without its critics. In 1832 John Stuart Mill complained:

> Modern education is all *cram* – Latin cram, mathematical cram, literary cram, political cram, theological cram, moral cram. The world already knows everything, and has only to tell it to its children, who, on their part, have only to hear, and lay it to the rote (not to the *heart*). Any purpose, any idea of training the mind itself, has gone out of the world. (Mill 1965, p.99)

A knowledge-based curriculum, divided into a timetable of academic subjects, is heavily content-laden. The present National Curriculum is organised in this way. Such a curriculum, particularly when it has to be covered in a defined timescale (a Keystage), lends itself to a particular style of teaching: didactic transmission to a passive class, a method that allows little prospect of the development of a critical disposition. R.S. Peters' (1979) notion of pedagogical 'initiation' is as one with the Priestley (1778) view of authority and acolyte. This type of curricular structure can easily create a pedagogically indoctrinatory climate where education becomes reduced, through pressure of time and content overload, to the didactic imparting of 'facts'. As Green (1971) has written: 'it is possible to indoctrinate people into the truth' (p.50). Teachers' comments such as 'Because I say so' or 'Just write it down' or the classroom practices of unquestioning copying from the board, taking dictation or adherence to a course textbook would indicate such a climate. Uncritical notemaking by pupils or didactic oral presentations by teachers would be other examples. Even if teachers clearly explain a process or an event, they could be said to be suppressing the development of a pupil's critical disposition, by doing all the thinking for them, and so indoctrinating rather than educating: 'when, in teaching, we are simply concerned to lead another person to a correct answer, but are not correspondingly concerned that they arrive at that answer on the basis of good reasons, then we are indoctrinating: we are engaged in creating a non-evidential style of belief' (Green 1972, p.37).

If a content-based liberal education can be viewed as potentially indoctrinatory in that its pedagogy is susceptible to the suppression of a critical disposition (and therefore antagonistic to the development of global citizenship), does a progressive or child-centred approach to education offer greater possibilities for the development of citizenship? Certainly, progressive education champions individuality, personal growth and active or 'discovery learning'. All of these characteristics were laid down by Rousseau in 1762 with the publication of *Emile*, the seminal tract: 'Every mind has its own form (p.58)... Nature provides for the child's growth in her own fashion and this should never be thwarted (p.50)... Childhood has its own ways of seeing, thinking, and feeling; nothing is more foolish than to try and substitute our ways... (p.54)'.

Progressive education takes as its starting point the unique soul of every child, a soul that is not a *tabula rasa* but, from the first moment of its existence, begins to develop as an act of self-creation. As Oelkers (1991) points out, this development is often referred to in Romantic metaphors of biological growth: 'All its symbols, slogans and metaphors are of Romantic origin. The "soul" of the child, education as "gardening", the "development" of "germs" – the whole language of educational reform was impregnated with the Romantic notion of *growing*' (p.76).

Proponents of progressive education claim that such 'growth' precludes indoctrination and promotes freedom. However, 'free', unrestricted growth does not require children to justify their decisions or actions. They need not develop any critical disposition. They could be guided in all their actions by the desires and aversions of animal freedom (Steutel 1991). The development of critical faculties requires practice (Mill 1965) and 'growth' education does not *per se* offer that practice to its pupils. The learning ethos might mitigate against such development. By certain definitions of indoctrination (Horvath 1991; Siegel 1991), such a system would be judged indoctrinatory in that as the pupil's choice is never questioned, a critical disposition is not promoted.

For different reasons, both liberal and progressive methods can lead to indoctrination – where indoctrination is understood as the suppression of the development of a critical disposition so that beliefs are held non-evidentially and are screened from criticism. If a pupil's critical faculties are not given the opportunity to flourish, her ability to act as a citizen will be impaired.

Dependent learning factor 2: the social and moral isolation of the curriculum

Another possible dissonance between practices in schools and the development of global citizenship might centre around their physical or psychological isolation from society. By specifying centralised national syllabi that all pupils will follow (in the UK, the National Curriculum) and compartmentalising knowledge in a way that makes it difficult for pupils to make the connections between seemingly discrete subjects, state-maintained liberal education may neutralise the curriculum so that knowledge appears to exist in an academic void. It has no social or moral relevance to pupils. They learn nothing about the world they inhabit as children and will participate in as citizens.

In a different way, progressive education may also divorce itself from the social reality, impelled by the idea that the purity of the child is contaminated by society. Rousseau (1762) advocated that the child, until the age of fifteen, should be isolated from society and 'remain in complete ignorance of those ideas which are beyond his grasp' (p.141). This has been a policy, adapted in varying degrees, of private progressive schools which have rejected the urban, industrial realities of society and established themselves in remote, rural areas with unsullied nature regarded as the best environment for the development of the correspondingly free will and fresh nature of the child (Summerhill 1924– date; Dartington Hall 1920–87; Beacon Hill 1927–43; Sands 1988–date). Where progressive practices have been adopted within the state system (almost exclusively in the primary sector), a similar philosophical viewpoint has sometimes led to a curriculum rich in imaginative and creative experiences but distanced from the 'real world'. The creation of a controlled environment isolated from the social reality and the emphasis on personal, rather than social, development is not consistent with the development of a sense of belonging to a global community and having responsibilities to that community.

Pestalozzi and Froebel inherited the legacy of Rousseau and continued with the idea of personal development through discovery learning, stimulated by ap- propriate texts (Pestalozzi) or activities (Froebel) and the caring encouragement of the teacher. Of the pioneers of child-centred learning, Dewey (1897) was the first to see the child as a social being and education as a social process: 'The teacher is engaged not simply in the training of individuals but in the formation of the proper social life' (p.29). Dewey envisaged an interaction between the communities of school and society – a major shift away from the Romantic idea of individuality and nature. Like his predecessors, he also advocated active, experiential learning but stressed the importance of group activities and maintained that the child learnt by interacting with its social environment:

> Where the school work consists simply in learning lessons, mutual assistance, instead of being the most natural form of cooperation and association, becomes a clandestine effort to relieve one's neighbour of his proper duties. Where active work is going on, all this is changed… A spirit of free communication, of interchange of ideas, suggestions, results…becomes the dominating note. (Dewey 1900, p.29)

He emphasised child development rather than a subject curriculum: '…the child becomes the sun about which the appliances of education revolve; he is the cen- ter about which they are organised' (Dewey 1900, p.51).

Dewey's ideas were continued through the work of William Kilpatrick during his tenure as a professor at Teachers College, Columbia between 1918 and 1938. Kilpatrick developed 'the project method' and insisted that learning should be purposeful and pleasurable so that pupils might become 'better citizens, able to think and act, too intelligently critical to be easily hoodwinked either by politicians or by patent-medicines, self-reliant, ready of adaptation to the new social conditions that impend' (1918, p.334).

This comment encompasses many of the attributes of educational citizenship, yet it is difficult to find evidence of any large-scale development of ideas like Kilpatrick's, in state-maintained educational systems, after the Second World War. Since 1945, in the Western democracies of Europe and America, the two dominant styles of state-maintained educational systems have been versions of creative, personal child-centred (progressive) education in the primary sector and objective, knowledge-based (liberal) education in the secondary sector. Both, for the reasons outlined, may be considered unlikely to develop the critical and ethical attributes of citizenship for the third millennium.

Dependent learning factor 3: The denial to pupils of the opportunity to practise the rights and responsibilities of global citizenship

The third way in which state-maintained educational systems may suppress the development of the attributes of global citizenship revolves around the institutional distribution of power. If pupils are not given the opportunity to practise the rights and responsibilities of their future citizenship, they may be ill-prepared for, or even disenfranchised from, full citizenship. Attention has been drawn to curricular practices likely to suppress pupils' rights in earlier sections of this chapter. There are also administrative practices likely to restrict pupils' rights: school dress codes, rules and regulations imposed by sanctions, gender and 'ability' differentiation, a militaristic management style, a competitive ethos, the exclusion of pupils from all policy-making organs.

I have argued that pedagogical practices associated with both liberal and progressive philosophies of education are unlikely to develop educational citizenship, when educational citizenship is understood as a concept of education based upon the perceived symbiotic relationship between the development of the qualities of the educated person and the attributes of the global citizen of the third millennium. There is, however, some history in the UK of a third philosophy of education that appears to have more in common with educational citizenship and independent learning:

> Libertarian education has strong roots in basic human rights. It apportions to learners a degree of independence and autonomy that libertarians seek for everybody. Furthermore it is a set of educational beliefs that seeks to break down the boundaries between teachers and learners, that is grounded in a desire to construct non-coercive and anti-authoritarian pedagogies, and that is not concerned with systems of reward and punishment. It is an all-embracing philosophy of education and learning that is compatible with anarchist views of freedom. (Shotton 1993, p.260)

Shotton (1993) offers a history of libertarian education and schooling between 1890 and 1990 in the state and independent sectors of education in the UK. He describes the the pre-First World War working-class initiatives (often funded by trade unions or community organisations), the private boarding schools established between the wars (reliant upon the fee-paying middle classes), the urban free schools of the 1960s and 1970s and the few state school ventures into libertarian education.

The book consists of a number of case studies of particular schools within these broad bands. Whilst Shotton is reluctant to generalise, and does not himself draw the following conclusions, his meticulous data suggest strongly that:

- there is no established tradition of libertarian education in the state sector

- the few state experiments in libertarian education have attracted the condemnation of local parents, national media and government agencies

- schools of an apparently libertarian nature that have survived over a lengthy period of time have actually had an authoritarian structure, in that their success can be traced to charismatic leadership

- the imposition of a National Curriculum, more frequent and more publicised evaluation (testing of pupils, appraisal of teachers and inspection of schools) and the prevalent political and socioeconomic culture make it unlikely that libertarian education will advance within the state system.

There would seem to be little realistic hope that programmes intended to develop educational citizenship are likely to be introduced into schools. The nature of liberal and progressive education is contradictory to that of educational citizenship. Although libertarian education has more in common with educational citizenship, it does not augur well for educational citizenship that attempts to establish libertarian schools have consistently failed.

However, it is possible both to embrace the above conclusions upon libertarian education and to take a more positive view of the possibility of the introduction or development of educational citizenship in state schools. Of the schools that Shotton describes, it is the free and state school initiatives between 1960 and 1990 that that have most in common with the ideas of educational citizenship – of democratising the school place to produce critical citizens – and the independent boarding schools – whose emphasis was not political but rested upon progressive theories of the development of self – that have least in common with educational citizenship:

> British Free Schools were based on the principle that pupils should have democratic freedom, and that they should play as active a role in the educational process and running of the school as the teachers and parents. In this sense Free

School theory was the epitome of libertarian educational theory. (Shotton
1993, p.203)

Whilst different free schools had different characteristics, all shared in common
the jettisoning of a set timetable and curriculum, class groupings and any
imposed power structure. Parents, pupils and teachers worked together to
realise their aim of self-government and self-fulfilment. These practices were
also applied in libertarian private schools but free schools were distinguished by
a more direct connection with the 'real world' – invariably they were situated in
urban communities, they were day schools with people constantly moving
between the cultures and environments of society and school, they attracted a
wider class-range of pupils than the private schools and they had a more
muscular perception of the relationship between education and citizenship. The
libertarianism referred to in the following excerpt from a Liverpool Free School
newsletter is not the freedom of dropping out of society but of engaging with it:

> for our kids to become free people – instead of dependable consumers – aware
> of our environment and capable of working together to shape (or preserve) it.
> Our education must be a way of life instead of a training for subsequent living…
> It must enable us to create community consciousness and control, and
> consequently a capacity for active social change. (Scotland Road Free School
> News Letter 1971)

Writing in 1993, Shotton was not able to identify one free or state school
presently in existence and successfully applying the principles of libertarian
education. A close reading of the accounts of the foundering of state or free
school initiatives during the last 30 years reveals certain recurring reasons for
their demise or restructuring along the traditional lines of a state liberal
education:

internal dissent

> State: Summerhill Academy, Aberdeen, 1974;
>
> William Tyndale School, Islington, 1975.
>
> Free: White Lion Free School, Islington, 1987.

inability to convince the parents or to sustain their support

> State: Countesthorpe College, Leics. 1973;
>
> Sutton Centre, Notts. 1977.
>
> Free: Saltley, Nottingham and Brighton Free Schools, 1974.

lack of LEA or HMI support

> State: Braehead School, Fife, 1967.
>
> Free: Scotland Road Free School, Liverpool, 1972.

Invariably, these conditions arose because the ideals of libertarian education
were not translated into a pedagogy that was supported by parents and LEA

observers as well as involved pupils and teachers. The brave experiments and experiences of these libertarian schools suggest that it is schools that offer (rather than deny) pupils the opportunity to practise the rights and responsibilities of global citizenship that have most to fear in the form of public pressure and criticism, unless a way can be found of implementing the aims of libertarian education in a manner that is effective and uncompromising but also acceptable to public opinion. The identification and implementation of the twelve factors of independent learning (Chapter Three) are an attempt to offer a clear framework for such a pedagogy.

SUMMARY OF THE CHAPTER

This chapter has sought to show that preparation for citizenship is regarded by government as one of the principal roles of a state-maintained education, but that present confusions about citizenship, that apply to all the UK parliamentary parties, have had a significant effect upon education for citizenship within schools which has led to the application of ideologies and practices inconsistent with the likely nature of citizenship appropriate to the third millennium.

A construct of citizenship based upon ethical criteria has been suggested as appropriate to the third millennium: global citizenship. A synthesis between the ideal of the global citizen and that of the educated person has been outlined and a philosophy of educational citizenship has been described. Current pedagogical practices in a state-maintained educational system that may inhibit educational citizenship have been considered.

It has been argued that attempts to democratise schools have failed because libertarian ideals have not been translated into convincing pedagogical practices. It has been suggested that the pedagogy of independent learning may offer a practical rigour so that the libertarian and democratic aims of educational citizenship can be implemented and sustained.

CHAPTER THREE

Research Method and Procedure

INTRODUCTION

This chapter attempts to record the method and practice of the fieldwork research and to locate that research within the critical paradigm. The fieldwork – spanning five years and involving 97 educational establishments in one shire LEA – is summarised, the relationship between the researcher and the research partners is described and a timetable of the research is given. (The phrase 'the research partnership' is used as a general reference to encompass myself and the various groups of research partners with whom I worked: pupils, teachers, parents, governors, observers.) An account is given of the development of clear criteria that were used to unify different aspects of the research, the attendant data collection and their analysis. Consideration is given to the appropriateness of various methods of research with the disempowered.

No doubt some readers will find this part of the book rather dry fare, so feel welcome to scan through – personally, I find the following chapters more interesting. Nevertheless, I thought it important in a book that makes some fairly strong claims and comments about current educational practices to show that the research that underpins my findings was conducted in a responsible manner. Thus a main purpose of this chapter is to establish an imprimatur of research respectability for the discussion that follows in Chapters Four, Five, Six and Seven. A second purpose is to set out a method of classroom research that other researchers, teachers, students or pupils may like to adopt, adapt, improve or reject for their own use in their own classrooms. The third aim of this chapter is to show some of the difficulties that a researcher may encounter when conducting active educational research within the school community. It was very important to me to find a way in which research could be carried out with the fully informed and active participation of pupils and teachers and to resist more easily practised methods of research that seemed – to me – to prey upon pupils and teachers.

THE RESEARCH BACKGROUND

The literature suggested two avenues of field research within the curriculum, the first to survey the field and record currently observable opportunities and practices in educational citizenship, the second to establish critical action research projects intended to develop educational citizenship (Figure 3.1). Research was conducted in all 31 secondary schools in the study LEA, in 60 of the 266 primary schools, and in one post-16 college, two special schools, two nursery units and one playgroup. The research took place between September 1988 and April 1993. This book focuses on the research and data collection in the secondary sector only.

Figure 3.2 gives a graphic representation of the research timetable, which spanned four-and-a-half years – during which time intervention and non-intervention research overlapped. A clearer view of the development of the research can be obtained by applying Kelly's (1955) three-phase creativity cycle of circumspection, pre-emption and control.

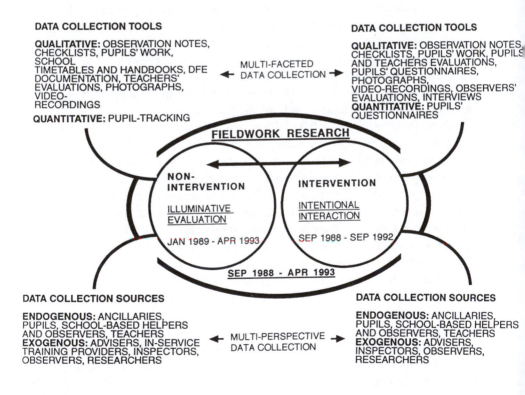

Figure 3.1: Description of the research illustrating the multi-faceted and multi-perspective data collection of the non-intervention and intervention aspects of the fieldwork
Source: Author

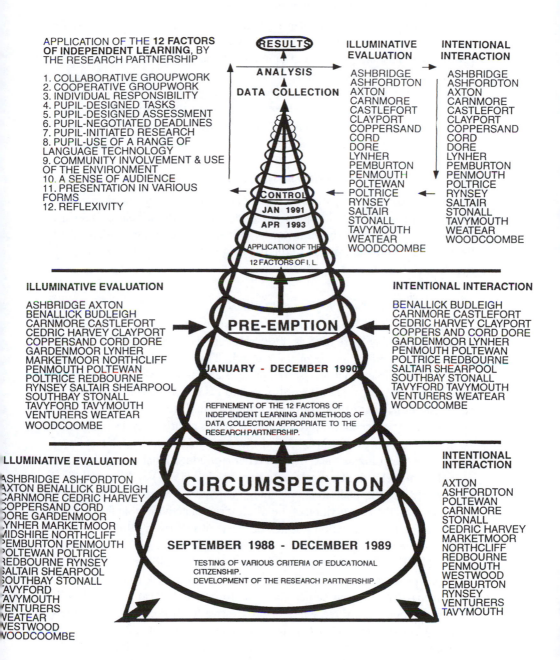

APPLICATION OF THE **12 FACTORS OF INDEPENDENT LEARNING**, BY THE RESEARCH PARTNERSHIP

1. COLLABORATIVE GROUPWORK
2. COOPERATIVE GROUPWORK
3. INDIVIDUAL RESPONSIBILITY
4. PUPIL-DESIGNED TASKS
5. PUPIL-DESIGNED ASSESSMENT
6. PUPIL-NEGOTIATED DEADLINES
7. PUPIL-INITIATED RESEARCH
8. PUPIL-USE OF A RANGE OF LANGUAGE TECHNOLOGY
9. COMMUNITY INVOLVEMENT & USE OF THE ENVIRONMENT
10. A SENSE OF AUDIENCE
11. PRESENTATION IN VARIOUS FORMS
12. REFLEXIVITY

RESULTS

ANALYSIS

DATA COLLECTION

CONTROL
JAN 1991
APR 1993
APPLICATION OF THE
12 FACTORS OF I. L.

ILLUMINATIVE EVALUATION

ASHBRIDGE
ASHFORDTON
AXTON
CARNMORE
CASTLEFORT
CLAYPORT
COPPERSAND
CORD
DORE
LYNHER
PEMBURTON
PENMOUTH
POLTEWAN
POLTRICE
RYNSEY
SALTAIR
STONALL
TAVYMOUTH
WEATEAR
WOODCOOMBE

INTENTIONAL INTERACTION

ASHBRIDGE
ASHFORDTON
AXTON
CARNMORE
CASTLEFORT
CLAYPORT
COPPERSAND
CORD
DORE
LYNHER
PEMBURTON
PENMOUTH
POLTRICE
RYNSEY
SALTAIR
STONALL
TAVYMOUTH
WEATEAR
WOODCOOMBE

ILLUMINATIVE EVALUATION

ASHBRIDGE AXTON
BENALLICK BUDLEIGH
CARNMORE CASTLEFORT
CEDRIC HARVEY CLAYPORT
COPPERSAND CORD DORE
GARDENMOOR LYNHER
MARKETMOOR NORTHCLIFF
PENMOUTH POLTEWAN
POLTRICE REDBOURNE
RYNSEY SALTAIR SHEARPOOL
SOUTHBAY STONALL
TAVYFORD TAVYMOUTH
VENTURERS WEATEAR
WOODCOOMBE

PRE-EMPTION

JANUARY - DECEMBER 1990

REFINEMENT OF THE 12 FACTORS OF
INDEPENDENT LEARNING AND METHODS OF
DATA COLLECTION APPROPRIATE TO THE
RESEARCH PARTNERSHIP.

INTENTIONAL INTERACTION

BENALLICK BUDLEIGH
CARNMORE CASTLEFORT
CEDRIC HARVEY CLAYPORT
COPPERS AND CORD DORE
GARDENMOOR LYNHER
PENMOUTH POLTEWAN
POLTRICE REDBOURNE
SALTAIR SHEARPOOL
SOUTHBAY STONALL
TAVYFORD TAVYMOUTH
VENTURERS WEATEAR
WOODCOOMBE

ILLUMINATIVE EVALUATION

ASHBRIDGE ASHFORDTON
AXTON BENALLICK BUDLEIGH
CARNMORE CEDRIC HARVEY
COPPERSAND CORD
DORE GARDENMOOR
LYNHER MARKETMOOR
MIDSHIRE NORTHCLIFF
PEMBURTON PENMOUTH
POLTEWAN POLTRICE
REDBOURNE RYNSEY
SALTAIR SHEARPOOL
SOUTHBAY STONALL
TAVYFORD
TAVYMOUTH
VENTURERS
WEATEAR
WESTWOOD
WOODCOOMBE

CIRCUMSPECTION

SEPTEMBER 1988 - DECEMBER 1989

TESTING OF VARIOUS CRITERIA OF EDUCATIONAL
CITIZENSHIP.
DEVELOPMENT OF THE RESEARCH PARTNERSHIP.

INTENTIONAL INTERACTION

AXTON
ASHFORDTON
POLTEWAN
CARNMORE
STONALL
CEDRIC HARVEY
MARKETMOOR
NORTHCLIFF
REDBOURNE
PENMOUTH
WESTWOOD
PEMBURTON
RYNSEY
VENTURERS
TAVYMOUTH

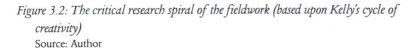

Figure 3.2: The critical research spiral of the fieldwork (based upon Kelly's cycle of creativity)
Source: Author

Phase 1: Circumspection (September 1988 – December 1989)

This first phase, although guided by the literature search and the common-sense theory of the practitioner, was open to a wide range of research issues and possibilities. The suggestions and opinions of the research partnership were welcomed and, from the outset of the fieldwork, the research was grounded in the personal experiences of those involved. Therefore, a variety of sources contributed to the emergence of a body of opinion that informed classroom practices intended to develop educational citizenship and the observation of 'normal' National Curriculum lessons.

Phase 2: Pre-emption (January – December 1990)

Progressive focusing on particular classroom practices led to the recognition and refinement of 12 pedagogical characteristics of educational citizenship. These became known as the 12 factors of independent learning – independent learning being the name given to the pedagogy of educational citizenship by the research partnership.

Phase 3: Control (January 1991 – April 1993)

This period of the research had the sharpest focus. The 12 factors of in-dependent learning were used as observable criteria in both the intervention and non-intervention aspects of the research. They were used to inform the practice of class-based action research projects and as an evaluative tool in the observation of lessons. They were also used to systematise the analysis of data collected in different forms, at different times, from different sources.

Thus, in the research, the three phases of Kelly's creativity cycle can be seen as the emergence, the refinement and the application of the 12 factors of independent learning as the classroom criteria of educational citizenship.

Kelly's model is itself a successor to Kurt Lewin's (1947) cycle of analysis – fact-finding, conceptualisation, planning, execution, more fact-finding or evaluation and then a repetition of the whole circle of activities. Sanford (1981) points out that the evaluation research of the 1960s (Scriven 1967; Campbell 1969) developed Lewin's cycle with precise operations. This process also reflects Elliot's (1991) action research spiral in which the focus of the research becomes progressively finer through the use of checklists of relevant phenomena derived from earlier analyses. Torbert's (1981a) model of coll-aborative enquiry has three stages of progressive focusing, similar to Kelly's creativity spiral. Heron (1981b) claims that in his full experiential research model, where 'each person involved is both researcher and subject' (p.156), many dyadic corrective feedback loops are created that serve to fully define the research focus during successive phases.

Therefore, it is claimed that the research timetable follows in the her-meneutic tradition of the Chicago school of ethnography, which, when 'rediscovered' in the 1970s, contributed to the development of critical paradigm research in the 1980s (Cohen and Manion 1980; Reason and Rowan 1981; Banister *et al.* 1994).

Non-intervention research: illuminative evaluation

The non-intervention research consisted of an extensive survey to gather data on what opportunities for the promotion of educational citizenship were offered to pupils within the typical curriculum and timetable of the study LEA's primary and secondary schools. There were four strands to this part of the research: passive observation of lessons; discussions with teachers about common pedagogical practices; the gathering of documentation; an intense study of the curriculum time of one pupil in each Keystage during a school week.

Lessons were observed in all 31 of the secondary schools in the study LEA between January 1989 and April 1993. Often, the same schools were visited in each stage of the research spiral. Throughout this time regular discussion took place with teachers at regional and national courses and conferences as well as within the schools where observation took place. For a finer search, three schools (two secondary, one primary) were selected and four pupils (one in each Keystage) were shadowed through all of their lessons for one week. This data gathering took place between February and March 1993.

The observation research followed the method of illuminative evaluation: 'Its tenets, methods and operating styles derive from cumulative practice and from reflecting, after each study, on what happened, went wrong, and went right' (Parlett 1981, p.219).

The neutral observer does not aim to proffer prescriptions, recommendations or judgments but tries to increase communal awareness and bring local as well as wider-scale policy questions into sharper focus. The evaluation, drawing on a variety of sources, seeks to promote discussions among those concerned with decisions about the system studied. There was a close correlation between the purpose of the observation and concerns expressed beforehand in discussion with teachers. As there were different purposes to different observations, particular (rather than unique) to different settings and to the policy discussions into which the evaluation would be fed, no fixed system of evaluation was initially imported into the research environment – that is to say, we used a variety of methods appropriate to different circumstances on a pragmatic basis.

Intervention research: intentional interaction

The purpose of the action research was to collect data on teaching and learning styles across the 5–16 age range that might be regarded as promoting educational citizenship via the factors of independent learning.

The intervention research consisted of critical action research in the classrooms of the study LEA schools and had two strands: cross-curricular, cross-phase projects, and secondary phase projects in one National Curriculum subject (English). The projects were referred to by the research partnership as independent learning projects. During the circumspection phase of the research in the study LEA comprehensive schools, 14 projects were undertaken, during the pre-emption phase, 24 projects, and during the control phase, 19 projects (see Figure 3.2). All of the projects were based on the libertarian premise that pupils should be allowed to study whatever they wanted, in whatever way they wanted, in partnership with whomever they wanted. As the LEA Senior Advisory Teacher for English (Secondary), I was the practitioner-researcher and director of each project. Details of the way in which the projects were organised are given below. Most English projects spanned one full term – the cross-curricular projects encompassed a full school year. Term-long independent learning projects took place in each of the LEA's 31 comprehensive schools, usually with the involvement of three or four classes. Around 4500 pupils were directly involved in these projects. Year-long projects took place in 27 schools (15 secondary and 17 primary), often with whole-school involvement. Around 2500 pupils were directly involved in these projects. In total, approximately 7000 pupils – spanning the age and ability range of the National Curriculum – and 250 teachers were involved in independent learning projects between 1988 and 1993.

The intervention research was conducted along the lines of Heron's peer-review audit of intentional interaction, with all members of the research partnership regarded as peers.

Heron (1981a) draws a distinction between the traditional social science experiment (a model of unilateral control) in which 'the enquiry is all on the side of the researcher and the action being enquired into is all on the side of the subject' (p.19) and co-operative enquiry, a method very similar to Torbert's (1981a) collaborative enquiry. Heron distinguishes between 'strong' and 'weak' co-operation. In the former, subjects [sic] are co-researchers and contribute to creative thinking at all stages; in the latter, they are thoroughly informed of the research propositions and invited to assent or dissent at any stage of the research. During the intervention research, members of the research partnership offered both types of co-operation.

Unifying features of the two research methods

Both intentional interaction and illuminative evaluation are methods associated with the critical paradigm and its concern with research that brings about change and develops social justice. Whilst the two methods have significant differences in practice, the values system embodied in both is consistent: a respect for different outlooks based on the conviction that all members of the research partnership have insights and a right to be heard and that the research is incomplete without such an acknowledgement and vastly richer when, through broad and equal participation in the research process, different outlooks are expressed. The two methods have other similarities. Like the various cycles of action research, illuminative evaluation also depends on progressive focusing on selected phenomena. Illuminative evaluation's procedure of formulating thematic lines of enquiry from an expanding knowledge base is akin to the construction of grounded theory that informed the intervention research. The successive transformation of tentative themes is very much like the constant comparative analysis of categories (Glaser and Strauss 1967). Both methods collect multi-faceted data from multiple perspectives and utilise triangulation as a tool of consensual validity.

In having shared values and methodological styles of developing the fieldwork, similar systems of analysis and theory generation and the same policies of data-collection and criteria of validity, the methods of illuminative evaluation (for the non-intervention research) and intentional interaction (for the intervention research) helped to control and unify what might otherwise have become a sprawling and undisciplined research programme consisting of the opportunist and unstructured study of a series of apparently disparate singularities.

A synopsis of the data collection

Both qualitative and quantitative data were collected from a variety of sources in a variety of ways. The intention was to build up an archive of multi-faceted and multi-perspective evaluative data that could be used to advance the fieldwork, contribute to the construction of grounded theory and test for consensual validity.

That both qualitative and quantitative data were collected is regarded (as well as the methodological unity referred to above) as a unifying strength of the research, rather than an example of its ostensibly diverse irregularity. Although the collection of quantitative data is not as often associated with action research in the critical paradigm as it is with research in the interpretative and, particularly, the positivist paradigm, there is no reason why the collection of qualitative or quantitative data should be exclusive to different paradigms. Latour (1987) suggests that quantification and qualitative analysis are different but equally valid forms of the re-representation of data. Bryman (1988) elaborates upon this view, stating that 'the distinction between qualitative and quantitative research is really a technical matter whereby the choice between them is to do with their suitability in answering particular research questions' (pp.108–9). Henwood and Pidgen (1993) argue strongly that qualitative and quantitative research should not be seen as typical of different paradigms as 'this would deny the possibility of strengthening research through the use of a principled mixture of methods' (p.18). Golby (1994) emphasises this point:

> Education, on almost any ideology, has broad terms of reference including such things as promoting tolerance and social cohesion; it is moreover a very broad field indeed containing a vast array of activities of different sorts. It is therefore much to be hoped that educational research, after all the cutting edge of educational advance, will profit from and utilise the diversity of methods available to it instead of consuming energy on futile theoretical debates about methods. (p.15)

When research studies have utilised both quantitative and qualitative data analysis, they have done so in three ways. Qualitative data analysis has preceded quantitative data collection and has been used to survey the field and focus later quantitative research on particular issues. Quantitative data analysis has preceded qualitative data collection – Emler and Reicher (1986) used an initial quantitative survey to identify groups for interview. Or the two can be used in parallel, so that statistical representations of the corpus of data and in-depth qualitative analysis can illuminate each other (Silverman 1985). During my research, qualitative analysis of pupils' project diaries, interview transcripts and written evaluations led to quantitative data collection in the intervention research (the use of a multi-choice questionnaire) and qualitative analysis of notes of lesson observations and discussions with teachers led to quantitative data collection in the non-intervention research (the use of printed forms during the Keystage tracking of pupils). The two approaches were also employed in tandem during control phase analysis, with qualitative data being used to generate statistical representations concerning different groups within the research partnership and also to exemplify these statistics. The amplification of the illustrative example can illuminate the actual experiences of the events that statistics and percentages encapsulate so neatly.

Multi-perspective and multi-faceted data

The data collection was multi-faceted in that different forms of data collection were employed and multi-perspective in that data were collected from different sources, both exogenous (the researcher and other observers) and endogenous (pupils, teachers and other members of the research partnership). Data collected included the evaluations of pupils, teachers, fellow researchers, observers within the school-based community (such as parents, ancillaries, school staff) and representatives of the LEA (advisers, inspectors, advisory teachers and advisory support teachers). Different methods were used for these evaluations: audio-taped interviews, video-taped interviews, multi-choice questionnaires, guided questionnaires, project diaries, pupils' open evaluations, pupils' guided evaluations, evaluations written by consensus of a collaborative group, mixed teacher and pupil evaluations, video-profiles. Other data were video-recordings of lessons, photographs of lessons, examples of pupils' written and video artifacts and video-recordings of pupils' live presentations (see Figures 3.3, 3.4 and 3.5).

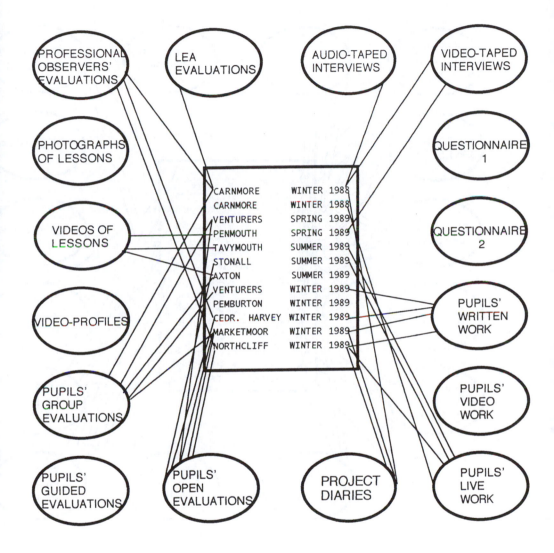

Figure 3.3: Data collection methods used during the circumspection stage of the intervention research (Sep 1988 – Dec 1989). Teachers' and researchers' evaluations were collected from every project and are not depicted on this chart, nor are schools from which only teachers' and researchers' evaluations were collected
Source: Author

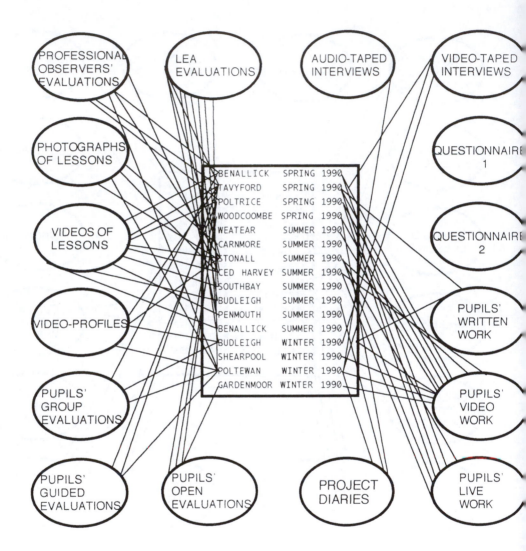

Figure 3.4: Data collection methods used during the pre-emption stage of the intervention
research (Jan 1990 – Dec 1990) Teachers' and researchers' evaluations were collected
from every project and are not depicted on this chart, nor are schools from which only
teachers' and researchers' evaluations were collected
Source: Author

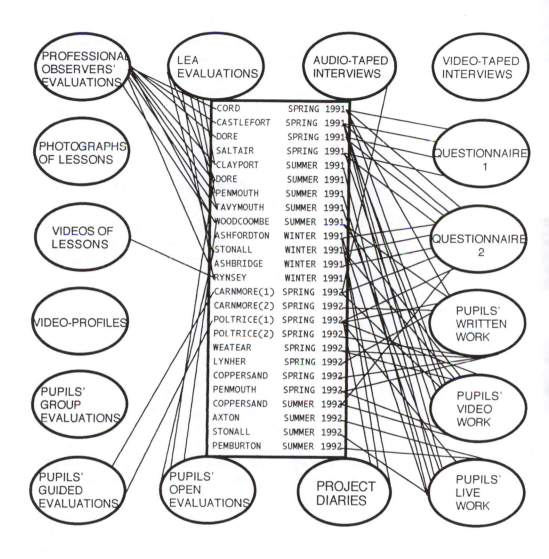

Figure 3.5: Data collection methods used during the control stage of the invention research (Jan 1991 – Sep 1992). Teachers' and researchers' evaluations were collected from every project and are not depicted on this chart, nor are schools from which only teachers' and researchers' evaluations were collected
Source: Author

Documentary data were also collected: DFE publications, study LEA publications, the school prospectuses of, and Inspectors' Reports on, schools involved in the research programme. Figures 3.3, 3.4 and 3.5 illustrate the development of the data collection in the intervention research.

Figure 3.3 shows a fairly even spread as different collection methods are tried. Figure 3.4 shows the same type of spread in the same areas of data collection as more expertise is gained through research in a wider number of schools. Figure 3.5 shows a concentration on some forms of data collection and a jettisoning of others. For the first time, as a result of knowledge gained, it is possible to use finer tools of collection, such as questionnaires. A balance of sources, and therefore perspectives, is maintained.

THE ESTABLISHMENT OF OBSERVABLE RESEARCH CRITERIA: THE 12 FACTORS OF INDEPENDENT LEARNING

For both aspects of the research, it was necessary to define specific and observable criteria of the classroom practices of educational citizenship based upon the literature which suggested general pedagogical characteristics likely to develop or to suppress global citizenship. General practices regarded as likely to develop educational citizenship were those designed to promote a critical disposition, moral awareness and an equal social interaction of adult-pupil and pupil-pupil relationships (symmetrical reciprocity). General practices likely to suppress such development had been identified in the theory as indoctrination, the isolation of the curriculum from social relevance, the promotion of the cognitive at the expense of the affective, hierarchical systems of authority/ responsibility and complementary reciprocity in adult-pupil and pupil-pupil relationships. The literature had suggested that such negative practices might be found within schools that pursued either a liberal or a progressive policy of education.

More precise indicators were needed for the purposes of classroom observation. It was also considered necessary to have a name for pedagogical practices that problematised the concept of educational citizenship, which described a philosophy of education that encompassed all areas of school life, rather than specific classroom practices intended to realise this philosophy. Havel (1986) referred to the 'essence of life' as 'independent self-constitution', a phrase which seemed to capture the spirit of the learning style endemic to educational citizenship. 'Independent learning', as a name for the pedagogy of educational citizenship, was therefore suggested by myself and endorsed and adopted by the research partnership.

Between September 1988 and December 1989 (the first phase of Kelly's creativity cycle – Circumspection), various methods of data collection were tried: video-recording, note taking and the use of different printed forms. This was also a period in which different criteria of observation were tested. A line of development can be traced of observation criteria and methods of data collection that concentrated first upon the teacher, then the class and selected pupils until, finally, a set of criteria were formulated that focused upon classroom activities – the 12 factors of independent learning.

Although Flanders' (1970) matrixes were not used, some early observations were based upon his interaction analysis categories. The categories were useful in focusing attention on specifics but it was found (not surprisingly, since they had been developed nearly two decades before) that the specifics to which they drew attention were selective and excluded certain practices because the categories were predicated upon a didactic style of presentation. For instance, there is no category in Flanders' list for pupil groupwork. The greatest perceived weakness was that the Flanders matrix concentrates attention upon the teacher rather than the learner: there are seven teacher categories and three pupil categories. Thus interaction analysis is likely to reveal more about the teaching style than the learning experience. It can also give an inaccurate view of the effectiveness of the teaching style. As there is no way of distinguishing interaction with individual pupils, the matrix could suggest a positive interaction between teacher and class that may have been limited to a small number of its members.

As a result of these trials, the gaze of the observation was changed from the teacher towards the learner. Time lines were used, at longer intervals than the three seconds of the Flanders' Interaction Analysis Categories (FIAC) matrix, to record what pupils, rather than teachers, did during a lesson. It almost immediately became apparent that blanket observation of around 30 pupils, as if they were a homogeneous mass, was a superficial exercise. Within every class lesson there were as many different lessons as there were people within the class. This led to the targeting of two or three individual pupils, or a small collaborative group, and their activity during a lesson was recorded every minute on a checklist. This revealed wide variations in the learning experience of different pupils in the same learning environment, which led to the construction of checklists designed to give information on particular activities designed to include all the members of a class so that no pupil was disenfranchised from her learning entitlement: opportunities for collaborative work, the use of appropriate texts, the range of talk.

From these checklists evolved lists that attempted definitions of 'good practice'. The criteria of good practice were influenced by a number of diverse sources: the RSA Education for Capability Award, the Swann Report, the Centre for the Study of Comprehensive Schools database, Technical and Vocational Educational Initiative (TVEI) enhancements, School Curriculum Industry Partnership (SCIP) and Mini Enterprise in Schools Project (MESP) publications, ILEA English Centre publications – principally *Gender* (1985a) and *Race* (1985b), National Association of Advisers in English (NAAE) commissioned publications – principally Allen (1988), the work of Human Rights authors such as Caroline Roaf (1991) and Ian Lister (1991) – both of whom suggest specific classroom practices – LEA curriculum support material and a search of the literature.

During the circumspection phase of the fieldwork research (September 1988 – December 1989), observation of 'normal' lessons took place in 30 of the study LEA's 31 comprehensive schools and intervention research, in the form of teaching projects designed to promote educational citizenship, took place in 14 of the study LEA's comprehensive schools. During the pre-emption phase (January – December 1990) observation was carried out in 29 of the county's comprehensive schools and a further 24 teaching projects were undertaken.

All of these sources – illuminative evaluation, intentional interaction and the literature search – were used in an attempt to discover classroom practices that activated the description of global citizenship. That is, the search was for descriptors of a pedagogy that would promote educational citizenship, a concept of education based upon the premise that similarities between the qualities of the educated person and the global citizen indicate a symbiotic relationship between education and citizenship. From this premise it is argued that pupils of all ages should be accorded citizens' rights throughout their education, both to prepare them for full and active democratic citizenship and to improve the educational provision of their state schooling. Such a pedagogy had been named 'independent learning', the pedagogical construct intended to translate a policy of educational citizenship into effective practice. Pupils of independent learning would have the independence to choose how they learnt and, through the development of the qualities of global citizenship, would have the opportunity to learn to become independent in their making of decisions – both as pupils and as citizens.

The 12 factors of independent learning and their relationship to educational citizenship

The following factors of independent learning were identified as a combined result of the literature search and classroom research – the provenance of the factors lies both in the theory and the practice:

1. collaborative groupwork: a group of three to five pupils, preferably mixed gender and self-selected, working in partnership to research a subject chosen by the group.

2. co-operative groupwork: non-competitive agreements and exchanges between the collaborative groups. The co-operative group to encompass all involved in the project, including adults.

3. individual responsibility: to contribute, and adhere, to the formulation of codes of practice for both groups above.

4. pupil-designed tasks: each collaborative group should define its own project tasks and the range of outcomes.

5. pupil-designed assessment: each collaborative group should decide what aspects of its work should be assessed, at what stage of the project, to what criteria and by whom – multiple assessors should be encouraged (e.g. a peer, a teacher or an adult other than a teacher).

6. pupil-negotiated deadlines: pupils should be entitled to plan the progress of their own project.

7. pupil-initiated research: pupils should have the opportunity to interview and conduct questionnaires, use databases, communicate directly with living authorities, access information centres off the school campus and make site visits.

8. pupil-use of a range of language technology (synthesisers, cameras, audio and video editing and recording equipment, word-processors, computers, E-mail, telephones, fax machines, photo-copiers): pupils should have the opportunity, by creating their own media artifacts, to experience and interpret the effect of language in a post-literary, audio-visual, high-tech society.

9. community involvement and use of the environment

   Community: education should be seen as relevant to real life. By allowing pupils to make a choice of topical social issues for their collaborative topic and by relating the work of all groups to the community of humankind, pupils may be encouraged to see global society as a series of concentric co-operative groups (starting with the co-operative group undertaking the project).

   Environment: taking the learning experience beyond the classroom walls (where it must be taken voluntarily by the learner if learning is to continue after the strictures of a statutory state education), a stimulus to experiential learning in the environment in which the local community lives, an awareness of a shared global environment.

10. a sense of audience: lending purpose to the project and shaping its presentation differently for different audiences, thus encouraging the critical awareness that messages can be put across more effectively if directed with a specific audience in mind. A way of giving something back to the community.

11. presentation in various forms: for a curriculum to be accessible for all, a wider range of project presentation than the traditional pupil's manuscript is desirable. For pupils to develop their ability to read the world, their own opportunity to create media artifacts is helpful in developing a wider literacy.

12. reflexivity: the sense of a personal stake in one's education and the development of the capacity for critical and self-critical reflection.

It is not claimed that these factors are exclusive to independent learning, but, if opportunities for some or all of them are available within a pupil's lessons (irrespective of subject content) then, according to the thesis, educational citizenship is more likely to be developed than if the factors are not present *because they are intended to support a learning environment of global citizenship* in which:

- an 'ethical concern for social justice and the dignity of humankind' is engendered as pupils work together in small groups yet are aware of a responsibility both to the larger society of the class within which they operate (and by extension, to the larger societies in which the school is located) and to the self (Factors 1,2,3: collaborative and co-operative groupwork and individual responsibility)

- the development of a 'an autonomous and inquiring critical disposition' is fostered in these citizens of the classroom as they become decision takers and policy makers by designing their own tasks, undertaking their own active research, having some control over the time and pace of their work and being involved in any assessment of the worth of their labour (Factors 4,5,6,7: pupil-designed tasks and assessment, pupil-negotiated deadlines and pupil-initiated research)

- through presenting their research and opinions in facsimiles of the way in which news and opinions about the world are presented to them (via television programmes, newspapers, magazines, public meetings), they learn how the media always has a point of bias. Thus, by creating their own media artifacts, they learn 'to read their world' (Jones 1990) (Factor 8: pupil use of a range of language technology)

- these citizens are encouraged to realise that their actions have a wider consequence and relevance by placing their work in the context of the real communities and environments (whether local, national or global) within which they live (Factor 9: community involvement and the use of the environment)

- by presenting their work to a wider audience, they are encouraged to see that groups within society can inform others with a view to bring about change (Factor 10: a sense of audience)

- a variety of styles of presentation allows the efforts of all pupils to be communicated to a wider audience and to be seen as having intrinsic value, thus promoting self-worth and a desire to participate (Factor 11: presentation in various forms)

- a capacity for self-critical reflection is an attribute of the post-modern citizen, as identified in Giddens' (1991) phrase 'the reflexive project of the self' (Factor 12: reflexivity).

Different factors have different emphases but, cumulatively, they are intended to stimulate the active development of the pupil as citizen: *The global citizen is not merely aware of her rights but able and desirous to act upon them; of an autonomous and inquiring critical disposition; but her decisions and actions tempered by an ethical concern for social justice and the dignity of humankind; therefore able, through her actions, to control and enhance 'the trajectory of the self' through life whilst contributing to the commonweal, the public welfare, with a sense of civic duty to replenish society.*

It was intended to employ the twelve factors of independent learning in four ways:

1. To provide comparability between, and within, the intervention and non-intervention aspects of the research.

2. To provide a focus for discussion with adults and children.

3. As a tool for interrogating the reports, diaries, evaluations or tape-recordings of pupils reflecting upon their experiences.

4. As a pedagogical framework for independent learning projects intended to develop educational citizenship.

Independent learning projects

1. All of the projects took place in the state-maintained comprehensive schools of the the study LEA: Projects were undertaken in all 31 secondary schools. Each project was undertaken at the request of the school, generally from the Head of English, sometimes by individual English teachers, sometimes by headteachers. No teacher or pupil was involved who did not wish to be.

2. All of the projects were based on the premise that pupils should be allowed to study whatever they wanted, in whatever way they wanted, in partnership with whomever they wanted: This premise was inevitably subject to some limitations, mainly to do with the legal obligations of the teachers and the timetable of the school. For instance, pupils were dissuaded from undertaking activities that were clearly dangerous; if working off the school premises, they had to return in time for their next lesson; their choice of partners was limited to the pupils in their English class (although they could arrange to work with adults other than teachers during lessons and with other pupils outside lessontime).

3. All the projects were based upon the concept of educational citizenship (although a clearer explicit understanding of the

classroom application of this concept developed throughout the three phases of the research with the identification and refinement of the 12 factors of independent learning): From the pre-emption phase onwards, at staff meetings prior to the inception of a project, the 12 factors were discussed and copies distributed. Before the start of every project I addressed any class that might choose to be involved and the same procedure was followed. Meetings with parents, governors and whole-school staff conformed to the same pattern. A list of the factors was used to orientate any visiting observers.

4. All of the projects shared the same five outcomes: Each collaborative group of three to five pupils chose their own subject of study but were expected to aim towards these five outcomes, which are listed with no sense of hierarchy:

    (i)   a short video, researched, story-boarded, filmed and edited by pupils (5 minutes). Editing to include computer-generated titles and credits, insert-editing and audio-dubbing where necessary, including theme music, sound effects and voice-over commentary where required.

    (ii) a magazine (or pamphlet, brochure, booklet) preferably drafted and published using a range of wpc and DTP software. The contents to include a variety of writing, both individual and collaborative: descriptive, discursive, explanatory, narrative, poetry.

    (iii) a short live presentation prepared for a particular audience (5–8 minutes). The presentation may be one of, or a combination of, the following (or something entirely different): dance, demonstration using technological and other audio-visual aids as appropriate, lecture, mime, play, poetry-reading, song, story-telling.

    (iv) a project bibliography of texts referred to by the members of the collaborative group, including databases and other research reading, visual texts, poetry, fiction, drama, factual and reference texts. The bibliography to include a review of some texts, with criticisms, comments and suggestions.

    (v)   each pupil to keep a diary of the project that need not be shown to anyone else. The diary might include ideas, drafts, memos, deadlines, group's code of conduct and reflections on problems encountered and group relationships.

    The video, the magazine and the live presentation should show a clear sense of audience and would usually be presented to that intended audience.

5. All of the projects spanned a full term of English lessons, in the schools where pupils completed the two Independent Learning Questionnaires: In some other schools, projects lasted for half a term

or the conventional timetable was abandoned and the project compressed into an intense period of three to five full days. The Independent Learning Questionnaires were distributed to pupils in ten schools during the control phase of the research.

6. Rhys Griffith was the director of each project. Other members of the study LEA Advisory Team were involved in some projects, notably the Outdoor Education Team, the County Multi-cultural Education Advisory Teacher and English Advisory Support Teachers. Technical support for video and audio-recording was provided jointly by the English and Performing Arts Advisory Teams. All of these personnel acted as catalyst or participant observers, as did the research partners of pupils and teachers.

7. Each project was known as an Independent Learning Project. 'Independent learning' became a commonly used phrase within the LEA. The action research projects were referred to by the study LEA teachers as 'independent learning projects' and the work as a whole became known under the collective title of 'The Independent Learning Project'. LEA funds were made available for personnel and equipment and a support team was established.

The term independent learning was less limiting than 'Education for Citizenship', with its associations with Political Education and Peace Studies and, thus, its perceived relevance to only a few NC subjects. Offering to work with members of a school staff to develop an independent learning project afforded greater access, first, to schools and, second, to departments within them. Many teachers, of different subjects and classroom styles, were interested in the idea of independent learning (with its connotations of research, the use of technology, a sense of autonomy or capability) whereas 'Education for Citizenship' would have attracted a much smaller constituency (according to teachers who chose to be involved in independent learning projects). The nomenclature was not a subterfuge and I do not consider it to raise an ethical problem for before every project all involved (including pupils, interested parents and senior management) were addressed and given or shown a copy of the 12 factors of independent learning, or early versions of them. There was no attempt to disguise the purpose of an independent learning project: the development of educational citizenship.

RESEARCHER AND RESEARCHED: A RESEARCH PARTNERSHIP

The research partnership was made up of four egalitarian sections: pupils, teachers, observers and researchers. Parity of esteem was accorded to each of these groups and every individual member was shown the same respect and consideration. Torbert (1981a) claims that educational research based upon the unilateral control of the researcher must fail: 'the model of unilateral control is intrinsically anti-educational and cannot, therefore, lead to good educational practice. If everyone in a given situation acts in accord with this model, then no-one is open to learning new strategies or to examining their own assumptions' (p.142).

Heron (1981a) argues that as the research behaviour of the researcher is explicated as 'intelligent self-direction', it would be grossly inconsistent not to apply the same model to the researched. His argument is based on the illogic of viewing the researcher as a self-directed intelligence within a scheme of relative determinism, yet simultaneously regarding the researched as fully under the control of a scheme of absolute determinism. Bannister (1981) concurs with the idea that to regard the identities and intellects of the researched as inferior to that of the researcher is misconceived and patronising, and also warns that to ignore their opinions can lead to incomplete research. He writes that any [psychological] experiment sets up a relationship between the 'experimenter and subject, and that relationship is not neutral' (p.196). To treat it as if it were so, or to deny the existence of the relationship, is not only insulting to the subjects but 'we have cut ourselves off from potentially valuable information about what is going on within the confines of our enquiry' (p.196).

Both Torbert and Heron advocate a research partnership of the researcher and the researched. Torbert refers to 'collaborative enquiry', Heron to 'co-operative enquiry'. Both methods share common characteristics: action research in which the researcher immerses herself in the research partnership in which the fieldwork is undertaken; 'experiments-in-practice' in which no attempt is made to control variables but rather to interpret, to vivify and to apprehend the dynamics of the research environment and its community(ies); and the shared explicit aims of the researcher and the researched.

My research methodology drew pragmatically upon the views of Torbert, Heron, Bannister and other 'new paradigm' researchers (Reason and Rowan 1981). But its view of the equality of all contributors to the research partnership was also based on the ethical grounds that underpin the subject of the research. If the research had been under the unilateral control of myself as the practitioner-researcher, it would have been inconsistent both with the concept of educational citizenship (within which collaborative and co-operative relationships are seen as crucial) and the democratic and reflexive attributes of global citizenship that a policy of educational citizenship is intended to promote. Unilateral control typifies the authoritarian, secretive and suppressive power that adult staff in educational institutions traditionally exercise over pupils, and that my thesis challenges, both within schools and society. Intentional interaction is a method of research that mirrors *the practices studied* in the intervention research: those promoted by the 12 factors of independent learning. Illuminative evaluation is a method of research that mirrors *the values sought* in the non-intervention research: also those promoted by the 12 factors of independent learning.

Pupils from playgroups to tertiary colleges took part in the research and contributed their suggestions and evaluations on all aspects of the research. Although this book concentrates on Keystages 3 and 4 (11–16-year-olds), the participation of pupils from 3–19 years of age offered deep background to the study and contextualised the chosen Keystages within a continuum of practice. Teachers were often participant observers of the action research conducted within their own classrooms. That is, they participated as *teachers* during projects which I led; they did not simulate the role of pupils. Thus their observations were from a different perspective than that of the pupils. Different viewpoints were given by other observers, some of whom were actively involved in the action research and some of whom were 'watchers from the shore': advisers, advisory teachers, ancillaries, caretaking and maintenance staff, carers, catering staff, classroom assistants, cleaning staff, clerical staff, ET trainees, head-teachers, HMI inspectors, LEA inspectors, lunchtime supervisors, members of the senior management team, parents, prospective parents, prospective pupils, road-crossing supervisors, S.E.N. staff, school deliveries personnel, teachers from other departments, teachers from other schools, technical staff, visitors to the school, YTS trainees. My role of the practitioner-researcher as advisory teacher is difficult to categorise. I was not a participant observer of the action research for I was neither participating as a teacher nor a pupil. As the director of each project, I was not a participant in the usual usage of the phrase 'participant observer' for I did not immerse myself in the *status quo*, I sought to change it. The phrase 'catalyst observer' is more accurate.

One of the points of resistance that I encountered from some teachers during the early stages of the research was their opinion that pupils were simply not equipped to take an active role in evaluating and guiding the quality and direction of the research programme. Yet the partnership between researched and researcher may be particularly apt in educational research. Davies (1984), in her research with Australian primary children, noted that: 'They are practical theorists: they ground their statements of theory in the events of the everyday world, and they use those theories as a basis for action in and upon the world.' (p.291). Ely (1991) points out that it is the interaction between the 'investigated and the investigator through which knowledge is sought' (p.122). Lincoln (1993) elaborates upon this mutual search for knowledge and suggests that the relationship benefits both parties for the voicing of the researched both empowers them and provides richer data for the researcher:

> Researcher and researched can engage themselves together in formulating questions that have high salience for the community which is the context of the study. In this way, the silenced, in becoming producers, analysts and presenters of their own narratives, cease to be the object of their histories and knowledge. They are enabled instead to become the agents of the stories which are produced

and consumed about them, and the agents and instruments of their own change processes. (p.43)

This concern for the immediacy of the research itself to empower the research partnership and to bring about change (rather than a delayed possibility of empowerment as a result of society's reaction to the publication of the research findings) can be traced from the work of Lewin in the 1940s, via Friere's concept of conscientisation in the early 1970s, to Hart's work on child participation in the 1990s.

The voicing of the silenced: implications for data collection

Typically, the 'silent' as a research category has been broadly defined to include non-mainstream gender, classes and races (Weis 1988; Giroux 1991), although they may be more specifically described as women, racial and ethnic minorities, Native Americans, the poor, and gay and lesbian persons. (Lincoln 1993, p.29)

In my opinion, to this list may be added 'children'. Schools that have policies and practices within which can be discerned the factors of dependent learning (the suppression of a critical faculty, the social and moral isolation of the curriculum and the denial to pupils of the exercise of the rights of global citizenship) are schools which are effectively disempowering and silencing their pupils.

It was decided as a precept of the action research that, as the thesis was primarily concerned with the democratisation of the curricular learning experience of pupils, the perceptions of pupils would be the primary data- source. The observations of researchers, teachers and other observers, as well as the written policies of schools, would offer data for triangulation.

In accordance with the cyclical nature of the research for my thesis, several different ways of recording pupils' opinions were tried. These included a variety of written evaluations: individual, collaborative, 'open', guided, project diaries. Questionnaires were also used, both of a multi-choice and sentence-answer style, and profiles of individual pupils were constructed from the questionnaires. Pupils were interviewed and data recorded in note form, and on video and audio-tapes, from which transcripts were made. Pupils recorded their own video-profiles, without the presence of a teacher or researcher.

Each of these methods contributed to the collection of various valuable data and to a clearer understanding of the most appropriate method for facilitating the voicing of those members of the research partnership who had been silenced, and the most appropriate method for offering the researcher the possibility of a generalisation. The relative advantages and disadvantages of different methods are discussed below for one of the main findings of the research was the discovery of an ethical and efficient form of data-collection of pupils' opinions.

The main problems found with gathering comments from pupils were broadly two-fold: etymological and ontological. Pupils often lacked a precise vocabulary with which to express unequivocal opinions: a project was 'brill', 'ace', 'excellent', but the reasons for this were nebulous – 'because it was fun', 'it was a laugh', 'we did things we don't do in normal lessons'. Second, in responding to independent learning projects, pupils sometimes appeared to be restrained from commenting freely and personally by the ontology from which they viewed education, hence oblique comments such as 'fun but worthwhile', 'it was good *and* it was educational [my italics]', 'just enjoy yourself even if you don't learn anything'. The effect of these two problems was that many of the pupils' comments were unstructured, elliptical, suggestive rather than con-clusive. Often a pupil offered seemingly contradictory opinions: 'I enjoyed it but it was boring', 'I learnt a lot but would not want to do it again', 'it was a good way of learning but interfered with my GCSE work'. Thus a main concern was to find ways in which the reflexive voice of the pupils could be liberated.

This approach raised certain questions. Is the researcher's dedication to the release of the individual voice compromised by providing a standard format (such as a questionnaire) for its expression? Or is the opposite arguable: that without a guiding framework, the voice might be inarticulate and remain unheard? If each individual voice is encouraged to speak in its own individual way, will it be possible to distinguish common themes, let alone quantify them? By relying on the child for the primary data, might the researcher be asking her to articulate views that she may not have clearly expressed to herself? And if so, what value would this data have, other than to confirm that pupils are rarely asked to reflect upon or to analyse their learning experiences? By relying on data provided by pupils, would the research lack objectivity?

Lincoln (1993) suggests four guidelines for research with the silenced. First, that knowledge generated is used in 'addressing or ameliorating conditions of oppression, poverty or deprivation'. Second, that it may take a long time for the silenced to find a form in which to use their voice, 'to find the shape and form of such stories, and a language and imagery for telling them'. Third, she empha-sises the researcher's responsibility to the faithful reproduction of these stories. Fourth, the researcher has a responsibility to ensure the validity and rigour of the narratives.

Her first point bears on the purpose of research in the critical paradigm, but also upon the evolving nature of successive independent learning projects within the hermeneutic cycle of the research. It can be argued that, as a trusted partner of pupils and teachers, I had a moral duty to improve and change each project in the light of what had been learned. A counter argument is that, as a researcher, I had an ethical duty not to make any changes or improvements that might contaminate the growing archive of research data. This has implications for research intended to provide a generalisation: does a corpus of research comprising a series of evolving projects provide data that can be used to generalise, or does the research consist of a series of related singularities? My viewpoint is that the consistencies that linked independent learning projects

over the eighteen-month period of the control stage of the research cycle provide a unification of experience that is more than the related similarities of a
series of singularities. Changes in the presentation to pupils of an independent
learning project, as a result of the hermeneutic research cycle, were changes of
degree rather than of direction. There were no radical changes in method or
practice between January 1991 (when the 12 factors were fully articulated) and
September 1992 (when the intervention field research was completed). Essentially, all pupils had the same substantive opportunities of the same learning
experience. The dependent variable of the 12 factors did not alter from one
project to another. An analysis of the data from different schools, over an
eighteen-month period, revealed that the projects were not perceived differently by pupils in different schools and at different times (see Chapter Five).

Lincoln's second point (that it may take a long time for the silenced to find a
form in which to use their voice) was exemplified in my research by the use of
different methods of data collection. Her fourth point relates to her second:
merely finding a form in which the researched can tell their stories is not
sufficient; for the data to be meaningful, the stories must be as honestly and
fully told as possible. For this reason, certain forms of data collection were tried
and then rejected. Also embedded within Lincoln's fourth point is a warning to
the researcher that data collection methods should not be chosen just for ease of
interrogation but because they are the best way of enabling the voicing of the
silenced. Her third point (the researcher's responsibility to the faithful reproduction of the stories of the researched) is relevant to the handling of the
data, particularly when it is changed into a different form for analysis – for
instance, the generation of categories and properties for the construction of
grounded theory – and the researcher has to make interpretative (and ultimately
subjective) selections of, and decisions about, text segments.

Lincoln rejects the image of the researched as the subjects of the research
(Hughes 1976). For her, they are participants in the research (Lincoln 1993).
She makes the point that:

> Participants as collaborators will need to commit to active learning. In some
> instances, their roles will involve moving to new and unfamiliar levels of
> abstraction in order to analyse the meanings of events surrounding their lives
> and to connect their personal, individual and group histories to larger social and
> historical contexts and issues. (p.42)

Maruyama (1981) draws attention to another problem of researching the
silenced: 'relevance dissonance' – that is, where there is a discrepancy between
the understanding of the research aims and its goals between the researcher and
the researched. The researched may counter-exploit the research (for instance,
pupils may enthusiastically but falsely claim how 'educational' they had found
an independent learning project because they would like to repeat the experience as it had actually been a soft option that allowed them to be indolent) or
supply phony information because they have no commitment to the project.

Maruyama claims that the best way to avoid relevance dissonance is not to instrumentalise the researched but to enlist them as endogenous researchers.

Teachers as the silenced

Some reflexive consideration on my part led to a re-evaluation of the notion of only the pupils representing the silenced, within a research partnership that also included teachers, researchers and observers, with all four groups purportedly being accorded parity of esteem. Mindful of the literature (Torbert, Heron, Bannister D. in Reason and Rowan 1981; Kincheloe 1991; Bannister *et al.* 1994) that stated that the researcher should not underestimate or patronise members of the research partnership, evaluations collected from pupils were re-examined. This exercise confirmed that there was a need to find appropriate ways for the silenced to articulate their views. However, it was decided that one could not assume that only the pupils in the research partnership comprised the silenced. In Chapter Two I have suggested that teachers may themselves be victims of a form of indoctrination that suppresses the development of a critical faculty, effectively silencing them – at least in certain areas, principally those concerning education. Parlett (1981) writes pertinently on this subject:

> The next point is that individuals are inevitably caught up in the informal thinking of their programme or setting, much of which they take for granted. As insiders who have become habituated to their environment, they no longer realise how much such thinking governs what transpires in the organisation. Studies have to be organised so that such pervasive influences are discerned and studied in detail. This means that there can be no exclusive reliance on what people say but attention also to what is done in practice. (p. 224)

The silencing of the researcher

Neither could the practitioner-researcher stand aloof. I had the potential both to be a member of the silenced myself and to act as an agent of silencing to others. The research was sponsored by my employer and there were certain pressures to show certain results. Amongst teachers within the study LEA, my own views on education were well known and might be regarded as having the effect of silencing those with dissenting opinions. Golby (1994) draws attention to these potential problems: 'But for an insider, with a past and a future in the case study institution, there may be a real temptation to use research as a vehicle for personal advancement or for the advancement of ideas or causes in a crusading spirit' (p. 25).

Various steps were taken to guard against these real dangers of the practitioner-researcher as an agent of silencing:

1. Open and honest statements by myself when questioned on my beliefs and values, so that members of the research partnership had no need to 'second-guess' my viewpoint.

2. My refusal to promulgate independent learning as anything more than an incomplete idea worthy of trial.

3. The encouragement of members of the research partnership as 'critical friends' showed that dissenting views were welcomed.

4. The use of data collection methods that guaranteed anonymity.

5. The jettisoning of data collection methods that were susceptible to respondent or experimenter bias (written evaluations solicited from teachers, interviews with pupils).

6. The use of multi-faceted and multi-perspective data collection from endogenous and exogenous sources.

7. An inductive approach to data analysis in which evidence generates theory, rather than a hypothetico-deductive approach in which evidence may be selected to fit theory.

Multi-faceted data collection methods used with pupils

As I have written above, the main problems found with gathering comments from pupils were broadly two-fold: etymological (pupils often lacked a precise vocabulary with which to express unequivocal opinions) and ontological (pupils sometimes appeared to be restrained from commenting freely and personally by the ontology from which they viewed education). Therefore, the use of multi-faceted data collection methods was initially undertaken in a search for a form of data collection that offered all pupils as equal an opportunity as possible to comment upon independent learning projects in which they had taken part – an important aspect of the voicing of the silenced. However, the use of a wide variety of data collection methods also provided the opportunity for assessments of divergent and convergent validity. Whilst some methods were discarded or amended because of a perceived susceptibility to experimenter bias (interviews) or to respondent bias (video-profiling) or because they were thought not to have representativeness (open evaluations), similar data were consistently recorded with varied methods. Thus the use of multi-faceted data collection methods had a dual purpose: to report the findings of pupils and to advance a case for the consensual validity provided by the data.

Table 3.1: Methods of data collection

Open evaluations:	pupils' group responses to independent learning projects in English lessons; pupils' individual responses to independent learning projects in English lessons; teachers' responses to independent learning projects in their English lessons; teachers' responses to INSET courses; observers' responses to independent learning projects in English lessons; advisory support teachers involved in independent learning projects;
Guided evaluations:	pupils' individual responses to independent learning projects in English lessons; teachers' responses to independent learning projects in their English lessons; teachers' responses to INSET courses;
Multi-choice Questionnaires:	completed by pupils undertaking independent learning projects in English lessons;
Written response Questionnaires:	completed by pupils undertaking independent learning projects in English lessons;
Lesson notes by:	pupils involved in independent learning projects; teachers involved in independent learning projects; advisory support teachers involved in independent learning projects;
Videotapes of:	work produced by pupils; work produced by teachers on INSET courses; pupils working; pupils reflecting on independent learning projects in English; pupils reflecting on cross-curricular independent learning projects; end-of-project presentation by pupils; interviews with pupils;
Audiotapes of:	pupils' work pupils reflecting on independent learning projects in English;
Photographs of:	pupils' work pupils at work during independent learning projects in English lessons; pupils at work during cross-curricular independent learning projects; teachers on INSET courses;
Examples of work	produced by pupils during independent learning projects in English lessons; produced by pupils during cross-curricular independent learning projects; produced by teachers on INSET courses

Source: Author

Open evaluations

Open evaluations were collected from both collaborative groups and individual pupils between 1989 and 1992 and found to have two disadvantages. The first disadvantage concerned the difficulty of sorting the data generated. The second disadvantage concerned the statistical conclusion validity of the data as representative of all pupils involved in an independent learning project.

Without the explicit requests of a questionnaire, pupils might not refer to aspects of independent learning about which information was being sought (although what effectively constituted a nil response was of some value). It was more time-consuming to sort the data as there was no common format and, therefore, no common order to references to particular aspects of independent learning. The lack of commonality caused by both these characteristics made it difficult to gauge comparability between schools. Open evaluations completed by individuals from a class involved in a project obviously generated more data (requiring more time for analysis) than collaborative group evaluations. It was cumbersome to collate and process the data into a form that could be interrogated. Often, individual open evaluations were summaries of diaries that emphasised the product, rather than the process, aspect of the project. Thus a great deal of time needed to be expended in processing data to learn little that was not apparent as a result of participant observation. Although such data was useful in confirming the findings of participant observation, an important aim of the research was to find ways of gathering information that illuminated the internal, rather than the external, features of the process of a project and the conduct of a collaborative group. The following excerpt from an extended individual open evaluation illustrates this superficial reporting of an independent learning project by Natalie, a Year 10 pupil in an upper set at Stonall (for photocopies and printed versions of the pupils' evaluations quoted in this section, see Appendices). Researcher's annotations (italic capital type) illustrate the data gaps:

> Cesspit Siege: A Personal View
>
> It was two weeks into the new term. The date was the 24th September 1991. Our video [sic] projects were just beginning. Groups had been sorted out. (*HOW?*)
>
> In my group were Sophie, Sarah, Tamsyn and I. We decided to do our project on sewage. (*WHY?*)
>
> One week before the 24th, Rhys Griffiths and Tony Stone had given us an insight on what we had to produce. (*WHAT INSIGHT?*) We were also shown how to edit and mix. It looked quite hard. (*WHY?*)

In Natalie's report (Appendix 1) there are examples of nearly all the factors of independent learning:

> *Factor 1: collaborative groupwork:* 'our group... We chose... We decided'.
>
> *Factor 2: co-operative groupwork:* 'a big day for most of the English group, the reason for this being that we were going flying'.

Factor 4: pupil-designed tasks: 'our group did some still photographs…we watched an Equinox video…we started to plan our live presentation'.

Factor 6: pupil-negotiated deadlines: 'Our magazine was shaping up nicely towards the last days of November. In the beginning of December we started to plan our live presentation'.

Factor 7: pupil-initiated research: 'Sarah recorded her speaking… We wrote to some companies'.

Factor 8: use of a range of language technology: 'We filmed a little pipe…Sarah and I did the computer graphics'.

Factor 9: community involvement and the use of the environment: 'Mrs Yanes, who is a councillor came in… We were taken to 850 squadron where we met the pilots and were given a briefing…Sarah, Tamsyn and I went down to the Timor Valley to film… We went up and flew around the coast. We got some good shots'.

Factor 11: presentation in various forms: 'Our magazine was just about complete… We did our live presentation and showed our video'.

Factor 12: reflexivity: 'I learned a lot from making the video'.

The project outcomes were all completed by Natalie's collaborative group. The evidence suggests that it had been a successful project for 'Cesspit Siege'. But little can be gleaned about the process of the project – there are virtually no details about how success was achieved. This is because Natalie has provided an account rather than an evaluation ('Groups had been sorted out… We decided to do our project on sewage…we started to plan our live presentation… The live presentation was ready… We did our live presentation').

Such accounts are useful, for, although they offer little insight into the internal workings of a collaborative group, they corroborate the conclusions of participant observation and Questionnaire 2: that well-organised groups can complete a successful project by fulfilling the 12 factors of independent learning. An account by Joanne (Appendix 2), a classmate of Natalie's, has a similar value in illustrating the factors in operation. Joanne's account ex-emplifies:

Factor 1: collaborative groupwork: 'Emma B., Antony and Cheryl went to the R.S.P.C.A. for a look around and did some filming there and we got a few pictures for the edited video from it. So Emma T. and I went to Mr Jacques and we put the moving pictures onto the video'.

Factor 3: individual responsibility: 'I had worked out how long Emma T.'s voice over will take to say and I wrote it down…I now buy my cosmetics from 'The Body Shop'.

Factor 4: pupil-designed tasks: 'Emma B. and I sorted out what order we were going to put the magazine in…Emma B. phoned two companies (cosmetics) to ask them some questions on animal testing'.

Factor 5: pupil-negotiated assessment: 'in the end we all thought "Crazy" by Seal was more appropriate as it had more appropriate lyrics…he thought he was being dramatic…Emma B. said to Emma T. that she had done it wrong'.

Factor 7: pupil-initiated research: 'Emma had written up a load of information...I asked around to people on my school bus some questions on animal testing and I wrote it as a survey'.

Factor 9: community involvement and the use of the environment: 'Emma T. and I went to Mr Jacques...Emma B., Antony and Cheryl went to the R.S.P.C.A...Emma B. phoned two companies'.

Factor 10: a sense of audience: '"Crazy" by Seal was more appropriate'.

Factor 11: presentation in various forms: 'To start off with, everybody in the group wrote a diary...the magazine...the edited video'.

Factor 12: reflexivity: 'I have learnt a lot by doing this project from research and now I am against animal testing'.

Some details about certain factors are given, for instance that the pupil-designed tasks involved task sharing rather than task allocation and that the pupil-initiated research included surveys and interviews. But the account is still tantalisingly discreet about group dynamics, how the group formed, how arguments were resolved and decisions made.

The second disadvantage of open evaluations concerned the validity of the data as representative of all pupils involved in an independent learning project. The open evaluation tended to favour the more able pupil. Without the assistance of any framework to guide and support, less able and less literate pupils often struggled to organise and express their responses. Participant observation suggested that discussions immediately prior to the writing of a group open evaluation sometimes excluded the less articulate or confident members of the group, so that the evaluations may not be truly representative of the opinions of all members of the co-operative group.

The greatest advantage of the open evaluation is also its greatest weakness: by offering no guidelines, no questions, no restrictions, it seeks not to influence the pupil's response in any way. However, these very features disenfranchise those pupils who find self-reflection awkward and who may have difficulty in constructing an unsupported personal narrative. The problems of data analysis could be overcome if it was felt that the data was valid. Open essay evaluations could be processed and interrogated using the techniques employed for Questionnaire 2 (see p.103) but if the data are not considered representative of the whole ability range of pupils who undertake independent learning projects, it might be thought more effective to try other, more equitable, ways of gathering information.

Guided evaluations

Guided evaluations were more productive than open essay evaluations for, to some extent, they overcame the weaknesses of an open evaluation whilst retaining its strengths. Pupils could write an extended evaluation, but within a framework that structured the narrative. This had the effect of offering support to pupils who had found it difficult or impossible to write an open evaluation. It also ordered the data so that analysis, using the techniques employed in Questionnaire 2, was more straightforward. Most effectively, the extended guided evaluation generated much more detailed data about the internal workings of collaborative groups. The two examples that comprise Appendices 3 and 4 illustrate how pupils across the age and ability range were able to organise their thoughts about independent learning using the same guided format for evaluation.

The first example (Appendix 3) was written by a Year 10 pupil in an upper set at Poltrice whose class had undertaken an independent learning project in the Spring term of 1992. The ability level of the pupils was closely akin to that of the Year 10 Stonall pupils, two of whose open evaluations are quoted above. It is quite noticeable that the Poltrice Year 10 evaluations are significantly richer in offering insight into the process of the project.

Vanessa's evaluation, like Natalie's and Joanne's, is useful both in ex-emplifying the factors of independent learning in operation and in confirming questionnaire trends – such as the generally held views concerning the importance of issues of time management, choice of subject and group dy-namics. However, Vanessa's evaluation contains greater detail about these issues and, as a document about independent learning from a primary source, is of greater value to the researcher.

As has been written, the guided evaluation was a better data-gathering instrument than the open evaluation as it was accessible to a wider range of pupils. Appendix 4 is the guided evaluation completed by an individual needs pupil, a boy, from Poltrice whose class participated in an independent learning project during the same term (Spring 1992) as Vanessa's group. Shaun's project revolved around a co-operative expedition and presentation. In collaborative groups the class prepared for a visit to the local hospital, where they were to interview staff and patients. The results of this community research were then to be used for video, magazine and live outcomes which would be presented to a another Year 8 class in the school. The project was successfully accomplished, apart from the inconvenience of not being allowed to video-record in the hospital (audio-recorders were used during interviews with patients). It is doubtful that Shaun, without the supporting structure of the guided evaluation form, would have been able to marshal his thoughts in a way that both allowed him to express himself succinctly and also facilitated data processing and analysis. It is maintained that the guided evaluation form, like Questionnaires 1 and 2, encouraged voicing.

In summary, both open and guided evaluations were useful for gathering data that exemplified the factors of independent learning in operation and for gathering data that confirmed and exemplified trends identified in the analysis of Questionnaires 1 and 2. Open evaluations were of limited use with less able pupils whilst guided evaluation forms were accessible to the full ability range.

Open evaluations were less effective in generating data on the process of a project and more difficult to collate and interrogate.

Project diaries

The most extended form of open evaluation was the project diaries kept by pupils during independent learning projects. The enthusiasm for keeping project diaries varied from school to school, and from class to class within schools. Sometimes they were functional and perfunctory, at other times they showed a high degree of reflexivity. An analysis of the project diaries of one collaborative group called 'MOB' (five Year 9 pupils – two girls and three boys – Winter 1988) was undertaken. The full text of the analysis (30,000+ words) is available to other researchers, but only a condensed summary of the findings is given below:

1. To show that the study of a singularity of 'the silenced' is a valuable research practice in illuminating the research community of the silenced and highlighting productive areas of research potential that may lead to a generalisation. The MOB diaries, and a follow-up interview with the members of the group (1991), indicated some seminal lines of research: the identification of boys with the product, and girls with the process, of learning; the tensions of collaborative groupwork; the relationship between boys and girls.

2. Pupils may devalue their learning experiences, or simply not recognise them. In an end-of-project group evaluation, MOB concluded that they had failed to achieve anything of value. Individual members' comments in the diaries repeatedly made the same point. This opinion was consistently based on the group's perception that success equated with the production of a great deal of neat writing. No recognition was given by any member of the group to the high level of personal and social skills they exhibited – success was defined by product, not process.

3. Certain aspects of independent learning are a natural, if unrecognised and unstructured, form of learning that pupils are likely to adopt unconsciously, given the freedom to choose their own learning styles. Although relationships between group members were sometimes volatile, the group functioned as a collaborative unit throughout the project and the diaries show evidence of all the factors of independent learning – although the factors were often unrecognised (see 2. above).

4. The use of the 12 factors as a tool of analysis upon an ethnographic text was efficient. The 12 factors allowed a systematic analysis of the

diaries and interview transcripts from a different ontological perspective than that held by the diarists.

The greatest value to the research programme was the realisation, via the MOB analysis, that independent learning may well be a natural activity but that without an external agent (such as a teacher) making explicit to pupils their personal and social achievements, and possibly offering practical advice on how to achieve greater success, pupils may not realise that the natural activity they are engaging in is a learning activity. The greatest disadvantage of using project diaries was the enormous amount of data generated and the consequent difficulties of systematising the data for analysis. Fascinating though the exploration of these ethnographic texts was, it would simply have been too time consuming to use project diaries as the main data collection tool. There may also have been a problem of representativeness: the project diaries were respected as the personal property of pupils, thus the only diaries that were used in the data collection were those that pupils had offered voluntarily.

Interviews

Interviews, whether video or audio-recorded, had one particular feature that could be an advantage and a disadvantage: an interviewer could usefully guide the discussion so that the specific areas that a researcher wished to gain information on were covered but the very presence of the interviewer could influence the type of answers pupils gave and steer discussion away from areas upon which pupils might have commented if not constrained by the interview format (Maruyama 1981; Finch 1993; Bannister *et al*. 1994). Thus interviews were found to be susceptible to experimenter bias and data contamination.

Interviews were most useful as a follow-up to questionnaires, evaluations or the reading of project diaries (Natalie's open evaluation, or the MOB diaries, are good examples). In this way, an interview could target a specific aspect or factor that had a particular relevance to the pupil or collaborative group being interviewed. Unstructured interviews, because they lacked a personal focus for the interviewees, tended to produce generalised answers and to be time consuming as the interviewer searched for a focus that might galvanise personal reflection based upon the interviewee's actual experiences during a project. Interviews were most productive when they were short and devoted to discussion based upon the known experiences of a group. Group interviews were more efficient than interviewing group members separately, both in terms of time (of the interviews themselves and the making of transcripts) and quality of discussion.

The main value of interviews is considered to be the same as that of open and guided evaluations: they offer consensual validation and qualitative exemplification of the questionnaire statistics.

Video-profiling

I had high hopes for video-profiling as a method of gathering pupils' reflections on independent learning projects. The method was not time consuming: as collaborative groups, towards the end of a project, finished their own work, they were asked to find a spare room, set up a video-camera on a tripod and record their opinions of the project. This seemed to be a form of open evaluation that should not deny any pupil the opportunity to make a statement.

In practice, video-profiling was, perhaps, the least valid and informative method, principally because there was no anonymity – something that may have liberated questionnaire respondents to be able to write with a greater degree of criticism than was evident in the video-profiling, the comments of which were almost universally complimentary in a generalised (about the project) or personalised (about the teachers) way. Thus video-profiling was regarded as susceptible to respondent bias.

Questionnaires

Questionnaires 1 and 2 were completed by 514 pupils (239 boys – 46.5%; 275 girls – 53.5%), from 10 comprehensive schools in the study LEA who undertook independent learning projects between January 1990 and June 1992. Completed questionnaires were returned by 94 per cent of the target population. The pupils spanned the 11–15 age range (24.9% Year 7, 36.0% Year 8, 24.5% Year 9 and 14.6% Year 10) and the full ability range. Some classes were setted, some mixed ability. Pupils from 'top' sets and individual needs classes took part in the project and completed the questionnaires. Pupils born in the study LEA and non-indigenous pupils were represented, as were pupils from family backgrounds across the social scale.

Despite these variables (and others such as school ethos and facilities, the expectations and expertise of teachers, and the quality of advisory team support), there is a consistency of opinion expressed in the questionnaires. Local fluctuations are hard to detect. This was a consequential finding as one of the aims of the questionnaire was to see if there is some evidence for consensus – that is, that independent learning is not something that only suits a particular section of the school population.

Other data suggest that the findings of the questionnaires are representative of all the pupils who were involved in independent learning projects, not just those pupils who completed the questionnaires. From January 1990 to June 1992 an independent learning project with English Advisory Team classroom support, lasting for either half of a term or a whole term, was undertaken in every secondary school in the study LEA. Although the questionnaires were administered in only 10 of the 31 secondary schools, observation notes, examples of pupils' work and end-of-project evaluations were collected from every school. The salient points that emerge from these secondary data are consistent with the findings of the questionnaires: both sets of data corroborate each other.

Questionnaire 1: format and rationale

The particular target of enquiry was to try to establish *how pupils felt they had learnt and what learning strategies they considered to be most effective.*

Questionnaire 1 (Appendix 5) had the following aims:

1. To find out what learning strategies pupils had chosen for themselves (A–H, 1–5 ratings).

2. To find out how effective pupils considered these strategies to be (V–Z ratings).

3. To assess whether such a questionnaire was a valid and efficient way of collecting data from pupils about their perceptions of their learning.

4. To provide information for further independent learning projects.

Questionnaire 1 was designed in collaboration with pupils in the four schools. The phrasing of the A–H options and the 1–5 and V–Z ratings was the pupils' own, as was the list of eight questions. The phrasing of instructions and explanations was mine, based upon discussion with pupils. The format of the answer box for each question in Section 1 was designed by me but was self-evident after the evolution of the A–H options and 1–5 and V–Z ratings. The learning strategies that comprise the eight options were suggested by pupils. This process took several weeks in the second half of the Spring term in informal conversations with small groups of pupils. That the pupils themselves (not all of them, but self-selecting groups who were interested in the idea of developing a questionnaire about the project) played a major part in its design led to hopes that the voicing of the child would not be constrained by a questionnaire format but that its expression would be strengthened by the framework that this particular questionnaire provided. Although having the constraints of any multi-choice format, Questionnaire 1 had the advantage that the options and ratings had been written by the people (involved pupils) who had the best experience, if not necessarily the best articulated insight, into the learning strategies most likely to have been used. A further easing of the bonds of a multi-choice questionnaire was that a combination of the A–H options and 1–5 and V–Z ratings gave an extremely wide range of possible responses to each question – over 10 million.

Questionnaire 1 was piloted with groups of Year 8 pupils at Castlefort and Saltair and with a class of Year 7 pupils at Dore. This piloting showed that pupils could understand the format. The time taken to complete the questionnaire was about 25 minutes. The pupils exhibited no difficulties in completing the questionnaire and expressed none in conversation afterwards. If anything, the opposite was demonstrated with pupils treating the questionnaire seriously but enjoying being asked for their opinions. This alleviated a research concern that some of the phrasing was naïve and ambiguous. It was regarded as one of the strengths of the questionnaire that the pupils themselves had identified the range of options but there was concern that their phrasing of the responses (particularly the 1–5 and V–Z ratings) might confuse respondents. The teachers who administered the full questionnaire, despite initial misgivings about its complexity, reported no problems. Of the pupils who returned a questionnaire, only three commented on finding it difficult to fill in.

A second possible weakness of the questionnaire, from a researcher's perspective, might have been that it could generate too much data too complicated to process and interrogate and that a clear view of the findings might be difficult to achieve (particularly with the permutations that the number and letter ratings allowed). Trials of various computer software programmes were undertaken before, during and after the completion of the questionnaire by pupils. It was concluded that if a suitable qualitative analysis programme could not be located, it would be possible to organise the findings with a simple spreadsheet and pocket calculator approach, although a full series of sophisticated sorts and searches might not be possible. The analysis strategy decided upon was to look at the responses to each question to see if there was a consistent pattern and, if there was, to undertake a statistical interrogation of the accumulated figures of the eight questions of the questionnaire as a whole rather than undertaking a minute exploration of each individual question. Classroom observation and participation during the project suggested that girls appeared to work more readily than boys and so the analysis ought to be capable of gender differentiation and comparison.

Thus the data analysis had three precise aims:

1.   To identify learning strategies chosen by pupils.

2.   To identify those strategies that pupils regarded as most effective.

3.   To identify any differences in the responses of girl and boys.

There were eight choices of answer for each of the eight questions. These were known as the A–H options – brief descriptions of the ways in which pupils perceived that they spent their time learning. The number of the options and their phrasing was suggested by pupils involved in the project and had these meanings:

A: I spent time learning based upon a foundation of knowledge, experience or expertise.

B: I spent time learning by being told or shown by a teacher.

C: I spent time learning by being told or shown by a member of my group.

D: I spent time learning by being told or shown by a member of another group.

E: I spent time learning by being told or shown by someone other than a pupil or a teacher.

F: I spent time learning by working things out for myself.

G: I spent time learning by working it out with someone else.

H: I spent time learning by telling or showing someone else.

Each response to a question required the pupil to make a reference to the A–H options and to qualify the reference using the 1–5 ratings. The 1–5 ratings were intended to give more detail about the learning process as perceived by pupils. As with the phrasing of the A–H options, pupils were responsible for formulating the wording of the 1–5 ratings which had the following meanings:

1: I did not learn in this way at all.

2: I spent a bit of time learning in this way.

3: I spent some time learning in this way.

4: I spent quite a lot of time learning in this way.

5: I spent most of the time learning in this way.

There were two ways in which pupils could give answers to the questions: either with a single response or a combination response. A single response required the pupil to ring *one* of the 1–5 ratings qualifying *one* of the A–H options. In the example below, for Question 1, the single response is B5 ('I spent most of the time learning by being told or shown by the teacher').

Q1

A	B	C	D	E	F	G	H
1	1	1	1	1	1	1	1
2	2	2	2	2	2	2	2
3	3	3	3	3	3	3	3
4	4	4	4	4	4	4	4
5	(5)	5	5	5	5	5	5

However, it was clear from lesson observation and participation, and confirmed by pupils involved in the questionnaire design, that whilst segregated choices of learning strategy might be appropriate for normal lessons, during an independent learning project it was possible to combine a range of strategies. Thus the notion of a combination response evolved: a response by a pupil to a question in which *more than one* of the A–H options has been chosen. A combination response consists of a string of references. For example, again in response to Question 1:

Q1

A	B	C	D	E	F	G	H
1	1	1	1	1	1	1	1
(2)	2	2	2	2	2	2	2
3	(3)	(3)	3	3	3	3	3
4	4	4	4	4	4	4	4
5	5	5	5	5	5	(5)	5

The 1–5 ratings were particularly illuminating in combination responses. A string of combination references such as A+B+C+G tells little. The addition of 1–5 ratings gives a weighting to the various options: A2+B3+C3+G5 (as in the example above) translates to 'Because I had a foundation of knowledge in this area, I learnt a bit in this way. I spent some of the time being told or shown by the teacher and members of my group, but most of the time working things out with someone else'. In this instance, a profile emerges of collaborative experiential learning facilitated by some didactic support and a foundation of existing knowledge.

The A–H options and 1–5 ratings were intended to identify the most common learning strategies and also to indicate whether pupils brought different strategies to bear on different types of problem. For instance, Question 1 deals with a particularly technical issue: the use of an external microphone when filming with a video camera. Would the responses to this question show a greater reliance on teacher instruction (B 3–5 answers) than, perhaps, the responses to Question 8, which dealt with groupwork? That is, when pupils were given a free choice, did they demonstrate the flexibility to use appropriate learning strategies in different circumstances?

The second aim of the questionnaire was to attempt to identify the learning strategies that pupils regarded as the most effective. For this purpose a further column, containing the V–Z ratings, was added to the response box. These ratings, also phrased by pupils, had the following meanings:

V: My knowledge or expertise in this area got worse than it was before I started.

W: My knowledge or expertise in this area stayed the same.

X: My knowledge or expertise in this area improved a bit.

Y: My knowledge or expertise in this area showed some improvement.

Z: My knowledge or expertise in this area improved a lot.

Thus a response to Question 1 might be:

A	B	C	D	E	F	G	H	
1	1	1	1	1	1	1	1	V
(2)	(2)	2	2	2	2	2	2	W
3	3	3	3	3	3	3	3	X
4	4	4	4	4	4	4	(4)	Y
5	5	5	5	(5)	5	5	5	(Z)
				WHO		WHO	WHO	

This would translate as 'I spent a bit of time learning as a result of my own existing knowledge or being shown or told by the teacher, but most of the time I was shown by someone other than a teacher or pupil and then I consolidated that knowledge by telling and showing someone else again. I feel that my knowledge and expertise in how to use an external microphone with a video camera has improved a lot'.

A final amendment was made so that pupils could identify the 'someone else' that Options E, G and H refer to:

A	B	C	D	E	F	G	H	
1	1	1	1	1	1	1	1	V
(2)	(2)	2	2	2	2	2	2	W
3	3	3	3	3	3	3	3	X
4	4	4	4	4	4	4	(4)	Y
5	5	5	5	(5)	5	5	5	(Z)
				WHO		WHO	WHO	
				Mr Bell			Harry	

The full response to Q1 is now: 'I spent a bit of time learning as a result of my own existing knowledge or being shown or told by the teacher but I was shown by Mr Bell, the AVA Technician, and then I consolidated that knowledge by telling and showing Harry, a member of my group. I feel that my knowledge and expertise in how to use an external microphone with a video camera has improved a lot'.

By drawing on the information available in Section 3, the response can be expanded further: 'I am a Year 9 boy in a top set at Cord who…etc'.

The potential of the questionnaire was exciting, particularly because it had evolved during group discussions with pupils and they had made significant contributions to its ethos, phrasing and format. The questionnaire seemed to offer a way of structuring qualitative data for statistical analysis. It was hoped that the format would enable pupils to analyse their learning strategies in a common manner (easing interrogation of the data) and allow them to respond more fully than if each pupil was presented with a blank sheet of A4 and asked to respond to the two-part question that the questionnaire is essentially asking: 'Faced with a number of decisions and problems of varying natures, what learning strategies did you develop and which strategy or combination of strategies did you find the most effective?'

The example above concerning Mr Bell the AVA Technician demonstrates how the questionnaire was intended to encourage the child to express her own views. With software similar to the SIMS comment-banking programme used for school reports and records of achievement, a profile such as the Mr Bell example could be generated for each respondent. Such a profile would be lent greater integrity as a reliable picture of all-round performance during the project by the addition of Questionnaire 2 comments. Here are two examples:

Example One (Questionnaire 010, Appendix 6):

'I am a Year 8 boy in a mixed ability class at Castlefort School. Some of how to use an external microphone with a video camera I knew already and some I learned from our teacher, Mrs Rivers, and I feel I improved a bit. I knew a bit about how to plan a video but learnt mostly from Mrs Rivers and some from being told or shown by members of another group. Again, I feel I improved a bit. We found the filming locations by relying on our own knowledge to some extent and quite a lot on Mrs. Rivers and I made some improvement in this area. We learnt quite a lot from Mrs. Rivers on how to involve members of the community but Darran (a member of my group) and I worked it out a bit for ourselves. I think my expertise in this area stayed the same.

I knew a bit about how to make arrangements to go out of school, learnt some from Mrs. Rivers, and feel I made some improvement in my knowledge here. I knew a bit about how to get jobs done on time and learnt some from Mrs Rivers and I improved a bit. I mostly knew how to do research but feel I learnt some more by showing Jason Wood, another member of my group, how to do it. I think I improved a lot in this area. I knew quite a lot about how to get on with others in the group and I worked out quite a lot for myself and improved a bit.

The hardest thing I had to learn was working without a teacher and the most important thing was to cooperate with people and work. I most enjoyed doing the computer titles. I already knew quite a lot about how to use a computer for putting titles and credits on the video and learnt quite a lot from Mrs Rivers and some from being shown by a member of my group. I feel I made a lot of improvement. I least enjoyed filming and refilming until we got it right.

If we were doing the project again I would choose a better poem to film as ours was a bit too short. To improve the project, teachers could provide the equipment in school all the time. My advice to other pupils starting the project is to choose people you can work with and don't muck around. The project was enjoyable and educational. I would like to do the project again.'

Example Two (Questionnaire 141, Appendix 7):

'I am a Year 7 girl in a mixed-ability class at Dore School. I worked out how to use an external microphone on a video camera mostly with someone else in my group and I feel I improved a lot. I knew a bit about how to plan a video but learnt mostly from Mrs. Ratcliffe and made some improvement. My group didn't need to find locations for filming as we didn't go out of school as part of the project. I mostly knew how to involve members of the community in our work and I also worked it out a bit for myself.

I knew a bit about how to get jobs done on time but I learnt quite a lot by working it out with my group and I think I made some improvement. I knew quite a lot about how to do research and made some improvement here. I also knew quite a lot about how to get on with others in my group, Mrs. Ratcliffe taught me a bit and I improved some.

The hardest thing I had to learn was getting on with the two boys in our group and sometimes my friend and I had to shout at the boys because they were mucking around. Nevertheless, the thing I most enjoyed about the project was working in a group although if I were doing the project again I would choose a different group of friends as we had a few problems last time.

The most important thing I learnt was not to get the video camera insides wet and the least enjoyable thing was when the graphics went wrong. My advice to others would be to work carefully because one mistake costs a lot. To improve the project I think the teachers involved could help a little more, although you were very helpful. I enjoyed the project very much.'

Such profiles give a detailed insight into the way in which individuals perceive they have learnt and can form a valuable part of the researcher's data. They offer an agenda for follow-up interviews with individuals or members of the same collaborative group. What they do not easily allow is a statistical overview of the whole population. However, the data that generate the profiles can also be used in statistical form to quantify the variety and efficacy of the learning experiences of all the respondents to the questionnaire. It is this use of the Questionnaire 1 data that is described in Chapter Four.

Questionnaire 2: format and rationale

Questionnaire 2 (Appendix 8) was intentionally subjective – it asked pupils to express their opinions, feelings and emotions. The format was not restricted in the way that a multi-choice questionnaire must inevitably be (in that it provides all the sensible answers the compiler can envisage and invites the respondent to choose one or more of them). The format was guided – a broad question and a space for a response in the pupil's own words. The questions were based on pupils' suggestions and the phrasing was approved by groups of pupils from each school.

From September 1988 to December 1990 (the circumspection and pre-emption stages of the research cycle), pupils' responses to prototype independent learning projects had been collected in a variety of ways: video and audio-recordings (Budleigh, Poltewan, Tavymouth, Southbay, Penmouth, Axton, Benallick), project diaries (Venturers, Marketmoor, Carnmore, Stonall) and end-of-project evaluation forms of differing format (Tavyford, Axton, Stonall, Marketmoor, Carnmore, Woodcoombe, Poltrice, Pemburton, Venturers). Common-sense analysis had revealed that pupils can often be inconsistent in their statements or hold views that seem contradictory. Such comments can be confusing to the research analyst and their form is not conducive to a systematic analysis that might clarify ostensible contradictions or inconsistencies. Yet without more precise information about independent learning, it would have been irresponsible to have formulated a questionnaire that allowed only tightly defined responses and which might have excluded the voicing of undefined but important aspects of the pupils' experience. This hesitance to restrict, inhibit or guide responses led to the construction of a questionnaire about independent learning in which no question used the phrase 'independent learning' and no question referred specifically to any of the 12 factors of independent learning. Whilst this would make the data processing and analysis more complicated, it avoided a superficiality of response and effectively mitigated against the possibility of researcher bias. It was hoped that the style of the eight questions would also overcome the etymological and ontological difficulties referred to above.

Questionnaire 2 was intended to gather data systematically so that data handling and analysis, based upon the principles of grounded theory, might expose any perceived contradictions and inconsistencies in an organised way so that they might be resolved. Diaries or project journals, interviews or profiles offer an extended narrative in which the expression of seeming or real contradictions has a wider context for interpretation and resolution than yes/no or tick-box responses when a pupil can only select from a limited number of responses that the researcher has chosen for her or from questionnaires that encourage a freer response. However, such forms of data collection produce a great deal of written material that does not lend itself to the systematisation required for a researcher to make a generalisation (although ethnographic content analysis of case studies can reveal related similarities). With these considerations in mind, a format was decided upon, in collaboration with pupils and based upon earlier data-collection, that was regarded as being as open as possible, given that the returned data were intended to provide some statistical evidence for a generalisation. Although the format differs from Questionnaire 1, the intention was the same: to gather information that could be used both in the construction of an individual profile and in the statistical representation of the trends within the whole questionnaire population.

The questionnaire, then, had the following purposes:

1. To elaborate on the responses to Questionnaire 1, with particular attention to the following areas: the most and least enjoyable aspects

of a project, the most important and hardest aspects, things that pupils would change on another occasion, advice to other pupils and comments on how teachers could contribute more fully.

2. To provide data for the construction of grounded theory leading to a generalisation concerning pedagogical practices likely to develop the attributes of citizenship considered to be appropriate to the third millennium.

3. To assess whether such a questionnaire was a valid and efficient way of collecting data from pupils about their perceptions of their learning.

4. To provide information for further independent learning projects.

The Questionnaire 2 format trialled with four schools (Castlefort, Cord, Dore and Saltair) was amended so that more information could be gathered concerning collaborative groups (what method was used for forming the group? was the group mixed or single gender? how many in the group?) The original questions (suggested and approved by pupils), plus comments space, were retained.

One of the aims of the research was to try a variety of approaches to see if there was a particular method that was most effective in encouraging the voicing of the child to describe and discuss her learning experiences. It is believed that the format of the questionnaires, and their capacity to generate personal profiles from the data, gave an element of additional articulacy to the pupils. As importantly, the method of data processing, in transferring the pupils' own words to a database, allowed a diverse range of eloquent groups to emerge from what might have been a cacophony of individual voices during the data analysis and the generation of grounded theory. The presentation of the findings combines qualitative and quantitative data using individual pupils' comments to exemplify the statistical representations of various groups within the pupil population of the questionnaire.

TECHNICAL ASPECTS OF THE RESEARCH

Internal validity

The critical paradigm's emphasis on personal encounter with experience and persons has led to a re-evaluation of the classical criteria of validity. The positivist's ideal strategy of the experimental control of sub-sets of variables in the testing of prior theory cannot be applied to research in the critical paradigm. The debate on validity has had three phases: an attack upon critical paradigm research as having no claim to validity, a counter-attack that disputes the possibility of the objectivity upon which the traditional terms of validity are predicated and the promulgation of new criteria of validity.

The classic criteria have rested upon the independence of the researcher and the researched and the objectivity that this segregation is held to promote. However, researchers in the critical paradigm claim that there is always a personal element involved in research and that there is a relationship between the knower and the known. For Reason and Rowan (1981) there is no one truth, knowledge is a matter of the relationship between the knower and the known. They assert that validity rests on the nature of this relationship and that 'this validity may sometimes be enhanced if we can say we know, rather than simply I know: we can move towards an intersubjectively valid knowledge which is beyond the limitations of one knower' (p.241).

Bannister (1981) believes that to deny the existence of the knower/known relationship must limit the internal validity of traditional experiments. Similarly, Heron (1981a) has sought to demonstrate that research about people that is not experientially based is incomplete and can, at best, be no more than tentatively predictive. Torbert (1981a) argues that educational research that attempts a positivist approach will lack both internal validity and generalisability, because most practitioners 'act under conditions that are almost exactly the reverse of pre-defined, unilaterally controlled (and hence uninterrupted) experimental conditions. Consequently, the conditions under which knowledge is gained when following the canons of rigorous experimental research are simply not generalizable to the conditions practitioners face' (p.143).

Schwartz and Ogilvy (1979) propose that researchers' attempts to suppress subjectivity and claim objectivity should be reconciled in the notion of perspective, 'a personal view from some distance' that suggests 'neither the universality of objectivity nor the personal bias of subjectivity' (p.53). This is close to the rigour of the 'objective subjectivity' of critical paradigm research in which reality is viewed dialectically as a process. Thus the idea of validity is not an image of the opposite ends of a see-saw, with objectivity on one side, subjectivity on the other and the researcher at its fulcrum, whose slightest move must weigh the balance in favour of either objectivity or subjectivity (and, to extend the metaphor, with objectivity being seen as down-to-earth, solid, having its feet on the ground and subjectivity as up-in-the-air, ethereal, with its head in the clouds). Rather, there is a continuum between the possibility of an external reality and hallucination, and at some point along this continuum there is, as Bateson puts it, 'a region where you are partly blown by the winds of reality and partly an artist creating a composite out of inner and outer events' (quoted in Brockman 1977, p.245).

The practical effect upon research has been to accept variables as a valuable and informative contribution to research and to regard their progressive elimination from fieldwork as a damaging decontextualisation of the research. The manipulation of variables in an attempt to achieve validity is dismissed in preference for a method of progressive focusing, checked and rechecked against the analysis of multi-faceted data, to provide consensual (or 'contextual' (Diesing 1972)) validity:

> The interest in empirical data is not concentrated on predicting relationships between independent and dependent variables; rather, the same study will seek empirical data relating to acting systems' aims, strategies, behaviours, and effects, in order to test, and offer feedback on, the degree of congruence and incongruence across these qualities of experience. (Torbert 1981a, p.149)

Both of the research methods used in the intervention and non-intervention aspects of my research (intentional interaction and illuminative evaluation) rely upon consensual validity for their justification. For the validation of illuminative evaluation Parlett (1981) advocates internal checks based upon different techniques being used in parallel, accepting that each method has limitations, and triangulating on issues from different methodological techniques. Heron (1981b) claims that in his full experiential research model of intentional interaction, where the researcher is a co-subject and the subject is a co-researcher, where 'each person involved is both researcher and subject' (p.156), many dyadic corrective feedback loops are created that serve to strengthen the consensual validity of the research: 'The model is thus charged with internal checks and balances for the empirical validation of research propositions through experience and action, where this validation is always from the agents' standpoints' (p.156).

Maruyama (1981) believes consensual validity is strengthened by a combination of exogenous and endogenous polyocular vision, embedded within a heterogeneistic and complementary epistemology in which differences in perspectives are seen as non-contradictory and enriching, to create the vision of what she calls polyocular anthropology. This is the view that underpins the multi-faceted and multi-perspective data collection that served to offer internal validity to my research.

Consensual validation should not just be about *consensus gentium* (which may conceal a widespread collusion to ignore, or an unawareness of, relevant variables). What is crucial is the quality of critical awareness, discrimination and evaluation that informs consensual validation. Reason and Rowan (1981) distinguish two main ways in which the validity of an enquiry may be threatened:

1. Unaware projection: in which the researcher unconsciously projects his [sic] own concerns onto the research partnership.

2. Consensus collusion: in which the researched and the researcher overlook activities, behaviour or influences that would affect the theory when activated in experience.

They conclude that 'validity in new paradigm research lies in the skills and sensitivities of the researcher, in how he or she uses herself as a knower, as an enquirer. Validity is more personal and interpersonal, rather than method-ological' (p.244).

Henwood and Pidgen (1993) describe practices designed to ensure internal validity (keeping close to the data, theory integrated at diverse levels of abstraction, reflexivity, documentation, theoretical sampling and negative case analysis, sensitivity to negotiated realities and transferability) but the seminal proposals made by Reason and Rowan (1981), listed below, are used as a framework for the internal validity of my research:

1. *Valid research rests above all on high quality awareness on the part of the co-researchers*: Members of the research partnership were fully aware of the research aims in both the intervention and non-intervention aspects. Meetings were held before observations or action projects and agenda agreed with pupils and teachers. All involved were volunteers. Copies of the 12 factors of independent learning were distributed. Video-recordings of other pupils at work, and project artifacts created by other pupils, were shown before a project began.

2. *Such high-quality awareness can only be maintained if the co-researchers engage in some systematic method of personal and interpersonal development*: Regular meetings were held during projects to discuss and clarify emergent issues. Data collection methods were devised within the research partnership.

3. *Valid research cannot be conducted alone*: Details have been given of the research partnership between the researcher and the researched, and of endogenous and exogenous research conducted and data collected.

4. *The validity of the research is much enhanced by the systematic use of feedback loops, and by going round the research cycle several times*: Details have been given of the research cycle stages of circumspection, pre-emption and control. Within each of these major stages there were also many minor feedback loops. Observations, discussions and projects took place on many occasions. Return visits for illuminative evaluation and intentional interaction were made to some of the same schools in each phase of the research spiral.

5. *Valid research involves a subtle interplay between different ways of knowing*: The epistemology of the research is social constructivist. The research acknowledged and embraced objective and subjective knowing and quantitative and qualitative data were collected. Reflexivity was encouraged within the research partnership and various problem-solving methods were employed, from the subjectivist to the causal-determinist. The general viewpoint of the researcher shifted between the eclectic-pluralist and the dialectic-organic.

6. *Contradiction can be used systematically*: Contradiction was a stimulus to the dialectic of the research and a useful tool of triangulation in divergent validity. Exogenous observers and the members of the research partnership were encouraged to play the role of the critical friend.

7. *Convergent and contextual validity can be used to enhance the validity of any particular piece of data*: The construct of consensual validity used during this research embodies convergent, divergent, contextual and face validity.

8. *The research can be replicated in some form*: Detailed descriptions are given of method and practice, and of the 12 factors of independent learning upon which the intervention and non-intervention aspects of the research were based.

To summarise, the old views of validity cannot be applied to the critical paradigm. First, there is not the obsession to control variables (although they are identified). Second, the classical criteria attempt to achieve pure objectivity by the segregation of the researcher from the researched and the researched from the purpose of the research (sometimes to the point of deception experiments), whereas the critical paradigm is based upon the intersubjectivities of a research partnership. Third, the research environment: classically, it is clinical and the researcher is a detached observer. In the critical paradigm, research is experiential, based in real-life settings and the researcher's role is often participative. Fourth, the critical paradigm's inductive forms of analysis (whether the findings are expressed quantitatively or qualitatively) admit subjectivity, particularly where grounded theory is involved. Fifth, research in the critical paradigm often has a personal stake for the researcher and this aspect of reflexivity is valued.

External validity (generalisability)

Researchers in the critical paradigm (Torbert 1981b), researchers whose main data is qualitative (Dobbert 1982; Denzin 1983; Kirk and Miller 1986) and researchers whose methods have relied heavily on case studies (Wolcott 1973; Guba and Lincoln 1981) have not tended to regard external validity as a centrally important aim or outcome of research: 'Moreover, in collaborative enquiry the primary interest is not in generalizing to other settings, but rather in applying knowledge to improve actors' effectiveness in the situation under study' (Torbert 1981b, p.442).

Researchers such as Denzin and Lincoln and Guba actively reject generalisability as a goal: 'It is virtually impossible to imagine any human behavior that is not heavily mediated by the context in which it occurs. One can easily conclude that generalizations that are intended to be context-free will have little that is useful to say' (Guba and Lincoln 1981, p.62).

In a later text, Guba and Lincoln claim that 'Generalizations are impossible since phenomena are neither time free nor context free...' (1982, p.238)

Reason and Rowan (1981) express a more cautious attitude:

> We are interested in generalization, not in order to make deterministic predictions, but as general statements about the power, possibilities and limits of persons acting as agents. We are interested in describing the general patterns within which the particular may exist, and accept that often the most personal and particular is also the most general. (p.490)

This is the view that has increasingly been adopted by critical paradigm researchers: that generalisability in the sense of producing laws that apply universally is not a useful standard or goal for research, but that generalisability in the sense of taking the findings from one study and applying them to the understanding of a similar situation can be legitimated. Guba and Lincoln (1982) refer to the 'fittingness' of different situations that allow the 'transferability of hypotheses' (p.238). Goetz and LeCompte (1984) write of the 'comparability' of the results of one study as a basis for comparison with another. Stake (1978) describes a process he calls 'naturalistic generalization' that has the same purpose as comparability. Each of these writers stresses the need for a detailed description of a study if it is to be useful for fittingness, comparability or naturalistic generalisation. A further strengthening feature would be that the study is of a typicality (for instance, in Wolcott's famous study *The Man in the Principal's Office* he went to great lengths to find a typical principal in a typical school). Finally, multi-site studies – particularly if a consistent trend emerges from heterogeneous sites – offer a stronger platform for external validity:

> Selection on the basis of typicality provides the potential for a good 'fit' with many other situations. Thick description provides the information necessary to make informed judgments about the degree and extent of that fit in particular places of interest... Generally speaking, a finding emerging from the study of several heterogeneous sites would be more robust and therefore more likely to be useful in understanding various other sites. (Schofield 1993, p.211)

Thus three criteria for critical paradigm generalisability emerge: detailed description, typicality and the use of multi-sites. The research findings of this study are based upon the analysis of qualitative and quantitative data gathered from heterogeneous multi-sites: the 31 comprehensive schools in the study LEA. Attendance at national and international conferences and courses suggests to me that these schools are also typical of UK secondary schools that study the National Curriculum in a series of timetabled lessons in discrete subjects. Where case studies have been used as data for the research findings (the independent learning project of the collaborative group 'MOB' and the Keystage 3 and 4 tracking of individual pupils), detailed descriptions accompany their procedural reports and analysis. No unjustified generalisations are made about populations that have not been sampled.

Construct validity

I believe that the indicators chosen to represent the underlying concept of the research – educational citizenship – are appropriate. These indicators are the 12 factors of independent learning. The factors are legitimated by the theory-in-the-literature, the common-sense theory of the experienced practitioner and reflexive evaluation and progressive focusing during the three stages of the research spiral. During the application of these factors, data collection was from multiple sources using methods that guarded against the possible unrestrained subjectivity or impressionism of the practitioner-researcher and the possibility of falsely confirming a priori assumptions.

Reliability

I maintain that the methods of illuminative evaluation and intentional interaction, as employed in the non-intervention and intervention research for this book, are reliable and that others using the same data collection methods with pupils whose learning is impelled by the 12 factors of independent learning would record similar results. Because of the nature of the research cycle, which led to progressive clarification of the 12 factors of independent learning, it is suggested that the control phase has greater reliability than the circumspection and pre-emption phases of the research.

Representativeness

I maintain that the pupils from whom data were collected are typical of others in Keystages 3 and 4. Illuminative evaluation was undertaken within Keystages 3 and 4 in every secondary school in the study LEA. The criteria of observation were the 12 factors of independent learning. Over 40 independent learning projects were undertaken in the 31 secondary schools. The criteria of practice were the 12 factors of independent learning. The 10 schools sampled in Questionnaires 1 and 2 were representative of the overall population.

Experimenter bias, respondent bias, and data contamination

> Confronting oneself and one's biases was one of the most difficult and thought-provoking aspects of being a qualitative researcher for many students.
> (Ely 1991, p.122)

I maintain that the researcher's skills of objective subjectivity and reflexivity, the involvement of the research partnership in designing all data collection tools and the polyocularity provided by exogenous and endogenous viewpoints, collected in a variety of ways, mitigates against both experimenter and respondent bias. As a researcher, I was aware of the possibilities of unaware projection and consensus collusion (Reason and Rowan 1981) but believe that the multi-site studies and the anonymity of the questionnaires, as well as the use of standardised forms and a research partner for the Keystage tracking data collection, were measures that limited these possibilities – as did my public statements of my own interests and values and my encouragement of all members of the research partnership as 'critical friends'. Methods that experience in the field suggested might have been susceptible to relevance dissonance (Maruyama 1981) were discarded.

SUMMARY OF THE CHAPTER

This chapter has described how a wide variety of data were collected from a wide variety of sources in a wide variety of ways over an extended period of time in addressing the research question: 'What effects do the 12 factors of independent learning, intended to promote educational citizenship, have in practice?'

This chapter has sought to show that the research was conducted in a disciplined manner and that the method and practice were legitimated by the conventions of the critical paradigm in which the research was located. The relationship between the researcher and the researched has been described as striving towards an equal partnership – all were treated as persons of equal status. An integral aim of the critical paradigm is that research within it should be an empowering experience for the research partnership, which has been delineated as comprising pupils, teachers, observers and researchers. The argument has been advanced that each of these groups, but particularly the pupils, can contain – or even comprise – 'the silenced'. To this end, different methods of voicing were tried, both in data collection and in its processing and analysis. The primary data were collected from pupils. Secondary data, from teachers and observers, were collected and used for triangulation.

Using a variety of data collection methods was worthwhile for although the quality of the data varied, all methods showed a consistency in identifying similar aspects or factors of independent learning. This provided a clearer research terrain and enabled the development of a system of data gathering, interrogation and analysis that utilised quantitative data for statistics and qualitative data for their exemplification (Questionnaires 1 and 2), and that was effective in encouraging the voicing of the silenced.

Procedural and methodological decisions were made only after consideration of the opinions of the research partnership, the theory-in-the-literature and the common-sense theory of the practitioner-researcher.

CHAPTER FOUR

Dependent Learning

A SURVEY OF NATIONAL CURRICULUM TEACHING AND LEARNING STYLES

The purpose of the survey, which comprised the non-intervention research referred to in Chapter Three, was to collect data on teaching and learning styles across the 5–16 age-range that might be regarded as promoting or suppressing educational citizenship via the factors of independent or dependent learning.

As I wrote earlier, there were four strands to this part of the research:

- passive observation of lessons
- discussions with teachers about common practices
- the collection of relevant documentation
- an intense study of the curriculum time of one pupil in each Keystage during a school week.

Lesson observation

Access to classrooms was either by request on the part of the classroom teacher or invitation from a member of the middle or senior management team of a school. For example, Jill Waghorne, a teacher at Stonall, asked me to observe her lessons twice a week for half a term as she wanted a second opinion on how appropriate her pedagogy was with high-performing GCSE pupils. Ronald Miller at Pemburton wanted his lessons with a low-achieving Keystage 3 class observed as he felt that a change in learning style might lead to a greater intrinsic motivation on the part of the pupils. On other occasions, headteachers or heads of department asked for the lessons of a teacher who was experiencing difficulties to be observed so that a programme of support could be established. Sometimes, heads of department gave demonstrations of techniques or practices that they felt might be of interest to other teachers. Often, a request for classroom observation led to the establishment of a critical action research programme. In these cases, when the observation spanned the non-intervention and intervention aspects of the research, the nature of the observation and the roles of the observer changed from that of the disinterested and discreet recorder to those of the participant or catalyst observer.

Discussion with teachers

Some discussions with teachers took place immediately after lessons had been observed and were based upon the shared experience of the lesson by researcher and teacher. At other times, discussions concerning a review of current practice took place during departmental planning meetings for an independent learning project. Other departmental meetings concentrated on a particular topic that was related to classroom practice: classroom layout, pupil grouping systems, looking at resources, time management, assessment, the role of other adults in the learning process. Such meetings generally had a written agenda or stimulus sheet, minutes were taken and action plans or policy statements were drawn up. Evening and residential courses within the study LEA provided other opportunities for discussion, as did national conferences and regional residential courses, the purpose of which was to reflect on teaching and learning styles. During the research programme I directed 17 residential courses, co-directed 9 and contributed to a further 25. The majority of these courses were within Greenshire but around a third were at venues throughout the United Kingdom, with course members drawn from a national, and on occasions, international catchment.

During the circumspection and pre-emption phases an eclectic range of different forms, as well as researcher's notes and visual representations, provided data for the observation of lessons. During the control phase the 12 factors of independent learning were used as evaluative criteria. This series of lesson observations and discussions with teachers throughout the United Kingdom over a five-year period provided a broad picture of typical classroom practices in the primary, secondary and tertiary phases, principally in the study LEA but also within a national context.

Documentation

A range of documents were collected from different sources: school prospectuses and handbooks, minutes of departmental, staff, parents' and governors' meetings, school-produced magazines and newspapers, departmental and public examination board syllabuses, departmental schemes of work and policy statements, LEA and Advisory Team policy documents, DFE (Department for Education), NCC (National Curriculum Council), SEAC (School Examinations and Assessment Council), SCAA (School Curriculum and Assessment Authority) and OFSTED publications. The data collection of documents was at my request (i.e. school handbooks), unsolicited presentation (i.e. school newspapers) and professional circulation (i.e. DFE and LEA material).

The Keystage tracking of pupils during a timetabled week

The tracking of individual pupils in each Keystage gave finer detail to the brushstrokes of the broad picture. It also offered a pupil's eye view of teaching and learning styles. The intense study of the curricular experience of a pupil throughout an entire timetabled week appeared to offer the possibilities of generalisability in a variety of ways. If a school was chosen that had a five-day timetable cycle, the curricular work of one week would demonstrate certain consistencies for the whole school year, or Keystage. Unless the pupil who was tracked was aberrant in some way, her curricular experience would be shared, although not exactly duplicated, by others within her class, NC Year and Keystage. If the school demonstrated practices that were known to be typical of others (for instance, the teaching of the National Curriculum, the division of the curriculum into discrete subjects, the teaching of subjects in discrete lessons, a timetabled day of six 50-minute lessons), the findings may be transferable to similar institutions. In short, both the shadowed pupil and the school could be regarded as particular, rather than unique, and a case study could illuminate a wider field of pupils and schools.

The pupil tracking at Keystages 3 and 4 encapsulated and exemplified, in the most vivid manner, the principal findings of lesson observation, teacher discussion and the analysis of documentation:

- that for most pupils school is a dulling experience
- that most lessons are contrived and irrelevant
- that in most lessons dependent learning is the norm
- that in most schools pupils are treated as serfs not citizens.

Although there was plenty of evidence for these conclusions in other lesson observation and discussion, no other section of research that I undertook illustrated so emphatically the shortcomings of a state-maintained education system in allowing any opportunity for the development of educational citizenship via independent learning. Therefore, I devote the rest of this chapter to a detailed recounting of the curricular weeks of Josie and Emily. I preface their stories with an argument for the generalisability of their experience for I have become convinced that dependent learning is the norm in UK state secondary schools.

The generalisability of case studies

This chapter concerns two case studies which describe in full detail the curricular experiences of two typical pupils during a typical school week in a typical comprehensive school in the study LEA. It has been maintained in Chapter Three (Technical Aspects of the Research) that such a study can offer the 'fittingness' of generalisability in a variety of ways (Wolcott 1973; Stake 1979; Guba and Lincoln 1982; Goetz and LeCompte 1984; Yin 1989;

Schofield 1993; Golby 1994). External validity is strengthened if the case study can be shown to offer typicality, if there is detailed description and if research is conducted on multi-sites.

Typicality

Josie Leigh was a 14-year-old girl in Year 9 of Keystage 3 when the week's tracking took place at Sir James Redbourne School from 1–5 February 1993. Emily Jay was a 15-year-old girl in Year 10 of Keystage 4 when the week's tracking took place at Penmouth Community School from 1–5 March 1993. Both pupils were regarded by their form tutors, their teachers and their Heads of Year as typical – that is, socially well-adjusted pupils of average academic ability. Both pupils followed a weekly timetable in which lessons were taught in 50-minute periods. The six daily periods were divided by a 15-minute break between lessons 2 and 3; and by a dinner-break between lessons 4 and 5. Josie and Emily regarded the week of their tracking as typical of their timetabled school week. They were asked (by myself) every day if this or that lesson was normal, ordinary, 'the kind of thing you usually do', and they said that it was.

Both were pupils in comprehensive schools that were regarded by me as typical of other comprehensive schools in their presentation of the National Curriculum. My opinion was primarily based upon four years' experience as the County Senior Advisory Teacher for Secondary English, during which time I had supervised independent learning projects in every comprehensive school in the study LEA, had attended departmental meetings in every comprehensive school and had organised residential in-service training courses attended by English teachers from every comprehensive school. I had also attended regional and national courses (Southampton, York, Swansea, London, Manchester, Leicester, Plymouth, Chester, Exeter) which had given me the opportunity to meet teachers and to visit schools across the country.

Secondary data suggesting typicality were provided by my attendance at annual Heads of English conferences in the study LEA, as a Head of English, between 1979 and 1988; and my experience as one of the two county teaching representatives to the South West Examinations Board (English) and as a Board CSE Examinations Moderator between 1976 and 1982, during which time I represented and visited many of the study LEA's secondary schools. Further data of typicality were provided by a scrutiny of GCSE results achieved by comprehensive schools in the study LEA and nationally, a comparison of the school prospectuses of the LEA's comprehensive schools, one-to-one meetings with each secondary headteacher in the study LEA and opinions expressed by the senior management teams of Sir James Redbourne and Penmouth schools.

Detailed Description

The full text of the two case studies comprises 52,000+ words of lesson-by-lesson commentary and analysis, photocopies of all of the pupils' reading and writing for the week and diagrams of seating arrangements for every lesson. A description of the schools' management systems is given, of how introductory contact was made with the schools and the way in which the case studies were initiated. This text is available to other researchers but, for reasons of length and equilibrium, only the main findings are reported in this chapter.

Multi-site studies

The week-long pupil tracking took place with four different pupils (one tracking for each National Curriculum Keystage) in three schools during February and March 1993 (although only the Keystage 3 and 4 trackings are reported in this book). This intensive study followed lesson observation in 74 schools – including every comprehensive school in the study LEA – between 1989 and 1993.

The purpose of the tracking was to make some assessment of the typical curriculum and timetable of 11–16-year-old pupils and to see what opportunities were offered for the promotion of educational citizenship. Thus the case study is of a curriculum rather than an individual. Josie and Emily represent typical Keystage 3 and 4 pupils in a typical comprehensive school: they are the lenses through which the researcher observed the week's lessons.

PUPIL TRACKING AT KEYSTAGE 3: DISTRIBUTION OF THE 1500 MINUTES OF JOSIE'S TIMETABLED WEEK

Table 4.1 shows Josie's learning activities, generically, throughout the curriculum. Figure 4.1 illustrates Table 4.1 in graphic form.

The greatest block of curricular time was not actually spent in lessons but in moving between them. Room changes and lesson registers took 21.5 per cent of the time. Teacher-led talk consumed the greatest amount of lesson-time (20.5%), followed by pupils working individually on note making and comprehension exercises from textbooks or duplicated worksheets (16.5%). Art and Design lessons took up 15.5 per cent of the week. The remaining 26 per cent of the week consisted of Maths (7%), groupwork, P.E. and video watching (4.5% each), silent reading (3%), a pupils' presentation to their year group during the weekly Personal and Social Education lesson (1.5%) and singing and redrafting (0.5% each).

Art, Design and PE apart, there was a common approach to teaching and learning styles and a common notion of a content-based curriculum, so that pupil activities tended to be much the same in different lessons: note taking, comprehension exercises, watching videos and a great deal of whole-class, teacher-led 'discussion'.

Activity	Mon	Tues	Weds	Thurs	Fri	Totals	%
Table 4.1: The distribution of the 1500 minutes of Josie's timetabled week.							
Room changes & register	45	76	41	98	66	326	21.5
Teacher-led talk	86	43	73	81	28	311	20.5
Note-taking and comp. exs.	94	38	9	10	96	247	16.5
Art and Design	0	97	90	0	45	232	15.5
Maths	18	20	0	26	37	101	7
Groupwork	0	0	47	15	5	67	4.5
P.E.	0	18	0	25	23	66	4.5
Video-watching	57	0	9	0	0	66	4.5
Reading	0	0	0	45	0	45	3
PSE show	0	0	25	0	0	25	1.5
Singing	0	8	0	0	0	8	0.5
Redrafting	0	0	6	0	0	6	0.5
Totals	300	300	300	300	300	1500	100

Source: Author

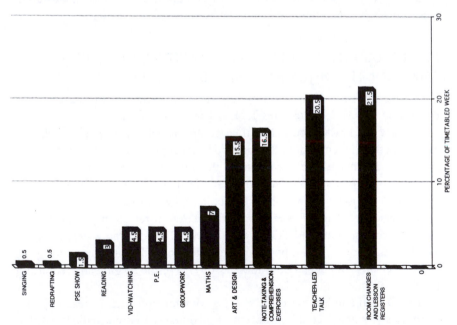

Figure 4.1: Bar graph showing the distribution of the 1500 minutes of Josie's timetabled week
Source: Author

An examination of Josie's talking, reading and writing during the week demonstrates the low level of cognitive and affective engagement required in her schooling, the piecemeal nature of the content-based curriculum and the essentially passive and limited nature of the learning process.

Talk

What talk there was was directed by and through the teacher, who decided the subject and direction of the talk and who should speak.

In this process boys appeared to gain a much greater share of the teacher's attention than girls.

Table 4.2 shows the 12 occasions upon which teacher-led talk was recorded systematically. It shows the number of boys and girls in each class and differentiates between unrequested and requested responses to the teacher. An unrequested response refers to when a pupil talked without being specifically selected by the teacher but the teacher accepted the response. For instance, in

				Boys'	Girls'	Boys'	Girls'
Activity Number	Subject	Number of boys	Number of girls	unrequested responses	unrequested responses	requested responses	requested responses
28	Music	16	10	67	5	4	0
30	English	10	13	4	2	0	0
31	English	10	13	4	5	0	0
33	English	10	13	7	0	0	0
37	R.E.	17	10	21	1	1	3
39	R.E.	17	10	4	0	0	0
41	German	17	16	6	2	0	1
43	Maths	20	11	5	5	14	4
53	Maths	20	11	5	0	0	0
55	Science	17	7	7	2	8	3
63	Science	17	7	5	0	0	0
65	History	17	10	8	0	1	0
Totals		188	131	143	22	28	11

Table 4.2: Pupils' contributions to whole class discussion Keystage 3

Source: Author

Table 4.3: Contributions to whole class discussion by percentage of the class population

Activity Number	Subject	% of boys in the lesson	% of girls in the lesson	Boys' % of unrequested responses	Girls' % of unrequested responses	Boys' % of requested responses	Girls' % of requested responses
28	Music	61.5	38.5	93	7	100	0
30	English	43.5	56.5	66.5	33.5	0	0
31	English	43.5	56.5	44.5	55.5	0	0
33	English	43.5	56.5	100	0	0	0
37	R.E.	63	37	95.5	4.5	25	75
39	R.E.	63	37	100	0	0	0
41	German	55	45	75	25	0	100
43	Maths	64.5	35.5	50	50	78	22
53	Maths	64.5	35.5	100	0	0	0
55	Science	71	29	78	22	73	27
63	Science	71	29	100	0	0	0
65	History	63	37	100	0	100	0

Source: Author

Geography Mr Peters asked: 'What's the answer to that one, then, anyone?' and Simon called out his response, which the teacher acknowledged. A requested response refers to when a teacher chose a particular pupil (who may or may not have signalled a desire to speak) to respond. For instance, in Science, despite the frantic urgings of 'Sir! Sir!' from boys with arms stretched high and ignoring called-out answers, Mr Carter asked Samantha.

Table 4.2 clearly shows that there was a higher incidence of boys than girls talking voluntarily (unrequested responses) and also being asked, by the teacher, to talk (requested responses). From a total of 165 unrequested responses, boys made 143 (86.67%) and girls 22 (13.33%). Of the 39 times on which teachers chose a particular pupil to speak, teachers chose boys 28 times (71.79%) and girls 11 times (28.21%). There was only one occasion when girls spoke more often than boys (4 minutes of teacher-led talk in English, when boys spoke 4 times and girls 5 times). However, in nine of the lesson activities from which data were gathered, there were more boys than girls in the class so the raw scores of Table 4.2 needed to be analysed in a way that took into consideration the gender ratio of pupils within a class when comparing the talk responses of boys and girls. Table 4.3 seeks to do this.

Table 4.3 converts the raw figures of Table 4.2 to percentages. If there was a more or less equal involvement in teacher-led talk by boys and girls, the response percentage, by gender, should be close to the class percentage by gender. For instance, if a class consisted of 60 per cent boys and 40 per cent girls, these percentages would be reflected in the response percentages (about 60% for the boys and 40% for the girls) if the teacher had sought to ensure a fair and balanced contribution from both boys and girls to 'whole-class discussion'. However, this was not the case. In Music, for instance, boys comprise 61.5 per cent of the class number but account for 93 per cent of the unrequested responses and 100 per cent of the requested responses. Only on one occasion (Activity 43, Maths) is the boys' response percentage less than their class population percentage. In crude terms, boys get more than their fair share of teacher-time and attention in teacher-led talk that is purportedly open to the whole class.

Over the 12 activities for which responses were recorded, boys consisted of 59 per cent of the pupil population yet had 87 per cent of the number of unrequested responses and 72 per cent of the requested responses. Girls, 41 per cent of the population, had only 13 per cent of the unrequested responses and 28 per cent of the requested responses. The closer relation between the figures for percentage of the class population by gender, and requested answers, suggests that teachers did attempt to balance boys and girls (although they tended to favour the boys) when choosing particular pupils. The disproportionately high percentage of boys' unrequested responses indicates that boys made a greater voluntary per capita contribution to teacher-led talk than girls.

Every school in Greenshire had an Equal Opportunities Policy that included statements on the curricular entitlement of all pupils. Between 1988 and 1994 there was a County Advisory Teacher for Multicultural Education and much of her work had publicised the socio-cultural differences in the way in which boys and girls are treated. One of the curriculum enhancement areas of the Technical and Vocational Educational Initiative, then in its fifth year of operation in secondary schools in Greenshire, was Equal Opportunities: Gender. Greenshire had a County policy on Equal Opportunities and a standing committee to monitor practice in schools. Residential and school-based In-Service Training had been provided by several of the Advisory Teams (including the English team). One of the National Curriculum cross-curricular dimensions, which are intended to permeate all lessons, is Equal Opportunities: Gender. Despite these initiatives, for whatever reasons, the type of lessons that were typical of classroom practice at Sir James Redbourne appeared to encourage the participation of boys more than girls.

In whole-class discussion, or teacher-led question and answer sessions, Josie barely contributed. In the week's 311 minutes of teacher-led talk, Josie spoke for 11 seconds. Her three contributions were all in Maths: on Monday, Ms Soames asked Josie to give her answer for one of the sums set for homework, to which came the correct response: 'Sixty seven point four'. Josie was asked for another answer and recorded her second whole-class utterance of the day: 'AC squared minus BC squared equals AB squared'. On Tuesday, Josie made her only voluntary comment of the week when she politely called out: 'You've put three times three equals fifteen', drawing attention to a mistake Ms Soames had made on the board.

Josie was not a girl who lacked subject knowledge. She was considered to be average or above average in all her subjects. I often observed that she knew the answers to the questions asked by the teacher – they were correctly written in her exercise book, or she mouthed the answer to herself, or murmured it to a companion. Josie did not appear to have relationship problems with teachers. She was confident and relaxed in dialogue with them. It should also be said that not once during the week was a teacher observed to react negatively if a pupil gave an incorrect answer. Quite the opposite. In all the lessons throughout the week, teachers were supportive and kindly. Josie was not a shy girl. She was confident in company – one of the reasons that she was asked by the school to be the tracked pupil was because of her self-composed nature. Nevertheless, Josie spent 99.94 per cent of teacher-led talk time in silence.

Her talk with teachers on a one-to-one basis was limited to two occasions, both of which occurred as a teacher walked around the class whilst pupils worked silently and individually on exercises set by the teacher. During Monday's History lesson Josie finished the worksheet before anyone else on her table and put her hand up to signal the teacher, who commented upon the quality of her answers and then gave her another worksheet to start. A similar situation arose in Tuesday's Maths lesson.

In the collaborative groupwork (67 minutes or 4.5% of the week's lesson-time) most of the talk was societal rather than task-related. In the Art and Design and Technology lessons, societal chat was accepted. In lessons where it was not, it occurred both openly and surreptitiously. There were examples of societal chat in every lesson.

In effect, throughout the week, talk played virtually no part of Josie's learning experience, either in whole class discussion, personal conversation with a teacher or during pupils' collaborative work. Assessed upon the statements of attainment for English in the National Curriculum, Josie's speaking and listening opportunities did not rise above Level 1: 'respond appropriately to simple instructions given by a teacher'.

Reading

Josie's personal, silent reading was limited to 49 minutes for the week. On three days she did no reading at all. The 49 minutes spent on reading covered three activities in two lessons and each time the activity was used as a time-filler. The first reading activity (Monday) was to read from a Geography textbook for 7 minutes at the end of a lesson – an activity mirrored in a French lesson (for 12 minutes) later in the day. The only other reading of the week was a 'make-do' lesson in French when half the class had gone to a sponsored Maths activity and the remaining pupils read French stories.

There were other forms of reading. The 81 minutes during the week devoted to comprehension (in Geography and History) required the reading of a worksheet. In English there was a shared reading of Romeo and Juliet, in small groups and as a whole-class. The 122 minutes of note taking required reading from textbooks or from the blackboard. The 66 minutes of video watching can be regarded as the reading of media texts. However, the learning context made it easy for pupils to abdicate from most of the reading if they wished: mindlessly copying from the board, cribbing a partner's comprehension answers, day-dreaming during the videos, not following the text in a class reading, not bothering to seek any meaning of the text when reading in small groups. Other than the French stories, Josie had no opportunity to choose any text for herself.

As with speaking and listening, it was difficult to plot Josie's reading onto the statements of attainment for English at anywhere approaching Level 6 (the suggested level of the average Keystage 3, Year 9 pupil (DES 1991)). Indeed, there was no evidence of the following statements of attainment for Level 3 in the work of any of the members of her various classes:

'Pupils should be able to:

Level 3 ii) Read silently and with sustained concentration.

Level 3 vi) Devise a clear set of questions that will enable them to select and use appropriate information sources and reference books from the class and school library.

(English in the National Curriculum 1990)

Writing

Josie's writing consisted of re-recording textbook data, either by copying from the text, summarising or short comprehension answers. There was no opp-ortunity to make a personal statement, for imaginative writing, for discursive writing or for extended writing. Little value seemed to be given to the writing: only six minutes in the week's 1500 (0.4%) were given to any further shaping of a first draft and a teacher gave away (to me) a pupil's work which she had spent a lesson creating, explaining: 'It's only classwork'.

For the National Curriculum (English) attainment target of writing, only the structure and organisation strand applied – and that only at Level 2. The average end-of-Keystage 3 pupil (and Josie was supposed to represent that vexed paradigm) should be working at Level 6. Level 2 would represent the average performance of a Keystage 1 infant.

Photocopies of all the reading and writing done by Josie during the week, and transcripts of all her authorised talking, were studied by 32 teachers of English on an LEA residential course directed by the Keystage tracking researchers (Farmer and Griffith). The data were referenced against the statements of attainment for English in the National Curriculum (DES 1990). The unanimous conclusion of this analysis was that over the profile components of speaking and listening, reading and writing, Josie – regarded by her teachers as a 14-year-old pupil of average ability – was operating at between Levels 2 and 3, the DFE suggested performance of the average 7-year-old pupil.

Other lesson activities

Other learning activities also seemed purposeless and profligate in the consumption of curricular time. Are production-line carpentry (the making of little boxes in Technology) and painting Dolly Vardens (decorative bows in Art) the kind of practices suited to a Design and Technology curriculum for the twenty-first century? Were 101 minutes of algebra and trigonometry, which were given no application to real life needs, useful?

Seating

A perusal of the diagrams depicting seating arrangements reveals the existence of two separate classroom communities: boys and girls. The analysis of teacher-led talk suggests that significant parts of lessons were biased towards one of these communities: the boys. That boys consistently occupied more of the teachers' time, whether they sat at the front (Science), back (English) or sides (Maths) of classrooms, implies that seating arrangements alone do not explain the greater involvement of boys in teacher-led talk. There are some tentative indications that boys sit to the front in the sciences (Science and Maths) and girls to the front in the arts (English and German). The role of the teachers in stipulating seating arrangements is not known.

What unifies the curriculum?

A knowledge-based approach

Although the philosophy of education was clearly of the Peters-Dearden-Hirst school of knowledge-based initiation with the curriculum divided into subjects, there was no evidence to suggest that these subjects united to represent a holistic body of knowledge. Their separatism was emphasised by different purpose-specialist rooms, different criteria for grouping pupils and different subject-specialist teachers who made no connections between any of the topics studied in different subjects: coal output in Russia in 1910, Romeo and Juliet, pathogens in the bloodstream, mortise and tenon joints, Pythagorean triangles. Nor were connections made between topics within subjects: the first Geography lesson was about map references, the second about population density; on Monday a new topic was begun in Science (Viruses) to be followed by another new topic on Friday (Respiration). Such a minimalistic, 'Trivial Pursuit' notion of education – picking up unrelated bits of 'facts' at differentiated levels depending upon which ability set a pupil is in – requires a particular regime to accommodate it: subject lessons, hierarchical groups, micro-activities during short lessons, a behavioural code that discourages enquiry or individuality, the official disempowerment of the majority.

A skills-based approach

There was no suggestion that the acquisition of bits of knowledge in different subjects was seen as part of a process that developed learning skills that were transferable across subjects, and that transcended those subjects, so that learning how to learn was the holistic aim rather than the *per se* accumulation of subject-based knowledge. One example of the lack of a policy of cross-curricular skills was the extremely low level of language development. The comfortable notion that pupils are taught English in all lessons because all lessons are taught in English was strongly challenged: 'Schemes of work in all subjects provide opportunities for pupils to meet attainment targets in English.' (NCC 1990a p.12). Nor were there any data, other than the single lesson of Personal and Social Education, that indicated that the promotion of National Curriculum Themes, Dimension and Skills were explicit pedagogical objectives.

There was certainly no attempt to present a unified curriculum by taking a pupil-centred approach and relating discrete subject knowledge to the personal and social lives of the pupils in their myriad interactions with the multi-communities and environments within which they lived, although the first of the school's aims, as published in its prospectus, seemed to claim this:

> To ensure that pupils develop their individual intellectual skills to the highest level of which they are capable, by providing a lively and enthusiastic atmosphere in which a love of learning and a questioning approach to life may be stimulated.

Thus there was not an effective knowledge-based, skills-based or child-centred meaning to the curriculum. As the curriculum lacked meaning, it was impossible to understand its purpose, other than in terms of infinitely recurring self-justification: coal output in Russia in 1910 is studied because coal output in Russia in 1910 is studied because coal output in Russia in 1910 is studied because...

Curricular disorientation

The difficulty of discerning any unitary purpose in the curriculum was exacerbated by its discrete timetabling. The collection of lessons that constituted Josie's timetable lacked cohesion: one subject followed another without any connection or appropriacy (on Tuesday: Maths, PE, Art, Science, Music), lessons in a particular subject occurred at any time of the day, pupil grouping systems varied, Josie missed some lessons to go to others because the timetable was overcrowded (English for German), she had more than one teacher for the same subject (English). From a timetabled 1500 minutes, 21.5 per cent was lost in the room changes that were required to sustain a curriculum that, for Josie, was divided into 13 discrete subjects and a timetable that, for Josie, was divided into 27 blocks, twenty-four of 50 minutes' length and three of 100 minutes.

During the week Josie changed rooms 30 times. By Tuesday she had attended lessons in ten different subjects (each in a different part of the school) and been in six different teaching groups, for which four different grouping systems were used (ability, gender, faith, social norming). On Tuesday a third of the lessons, but half the day's lesson-time, were not taken by the usual teacher (Maths and Art). In her six lessons on Thursday Josie had a student for Maths, a different teacher from her last lesson in English, missed the second of her English lessons to go to German and then missed half her German to go to a violin lesson, had a French lesson from which half the class was missing because they had gone to an extra Maths activity and ended the day in a Geography lesson led by an English teacher giving instructions in IT. On most days Josie was in a different pupil group for each lesson.

Didacticism and subject-specialism

The curriculum was unified, not by content links, cross-curricular skills, themes and dimensions, or a pupil-centred approach, but by a common teaching and learning style. Lessons began with an introduction by the teacher, pupils worked individually on short exercises, the class 'discussed' their findings and the process was repeated. In short, education appeared to be a process in which knowledge was neutralised and reified and then transmitted to learners who were instrumentalised by the transmission process. The accumulation of knowledge was purposeless and irrelevant to their daily lives.

It was the insistence on subject specialism that necessitated the compartmentalisation of knowledge, of disruptive room changes and, because of the short time-span of lessons, the expediency of short activities that did not allow the development of personal engagement with the subject being studied. Subject specialism is not the only way that the National Curriculum can be presented. The Keystage 2 tracking (undertaken by study LEA Primary Advisory Teacher Alice Farmer) revealed that a very similar curriculum to Keystage 3 was presented to pupils through extended, active topic work that contextualised and personalised the learning experience. Looking at the work produced by Josie, there is little evidence that she benefits from subject specialism at Keystage 3. It was our opinion that there was no subject content in any of Josie's lessons that a competent primary teacher would not have been capable of teaching in a more enlightened way.

Independent learning

The normal working pattern of silent individuality in response to teacher-selected textual exercises meant that it was hardly possible to record any examples of independent learning, which is based upon the interaction of individual, collaborative and co-operative research of self-chosen issues of personal interest.

Pupils did not learn collaboratively (Factor 1), or did so only very briefly on minor tasks decided by the teacher. They did not work co-operatively (Factor 2) for the teacher's role was clearly external to the pupil body. There was no sense of individual responsibility (Factor 3). The lack of opportunity for independent learning was reinforced by the teacher-control of the tasks undertaken during lessons, their assessment, the time which would be spent upon them and the manner in which they would be executed. Pupils completed short-term individual tasks at the command of the teacher but the rest of the class were engaged on exactly the same tasks. Completing these tasks involved no intrinsic individual responsibility; their completion was a matter of low-level self-convenience and expediency to avoid teacher-imposed sanctions. Pupils did not design their own tasks (Factor 4) or have any control over the time allocated for their completion (Factor 6) or any involvement in initiating research (Factor 7) – all tasks were from teacher-selected texts. Pupils had no voice in the assessment of their work (Factor 5), although in English they were invited to comment in pairs on the teacher's assessment. In other subjects 'answers' were always a matter of factual right or wrong, the decision made by the teacher or author of the textbook being used. The pupils' use of a range of technology (Factor 8) was limited to a brief instructional session in the computer room and the use of calculators in Maths. There was no suggestion that the content of lessons related to the community or the environment and certainly no movement into the local environment and community for pupil-initiated research (Factor 9). With the exception of a Personal and Social Education (PSE) presentation, there was no sense of audience for the work of pupils (Factor 10), other than teacher as marker, and the range of presentation of work (Factor 11) was in only two forms: hand-written or spoken response during lessons (a form of presentation that seemed to favour boys). There was no evidence of reflexivity (Factor 12).

Dependent learning

In the absence of a pedagogical commitment to educational citizenship via the factors of independent learning, there was no evidence of any clear alternative philosophy – knowledge-based, skills-based, child-centred – that related to the observed practice. Instead, there was confusion and inconsistency that suggested an ambivalent, uncertain attitude to what the school was trying to achieve. English was taught in mixed-ability groups, but also had one fast-track top set. Classroom furniture was arranged for groupwork, but for 95 per cent of the time individual work took place. The juxtaposed messages of the school prospectus attempted to embrace both pupil-responsibility and adult-control. There was a perceived need for different class-grouping criteria for the same pupils for different subjects. Throughout lessons there were continual knee-jerk calls for silence but an acceptance by all teachers of tolerable noise levels of societal chat.

It seemed that silence had a talismanic property and its imposition was the first criterion of the successful teacher. ('You'll learn not to talk in my lessons', said a student teacher.) It was as if teachers had chosen the criterion that was the most difficult to impose – and maybe this was how it was viewed, that the best teacher was the one who could bend the class to her will, the most potent representation of which would be to make pupils act against their powerful natural desire to communicate with each other. This provokes the image of teacher as controller not facilitator, and there was much evidence of this both in the daily life of the school and within lessons.

However, there were indications that the authoritarian ethos of the school was superficial and that the pupil body, although lacking any officially recognised role in the power structure, was no downtrodden proletariat. In almost all lessons teachers had to walk the fine line between overtaxing or overboring the class for, in either case, the pupils would withdraw their consent to the idea that the teachers were in charge and start to talk or mess around.

The major impetus of the lessons seemed to accept this unspoken premise, with teachers entertaining and mollifying and keeping noise and movement down to some unconsciously negotiated level of acceptability. Given that the basic curriculum was uninteresting, teachers seemed to adopt as a defensive mechanism a series of short tasks, endlessly moving pupils on as soon as they became noisily bored with any particular activity. It appeared to be an unarticulated but accepted agreement that the teachers had some right to be heard if they struggled to impose their voice but that they would soon shut up and give up and set another short, easy task which would allow pupils to chat quietly and societally for ten minutes or so as they completed the task.

Like individual lessons – at a quick glance – the macrocosm of the school system seemed efficient, for overlaying the actual practice (which may have been inefficient in achieving the stated aims of the establishment) was a veneer of apparent professionalism that was – at that quick glance – more than plausible but nighwell inviolable of any criticism.

There were many examples of a patina of monolithic certaintude: institutional codes of address, of movement around the buildings, of performance (school teams, 'houses', photos and plaques in the foyer, prospectus with public examination results, music certificates awarded in assembly), of suppression of personal freedom via school rules, of the emphasis upon neatness and conformity that a school uniform requires. The power discourse could be most vividly read in Monday's Year 9 assembly, during which pupils sat cross-legged on the gym floor. Teaching staff stood around the walls. Senior staff sat on chairs on a raised dais, the headteacher in the middle. With those ennobled adults at the apex of the hierarchy flanking him, the enthroned leader literally looked down on his young subjects as they sat at his feet, surrounded by guards.

The school regime was authoritarian, albeit benevolent in a maternalistic and paternalistic 'we know what's good for you' authoritarianism. This ethos was evinced in its many rules aimed at conformity rather than individuality. This spilled over into the set-up of the lessons, where all decision making was controlled by the teachers, all activities were presented as worthwhile without explanation and all learning was seen as accumulating factual information for no established or questioned purpose.

The longevity of such a system relies almost totally on its perceived success, its credibility with those involved in the system: pupils, parents and practitioners. Much of this credibility is promoted by drawing attention away from the difficult areas (like the curriculum and its pedagogy) towards various totems that have been artificially created as observable indicators of success: uniform, rules, punishment systems, homework, a spuriously impressive timetable, a glossy prospectus and the other trappings of Institution. To maintain this credibility, a climate is created in which the rightness of Institution becomes unquestionable: parents don't ask why their children need to be segregated by ability, teachers don't ask why their classes' weekly lesson time has to be scatter-shot across the timetable, pupils don't ask why they are doing what they're doing in a lesson. This is a climate of indoctrination in which members of all three groups – parents, practitioners and pupils – collude in their own oppression.

Chapter Two identified general practices likely to promote or suppress educational citizenship via the 12 factors of independent learning. The general practices regarded as likely to develop educational citizenship were those designed to promote a critical disposition, moral and social awareness and an equal interaction of adult-pupil and pupil-pupil relationships (symmetrical reciprocity). There was little evidence of such practices in Josie's lessons. General practices likely to suppress the development of educational citizenship had been identified in the theory as the three factors of dependent learning: indoctrination, the social and moral isolation of the curriculum, and the denial to pupils of the opportunity to practise the rights and responsibilities of global citizenship. There was a great deal of evidence of such practices in Josie's lessons.

The prevalent classroom ethos was one of indoctrination by suppressing the development of a critical disposition and by promoting cognitive development at the expense of the affective. In lesson after lesson pupils were actively prevented from thinking for themselves. Instead, they were offered a succession of unrelated exercises that required no personal engagement. The curriculum was almost exclusively socially and morally isolated from the real world. Not one teacher attempted to explain or justify a lesson with any reference to the community and environment at local, national or global level. Lessons lacked any topical relevance. One felt that they could have been taught in exactly the same way either twenty years ago or in twenty years time – the underlying message was that knowledge is neutral and immutable, unaffected by society or morality. In not one lesson were pupils given the opportunity to discuss social or moral issues at all, let alone issues set in a topical context relevant to their young lives. Pupils were denied the opportunity to practise the rights and responsibilities of global citizenship by a hierarchical system of authority that reserved all decision making at all levels to adults. The adult-pupil relationships were of a complementary nature, with the teachers' actions determining adolescents' concepts of themselves as pupils rather than people.

PUPIL TRACKING AT KEYSTAGE 4: DISTRIBUTION OF THE 1500 MINUTES OF EMILY'S TIMETABLED WEEK

Table 4.4 shows Emily's learning activities, generically, throughout the curriculum. Figure 4.2 illustrates Table 4.4 in graphic form.

It can be seen that the predominant lesson style of the week comprises didactic teacher-led presentations followed by individual note-taking – 49.8 per cent of the actual lessontime was spent in this way, 20.6 per cent of lessontime was taken up by room changes and register-taking, 11.4 per cent of the time was spent on Maths and the rest of the time was made up of odd bits and pieces: two short volleyball sessions (3.7%), the writing of a letter in German (2.4%), watching videos (2.2%). Groupwork appeared to account for 9.9 per cent of time but reservations about the validity of this figure are expanded upon in the full text of the case studies (the groupwork was a matter of expediency rather than pedagogy and was, in the main, of poor quality). The limited and repetitive experiences offered to pupils is powerfully demonstrated in Figure 4.2: over 80 per cent of the pupils' time is spent either in, or moving between, lesson after lesson of the same format – lecture followed by silent individual note making or sums.

Talk

The Penmouth tracking provided confirmatory data (Tables 4.5 and 4.6) for the trends suggested at Sir James Redbourne.

It was observed that:

- most talk was teacher-led rather than pupil-to-pupil
- most talk was of a factual, not a discursive, nature
- pupils' contributions were generally limited to short phrases lasting only a few seconds that were offered as answers to the teacher's question

Table 4.4: The distribution of the 1500 minutes of Emily's timetabled week.

Activity	Mon	Tues	Weds	Thurs	Fri	Totals	%
Note-taking and comp. exs.	131	37	93	31	168	460	30.7
Room changes & register	45	108	71	39	46	309	20.6
Teacher-led talk	83	89	32	37	46	287	19.1
Maths	41	0	46	44	40	171	11.4
Groupwork	0	0	0	149	0	149	9.9
P.E.	0	30	25	0	0	55	3.7
Letter	0	36	0	0	0	36	2.4
Video-watching	0	0	33	0	0	33	2.2

Source: Author

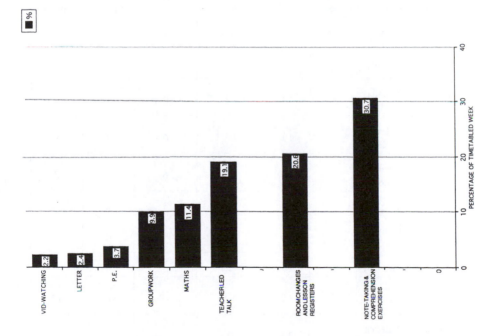

Figure 4.2: Bar graph showing the distribution of the 1500 minutes of Emily's timetabled week
Source: Author

- boys were three times more likely to contribute voluntarily to teacher-led talk
- boys were three times more likely to be asked to contribute by teachers
- teacher-led talk was the common form of introduction to a lesson
- teacher-led talk as an introduction was invariably succeeded by pupils working, individually, in silence
- pupil-to-pupil talk was discouraged and, sometimes, pupils were punished for talking
- boys and girls rarely talked to each other.

There seems to be the suggestion in Table 4.6 that a class has to consist of nearly two-thirds girls before they make a similar contribution to discussion as boys will make when they only represent about half the pupils, that a class is not

Table 4.5: Pupils' contributions to whole class discussion Keystage 4

Activity number	Subject	Number of boys	Number of girls	Boys' unrequested responses	Girls' unrequested responses	Boys' requested responses	Girls' requested responses
3	English	15	13	3	1	6	2
5 and 7	History	15	15	18	5	0	0
8	Science 1	12	13	12	0	6	3
10, 12 and 14	Science 2	12	13	19	6	3	1
17 and 19	Business Studies	16	4	30	6	6	2
22	English	15	14	5	3	2	3
25 and 27	Business Studies	16	7	8	4	0	0
29	German	6	13	2	3	0	0
46 and 48	German	8	15	12	49	6	13
51 and 53	Science 2	12	13	0	0	5	4
Totals		127	120	109	77	34	28

Source: Author

Activity Number	Subject	% of boys in the lesson	% of girls in the lesson	Boys' % of unrequested responses	Girls' % of unrequested responses	Boys' % of requested responses	Girls' % of requested responses
				Table 4.6: Contributions to whole class discussion by % of the class population			
3	English	53.6	46.4	75	25	75	25
5 and 7	History	50	50	78.3	21.7	0	0
8	Science 1	48	52	100	0	66.7	33.3
10, 12 and 14	Science 2	48	52	76	24	75	25
17 and 19	Business Studies	80	20	83.3	16.7	75	25
22	English	51.7	48.3	62.5	37.5	40	60
25 and 27	Business Studies	69.5	30.5	66.7	33.3	0	0
29	German	31.6	68.4	40	60	0	0
46 and 48	German	34.8	65.2	19.7	80.3	31.6	68.4
51 and 53	Science 2	48	52	0	0	55.5	44.5

Source: Author

representative of equal opportunity in discussion by number alone – an approximately 1:1 ratio of boys and girls (English, History, Science) gives around a 1:3 ratio of voluntary responses that favours the boys. In the German lesson a class of 35 per cent boys were still getting 31 per cent of requested responses, whereas requested responses for girls in 1:1 gender ratio classes was somewhere around half their population percentage.

Business Studies was the only lesson in which the percentage of boys and girls in the class closely related with the percentage of voluntary and requested responses during teacher-led talk. Although the mean population percentage of boys and girls was close (55% boys and 45% girls), boys recorded 79 per cent of the unrequested responses (girls 21%) and 65 per cent of the requested responses (girls 35%). Overall, boys made 76 per cent of the responses, girls 24 per cent.

In all lessons, apart from Maths (where they chatted comfortably throughout lessons), pupils were discouraged from talking to each other, although Communication is a NC cross-curricular skill. This embargo included English lessons –

one of the NC Profile Components of which is Speaking and Listening. Groupwork was rarely encouraged of itself, except as an expediency in the use of limited resources, and pupil-to-pupil talk was not valued – not even recognised – as an aid to learning. This is not surprising if learning is seen to mean note taking, the predominant activity of the week, for which the best classroom condition was held to be individuals working in silence. The image is of an old-fashioned library rather than a contemporary learning centre. During the week Emily had no one-to-one conversation with a teacher. Her contribution to whole-class teacher-led talk was restricted to two brief comments in one lesson, Business Studies. In the week's 287 minutes of teacher-led talk, Emily spoke for six seconds. She spent 99.65 per cent of teacher-led talk time in silence.

Reading

All of Emily's reading was done for the purpose of note making, which took up 30.7 per cent (460 minutes) of the week. Apart from the novel *Lord of the Flies*, all the texts were of a factual nature. Unlike Sir James Redbourne, in which worksheets containing comprehension questions were used (History, Geography, RE, French), the Penmouth emphasis was upon the précis, by pupils, of published texts. Often, the pupils were not asked to respond to questions upon the text but merely to reduce the text to note form (History, Science 1, Business Studies) for no stated purpose. Other forms of note taking were copying from the board (Science 2, Business Studies) and dictation (Business Studies). The length of texts that pupils were given to summarise was sometimes absurd: in History, pupils were given 25 minutes to read and make notes upon 12 densely packed pages of a large-page, small-print textbook; an English assignment for a single 50 minute lesson was to make notes on the following:

> 'Ralph and the conch, Ralph and death, Ralph and fear, Ralph and the fire, Ralph and the hunting, Ralph and Jack, Ralph and the leadership, Ralph and nature, Ralph and order, Ralph and Piggy, Ralph and reason, Ralph and the rescue – throughout the novel in order to explain the changes in Ralph.'
> (Written on the blackboard, English, 3 March 1993)

Neither of the teachers who set these tasks can have had the slightest expectation that they would be – or could be – fulfilled in the available time, yet both moved on to other topics in the following lesson.

Writing

Apart from the writing of a letter in German (2.4% of the week at 36 minutes), the only opportunity during the week for Emily to make a personal statement, Emily's writing consisted solely of note making. Collaboration was not allowed – the note taking was an individual activity carried out in silence. A third of the week was spent in this way.

Other lesson activities

Apart from teacher-led talk, note taking, the writing of a letter and the movement from one lesson to another, Emily spent 55 minutes (3.7%) playing volleyball, 171 minutes (11.4%) doing sums from a Maths textbook, 33 minutes (2.2%) watching a video and 149 minutes (9.9%) in small groupwork. Nearly two-thirds of the groupwork time (95 minutes) comprised a Drama lesson, which, on analysis, proved to be less than successful. The Science groupwork (46 minutes) appeared to be based upon expediency rather than pedagogy – there was not enough equipment for pupils to work individually. There were eight minutes of pair work in German when pupils tried out newly learnt phrases on each other. The groupwork occurred in only four of the week's 30 lessons: Drama (95 minutes), Science 2 (15 minutes), Science 1 (31 minutes) and German (8 minutes.) All the groupwork occurred on one day and 90 per cent of lessons contained no groupwork.

Seating

The Penmouth tracking confirmed the trends suggested at Sir James Redbourne:

- boys and girls chose to sit apart
- boys were asked by the teacher to contribute to teacher-led talk more than girls, wherever they sat in the classroom
- classroom furniture was arranged to signify discrete areas between the teacher and the pupils.

In addition, the Penmouth tracking illuminated the territorial possession signified by classroom seating. Other pupils would not sit in an absent peer's usual place. Pupils had 'their own' seats in every different classroom.

What unifies the curriculum?

Cross-Curricular Elements

It proved problematical to gather data on the National Curriculum cross-curricular elements of dimensions, skills and themes and the institutional cross-curricular elements of the school's aims. The difficulty stemmed from the vagueness of their wording and, therefore, the subjectivity required in deciding whether they were present within lessons, intended to be present or effective if they were present.

For instance, one of the NC cross-curricular dimensions 'which should permeate every aspect of the curriculum' (NCC 1990) is Preparation for Life in a Multicultural Society. In many lessons (Science, Maths, PE) there was clearly no evidence of this dimension – it was not present in lessons. However, although in no lessons was there any explicit reference to Preparation for Life in a Multicultural Society, it was possible to argue that the content of some lessons might be implicitly useful in promoting this dimension. For instance, some knowledge of Communist China might offer pupils a perspective from which to view indigenous Sino-British communities (History). A broader view of multiculturalism, to encompass class and gender, might allow that *Lord of the Flies* could be maintained to have a contributory effect to an understanding of different cultures (English). In that global economies certainly affect local cultures, Business Studies may be said to play a part in promoting the dimension of Preparation for Life in a Multicultural Society.

This led to the second consideration: if such undercurrents were detectable, were they intentional? Was Preparation for Life in a Multicultural Society one of Mrs Harvey's criteria (or one of the Southern Examining Group's criteria, or one of the School Examination and Assessment Council's criteria) for selecting *Lord of the Flies* as a public examination text? Was Preparation for Life in a Multicultural Society one of the recognised aims of the History and Business Studies lessons on Communist China and Taxation? There was no evidence, in discussion with these subject teachers, that they had given consideration to this issue, that the presence of cross-curricular elements should be deliberately implicit. This was more or less the claim of the Deputy Head in charge of Curriculum Development when asked for a copy of the Penmouth cross-curricular policy: 'It's happening all over the place. We just haven't got round to documenting it yet'.

The third question concerned the effectiveness of lessons to promote cross-curricular elements whether they were intentionally or unintentionally, explicitly or implicitly, present in lessons. It can be argued – as in Chapter 2 – that it may not be necessary for either teachers or pupils to be aware of that which is being learnt, that teachers can unintentionally indoctrinate pupils by suppressing the development of a critical faculty. Might there be evidence of a 'benign' form of indoctrination so that although Preparation for Life in a Multicultural Society was not acknowledged by teacher or pupil as an explicit aim of a lesson, the general atmosphere and pedagogy was actively promoting this dimension? There was no evidence, in the lessons observed, of any link between lesson content and contemporary society. Moreover, life in a multicultural society involves attitudes and beliefs that constantly need to be re-examined and possibly redefined. In the lessons observed there was no evidence of this kind of personal reflexivity or of the social and intellectual dialectic that might stimulate it. Knowledge consisted of immutable facts and learning concerned the cognitive and not the affective domain.

These three considerations made it impossible to collect quantitative data about NC cross-curricular elements or school aims. The qualitative data of observation and the collation of texts studied and created during the week by Emily strongly suggested that there was little or no evidence of cross-curricular dimensions or school aims within lessons, either at an implicit or explicit level or as a conscious or subconscious aim of the teacher, and, therefore, no evidence of their effective or ineffective application. Indeed, for one of the dimensions, Equal Opportunities (Gender), there was evidence to suggest that the school system actively promoted the unequal and superior opportunities of boys.

The above considerations also applied to the NC cross-curricular skills of communication, numeracy, study, problem solving, personal and social education, information technology, flexibility and adaptability, of which the NCC considers it '...absolutely essential that these skills are fostered across the whole curriculum in a measured and planned way...what is beyond dispute is that in the next century these skills will be at a premium.' (NCC 1990, p.3).

There was evidence of communication and numeracy, but at a very low level: the understanding of simple instructions and the offering of short-phrase factual answers by pupils during teacher-led talk, mindless doing of sums whilst chatting societally. The NCC publication *The Whole Curriculum* does not define any of the NC cross-curricular skills but 'Study' is defined in the English Orders (1990) as the ability of pupils to 'Select reference books and other information materials and use organisational devices to find answers to their own questions.' (Cox 1989). No pupil selected a reference book – there were no other information materials available than textbooks distributed by the teachers – and no pupils found 'answers to their own questions'. There was no evidence of problem solving, personal and social education or information technology. What evidence there was of flexibility and adaptability was not promoted by the school management but was detectable within the pupil body as a subversive defence against the invasions of the system, for example pupils' interpretation of the command 'Silence' was adjusted to different teachers, or Emily's exploitation of the timetabling error that allowed her to use Maths as 'my time off' (at the beginning of the school year she had mistakenly been enrolled in the individual needs Maths class).

The same is also true of the NC themes of Economic and Industrial Understanding, Careers Education and Guidance, Health Education, Education for Citizenship and Environmental Education. It was possible to find a few scattered, coincidental examples that might be used to illustrate some implicit policy (Business Studies for Economic and Industrial Education, the drink-driving lecture in the Social Education lesson for Health Education) but no suggestion that these themes are 'essential parts of the whole curriculum' (NCC 1990, p.4).

Thus it was not possible to find positive evidence to suggest that cross-curricular elements or the school aims were intended to contribute not just to separate dimensions, skills and themes but through them to a holistic learning experience for pupils. The opposite was more likely to pertain, with negative evidence of certain cross-curricular elements and a disorientating organisation of the curriculum.

Curricular Disorientation

There were several practices that contributed to a disorientation of the separate subjects that constituted the school curriculum.

Lessons in the same subject could occur at any time of the day or week. On Monday English was the first lesson in the morning, on Friday it was the last of the afternoon. All the afternoon lessons (apart from the single period of Social Education) were also timetabled during morning sessions at some point in the week. There seemed to be no pattern; apparently any lesson could happen at any time.

This lack of pattern was also shown in the lack of connections between lessons. There was no attempt to block disciplines together so that links could be explored as in projects like Centennial and Europeans (see Chapter Five). What cohesive flow is there to, say, Tuesday: English to Business Studies to Drama to German to PE?

There was also a lack of connections between lessons in the same subject: History and Science were both taught by two different people in two different classrooms, studying two different topics, so that pupils never had two consecutive lessons on the same topic – Communist China in Room 43 with Mr Oldman, followed by Health and Sanitation in Victorian Britain in Room 42 with Mrs Harvey, then back to Communist China with Mr Oldman and so on. Or in Science – a lesson on sound with Mrs Graham in Lab 1 was followed by a lesson on the greenhouse effect with Mr O'Dowd in Lab 2, then a return to Lab 1 for a lesson on light, back to Lab 2 for a new topic on Forces and Energy, then to Lab 1 for the fifth new science topic of the week, 'Pendulums'.

Teacher absence also disrupted continuity. During this week, Emily had cover teachers or supply teachers for lessons in English, German, History and Science.

The various elements of room change within a subject, teacher change within a subject, teacher absence and change of topic within a subject left only Business Studies and PE undisrupted during this week, that is following the same topic in the same room with the same teacher throughout the week. Mrs Sears spent the three lessons of Business Studies dealing with taxation and in the two PE lessons the same teacher took the same group for volleyball.

Lesson Times

There seemed to be a uniformity here, but at the expense of any recognition that some lessons may have benefited from being longer than others. One example would be to have a double PE lesson, for in the 100 minutes devoted to single periods, 45 per cent of the time was lost in changing. The eight Science periods may be better blocked as four doubles, so that experiments could have more time to be done – 50 minutes was not really long enough to arrive, be registered, get the gear out, make a few mistakes, get the experiment done and pack away and write it up.

Grouping Systems

A further disorientation was caused by the different grouping systems used, so that Emily did not have two consecutive lessons with the same group of pupils. Emily did not work with the same class-grouping of pupils in any of her different GCSE subjects. She had four of her subjects taught in different ability sets (English, Science, Maths and German) and three of her subjects were taught in different option groups (History, Business Studies and Drama). Of her three non-examination subjects, PE was grouped by gender and non-examination Tutor Group and Social Education were the only lessons she shared with a common class, her tutor group.

Option Choices

Emily's timetable is limited in learning styles and in content: no RE, no Music, no Computer Studies, no Art, no Design, no Technology, no Outdoor Education. As a profile of a well-educated GCSE student, Emily's list of subjects appears eclectic: English, Science and Maths, History, German, Drama and Business Studies. What educational philosophy (rather than institutional logic) justifies the personal, social and vocational legitimacy of these arbitrary subject choices, their disparate grouping systems and their attendant repressive pedagogy?

Independent learning

Apart from the few instances of collaborative groupwork (Factor 1), there was virtually no evidence of any of the factors of independent learning. On the contrary, the didactic teaching styles, the passive learning experiences, the emphasis on individual work (duplicated by every other member of the class) and the prejudice against pupil communication all legislated powerfully against independent learning.

There was no sense of co-operative groupwork (Factor 2) or of individual responsibility (Factor 3) in the independent learning definition of the term, in which the responsibility of the individual is defined in relation to the collaborative groups that an individual is a member of, within the embrace of concentric co-operative groups. Independent learning promotes the responsibility of the individual to others. The Penmouth ethos championed the responsibility of the individual to herself at the expense of others and actively discouraged collaboration and co-operation. Pupils did not design their own tasks, had no stake in the assessment of their tasks and no control over the timing of tasks (Factors 4, 5 and 6). Although pupils did a great deal of individual reading and concomitant note making, not once did they initiate their own research (Factor 7). Pupils did not use a range of technology (Factor 8), in fact pupils did not use any technology. Apart from the guest speaker for Social Education, there was no interaction with the community and no use of the environment (Factor 9). There was no sense of audience for the pupils' work other than teacher as marker (Factor 10). There was no range of presentation of pupils' work (Factor 11). The sole medium of presentation was hand-written manuscript. There was no evidence of reflexivity, of personal engagement or of self-critical and critical reflection (Factor 12).

Dependent learning

The cumulative effect of subject-specific timetabling, option groups and the use of different criteria for class membership is to create a system that casts the individual into a void where making cross-curricular connections with other pupils, or with unifying aspects of the curriculum, is almost impossible. It may be that Emily is the only pupil in the school following her particular pattern of lessons. She spends her lesson time in alienated classes, within which groups and individuals are discouraged from relating to each other, studying subjects that are isolated from each other in terms of either a holistic concept of knowledge or of transferable skills, and in which no attempt is made to relate their content to the relevance of her own personal and social life. Such a system is a very effective means of institutional control, for these constantly forming and disbanding groups of pupils are unlikely to develop a dynamic strong enough for them to achieve a corporate identity and purpose.

Evidence of the factors of independent learning intended to promote educational citizenship was scant. There was clear evidence of the factors of dependent learning likely to hinder the development of educational citizenship: indoctrination via the suppression of a critical disposition, the isolation of the curriculum from a social and moral context, the repression of the rights of global citizenship.

PUPIL TRACKING AT KEYSTAGES 3 AND 4: CONCLUSIONS

There are many similarities between Sir James Redbourne and Penmouth schools in their philosophy, their organisation and their rhetoric. Both appear to share a philosophy of education located firmly within the Peters-Hirst-Dearden tradition that underpins the National Curriculum: that educational attainment is best measured, and therefore served, by the accumulation of knowledge. In organisational terms, this philosophy leads to the division of knowledge into prescribed subjects with prescribed syllabuses for pupils of different ages and abilities. This curriculum is administered via a timetable which requires the individual pupil to join a series of different teaching groups, established by different criteria, for short, discrete lessons in different rooms with different teachers.

One of the effects of this policy is to isolate the individual within the system. It is my contention that such isolation leads to disempowerment and the silencing of the disempowered.

Neither Josie nor Emily had any officially recognised decision-making role to play within their school structures. Both school handbooks laid out expected codes of behaviour and sanctions for deviations from the code. Neither handbook suggested that pupils were consulted or played any part in the formulation of these rules. The audience for the handbooks was not the pupil but the parent (made obvious by the many textual references to 'your child'). Within lessons, pupils had no say in their education. The content, style and pace of all lessons were dictated exclusively by the teachers. Thus the system disempowered the majority and then the disempowered were effectively silenced by their disempowerment itself, which suggested that their voice was not important, not even necessary for the running of the institution, by the absence of any official route for voicing, such as a pupils' council or representation on school committees or the board of governors, but most powerfully by the ethos of lessons which discouraged collaboration and the development of a critical disposition, the two most critical conditions for effective voicing.

The inevitability of this system seems to unfurl from its basic philosophy of education: the notion of learning based on content knowledge rather than (independent) learning skills – *which leads to* the division of the curriculum into discrete subjects, each seen to require a different specialist teacher – *which leads to* the division of the school day into short, uniform periods of time for the dissemination of neutralised subject knowledge,which is regarded as having a hierarchy of difficulty – *which leads to* the division of the pupil body into myriad subject groupings, each using different evaluative criteria – *which leads to* the isolation of individuals within a hierarchy of power based upon the controlling oligarchy's definition and dissemination of knowledge – *which leads to the disempowerment of the majority.*

The combination of a knowledge-based philosophy of education, a positivist attitude to knowledge and a public examination system that imposes timed tests upon individuals of their memory of content-based syllabuses has the following practical effects upon lessons: a didactic transmission of 'factual' information unrelated to the real world, its communities and environments – *and* a view of talk as time-wasting and collaboration as cheating and, therefore, a concentration on silent, secretive, individual work – *and* a reliance on teacher-disseminated texts as the source of authority of knowledge rather than pupil research – *and* no sense of negotiation with the teacher about lesson content or structure, or the assessment of pupils' efforts – *which leads to the silencing of the disempowered.*

Furthermore, the observable attendant effects, in policy and practice, of the philosophy of education espoused by both schools were inconsistent with those school aims that claimed that Sir James Redbourne and Penmouth were committed to develop pupils' interests and intellectual capacities in stimulating lessons. There was a gulf between the rhetoric and the reality of Institution.

Both schools were claiming to offer the benefits of educational citizenship but it was difficult to collect any evidence of a pedagogy, such as independent learning, that was explicitly and commonly intended to promote educational citizenship within lessons.

The research issue which prompted this book was: 'Are the ends that are claimed for 5–16 education in relation to citizenship consistent with the means advocated for their development?'

A conclusion can be drawn from the findings of this section of the research programme: that the ends that are claimed for 11–16 education in relation to citizenship by the managers of two comprehensive schools in the study LEA are not consistent with the means advocated for their development. The two schools were selected for their typicality by researchers who had experience in many comprehensive schools in the United Kingdom. Such is the conformity that the National Curriculum imposes upon schools that I doubt there would have been any significant difference in my findings had the research been conducted anywhere in the country. This was certainly the view of teachers whom I met at a series of national and international conferences.

The research enquiry was: 'What practices within schools are likely to develop or to suppress attributes of citizenship considered to be appropriate to the third millennium?'

The findings of this section of the research programme clearly depict dependent learning practices within schools that are likely to suppress attributes of citizenship considered to be appropriate to the third millennium.

The next two chapters focus upon the research question, which is based upon the hypothesis that 'Pupils need to learn *as* citizens to become citizens': 'What effects do the the 12 factors of independent learning, intended to promote educational citizenship, have in practice?'

CHAPTER FIVE

Independent Learning

It is beyond the scope of this book to present and discuss the entirety of the fieldwork, its attendant data collection and consequent analysis. Nor do I feel that such a task is necessary – those who are ideologically opposed to the concept of educational citizenship are unlikely to be bludgeoned into conversion whatever the weight of evidence (and probably aren't reading this anyway) and those who are sympathetic to notions of democratic schooling are likely to accept that the exemplar evidence I offer is representative of the full research archive. What I intend to do in this chapter is to offer descriptions of some of the projects and to report more fully on one. Hopefully, this will give a feel for the nature of independent learning as a whole. Then I am going to review the major findings of the analysis of data collection from pupils. Finally, I shall use a few comments from teachers and observers as exemplification of the consensus of opinion that existed within the research partnership.

INDEPENDENT LEARNING PROJECTS IN ENGLISH LESSONS

As the guiding tenet of independent learning is that pupils should be allowed to study whatever they want, in whatever way they want and in partnership with whomsoever they want, I suppose that, depending on one's own classroom experience as a pupil or teacher or one's educational ideology, quite different scenes of the independent learning classroom can be imagined. These may vary from the Woodhead Hallucination (a nightmare of anarchic chaos as pupils run riot and hapless teachers, having lost all control, vainly attempt to cork the genie back into the bottle before the Witchfinder-Inspector descends), via the Plowden Viewpoint (a pragmatic and utilitarian image of reasonably-occupied pupils producing a fair standard of work without too much disruption and inconvenience), to the Dartington Dream (an idyllic vision of pedagogical kharmic peace, co-operation and enlightenment). Because of the encouragement to classes to organise in groups that may choose to work in their own way on self-selected topics, I doubt that it is possible to give a defining picture of an independent learning project. With this caveat in mind, I consider the following two descriptions to be fairly typical of the experience of an organised and committed collaborative group – and organisation and commitment were typical of the vast majority of groups and classes. The first description is written by a teacher of English, the second by a pupil member of a collaborative group.

'Another Day in Paradise'

David-John, Gemma, Harry and Martha were Keystage 3, Year 8 pupils at an urban comprehensive school and, at the time of the project in the summer term of 1990, were all thirteen years old. As a collaborative group, the four pupils chose to undertake a study of homeless people in their locality, a town of about 25,000 inhabitants. After much discussion within the group they decided that they would like to write a short script about a day in the life of two homeless adolescents and to video-record the film in the town. Their intended audience was the local adult community.

The opportunities for purposeful speaking and listening were already extensive: the original idea-sharing within the group until a consensus was reached and then the need to persuade me (the class teacher) that their idea was feasible. I arranged an interview for the group with the Headteacher, whose permission was required for the pupils to work and film off the school premises. The group decided to send their most articulate member to the Head and spent some time preparing for the interview, coaching Martha, their representative, drafting her exposition and hot-seating her for possible questions. Body language, dress, form of address, register and style of speech were discussed and practised.

At this stage the first part of a considerable programme of factual research was undertaken, the group feeling that their case would be strengthened if they appeared well-informed at the Head's interview. The final presentation to the Head was based around two discovered facts: that, apart from London, their town had the highest per capita homeless population and that 75 per cent of this population was of local origin. The Headteacher gave permission for the filming, subject to the written approval of the two shopkeepers and the hotel manager on whose premises the group intended to film, the permission of parents and the attendance of a responsible adult carer when the group were on location.

Telephone conversations took place, meetings were arranged with, and letters sent to, all those involved (including the parents) and a schedule organised, all by the pupils themselves.

The group had by now amassed a great deal of information that went far beyond the original local focus and included research on contemporary destitution in Africa, the dust bowl depression of middle America in the 1930s and the British history of the Poor Laws and the workhouse. Choosing what material to base further work on for the magazine that the group intended to publish was a formidable task and required a high order of selection, comprehension and summary skills.

About this time (early June), the group began to feel that their original objectives were being lost and that the experiences of the local homeless were being overlooked. With adult supervision, each member of the group spent a morning with a different homeless person (in one case, a couple). Their experiences were recorded on video, on pocket audio-recorders, in note form and, perhaps most vividly, in their memories.

None of this material appeared in the final video. Somehow, the group felt that this cheapened the trust the homeless had shown in them, particularly as the video was to be viewed by the local public. In discussion, I suggested that, with the subjects' permission, there were ways in which the material could be handled sensitively, but the group was adamant – words such as dignity, integrity, fairness were used. (It might be felt that the group was rejecting the notion of the local homeless as research subjects and responding to them as fellow members of the research partnership of the project. RG).

However, transcripts were taken, some of which were written up in interview or article form for the magazine. This highlighted to the group the ways in which language changes as it moves from one form to another and is used for different purposes with different audiences. On a rather more mundane, but nevertheless important, level there was much discussion about punctuation and spelling, the excision of expletives and the retention of slang.

This work led to narrative, descriptive and poetry writing as the pupils now felt able to empathise, without the sentimentality of ignorance, with the homeless. The magazine also contained factual articles placing contemporary homelessness in an historical perspective and clearly argued discursive pieces outlining possible solutions to 'the problem'. There was lively debate about what constituted the problem and whose problem it was. After all, one of the people interviewed had said that he wouldn't swap his lifestyle at any price. So did he have a problem? Or did conventional citizens have problems coming to terms with a sub-culture they regarded as anti-social? A pivotal point in the project was the realisation that homeless people were as diverse as any other group – beware stereotypes.

The group wrote to the Urban Council Housing Committee (the Chair granted them an interview) and the local representatives of all the political parties, all of whom eventually responded in some form or other. They also visited the local DSS office and a local support centre for the homeless.

I offered suggestions for works of literature as diverse as a revisit to *Gumble's Yard* (which the group agreed created an exciting fantasy of child destitution quite at odds with the reality) and the George Orwell essays *The Spike* and *How The Poor Die*. Gemma later read *Down and Out in Paris and London* and interviewed a local Major in the Salvation Army about his opinions of Orwell's criticism of their 'tea and prayers' approach to charity for the homeless. Martha compiled a list of colloquialisms from Orwell's essay and compared them with present-day language usage – for instance the shift from tramp to traveller, homeless to rough sleeper, jobless to unwaged, charity to support. The events leading up to the death of Fanny in *Far From The Madding Crowd* were read and David-John and Harry then compared literary text with a video version of the film.

Their own video was successfully filmed, with Harry and Martha operating the camera and David-John and Gemma starring. The film was edited one afternoon with the help of two members of the county advisory service. The group audio-dubbed the prerecorded soundtrack of Phil Collins' song *Another Day In Paradise* onto video and then insert-edited both their live footage and a series of still shots culled from texts discovered during their research. Much use was made of an Atari software package that helped create digitised special effects and a different software programme was used for computer graphic titles and credits.

The film was shown to a public audience, followed by a live presentation by the group which included an impassioned plea for greater understanding of the homeless, a demonstration of how to audio-dub and insert-edit so that synchronisation is achieved between lyric and visual image and members of the group welcomed spontaneous questions.

'Sources of Electrical Energy'

The following description was written by Vanessa, a Year 10 pupil in an upper set at Poltrice, whose class had undertaken an independent learning project in the spring term of 1992. Vanessa's group, 'Lightning', chose the subject 'Sources of Electrical Energy'. There were five in the group, three boys and two girls. Each member of the group was 'in charge' of an outcome (diary, literary review, magazine, live presentation, video) and had the responsibility of ensuring that every group member contributed to 'their' outcome. Each member of the group was also responsible for researching a different source of electrical energy: oil and gas (Darren), geothermal and coal (Matthew), nuclear power (Juliet), wind and water (Vanessa) and hydro and solar (Alistair). The 'many visits' that Vanessa refers to were organised by the group itself and took place both during lessons and out-of-school times:

1. General Impressions

> The general impressions I had after finishing this project were of some regret and resentment aswell as feeling relieved, quite pleased and satisfied at the work we produced.
>
> I think this regret was mostly about the last minute panic to finish the magazine and complete other work where this work could have been done under much less pressure, more relaxed to perhaps a higher standard.
>
> In our group we went on many visits, met many interesting people and discovered alot about researching for information. In the class our groups seemed to have taken totally different

approaches to the work than our group did. I enjoyed this term in English ~~as this~~ though project was something I had never imagined to work like it did.

2. Good things about the project

The good things about the project were working in small groups, being able to take the respondisibilty of organizing our time for ourselves, being able to choose a topic we were interested in, working at our own pace, using computer equipment, the video editing suite, having a whole term left for us to specifically work on the project and visiting places eg. Hinkley point, Delabole windfarm, Truro library. ~~ete~~

I enjoyed researching the subject of energy sources instead of having information thrown at us on printed notes and told to inwardly digest it. I think I have learnt alot of information without conciously trying as I have been interested in the subject ~~asand~~ and so naturally I have learnt alot of material I would have previously shut my mind to because I ~~hadn't~~ wouldnt have researched the topic myself, I would have had no active involvement and that information would pass without ~~me understanding it~~ the processing, selecting, reading etc that took place in our ~~in our~~ project.

3. Bad things about the project

The bad things about the project were mainly about the group. My position in the group seemed to change every week. ~~and was often not sure of what place In~~ At first our group seemed simple and quite natural but as time went on things became more complex and confused.

I think everyone could have made ~~th~~ everything much easier and simple for everyone else if t we had discussed how we personally felt ~~regulally~~. regularly.

Other bad things ~~was were the xxxx xx xxxxxxx xxxx~~ were how we were expected to do this project in one of our GCSE years. The time we were allow was long enough if we had organised and planned the term better.

4. How things could have been better

As I have said more guidance from teachers should have been given to the time management knowledge ~~involved~~ we needed. I think having mixed groups was okay but there were many drawbacks suchas ego conflicts, ~~domiance domience~~ dominunce, power, not confronting real emotions, not wanting to express inner feelings, resentment and competitiveness between the sexes and each other.

If we had undertaken this project in Year 9 it would have been 50% easier. I think we all coped quite well and maybe it has given us all an idea of how we can cope, restrain, opt out, thrive or ~~the give in~~ have a total nervous breakdown under xxxxxxx pressure and the threat of deadlines.

5. What I learnt

I learnt alot about wind power to a great depth and to a lesser extent about other sources of electrical energy. I've learnt some skills in communicating opinions and relating to other people.

I've carried out an interview with the owner of the wind farm at Delabole, Mr Edwards which has now given me a bit of confidence for the future if I happen to be put in similar situation.

I've learnt about researching and investigating a subject through the use of people, libraries, museums etc.

6. Advice for other people working like this

Don't. Seriously if you were to undertake a project similar to this I would give the following advice concluded from the mistakes I and our group made.

1) Organisation – organise everything really well so you can enjoy the project right to the end instead of panicking.

2) Separate workload equally and make each person of the group respondisible for his/her allocated part.

3) Help and support each other. You are all in the same group so work together. Help other groups if you can.

4) Keep an open mind. If your project dosent turn out exactly like you imagined in the first place then it is probably for the best. Try out and discuss all possible ideas.

5) Enthusiasism is really important. Be interested in the subject you choose and think positively.

\+ The Best of Luck.

7. Our Group

The subject we chose was ~~soucre~~ sources of Electrical Energy. In our group there was Alastair Lee, Darren Wilcock, Matthew Evans, Juliet Burnard and myself.

Our group sometimes merged as one, sometimes seperated as the bond cracked. At the start of project our group was quite a unsual mixture An Interesting combinations of personalities which seemed on a superficial level to work. About a month into the project underflowing emotions rose and disagreements happened. There was arguing, shouting and screaming, especially between Juliet and myself, until we both started to calm down and restrain ourselves from throttling each other.

Towards the end of the project our group worked really well all together. We achieved ~~all the xxx~~ all we had ~~ami~~ aimed to achieve ~~and a bit extra I think~~. What we achieved was good considering all the things that went wrong.

8. Would you like to do something similar again? If so, why?

Yes I would because I think I have learnt much more from this project than I realise at the moment. This project ~~xxxxx xxxxxxx~~ created alot of oppertunities and chances to experience new and ~~xxx~~ interesting activities which might not happened ~~xxxx~~ if we didn't ~~do~~ participate in project. eg visiting a Nuclear Power station, Delabole wind farm, using video equipment, computers and word processors etc etc.

Teachers gave us exactly the right amount of support, encouragement and interest in what we we doing ~~xxxx xxxxxx~~ throughout the project. Parents and libirarians were equally helpful and so were many friends.

I enjoyed this term in English and think the project ~~xxxxx~~ has had many benefits. ~~My~~ I would like to do a project similiar similar to this in the future because next ~~th~~ time it would be better ~~th~~ now we ~~had~~ have completed this project. and have gained experience.

CROSS-CURRICULAR, CROSS-PHASE INDEPENDENT LEARNING PROJECTS

It is easier to give a coherent description of the cross-curricular, cross-phase projects because the one significant difference between the work within English and the cross-curricular work was that each of the cross-curricular projects had an identifiable theme and each school elected to focus on a different aspect of that common theme. (Thus it cannot be claimed that pupils had complete freedom to 'study whatever they wanted'. Nevertheless, there was still scope for all the factors of independent learning, including Factor 4 – Pupil-Designed Tasks). The theme for each of the projects was some aspect of citizenship upon which pupils could conduct their own research so that a synthesis might be achieved between the knowledge and skills of citizenship. The various schools involved in each cross-curricular project, and the three projects themselves, were unified by a common theme, a common pedagogy based on the 12 factors of independent learning and a common outcome – a joint presentation to the public.

Three projects (Minorities, Centennial and Europeans) spanned three school years: 1989–1992. Each project had a planning phase, a presentation phase and, in between, four to eight months of curricular work in a range of lessons that included all the National Curriculum subjects. In total, 2264 pupils (1147 primary (50.7%), 1117 secondary (49.3%)) and 90 teachers from 27 schools were directly involved, although many more were audiences for the work or had a peripheral involvement during the course of a project.

Minorities, October 1989 – July 1990

As well as developing independent learning, this project was intended to develop an awareness of the citizen's rights and responsibilities in a multi-cultural society.

Preliminary classwork in the winter term of 1989 was followed by a residential course for teachers in the spring term, during which experiences were shared and a class-based project was planned for the summer term. Six schools were originally involved, with one class (and teacher) from each participating in the project. Each class was divided into six groups of pupils.

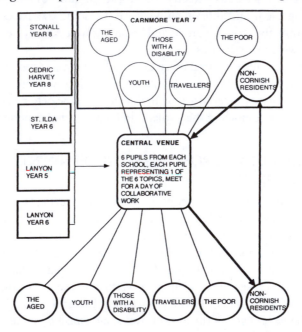

Figure 5.1: The interaction of individual pupils, groups of pupils, classes and schools during the 'Minorities' cross-curricular, cross-phase project for 9–13 year olds (October 1989–July 1990)
Source: Author

Each group in each class studied one of the following minorities: the aged, youth, those having a disability, travellers, the poor, non-indigenous residents of the study LEA. It was agreed that the project should embrace local, national and international issues and that pupils should be encouraged to conduct their own active research within the local community, meeting representatives of the minority groups. When one school had to withdraw from the project, one of the other schools contributed a second class so that the equilibrium was maintained. Two of the schools (but three of the classes, therefore approximately half the pupils) were in the primary sector and three in the secondary. All were schools in the same administrative district of the study LEA.

The pupils were from Years 5–8 (9–13 years old). Pupil-representatives from each group in each school met at a central venue for a whole day once each week to work in partnership with the other five pupils from the other five schools who were studying the same minority. During the central venue days, therefore, each group of six consisted of a pupil from each participating school and each group spanned the 9–13-year-old age-range. Figure 5.1 attempts a graphic representation of this process. One school class (Carnmore) has been

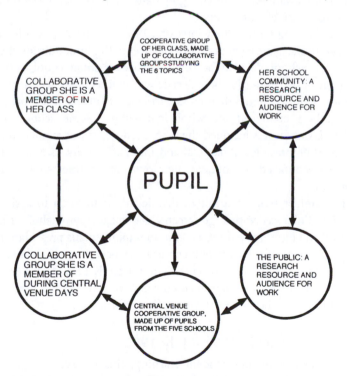

Figure 5.2: Interactions intended to promote collaborative groupwork, co-operative groupwork and the individual responsibility of pupils during the 'Minorities' cross-curricular, cross-phase project (October 1989 – July 1990)
Source: Author

highlighted, and one collaborative group within that class, to depict inter-relationships generated by the central venue days. All the other groups in all the other schools were simultaneously engaged in the same interaction. Figure 5.2 indicates the possibilities of individual, collaborative and co-operative interactions for every pupil involved in the project.

Around 200 pupils were actively involved, although many more were audiences to presentations, both in individual schools and at the public performance.

The project ended with a whole-day multi-media presentation, by the pupils, to the public, staged at Westwood Town Hall. The interactive presentation included demonstrations of equipment, screenings of video programmes made by pupils, lecturettes, song and dance, plays, poetry readings, music and exhibitions and displays of pictorial and printed information.

Centennial, October 1990 – June 1991

As well as developing independent learning, this project was intended to develop pupils' awareness of the changing nature of citizenship over time but of the enduring sense of community.

After a planning term in the winter of 1990, ten schools (six primary, four secondary) studied a different decade of the twentieth century during the spring term of 1991. Schools decided their own approaches, some schools choosing to focus on one or two events in 'their' decade whilst others spanned the whole ten years. Some schools limited their cross-curricular involvement to three or four subjects, others embraced the whole curriculum. Some schools targeted particular classes, others included the whole school. It was stipulated that the study should embrace local, national and international issues and that pupils should be encouraged to conduct their own active research within these communities.

In the summer term each school distilled their research to a six-minute presentation. Enhanced with large-screen video images, pyrotechnic effects and stage sound and lighting systems, a continuous multi-media presentation of the pupils' perceptions of the twentieth century was performed to an audience of 2000 at a public theatre situated centrally in the study LEA. About 850 pupils were actively involved, although many more were audiences to presentations, both in individual schools and at the public performance.

Europeans, September 1991 – July 1992

As well as developing independent learning, this project was intended to develop pupils' awareness of the international nature of citizenship and to challenge the stereotypical images that some people have about different national and ethnic groups.

Twelve schools (six primary, six secondary) chose a different European Union partner country and a series of half-termly investigations was carried out by pupils to find out what they and members of their local community knew – or thought they knew – about Europe and their current attitudes to the notion of being European, to focus this initial research with each participating school concentrating further study on a different EU country, to test the findings of the first two investigations by making direct contact with a partner school in the designated country of study and to encourage pupils in each pair of schools to exchange opinions on a variety of issues. Direct contact was made in a number of ways: letters, audio- and video-recordings made by pupils, the transmission of E-mail, telephone conversations and exchange meetings.

Each school held an open evening or open day for the local community during which presentations were made by the pupils. Representatives from six of the the study LEA schools visited their partner schools abroad. Around 1300 pupils were actively involved in this project.

Because of the diversity of age range (5–16), ability range (Individual Needs pupils representing the least and most able) and geographical range (across the whole of the study LEA, involving schools in each of the six districts), it was important that mechanisms were established to provide homogeneity of purpose and practice. All schools were invited, by letter, to be involved in each project; and the letter clearly stated the aims, structure and expected outcomes of a project. The pedagogy that underpinned classroom practice was based upon the 12 factors of independent learning, although there were variations between schools in their application. The idea for the Minorities project grew from a residential in-service training course attended by the teachers who would be involved in the project. During the project, involved teachers held fortnightly evening meetings. During the other two projects, involved teachers met for half a day (usually an afternoon) once every half-term. Further contact was maintained by monthly newsletters, edited by myself, and the classroom involvement of advisory staff (Minorities: Griffith and Wing; Centennial: Griffith and Stone; Europeans: Griffith, Stone and Wing). Involved teachers also visited colleagues and their classes to observe work in progress or to attend end-of-project presentations. An end-of-project debriefing (another half-day meeting) was held in each case and involved teachers and advisory teachers submitted written evaluations.

The findings of each project were analysed in terms of the 12 factors of independent learning and common trends between the three projects were evident. In the following sub-section the findings of the Europeans project are offered as an example of the analysis model. Quotations from pupils, teachers, researchers and observers exemplify the findings, although the primary data were the written evaluations of involved teachers' and researchers' field notes. (The analyses of the two earlier projects, comprising approximately 10,000 words, are held in the research archive and are available to other researchers).

Europeans: analysis using the 12 factors of independent learning

Factor 1: collaborative groupwork

The collaborative groupwork followed the same model as for Centennial: most of the pupils' work taking place in collaborative groups but lessons usually having a whole-class introduction or conclusion by the teacher. Occasionally there were whole-class sessions, particularly when a visiting speaker addressed the assembled pupils of a class, year group or (primary) school or when collaborative groups presented their work in progress to the co-operative group of the class to which they belonged.

> Their involvement and interest was considerable. Their role comprised: gaining information on a Spanish topic of their own choosing, making videos and audio-recordings about themselves, their school, and the local area; compiling a questionnaire concerning local people's knowledge of, and interest in, things European, corresponding with Spanish institutions and individuals regarding events occurring in Spain this year. (Head of Modern Languages, Coppersand)

Table 5.1: Details of schools involved in the Europeans cross-curricular independent learning project

School	Phase	Age range	Country of study	Number of pupils
Weatear	Secondary	13–14	France	33
Carnmore	Secondary	14–15	Luxembourg	107
Slaters	Primary	8–9	Italy	28
Lynher	Secondary	13–14	Germany	84
Pruddock	Primary	7–11	UK	65
Coppersand	Secondary	14–15	Spain	24
Chapeltown	Primary	9–11	Denmark	27
Poltrice	Secondary	11–16	Greece	270
Penmouth	Secondary	12–13	Portugal	120
Castlefort	Primary	5–11	Belgium	200
Winterfield	Primary	5–11	Netherlands	56
Edgehill	Primary	5–11	Eire	233
Totals	6P+6S=12	5–15		1247

Source: Author

The above account of the collaborative groupwork of a Year 10 GCSE Spanish class illustrates the intertwined nature of the various factors of independent learning:

> Their [Factor 2: co-operative groupwork] involvement and interest was considerable. Their [Factor 1: collaborative groupwork] role comprised: gaining information on a Spanish topic of their own choosing [Factors 4 and 7: pupil-designed tasks and pupil-initiated research], making videos and audio-recordings [Factors 8 and 11: pupil use of a range of language technology and presentation in different forms] about themselves [Factor 12: reflexivity], their school [Factor 2: co-operative groupwork] and the local area [Factor 9: community involvement and the use of the community]; compiling a questionnaire [Factor 7: pupil-initiated research] concerning local people's knowledge of, and interest in, things European [Factors 9 and 12: community involvement and the use of the environment and reflexivity], corresponding with Spanish institutions and individuals [Factors 3 and 10: individual responsibility and a sense of audience] regarding events occurring in Spain this year [Factor 7: pupil-initiated research]. (Head of Modern Languages, Coppersand)

Factor 5 (pupil-negotiated assessment) is implicit within several of the tasks, such as the video making and the analysis of the questionnaire referred to in the quote above. Factor 6 (pupil-negotiated deadlines) is implicit within the pupil-designed tasks that must be accommodated within the time limits of the project-designing tasks and requires a consideration of the time management of their execution.

Eight of the 12 factors are explicit in the following one-sentence reference to pupils' work at a primary school. Other factors, implicit in the short account, may have been observable in practice:

> Working in groups [Factor 1: collaborative groupwork], a class of Y5 children [Factor 2: co-operative groupwork], with the assistance of Tony Stone, filmed [Factor 8: pupil use of a range of language technology], edited [Factor 4: pupil-designed tasks] and scripted [Factor 12: reflexivity] a video about our village [Factors 7 and 9: pupil-initiated research and community involvement and the use of the environment] to send to their pen-pals in The Republic of Ireland [Factor 10: a sense of audience]. (Headteacher, Edgehill)

These two examples, one from the secondary sector, one from the primary, demonstrate the unity of the 12 factors of independent learning but suggest that the application or development of the other factors is contingent upon Factor 1: collaborative groupwork.

Factor 2: co-operative groupwork

The two principal aims of the Europeans project, as stated in the letter sent to all LEA schools inviting responses from those that would like to participate, were: to challenge the stereotypical images that some people have about groups within the European Community and to identify the multicultural nature of all communities.

The European Community (sic – this was before the establishment of, and consequent change in nomenclature to, the European Union) was intended to be seen as a positive image of a co-operative group within which collaborative groups and individuals could flourish and to offer a macroscopic example for the individual, collaborative and co-operative ventures that might take place within and between schools during the course of the project. This reflection of the attitudes and actions of nations in the individual lives of their citizens was powerfully enacted by the schools during 1991–92, the period in which individual nations themselves were approaching European Union:

> Perhaps the highlight of our contacts was the lady who came to the school to make pasta with the children. She is a delightful Italian lady who is skilled in the traditional cooking arts of her native country and she was a delight! The children warmed to her and if there was evidence needed that international boundaries can be broken down, the occasion of her visit provided plenty. (Headteacher, Slaters)

> The essential purpose of the exchange visits has obvious merits: the experience of living with a French family, eating their food, following their daily routines and being immersed in their language. But for many, the less obvious factors, such as the 'hidden curriculum', have been of a value far greater. These elements include the opportunity for less well-travelled pupils to venture beyond our county boundaries, the necessity to play a part within a newly-formed group, learning the art of 'breaking the ice' with new people, being the guest of French hospitality, experiencing the cross-Channel ferry services, pulling together for support and representing, with pride, our school in the outside community. (Head of Modern Languages, Coppersand)

> We hope that as a result of the project, we have widened our community and clarified our notion of identity and attitude towards being European. We have learned we can work together, co-operate, communicate and approach the future positively with informed but open minds. (Headteacher, Chapeltown)

> Summing up, we feel we have learnt a great deal about what being a European will [sic] mean to us, living together in a larger community but not losing our identity or culture. We enjoyed the project and learnt facts about ourselves, e.g. be tolerant and to listen (most of the time!), to discuss and come to a mutual agreement if possible. Working together brought good results which wouldn't have materialised if we had worked individually. Perhaps that is what Europe means to us at Castlefort – working together in harmony.

> P.S. These are our joint comments after a last Parliamentary Session. (Class teacher, E. Mylde and Year 6, Castlefort)

During the curricular work of the project, co-operative groupwork could be discerned at various levels: within a class (Example A), within a school (Example B), between schools in the LEA (Example C) and between schools and the local community (Example D). Of course, the whole project relied upon co-operation between the twelve project schools and their European Union partner schools:

> Example A: Co-operative groupwork within a class:

> We decided to rearrange our classroom into a parliamentary system and to debate formally certain topics. We did not go political! Here we learnt the hard

way that we had to listen as well as speak. Our first few sessions were really learning how to debate. (Year 6 pupil, Castlefort)

Pairs of children took one of the 11 countries to study and prepared to report back to the class. (Headteacher, Chapeltown)

Example B: Co-operative groupwork within a school:

A class of Y5 children, with the assistance of Tony Stone, filmed, edited and scripted a video about our village... Another class of Y5 children photographed the village to send to their pen-pals. (Headteacher, Edgehill)

Although only one class was working on the whole project, we tried to involve the rest of the school community also. All the classes featured in our video, a school assembly by Year 6 early in the Spring Term gave all the children a taste of what Class 6 would be up to...and we all enjoyed European Food Week immensely. In fact, school dinners were up by over 40%! (Headteacher, Castlefort)

We have had a European Week in which the canteen staff provided a Continental menu (Project Co-ordinator, Lynher)

Example C: Co-operative groupwork between Cornish schools:

Tenth Year pupils were involved in videoing...at one of the primary schools. (Head of Modern Languages, Coppersand)

Mr Kennedy, a European Studies Teacher from the comprehensive, came to find out our knowledge of Europe (Year 6 pupil, Castlefort)

Pupils have visited Weatear primary school to gather opinions about their notions of Europeanhood. (Head of Modern Languages, Weatear)

A significant and widely-observed aspect of co-operative groupwork within schools was the co-option of members of the public or public agencies into the work of the project:

Example D: Co-operative groupwork between schools and the local community:

Through some parents at school we wrote to three Irish schools attempting to set up pen-pal links. We received positive replies... One of the parents at our school grew up as a boy in Dublin. He gave an interesting talk to the children, explaining his childhood... We attempted to set up a radio link using a short-wave radio owned by a parent. (Headteacher, Edgehill)

Lucy Wing, Multicultural Advisory Teacher, worked with the children on the meaning of 'community' and 'stereotyping'. Rhys Griffith, the Senior Advisory Teacher for Secondary English, visited and helped the children on putting together a questionnaire for our local community. Tony Stone, video technician, helped us enormously with the production of our video of which we are very proud. Considering it was the first time the pupils had used a video camera, the filming was very good. Other visitors and contributors included:

Ginny La Page – Storyteller

Mrs Smith – Parent and French speaker

Mr Kennedy – Teacher from local comprehensive: expert in European Studies and European History

Mrs Goodyer – Cooking expert in European recipes

School Kitchen – Creators of our successful European Food Week

Christopher Beazley – MEP for Plymouth and Cornwall

Fourteen visitors were accommodated during the Spring Term, bringing in various methods of information for us to sift through and use. (Headteacher, Castlefort)

Visits to the country of the partner school afforded pupils and adults examples of co-operative groupwork:

We took in a guided tour of a French farm. They are better organised, it seems, than ours, with all the small farmers linking together to harvest and market their products rather than going it alone in true British style. Interesting tour. (James, Year 10 pupil, Weatear)

The most interesting visit was paid to our link school in Amsterdam. A community school of 280 pupils right in the middle of the city, it was as different from Winterfield School as it is possible to be. Many aspects surprised us, from the teachers being called by their first names to the casual way pupils walked from room to room. The system seemed to work. The children were bright, happy and confident, and their command of the English language impressive. It was in every respect a real education. (excerpt from an article written by a Winterfield parent-governor for the Europeans newsletter, No 7)

Factor 3: individual responsibility

Given the emphasis upon community, co-operation and collaboration, it is, perhaps, not surprising that teachers or pupils made little explicit, separate reference to individual responsibility. Comments relevant to this factor were subsumed within comments upon collaborative and co-operative groupwork that recognised the balance between individuality and collectivism and the duality of individual responsibility both to oneself and to various co-operative groups:

This was a good exercise [the questionnaire], one result being that students realised that it is difficult to treat people as a mass – we are all individuals in the European world. (Project co-ordinator, Lynher)

Working together brought good results that wouldn't have happened individually. Perhaps this is what Europe means to us at Castlefort – working together in harmony. (Class teacher and Year 6, Castlefort)

The symbiotic relationship between Factors 1, 2 and 3 (collaborative and co-operative groupwork, and individual responsibility) was commented upon:

As staff, we too have learned a lot. We are grateful for the support of the pupils involved in bringing about the obvious success of our twinning. They did themselves and our community proud and we look forward to the mutually profitable continuation of this association. (Head of Modern Languages, Coppersand)

We soon realised that working together was essential: groupwork would be necessary to cover the wide range of the E.E.C. [sic]. This proved to be successful because when Mr Kennedy, a European Studies Teacher from Castlefort Community School, came to find out our knowledge of Europe, we all knew a little of each country and he didn't waste time on the primary points. (Year 6 pupil, Castlefort)

Factor 4: pupil-designed tasks

There was evidence in all schools of pupil-designed tasks. These tasks related to the execution of pupil-related research, forms of presentation for the results of research and consequent tasks stimulated by the research:

> With visits and advice from Lucy Wing and Rhys Griffith, our pupils, in particular classes in Year 7 and Year 9, compiled questionnaires and carried out surveys, worked on aspects of stereotyping, then proceeded to produce materials for their partner school in Greece. (Head of English, Poltrice)

> The Italian Day ended with an assembly that was written by the children and based around the theme of breaking down barriers. (Headteacher, Slaters)

The following example shows evidence of Factors 4 (pupil-designed tasks), 7 (pupil-initiated research), 10 (a sense of audience) and 11 (presentation in different forms). As different collaborative groups took the responsibility for different sections of the presentation, Factors 1 (collaborative groupwork) and 2 (co-operative groupwork) also applied:

> The day started with Year 3 children [8-year-olds] taking a school assembly and showing us the story of St Patrick through drama. (Headteacher, Edgehill)

A common example of tasks relating to the execution of pupil-initiated research were the production, distribution, collection, collation and analysis of questionnaires. Tasks relating to the forms of presentation of the results of research varied from displays of computer-generated images (all schools) to video programmes made by pupils (all schools) and the contribution by each school of pupils' work displayed in six A5 plexiglass frames (to form a travelling exhibition of the project comprising 74 frames). Consequent tasks stimulated by the research were generally of a creative nature: stories, poems, paintings, cookery, songs, dance and drama.

> During our visit, Clare, Lisa and Julie were busy making copies of Belgian shoes, while James and Paul were playing a European game – with rules they made themselves. Linda and Emma were designing brightly coloured covers for their project books European style while Hayley and Alison were designing the logo for the start of their video. The music for the video was in the capable hands of Tani, Andrew and Adrian, while Carl and Daniel were busy putting the information gained from the questionnaires into the computer and designing the opening titles for the video. (excerpt from an article in Europeans Newsletter No. 5, by Tristan Howitt, County Press Office)

Factor 5: pupil-negotiated assessment

Pupils planned the content and course of their collaborative groupwork. In most schools there was a moratorium on 'normal-formal' teacher assessment involving alphabetical or numerical gradings. Some teachers attempted some assessment of some of the work of a collaborative group by formulating a negotiated statement with the members of that group. Pupils decided what work to submit for the open days and the travelling exhibition. In a sense, the public made the final assessment – data that were not systematically collected. The project was intended to encourage the development of pupils' ipsative and reflexive assessment (see Factor 12).

Some of the work produced by pupils was later used for formal assessment in public examination (Years 10 and 11 pupils, Clayport). In the main, the influence of Factors 4, 7 and 11 (pupil-designed tasks, pupil-initiated research and different forms of presentation) mitigated against the lone authority of the teacher as marker. Pupils were likely to negotiate with a range of informal, but informed, assessors: peers in collaborative and co-operative groups, teachers, parents, members of the local community. The overall impression, based upon researchers' observations, was that assessment in the sense of the teacher awarding grades or marks was suspended during the project but that a great deal of reflexive assessment – that was not always recognised as such – took place in the form of discussion, comment, evaluation for future action, planning and other shared talk.

Factor 6: pupil-negotiated deadlines

Pupils negotiated their own collaborative group deadlines within the time limits imposed by the timetable of the project – the starting date and the date of the public presentation. Pupils often worked outside of lessontime to meet their own deadlines, particularly in the recording of interviews or other video images that could be edited with advisory support.

> The need to work within a time constraint at first appeared irksome but emerged finally as an enjoyable challenge. Secondly, although this was a curriculum project, the pupils involved also worked in lunch hours and after school. They did so, not through any teacher pressure, but because they wanted to. Any scheme which generates this level of care and commitment must be counted a success. (Head of Drama, Tavymouth)

Factor 7: pupil-initiated research

Much of the pupil-initiated research involved the local community (Factor 9) and the use of a range of language technology (Factor 8). Pupils from all schools distributed questionnaires within the local community that were produced and analysed using computer technology. Pupils from all schools made video programmes in the local environment. There were also other aspects of pupil-initiated research:

> As part of their Home Economics GCSE coursework [pupils] were involved in producing many European recipes – very much an opportunity for research, exploration and fulfilment for them. (Head of Home Economics, Coppersand)

Year 5 children rang 5 companies and received some interesting replies. Letters were written to the Irish Tourist Board and the Irish Embassy. (Headteacher, Edgehill)

A number of classes throughout the school also used the excellent resources of the library to research on European awareness: e.g. food and drink, currency, systems of government and other information and statistics. (Head of Languages, Coppersand)

A great deal of research was carried out and this stimulated a lot of discussion amongst our students. They were very interested to find out that after 1992, a 'Cornish Pasty' can only be so called if it is actually made in Cornwall! (Project Co-ordinator, Lynher)

Factor 8: pupil-use of a range of language technology

Computers, using text and spreadsheet software, were used for the design and production of questionnaires which were distributed to the local community (all schools). Database and spreadsheet software were used for the processing and analysis of the questionnaire data and draw and paint packages were used to produce graphic representations of the questionnaire findings (all schools). Some schools (e.g. Edgehill) bought specialist software such as 'Touch Explorer on Europe'. With the support of Advisory Technician Tony Stone, pupils in every school were able to make their own video programmes, copies of which were then sent to their partner school. Some schools used Campus 2000 to communicate with schools abroad (Lynher, Chapeltown, Castlefort, Weatear, Carnmore and Penmouth). Some schools used audio-recorders for interviews and to produce edited tapes to send to partner schools (e.g. Coppersand, Poltrice). Some schools used still cameras in their research (e.g. Weatear, Winterfield). Pupils from all schools were the subject of media coverage (LEA Press Office, local press, radio and TV) and some pupils in each were able to play an active role: posing for photographs, being interviewed (e.g. Castlefort, Penmouth), having their presentations or lessons filmed (e.g. Edgehill). Pupils in all schools compiled a library of video-recorded images:

television has come into its own here in helping to bring home the fact that we are a multicultural society. (Headteacher, Slaters)

Factor 9: community involvement and the use of the environment

It was an important issue of the research ethics of independent learning projects that members of the public were not just seen as a resource but were welcomed and enjoyed equal status as members of the research partnership. (The same principle underpins the fieldwork undertaken for my research). Some examples have already been given of how Factors 2 (co-operative groupwork) and 9 (community involvement and use of the environment) synthesised, with members of the community becoming part of the co-operative group of each project school. There were many others.

Details of the progress of Slaters' project were published in the village magazine *The Slate.* Pupils from Lynher planted a perennial flower bed representing the EU flag in Queen Mary's Gardens near Goodrington beach, with a plaque inscribed 'Lynher School Links with Europe – 1992' as a lasting reminder. Members of the local community accompanied pupils from Winterfield and Pruddock on their visits to their partner schools. The end-of-project presentations by each school to its local community were an opportunity both for the pupils 'to give something back' and to strengthen the community partnership.

Similarly, it was important that the partner schools did not feel used solely as a resource but were as equally involved as the study LEA schools. That there was a mutually equitable relationship is suggested in the enthusiasm with which LEA pupils acted as an audience for their partner schools' work and the number of exchange visits that were arranged (9 of the 12 schools).

> Paula Mendes (Head of English at Escola Secundaria Dr Antonio Carvalho Figueiredo) and the Portuguese students were delighted to be able to communicate with Penmouth Community School. The obvious excitement and pleasure when students at Penmouth received their first letters from Portuguese students was indeed rewarding to witness. (School Librarian, Penmouth)

> The communication with a partner school, which in our case was in Scotland, was a joint approach. Many skills were enhanced during this activity – e.g. technical skills as we made our video, letter-writing techniques, the selection of materials typifying our area – and the anticipation and then pleasure of receiving a reply. (Headteacher, Pruddock)

> Successful communication was made with Denmark and pen pals were established. I'm grateful to Grete Elerby who carefully 'twinned/paired' children from Chapeltown with like-minded children in her class, so ensuring friendship continues, with some children writing direct to each other's homes now. (Headteacher, Chapeltown)

Representatives of six of the schools made trips abroad during the project and met their audience for past and future correspondence (Weatear, Lynher, Pruddock, Coppersand, Penmouth, Winterfield); three of the other schools hoped to make exchange visits the following academic year (Chapeltown, Poltrice, Winterfield).

The most striking example of local community involvement came from the small village school of Winterfield (56 pupils). Parents, governors, pupils and teachers raised £2660 in six months to subsidise every 6–11-year-old pupil to go on a five-day school trip to the Netherlands. On 2 April 1992, 37 pupils, 3 teachers, 1 ancillary and 9 parents (including a school governor and the coach-driver) set off for Bergen-an-Zee.

One of the most imaginative uses of the local environment was that practised by pupils from Roecastle School:

> One sunny day, the class went to the local beach and sculpted a map of Northern Europe in the sand. They then built the Channel Tunnel, using plastic

drainpipes, constructed dikes in the Netherlands and tried out windmills they had made in class. (Excerpt from article in Europeans Newsletter No 7)

In lessons, the pupils' sense of location within the local community was used to illustrate the concept of the European Community:

> The children of Winterfield school have, with their involvement in the European project, realised the full meaning of being 'European'. They have discussed their role in the local communities of Winterfield and Midgehill, extending the concept further to their own county, the West Country, England, Great Britain and into Europe. (Headteacher, Winterfield)

> Lucy Wing, Multicultural Advisory Teacher, came in to work with students and they were encouraged to think about and discuss their ideas of community – Penmouth Community School – local community – United Kingdom – European Community. Through this experience they found their stereotypical images of people challenged and began to think in terms of themselves as being 'West Country', British and European! (School Librarian, Penmouth)

> We began with 'Where We Live', looking first of all at a map of the world. We gradually focused in on Europe, The British Isles, this county, our locality and finally Slaters. (Headteacher, Slaters)

It was important that the project did not just replace insular notions of individual sovereignty and national community with élitist notions of a collective White European community. It was intended that the project should illuminate multi-racial Europe and look beyond Europe to a global understanding of community.

> It is important during this project that attention is drawn to the multicultural, multiethnic makeup of *all* European countries. The notion of a 'White Europe' is one that must be challenged and an increased awareness of cultural and linguistic diversity achieved. (Excerpt from an article by Lucy Wing in Europeans Newsletter No 1)

The Birmingham City Council '1992 and Race Equality Fact Pack' was sent to each of the twelve participating schools. All schools in the study LEA were sent details of World Poetry Childhood Day. A lead article entitled *Our County: A Multicultural Society* was printed in the Europeans Newsletter (No 3). The World Conference on Research and Practice in Children's Rights was publicised in the newsletter (and pupils from six schools from the study LEA later took part in a curricular project that culminated in a multi-media presentation at the Conference in September 1992). The distribution of the Europeans newsletter to all schools in the study LEA led to many requests for advice and information and the newsletter was also used to publicise the independent initiatives of LEA schools to forge links with partner schools abroad. By the summer of 1992 the newsletter was able to publish a contact list of 53 schools in the study LEA which had made new partnerships with schools in 19 European countries, ranging from Lapland in the north (Jamestow and Gonvik) to Greece in the south (Poltrice and Capodistriako), Rumania and Russia in the east (Gardenmoor and Remiti, Tavymouth and Moscow) and the Republic of Ireland in the west (Edgehill and Dublin). Details of The Council for Education in World Citizenship and also U3A (The University of the Third Age) were publicised via the Europeans Newsletters. A County tour by the Oily Cart Theatre Company to present their participative production *Gobble and Gook* to schools was organised:

> In Gobble and Gook, the Oily Cart will be exploring how language sometimes increases understanding and brings people together, whilst at other times it's the very thing that drives them apart. (From Oily Cart's publicity pack)

The work of A. Sivandandan was promoted in the Europeans Newsletter:

> Citizens may open Europe's borders to Black people and allow them free movement, but racism which cannot tell one Black from another, a citizen from an immigrant, an immigrant from a refugee – and classes all Third World people as immigrants and refugees and all immigrants and refugees as terrorists and drug-dealers – is going to make such movement fraught and fancy. (A. Sivandandan, from *Communities of Resistance*, quoted in Europeans Newsletter No 7)

That pupils did learn about the European Union within the wider dimension of global citizenship is instanced by the following comments:

> The multicultural nature of all communities has been illustrated particularly in the visit to our link school in Amsterdam. The school is the complete opposite to our small village school, our pupils were welcomed very warmly by a group of children so obviously from very varied cultures. The number of pupils actually in school on one of the days of our visit was greatly reduced, we were told, as the Muslim pupils were not in school, it being the end of Ramadam. (Headteacher, Winterfield)

> They [pupils] have been presented with positive images of children and adults from a wide variety of cultural and racial backgrounds. (Headteacher, Chapeltown)

> We feel the children's knowledge of Europe has increased greatly through participating in this project. It has also improved our appreciation and understanding of the diversity of cultures that go to make up Europe. (Headteacher, Edgehill)

> So far then, progress made towards our goal of European understanding, but, despite the generous timescale, much has still remained uncompleted – further school contacts with Wales and Northern Ireland, an understanding of the Europe beyond the twelve member countries and much more work, and hopefully first hand experience of the multicultural nature of the communities we all live in. (Headteacher, Pruddock)

Factor 10: a sense of audience

Pupils had a sense of three very clear audiences: their peers in their partner school, the local community to whom they would make their own end-of-project presentation and the wider community who would view the travelling exhibition of pupils' work.

Every school made video programmes to send to their partner school and wrote to their partner school. All schools gave presentations to the local community in the form of open days (e.g. Slaters, Carnmore, Winterfield), open evenings (e.g. Castlefort, Weatear) or even week-long events (e.g. Coppersand, Lynher). All schools contributed six A1-size frames to the travelling exhibition of pupils' work.

Factor 11: presentation in different forms

Over the twelve schools, just about every form in which it was possible for pupils to present their work was observed. Written work included stories, poetry, discursive and factual articles, and empathic descriptions (hand-written, as appropriate to the text, by Biro, quill, chalk, fountain-pen or brush, or word-processed using a variety of software). Writing was presented in different forms: in stapled booklets, facsimiles of brochures and magazines, on 'parchment', aged with cold tea and burnt at the corners. Some booklets were photo-copied and multiples distributed or sold in the school locality. Displayed visual work included posters, paintings, drawings, photographs, tracings, sketches, paper and wooden sculptures, and exhibitions of period artifacts. Recorded work included video programmes that ranged from simple vox-pop interviews to highly sophisticated edited programmes, audio-taped recordings of interviews and reminiscences, and the recording of pupils' singing. Apart from the use of electronic text for word-processing, computers were used to print out E-mail, questionnaire forms and to compile database information. Work was also presented in dance, mime, tableau, play, poetry reading, lecture and song:

> We have exchanged letters, audio cassettes, videos and brochures made by our pupils, as well as a range of publicity, brochures and items recorded from television, as an aid to learning. We have used various methods of communication to achieve this – letters, telephone, fax and, of course, personal encounters through the exchange visits themselves. (Head of Modern Languages, Coppersand)

The Europeans travelling exhibition was premiered at County Hall in July 1992. It then toured the project schools until April 1993 when it was made available on free loan to other schools, libraries, museums, institutions and shopping precincts. The exhibition consisted of 74 large picture frames, six from each participating school plus two frames explaining the project's aims and development, an audiotape of music, interviews and project news items that had been broadcast on local radio and a video-tape compilation of videos made by pupils in participating schools:

> The main purpose of the exhibition is to hear and see the opinions of pupils expressed in their own voices and their own texts. Each school's frames include evidence of the notion of Europeanhood as well as material specific to the partner country. (Excerpt from an article in Europeans Newsletter No 7)

Factor 12: reflexivity

Teachers reported that the project, with its thematic emphasis on the individual's personal membership of local and international communities and its structural emphasis on pupil-initiated research within those communities, gave opportunities for the development of reflexivity:

> Indeed, the link and quickly resulting friendship which has developed, have already given us ample access to a variety and breadth of experiences – enhancing not only our language learning but also our cultural and social awareness. (Head of Modern Languages, Coppersand)

> The older juniors [9–11-year-olds] would concentrate mainly on the United Kingdom stereotypical images, and to try and understand the multicultural nature of the Community member countries. (Headteacher, Pruddock)

> There is no doubt that the children held traditional stereotypical images of Dutch people which they have inherited from their parents and families. The questionnaire that we sent out to families and friends clearly reflected this. However, our visit to the Netherlands and the interaction of the children with the numerous groups of people with whom we came into contact dispelled these ideas. (Headteacher, Winterfield)

> The project has given the pupils the opportunity to view their world from different stand-points, helping them question prejudice. (Headteacher, Chapeltown)

> Our problem was how to approach the historical study of our particular country – Germany. It was decided to study the years between 1919 and the present day, emphasising the harshness of the Versailles Treaty, the economic problems it helped to bring about and how it might have influenced later history. When looking at the Second World War we attempted to compare the bombing of British towns with the bombing of Dresden. This proved especially topical and stimulated much discussion, as the statue of Bomber Harris, in London, was causing much comment nationally. Hopefully, our students have gained some insight into the futility of war rather than apportioning blame. (Project Coordinator, Lynher)

> As I read some of the work they [10-year-olds] did on 'We are British', which they did early on in the project, I am aware that the attitudes of some of the children have changed to such a degree that they would find it difficult to be quite as positive now as they were when they did this work as to what it means to be British. I feel this is an encouraging sign. (Headteacher, Slaters)

The factor of reflexivity may be summed up by two simple statements: 'Our students were thinking about what *they* wanted to find out' (Project Co-ordinator, Lynher) and 'We have learned we can work together – with informed but open minds' (Headteacher, Chapeltown).

The Minorities project contributed evidence of all 12 factors of independent learning, indicating that they could provide a pedagogical framework for older primary pupils as well as secondary pupils. Most of the work took place in English and Humanities lessons, which showed that independent learning was not a subject-specific method of learning that could only be applied to English.

Pupils across the ability range, including individual needs pupils from both of the primary schools and one special school, worked together – as did pupils between the ages of 9–13.

The Centennial project offered further evidence to suggest that independent learning can apply in many areas of the curriculum, to all ages of pupils in statutory state education and to pupils across the full ability range. Lessons took place in all of the National Curriculum subjects in both the primary and secondary sectors. Pupils aged 6–16 were involved in the curricular work and worked together for the final public presentation. The ability range included Year 4 pupils in a special learning unit and Year 11 pupils predicted to gain A Grades in their forthcoming GCSE examinations.

The Europeans project substantiated the evidence of the Minorities and Centennial projects that suggested that independent learning can apply in many areas of the curriculum, to all ages of pupils in statutory state education and to pupils across the full ability range. Subjects in which work took place in the primary sector were: Art, Cookery, Craft, Creative Writing, Dance, Design and Technology, Drama, English Language, English Literature, Geography, Geology, Health Education, History, Information Technology, Mathematics, Media Studies, Music, Physical Education, Religious Education and Science. Subjects in which work took place in the secondary sector were: Art and Design, Design and Technology, Drama, English Language, English Literature, French, Geography, History, Home Economics, Information Technology, Mathematics, Media Studies, Modern Languages, Music, Physical Education and Science.

The Europeans project advanced understanding of the factors of independent learning (particularly Factor 2 (co-operative groupwork), Factor 9 (community involvement and the use of the environment) and Factor 12 (reflexivity)). The project clearly illustrated the intertwined nature of all the factors and suggested that the key factor is collaborative groupwork (Factor 1).

Independent learning, as expressed through these three projects, was regarded as educationally effective by teachers and other professional observers and felt to offer benefits for both cognitive and affective development. Involved pupils expressed enthusiasm for this way of working in lessons and parents and other members of the various schools' communities praised both the process and the product of the project. The structure of the projects encouraged pupils to throw off the traces of dependent learning to which they may have been subject during 'normal' lessons and to become independent learners.

The research question of this book is: 'What effects do the the 12 factors of independent learning, intended to promote educational citizenship, have in practice?'

The three-year-long, cross-curricular and cross-phase independent learning projects undertaken between 1989 and 1992 offer positive evidence of:

- the application of the 12 factors of independent learning within all National Curriculum subjects
- the use of the 12 factors of independent learning as a means of curricular unification so that learning was a more holistic experience
- the application of the 12 factors across the full age and ability range of 5–16-year-old pupils
- the popularity of independent learning with pupils, teachers, parents and professional educational observers
- the high quality and wide range of work produced by pupils.

The evidence of the three projects suggests that the teaching and learning styles that predominated during the tracking of Keystage 3 and 4 pupils, Josie and Emily, are not the only way to implement the National Curriculum. However, as these cross-curricular independent learning projects were regarded by the involved teachers as a chance to experiment and to forsake their usual classroom approach, the Keystage 3 and 4 tracking pedagogy of factual didacticism is regarded to be more typical of schools in the study LEA than the project pedagogy of independent learning.

PUPILS' OPINIONS OF INDEPENDENT LEARNING PROJECTS

The main findings are that pupils want their learning to be interesting, enjoyable and fun, but they also value learning that they consider challenging, demanding, hard. Although independent learning is regarded as more exacting, pupils prefer it to their accustomed classroom practice. Boys tend to have a more functional attitude, associating success with completing the outcomes of an independent learning project, whereas girls express both greater concern and greater fulfilment with the personal and social relationships that independent learning encourages. There is also some suggestion that girls are more flexible in their use of learning strategies and capitalise more fully than boys on the opportunity to work collaboratively. This difference is one of degree; by and large, boys and girls appear to work in similar ways and hold similar opinions about independent learning. Despite its difficulties, they enjoy collaborative groupwork and identify choice of subject, group relationships, organisation and time management as the critical factors of harmony and success. They view the role of the teacher as being supportive but not intrusive.

The percentages quoted below are taken from the two questionnaires described in Chapter Three and are regarded as representative of the full pupil population involved in independent learning projects. Analysis of other forms of evaluation, both multi-faceted and multi-perspective, shows a strong corr-elation with the findings of the questionnaires. Percentages have been rounded to the nearest full figure.

Given that pupils had a free choice 'to study whatever they wanted, in whatever way they wanted, in partnership with whomsoever they wanted', when asked in which ways they felt they spent *most time* in working only about a quarter of the pupils (24%) referred to didactic teaching by the class teacher or others, whereas nearly three-quarters (74%) referred to individual, unsupported learning strategies or to shared learning within their collaborative group.

Differences can be discerned between boys' and girls' choice of learning styles, with a consistently higher percentage of girls than boys (between 5–10%) referring to collaborative learning. Boys were more inclined to depend upon their own individual resources, even within collaborative groups.

Pupils involved in the project felt that they *learnt most* via the following learning strategies: building on a foundation of their existing knowledge without teacher intervention (46%), teacher-directed learning (18%), individual discovery (15%) and collaborative problem-solving (13%). It is significant that when offered a choice of learning strategies, only 18 per cent of pupils considered the normal condition of the classroom – didactic learning – to be the most effective (and effective only in some circumstances rather than as a general premise).

Pupils appear to have adapted easily to the change from didacticism to independent learning. Fewer than one per cent of pupils wrote that working without a teacher directly controlling the group's activities was the hardest thing they had to learn. This opinion is endorsed by the tiny number of pupils (1%) who wrote that working without a teacher was the most important thing they had to learn. For the vast majority of pupils, the withdrawal of the didactic, decision-making teacher was simply not seen as an obstacle to learning.

Pupils did not reject teacher support where they deemed it appropriate. For instance, when faced with learning a technical issue, such as how to use an external microphone with a video-camera, the majority of pupils chose a didactic learning strategy – they asked a teacher or other adult for help and instruction. On other occasions, such as learning to get jobs done on time, learning to do research and getting on with others in the group, 75 per cent of pupils stated that they regarded finding out for themselves to be the most successful way of learning. Pupils often used a combination of strategies to solve a particular problem, and would then select a different combination for a different problem. This flexibility is referred to by Meighan (1995) in his analysis of authoritarian, autonomous and democratic educational disciplines:

> It follows that there are three types of error as regards discipline. One, the current error of most UK schooling, is to select the authoritarian as the predominant approach. The second, the error of some radical thinkers, is to make the autonomous the One Right Way. The third error, from another radical tradition, is to make the democratic the exclusive approach. All these One Right Way Approaches fail to match the need for young people to learn what most of their elders have clearly failed to learn, that is how to be competent in the

logistics and practice of all three types of discipline, and to select them
appropriately. (p.14)

Boys were more conservative than girls in their learning strategies, with 71 per
cent of their responses limited to only two of the eight options depicted in
Questionnaire 1 – and these two the least demanding learning strategies: 'I
spent time learning based upon a foundation of knowledge, experience or
expertise' and 'I spent time learning by being told or shown by a teacher'.

Pupils were generally adept in selecting the learning strategies that most
suited them. Nearly three-quarters of the pupils (74%) felt that they had
improved, with just over half (50.55%) recording that they had made 'some or a
lot of improvement'. There is a clear gender difference with 44 per cent of the
boys feeling that they had made 'some or a lot of improvement' compared to 56
per cent of the girls and 32 per cent of the boys feeling that they had 'stayed the
same or got worse' compared to 22 per cent of the girls. Girls not only seemed
to embrace independent learning more readily but to feel a greater sense of
success.

An analysis of the various tools of data collection revealed that there were
four consistent aspects of independent learning that pupils referred to in their
evaluations: group dynamics, time management, the technology used in video-
making and other project outcomes (the magazine, the live presentation and the
diary).

These aspects of an independent learning project dominated the responses
and the information elicited by different forms of evaluation allowed a multi-
faceted picture of the aspects to emerge. The four aspects can be seen to have
two different emphases: one for the process of the project (the management of
time and human resources) and one for the product generated by the project (the
various outcomes).

The two emphases of a project, the process (based upon the 12 factors of
independent learning) and the product (the content outcomes) have a symbiotic
relationship: the commitment to a product provides a vehicle for the process and
the commitment to the process is intended to enhance the educational quality
and scope of the product as well as the attributes of global citizenship.

When asked to state in what way or ways pupils would make changes to
improve an independent learning project, there was a tendency for girls to
associate improvement with a higher quality of personal and social skills
(process) and boys to associate improvement with production and performance
(product). Girls appeared to perceive success in terms of relating, boys in terms
of doing. For girls, an independent learning project would be better if people
got on better. For boys, an independent learning project would be better if
people produced better artifacts. Girls relate, boys function. However, as has
been stated before, these are differences of degrees, not absolutes. There is much
more common ground between the sexes than is perhaps generally recognised.

When asked to name the most enjoyable part of an independent learning project, more girls than boys commented on group dynamics in response to all questions – 51 per cent of the girls stated that the aspect of group dynamics was the most important thing they learnt about compared to 35 per cent of the boys. More girls than boys most enjoyed group dynamics – 24 per cent of girls and 19 per cent of boys. Girls (49.6%) were more concerned than boys (34%) to make changes to group dynamics.

Of the pupils who wrote that group dynamics was the aspect of an independent learning project that they most enjoyed, 40 per cent were boys and 60 per cent were girls; of the pupils who least enjoyed group dynamics, 45 per cent were boys and 55 per cent girls – that is to say that more girls than boys both most and least enjoyed group dynamics. Secondary data suggest that this is explained by the stronger identification that girls make with the process of the project – these figures illustrate that, to girls, groupwork is a more significant influence upon project success, both positively and negatively, than it is for boys.

However, boys and girls seemed to have few problems, caused solely on gender grounds, of working together in collaborative groups. Only three per cent of the pupils found that avoiding or resolving gender clashes within the collaborative group was the hardest thing that they had had to learn and only one pupil stated that learning how to resolve a gender clash was the most important thing that she had learnt. Few pupils wished to change the make-up of groups on the grounds of gender – one per cent of pupils in mixed groups would make changes, although not necessarily to single-gender groups, and one per cent of pupils in single-gender groups would change to a mixed group. When one considers that in the 'normal' classroom, as described in Chapter Four, girls and boys had virtually no interaction, these statistics take on a greater significance – in the classroom climate that usually pertains there is little gender interaction, in the independent learning classroom it is the norm.

Only two per cent of the pupils commented that avoiding or resolving arguments was the hardest thing they had had to learn. Only one per cent felt that overcoming arguments was the most important thing that they had had to learn and only one pupil thought that learning not to mess around was the most important thing. If undertaking another project, only six per cent of pupils would make a change in personnel because of dissent within the group.

These figures suggest that there was very little serious quarrelling or misbehaviour in the collaborative groups during term-long projects that required group members to plan and execute self-designed learning strategies that would enable each group to achieve a series of demanding outcomes. Nearly 95 per cent of the pupils, if they were doing the project again, would not change the group personnel because of an inability to work together due to personal antagonism. Second, the figures demonstrate a commitment to collaborative groupwork despite, or perhaps because of, the demands that it makes upon pupils – 99 per cent of pupils wanted to be involved in collaborative groupwork in the future.

Pupils are explicitly aware of the elusive qualities of effective groupwork. To describe their experiences they use words such as discipline, compromise, patience, responsibility, justice, trust. Nearly a third (30%) of the pupils specified working as a group or in a group, co-operating, getting on with the group or all contributing or working with others or working together as the most important things that they had learnt during the project. A group comprising 19 per cent of the population consisted of pupils who found collaborative groupwork to be both the hardest and the most important thing that they learnt.

The constituents of collaborative groupwork that were least enjoyed were arguments within the group, tolerating other members and lack of planning. The constituents of group dynamics that pupils most enjoyed were being allowed off the school premises to film and to conduct research amongst the community in the local environment, collaborative groupwork and the freedom to set their own agenda. Particular constituents of groupwork that were most enjoyed were working in or as a group, working together and working with others.

Pupils who considered changes in groupwork practice stated the need for better organisation and planning, for group members to make a more conscious effort to 'get on with' and 'talk with' each other, to 'co-operate' and 'concentrate' and avoid 'arguing', 'messing' or 'panic' and to 'work together' with 'all contributing'. Making a good start was seen as important for group success.

Although friendship was the most-used criterion for group formation, only two pupils, both boys, felt that working with friends was the most important thing. Only four pupils mentioned that working with friends was what they most enjoyed about the project. Only one pupil stated that what she would do differently, if she were doing the project again, would be to work with friends. Other pupils specifically wrote that they would not work with friends again, preferring to work with a wide range of people to develop their collaborative skills.

Girls expressed more concern than boys for time management. Pupils' advice on time management is basically to organise and plan so as to meet deadlines and avoid being rushed. The principal problem of time management was regarded as meeting deadlines within the span of the project, deadlines that groups imposed upon themselves. The main constituent of time management that pupils felt that teachers could help with was to 'allow pupils more time' to complete the project – another indication of the positive attitude that pupils had towards the project – with the largest group who mentioned time management asking for more time with the video-making equipment.

However, simply giving more time to pupils does not necessarily equate with better time management. With experience of independent learning projects in every secondary school in the study LEA, it is clear that a term is ample time in which to complete the project outcomes as long as the time is well managed. This is an aspect (like language technology) in which teachers and pupils have little expertise. Under the normal secondary school timetable, teachers are used to organising their, and their classes', time in small, often unrelated, sections (see Chapter Four). Pupils have almost no responsibility for time management, other than a Pavlovian conditioning to move in an orderly manner from one lesson to another. During lessontime, all responsibility for time management rests with the teacher. Neither teacher nor pupil is experienced in planning the development and completion of several volatile outcomes across a whole term.

Boys and girls hold similar ideas on the role of the teacher. Relationships with teachers seem to have been good – only three pupils (all Year 9 girls from Coppersand, in the same group) referred to problems with 'getting on with the teacher' or 'teacher's complaints'. Generally, pupils' comments about the role of the teacher were to cast her in the role of audio-visual technician, providing more equipment for video-making and being available to 'demonstrate', 'explain more fully' or 'help with editing'. However, the teacher's role during an independent learning project is that of adviser, not technician. Video-making is only one aspect of a project and one upon which a teacher should not spend a disproportionate amount of time – it may be better to remove this aspect from the project or, perhaps, offer it as an option for any groups who can organise their own support.

Eighty-two per cent of the pupils expressed no dissatisfaction with the role played by the teacher, ten per cent wanted more teacher support and seven per cent wanted less teacher intervention. Those wanting more support requested that teachers 'spend more time with groups', particularly to 'check' on progress, give 'more advice on groups' plans' and more help to 'groups without any ideas'. Those pupils wanting less intervention asked for the opposite: 'less help' and 'more freedom' for groups and also 'less whole class talk' and more opportunities for groups to work 'off school premises'.

The schism between some pupils requesting more and others less support on group organisation from their teachers is predictable and crucial to the role of the teacher in independent learning. Throughout the project, some groups, and individuals within them, will need more support than others. The primary responsibility of the teacher is to recognise which category any group is in *at any time* – for observation indicates that all groups will spend some time, to some extent, in both categories. What was never experienced was all groups being in the same category at the same time – so the discerning teacher is liberated to target her support and give it to whom it is most needed in different lessons and phases of the project. If the teacher attempts to offer equal support in every lesson to every group, she will have a deleterious effect upon all the groups. She will not be able to give the extended counsel that some groups will require because she is determined to be 'fair' and spend as much time with groups who do not wish for her intervention and, therefore, whose work she is effectively disrupting. This disruption can consist of breaking a group's rhythm and wasting some of its time. More seriously, ill-timed intervention on the part of a well-intentioned teacher can wrest the impetus and sense of ownership of a project away from the collaborative group. The hardest skills that teachers new to independent learning found were: 1) to target groups that would benefit from support and not to visit groups that were busily engaged; 2) to resist offering constructive advice to a group – even if the group needed it – until the group recognised its need and requested assistance.

Thirteen per cent of pupils would change the way in which their group chose its subject. Many of the comments were vague and referred to a choice of subject that was 'different' or 'more interesting', 'better' or 'good'. There were more specific and helpful suggestions: choose a subject you like or are familiar with, choose a subject that has lots of information available upon it, choose a topical subject, take your time in making a choice. Most pupils who commented on choice of subject advocated that groups should choose a subject they already had an interest in. (This illuminates Questionnaire 1 findings, that pupils regarded a learning strategy based upon extending existing knowledge as the most successful).

The idea of giving a framework to the project via certain common co-operative outcomes, irrespective of what choice of subject each collaborative group made, was endorsed with 73 per cent of pupils stating that they most enjoyed either the video making (47%) or the other project outcomes (26%). The gender divide was again apparent with 55 per cent of the boys most enjoying video making compared with 41 per cent of the girls – 47 per cent of the pupils most enjoyed video making, falling to 9 per cent who least enjoyed it. This was reflected in a converse shift in the responses to the other project outcomes: 26 per cent of the pupils most enjoyed the other project outcomes, rising to 7 per cent who least enjoyed them. It was apparent that traditional tasks (both written and oral) constituted the least popular aspect of the project. This can be interpreted as further confirmation that pupils like to be challenged. There was a much stronger relation between what pupils found to be the hardest and the most enjoyable aspects of the project than there was between familiar tasks and enjoyment. These findings have implications for the teaching of English. Pupils may well be rejecting the traditional English curriculum in preference for modes of language development that they find more stimulating, more empowering and more relevant to their own interests and forms of expression.

Girls clearly enjoyed the written and oral aspects of the project more than the boys, with 32 per cent of girls stating that they most enjoyed project outcomes other than video making compared to 19 per cent of the boys. The constituents of other project outcomes most noted in response to this question were: research, watching the finished videos and live presentations, performing the live presentation, the magazine, drawing, acting and interviewing. Of these, both 'magazine' and 'research' showed a gender imbalance. Of the 29 pupils who most enjoyed research, 27 were girls. Of the 16 pupils who most enjoyed compiling the magazine, 11 were girls.

The other project outcomes that pupils would handle differently are the live presentation, the diary, writing, interviewing, research and the magazine. Boys were more concerned than girls with changes to the content of the project (video making, choice of subject, other project outcomes).

One of the recurring findings, whatever form of evaluation was used, in schools across Greenshire were comments from pupils spanning the comprehensive school age and ability range that independent learning was 'fun', enjoyable and something they looked forward to during their other lessons. When I have suggested, over a period of years, that enjoyment might be used as a eudemonic test, a criterion to gauge the pupils' perceived success of a lesson, a scheme of work or an examination syllabus, five counter-arguments have been advanced by teachers:

> An enjoyable experience is not necessarily an educational experience, as pupils will enjoy a lesson that makes no demands upon them, in which they can mess around, talk to their friends and generally avoid work.

The findings of my research refute the infallibility of this argument by demonstrating that pupils have often shown that they enjoy work that is demanding and that they do not constantly want to avoid work for, given the opportunity to mess around for a term in largely unsupervised conditions, virtually no pupils took this option – 16 per cent of pupils most enjoyed what they found hardest to learn. The existence of this group is further evidence that a proportion of pupils involved in an independent learning project will be stimulated by its inherent challenges of problem solving, overcoming difficulties and adapting to new areas of learning. It is doubtful that this group is an isolated entity; it is more likely that it exists at one end of a range – the other end of which is populated by pupils who most enjoyed what they found easiest to learn. If this is so, there are more pupils – possibly a majority – who most enjoyed what they found hard, but not the hardest thing, to learn. A common exhortation to other pupils in the Advice and Comments sections of Questionnaire 2 was to 'work hard and enjoy the project'.

> Pupils are undiscriminating and derive the same level of enjoyment from all their lessons, irrespective of how 'good' different lessons are educationally.

The complacency of this viewpoint is discomfited by the discriminating and perceptive comments that many pupils made about their learning experiences in questionnaires, guided and open evaluations, project diaries and interviews.

> Pupils cannot judge how much they have enjoyed a lesson because they have no valid points of comparison ('What's the point of knowing that they like my

lessons less than watching Neighbours but more than having toothache?' a
teacher once asked me).

Their participation in an independent learning project afforded pupils a clear
and direct comparison of pedagogical styles: those described in Chapter Four
and this chapter – dependent and independent learning. The two questionnaires were not distributed during or immediately succeeding an independent
learning project but between two and six months after a return to the usual
curriculum and its presentation, thus offering the opportunity for reflection and
comparison. No pupils wrote that they preferred their normal curriculum
presentation.

> 'A change is as good as a rest' – pupils will express enthusiasm for any deviation
> from normal routine (the Hawthorne Effect).

It is true that pupils did comment upon the novelty of independent learning: 'A
very enjoyable term and a new exiting approach to english. Great fun!!!'
exclaimed a Year 9 boy from Cord. 'I liked this project because it makes a change
from normal English work' was the blunt statement of this Year 7 boy from
Dore, an opinion stated more positively by a Year 9 girl at Stonall: 'This project
was different to what we usually do in English, and much more interesting'.
Others made similar points about the novelty of the project: 'It was an
interesting alternative to normal classwork. I thought that it was a worthwhile
and enjoyable experience' (Year 10 boy, Poltrice) and 'Over all I really enjoyed
this project as it was different to normal lessons and I would like to do it again if
I had the chance. Thanks for letting us do this project Rhys it was great fun'
(Year 9 girl, Stonall) or 'It was fun and a change from the usual' (Year 8 girl,
Carnmore). Some pupils, like this Year 10 girl from Ashfordton, were more
precise: 'I think that this project is very valuble + that GCSE courses don't offer
for this *at all*. It is important to learn self reliance, time management,
independence and a sense of personal achievement that this project provides'.

The Hawthorne Effect is predicated upon an initial upswing of enthusiasm
for any change, based upon the novelty, not the efficacy, of the intervention. The
duration and intensity of each of the independent learning projects, and the
completion of Questionnaire 2 between two and six months after the end of a
project, are considered to compensate for the possibility of the Hawthorne
Effect.

> There is no causal relationship between education and enjoyment: pupils can be
> educated without enjoyment.

This statement lies at the very heart of the liberal/libertarian debate on
education in which the two philosophies become polarised with a knowledge-
based liberal education representing the disciplined virtues of determination,
self-denial, effort, of 'work' and a pupil-centred libertarian education representing the carefree indulgences of capriciousness, self-gratification, indolence,
of 'play'.

In their responses, many pupils do not regard education in this simplistic either/or way (either work or play, either enjoyable or educational) but, instead, comment upon the inextricable connection between enjoyment and education: 'This project was enjoyable and educational. I would like to do this project again' wrote a Year 8 boy from Castlefort. 'It was an experience that was very worthwhile and I thoroughly enjoyed it' was the opinion of a Year 10 girl from Poltrice. A Year 7 girl at Dore wrote: 'I've learnt a lot and really enjoyed it'. For a Year 7 boy at Poltrice, the project 'has been very interesting, educational and overall a pleasure to do' and for a Year 10 girl at Poltrice, 'The project was a worthwhile experience and very enjoyable'.

Thus pupils demonstrate a synthesis between enjoyment and education and the number of references to group dynamics clearly indicate that some pupils perceive education as more than the completion of a series of functional tasks – it also involves learning how to relate to others. That the enjoyment to which pupils refer is characterised by the grim virtue of a dutiful, self-denying and assiduous puritan work ethic is doubtful. Classroom observers' descriptions of pupils involved in independent learning projects often feature words such as activity, exuberance, excitement and energy. A word used by pupils is 'fun': Year 8 Castlefort boy: 'It was great fun really'. Year 7 Cord girl: 'The project was great fun, thanks to everyone involved'. Year 9 Cord boy: 'It was good fun'. Year 7 Dore boy: 'No comments because it was cool fun'. Year 7 Ashfordton boy: 'It was a good, fun project'. Year 10 Stonall girl: 'Using the video camera was ace fun and I really enjoyed it'. Year 8 Carnmore girl: 'Good, interesting, fun'. Year 8 Carnmore boy: 'It was intresing and it was fun to do'.

Only one pupil commented that the project was not fun, a Year 7 boy from Coppersand: 'The video should be a bit more fun. Make a bit more fun for others'. And only one pupil felt that it was fun because he did not have to do any work, another Year 7 Coppersand boy: 'It was good fun and 90% of the [time] no one gave me any work to do'.

Indeed, pupils expressed the opposite, that the project was fun or enjoyable and involved hard work. 'It was fun to do the project but a lot of work' wrote a Year 7 girl from Coppersand. A Year 8 boy from Carnmore recorded that 'This project was hard as well as fun and the end result was good'. A Year 7 Ashfordton girl, undertaking an independent learning project during her first term in secondary school, wrote: 'The project was fun but I found it quite hard and I would have rather done it later in the year'. A Year 7 girl at Poltrice wrote: 'I did enjoy it, but you need to work fast and hard' and a Year 7 boy at Coppersand stated: 'I thought the project was quite hard, it was quite enjoyable. For anybody starting the project, work your hardest'.

Something can be fun and difficult. The pupils' definition of fun implies more than meaningless frivolity. 'Fun' seems to encompass in its definition excitement and challenge. Certainly, just as something can be hard and enjoyable, and enjoyable and educational, so it can be fun and educational: 'I thought the project was good fun and very worth while' wrote a Year 8 boy from Castlefort. A Year 9 girl at Cord thought 'this project was a brilliant idea and I would do it again Because you learn alot of things but in a fun way', a view shared by her classmate: 'I really enjoyed doing this project and looked forward to the end results. It was a fun and education project'. A Year 10 Stonall boy put it succinctly: 'Good fun, learnt alot. Educational'. For his classmate, a girl, 'It was good fun and very educational as we learnt about technology as well as English work'. A Year 8 Carnmore boy and girl wrote, respectively, that 'It was good fun. We learnt alot. Using the video camera was good fun, it was never boring, I would like to do the same type of thing again' and 'I think it was brilliant fun it was something new that most of us had never done. I think everyone learnt something'.

Whatever the relationship between education and enjoyment, that the project was regarded as educational is indicated by the following comments: 'This project was more than valuable. We had to work on our own, aquire new skills in editing etc and be able to communicate ideas and opinions well' wrote a Year 10 girl from Ashfordton. A Year 10 girl form Stonall believed that 'Over all it was a good project. It was very benefical and we learn alot. We had alot of finished work. We picked a subject we enjoyed and put alot into it'. A Year 10 Poltrice girl wrote: 'I thought this project was a very good idea, involvinging many skills and group work'. The word 'worthwhile' was commonly used, as by this Year 10 Stonall girl: 'A worthwhile project which helped certain english techniques, though did not realize you were doing it eg find information – reading. Using such advanced equipment for the video' or by this Year 10 boy from Poltrice: 'The project was a worthwhile use of the time. It could have been better if more time had been allowed for the project'.

Many pupils wrote that they 'would love' to do another project. Heartening though these endorsements were, they always made me melancholy. Embedded in references to future projects appeared to be the assumption that an independent learning project was unlikely to make any change to the regular curriculum experience of the pupils. The project was seen to have a finite life-span and a particular personnel (me and Tony Stone, sometimes Lucy Wing, or members of other LEA Advisory teams). It was an extrinsic event that might visit a school and then pass on, and then classroom life would return to 'normal'. There is no evidence from the questionnaires that pupils felt that their everyday school learning would change as a result of the term that they had spent on independent learning. Most poignant was the prescient project epitaph of the Year 7 girl at Cord, with four years of statutory education ahead of her, who wrote, in block capitals, that she most enjoyed 'DOING THINGS WHICH I WON'T BE ABLE TO DO AGAIN'.

CONSENSUS WITHIN THE RESEARCH PARTNERSHIP

The use of multi-perspective data collection sources served to offer consensual validity of the data collected: similar data were consistently recorded by varied sources. Table 5.2 gives the sources of data, each offering a different perspective.

The perspective of pupils involved in independent learning projects has been documented in this chapter, as has the perspective of teachers and some observers of cross-curricular and cross-phase independent learning projects. Further multi-perspective data corroborate findings that suggest that independent learning is regarded as educationally effective and felt to offer benefits for both cognitive and affective development within a social and moral

---

Table 5.2: Sources of data collection

- pupils involved in independent learning projects in their English lessons;
- pupils involved in cross-curricular independent learning projects;
- teachers involved in independent learning projects in their English lessons;
- teachers involved in cross-curricular independent learning projects;
- advisory teachers involved in independent learning projects in English lessons;
- advisory teachers involved in cross-curricular independent learning projects;
- observers of independent learning projects in English lessons;
- observers of cross-curricular learning projects;
- observers of end-of-project presentations.

Observers comprised advisers, advisory teachers, ancillaries, caretaking and maintenance staff, carers, catering staff, cleaning staff, clerical staff, ET trainees, headteachers, HMI inspectors, LEA inspectors, lunchtime supervisors, members of the senior management team, parents, prospective parents, prospective pupils, road-crossing supervisors, SEN staff, school deliveries personnel, teachers from other departments, teachers from other schools, technical staff, visitors to the school, YTS trainees.

Source: Author

context and for pupils to practise the rights and responsibilities of global citizenship.

Of the 79 secondary English teachers whose classes undertook independent learning projects, only two wrote that they would not wish to develop aspects of independent learning in their own lessons. Teachers commented upon the self-discipline of the pupils, the quality of work produced and the capacity of the project to motivate pupils across the ability range. They also drew attention to the personal and social educational benefits of independent learning. Reservations about projects concerned practicalities rather than the philosophy of educational citizenship.

From 1989 to 1993 I was responsible for organising and directing the residential in-service training of secondary English teachers in the study LEA, some two or three courses a year. All of these courses promoted educational citizenship through the pedagogy of independent learning. Some courses involved teachers learning alongside pupils. Most courses were cross-phase so that teachers from primary, secondary and tertiary institutions worked together. Some courses combined with other advisory areas: multi-cultural education, outdoor education, the musical service, drama. In promoting educational citizenship, all of the courses, often for the entire duration of a course, required teachers to work in collaborative and co-operative groups themselves, to the five independent learning project outcomes.

Teachers responded favourably to these courses. It is possible to gain some statistical data concerning their enthusiasm for all of the courses were subject to internal LEA evaluation and some were also externally evaluated by a team from Exeter University. These assessments were based upon evaluation forms which all course attenders were asked to complete (anonymously, if they wished) and give, not to me as the course director, but to the Centre Warden. An external evaluation of a 1989 course entitled *Touching Bases* reported that 'There were 32 course members, all of whom responded to the questionnaire. 88% of responses relating to the course criteria are in the two highest positive categories weighted slightly to the higher of the two'. External evaluation of a three-day residential conference attended by all 31 of the study LEA's secondary Heads of English revealed that 96 per cent of questionnaire responses relating to the course criteria were in the two highest positive categories, 'weighted significantly to the higher of the two'.

In October 1990 a weekend course called *Pupils Writing, Teachers Writing* gave teachers the chance to undertake fieldwork in the local environment and community as a stimulus to the creation of a range of texts. The fieldwork included opportunities for climbing and abseiling on the nearby moors, river-canoeing and horse-riding or walking in the woods and along the coastline. Course members could meet the local mayor, the lifeboat coxswain, the sister-in-charge of the hospital, the harbourmaster, the comprehensive school caretaker, a local hotelier and a local shop owner. Effectively, this was an independent learning project for teachers.

The course was well received and was extended to three days and repeated in the following spring term of 1991. One of the most striking findings was the enthusiasm shown by teachers across the 5–19 age range, as is illustrated by the following quotations from evaluation forms completed at the end of the course:

> The best – most stimulating – course I've attended. It was relevant, friendly, creative – allowed tons of individuality and yet provided loads of learning opportunities too. An immediate impact on my own work will be giving children more time to produce work, providing more varied stimuli, more use of I.T. and more multi-media work. (Primary school teacher)

> It was totally brilliant! Hard work but refreshing too! It's recharged the batteries so I'll be more lively and enthusiastic! (Secondary school teacher)

> Stimulating and extending. Real learning experience. All parts of the course were useful – but particularly working co-operatively in groups and learning to do new things. (Tertiary college lecturer)

> Tremendously enjoyable. The most worthwhile course I have been on. I found all of it useful. The immediate impact it will have on my work will be to reinforce my enthusiasm for such a diverse way of working – giving choice to the learners. (Anon)

The comments of observers with a professional educational background who observed independent learning projects offered consensual validity for the multi-faceted evaluations completed by pupils and their teachers who undertook independent learning projects.

John Stock (1991) observed two term-long independent learning projects, one at Tavyford (Spring 1990) and one at Poltewan (Winter 1990). Julia Preece, National Projects Co-ordinator for TVEI, spent one day a week in the winter term of 1990 observing the Poltewan independent learning project. Carol Foley, a Southern Examining Group Assessor and herself a mature student undertaking part-time post graduate research, observed weekly lessons with Year 9 pupils at Poltrice for a term in the Spring of 1990. Three Primary Advisers from the study LEA, two of its County English Advisers and the Senior and Chief Inspectors of Schools for the study LEA were other observers between 1990 and 1992.

Their written reports drew positive attention to various aspects of independent learning such as 'the contribution to the whole curriculum of the school' (Primary Adviser, 1990), the personal involvement of pupils with their learning, the dual nature of cognitive and affective development, the high standards that pupils set themselves for both the process and product aspects of a project, the pupils' confident interaction with adults and their adept use of sophisticated technology.

Independent learning projects were widely perceived to have educational merit and to provide stimulating learning opportunities for pupils across the age and ability range. The projects were also regarded as a novelty, a departure from normal practice in schools. The final chapter of this book attempts to provide some answers to the question posed by a past English Adviser for the study LEA:

> Independent learning is a new approach but unthreatening to teachers. It requires the active participation of children and involves a range of language styles. Independent learning integrates the technology into the project and generates enthusiasm in children. How can this be brought into normal practice? (Internal report on independent learning projects at Budleigh, Haldon Primary and Poltewan schools 1990)

Consideration of how to introduce independent learning into classroom operation will be given in Chapter 6. Chapter 7 questions why, given the positive reactions of LEA personnel, teachers, governors, parents and pupils, independent learning is *not* normal practice.

SUMMARY

Analysis clearly reveals that within the specialised environment of an independent learning project, pupils across the 11–16 age and ability range are quite capable of working in largely unsupervised conditions; that groups will not disintegrate into a chaos of dissent and inertia; that girls and boys will not automatically polarise into single-sex groups; and that pupils will not inevitably choose to congregate with their friends, motivated by an irresponsible desire to waste time and mess about. In fact, pupils were capable of making sophisticated choices from a combination of learning strategies and adopting different strategies appropriately to suit different learning challenges.

Moreover, as the analysis of pupils' work and evaluations indicate, and the observation of project teachers confirms, pupils set for themselves tasks and standards more demanding than those which teachers would ordinarily impose upon them.

The data suggest that a learning programme intended to develop educational citizenship and based upon the 12 factors of independent learning offered the opportunity for pupils to develop personal autonomy in their learning and their decision making and that this was a major difference from the narrowly structured and limited learning possibilities that typified the curriculum experience of Josie and Emily (see Chapter 4).

CHAPTER SIX

The Classroom Application of the Twelve Factors of Independent Learning

INTRODUCTION

Whilst all twelve factors of independent learning are intended to develop educational citizenship, different factors emphasise different facets of the definition of the global citizen. The first three factors are designed to engender a sense of social justice as pupils work together in small teams, yet are aware of a responsibility both to the larger society of the class within which they operate and to the self. The aim of factors 4–7 is to foster the development of a critical disposition in the citizens of the classroom as they become decision takers and policy makers by designing their own tasks, undertaking their own active research, having some control over the time and pace of the work and being involved in any assessment of the worth of their labour. Factors 8 and 9 locate knowledge, and the pupils' quest for it, within the reality of a socio-moral peopled environment. Factors 10–12 are intended to show that education, like global citizenship, requires personal responsibilities and commitments and that both are active processes that bring about change.

FACTOR 1: COLLABORATIVE GROUPWORK

A distinction is made between co-operative groupwork and collaborative groupwork. A collaborative group is a small group, usually of three to five members, preferably mixed gender and self-selected, working in partnership to complete outcomes on a subject which the group has chosen to study. The immediate co-operative group is the larger group, often a class of pupils, from which collaborative groups are drawn and to which they contribute.

However collaborative groups were formed, they appeared to contain a hierarchy of two types of skill: process and product. On the basis of the research data, there is reason to believe that girls are more concerned with the process of a project and boys with the product. Process skills are those that concern the organisation of the group, the distribution of tasks, the management of time and the internal arbitration of disputes. Product skills relate more specifically to the tasks required to complete the outcomes: the sub-skills of video making (such as scripting, filming, editing, creating a soundtrack or using a computer to generate titles and credits) or compiling the magazine (writing, drawing, word-processing, desktop publishing, photo-copying) or preparing for the live presentation (script, rehearsing, wardrobe, lighting, make-up, sound effects, direction and production). Participant observation, the findings of Questionnaires 1 and 2 and other forms of pupil evaluation strongly indicate that the way in which a collaborative group synthesised these skills (process and product) – or even recognised their existence – had a profound effect on the group's own perception of its 'success'. These skills were vivified in collaborative groups' organisation of project tasks.

It is unlikely that all members of a collaborative group will all do the same thing at the same time. Almost certainly, the group will allocate or share tasks among its members. Task allocation is defined as one or more members taking on the sole responsibility for one aspect of the project. Task sharing means that the responsibility is rotated, is capable of being carried by anyone in the group, so that, for example, in a group of four, one pair may spend one lesson writing for the magazine whilst the other pair use the video-camera and then swap roles in the next lesson.

Task sharing requires a higher order of both process and product skills than task allocation. Allocating tasks is expedient, but, as well as excluding group members from the full range of outcomes, it reduces the opportunity for the full development of process skills. Allocating tasks can also lead to a gender polarisation within a collaborative group. Evidence from the analysis of Questionnaire 2 and participant observation suggests that boys are more likely to enjoy the use of video-making technology and that girls are more likely to spend time in the research and compilation of the magazine. This can lead to the juvenile equivalent of parallel play, with the boys making a disorganised video and the girls doing a lot of neat writing and drawing and neither gender having anything to do with the other.

A compromise is a form of task sharing, with a different group member taking the responsibility for leading a different aspect of the project but all members of the group being involved. Here the teacher needs to ensure that the same personnel do not retain leadership of the same aspect in project after project.

Educational citizenship, via independent learning, is more concerned with the process than the product of curricular work and this should be borne in mind by the teacher and communicated to the pupils. A group of four pupils that has allocated tasks so that a pair of boys makes the video and has no interaction with a pair of girls, ostensibly their collaborative partners who produce the magazine and perform the live presentation, has not been fully involved in independent learning. Conversely, a group of pupils that works in collaborative harmony, sharing tasks and meeting deadlines, but which produces a seemingly indifferent set of outcomes may well have been more successful, judged by the definition of educational citizenship, than a disparate group that has produced a high standard of outcomes.

Although it is not likely, nor particularly desirable, that all the members of a collaborative group will work together all the time, there should be times when the group does work all together. It should also be possible for members to work in different combinations to suit different circumstances so that pupils gain experience of interaction across the social spectrum.

Over a series of projects, one would expect to see a developing synthesis of process and product skills, leading to greater success in both areas.

Criteria for the formation of collaborative groups

Some of the inherent problems of collaborative groupwork can be alleviated by a careful consideration of various criteria that may be used in forming groups. The Questionnaire 2 findings suggest that no particular method is universally effective but that whatever method is used is likely to be more effective if it is a method that the group has chosen for itself. There is no reason why all the collaborative groups in a class should use common criteria. The critical fulcrum, whatever criteria are used, is the attempt to balance process and product skills within the group.

The high percentage of Questionnaire 2 responses to 'teamwork' suggests that it is worth spending some time with the co-operative group of a whole class, perhaps a preparatory half-term, on discussing and experimenting with criteria so that pupils are explicitly aware of the relative advantages and disadvantages of different criteria. During this time, issues noted by pupils in the questionnaire that cause problems of group dynamics can also be raised: all members contributing, keeping to self-imposed deadlines within the time limits of the project, an equitable allocation or sharing of tasks, getting on with other group members, planning and organisation. The writing of a contract by the members of a collaborative group has been found to be helpful in formulating a code of conduct that each group designs for itself. It is also worth having a more general code to which the co-operative group agrees to adhere. Pupils may benefit from a series of team-building tasks that might include trust exercises and problem-solving games.

The relevance of groupwork to global citizenship can also be made explicit to pupils during this exploratory stage. Society can be viewed as a series of interconnecting or concentric collaborative and co-operative groupings. Pupils can discuss the different groups to which they belong (families, friends, sports teams, special interest groups) and analyse the criteria that are used for the formation of these groups and the criteria that indicate their successful performance and behaviour. Pupils can apply their findings to well-known collaborative groups, such as successful rock bands or sports teams. Larger groupings can also be discussed (gender, ethnicity, faith, race) and the problems of conflict both within and between groups can be addressed. Concepts such as monoculturalism, multiculturalism, assimilation, integration and cultural diversity can be introduced as appropriate.

The decision as to who is to apply the chosen criteria must be made. Should it be the pupils or the teacher? Who makes the choice is a potent symbol of where power is seen to reside in the classroom. My own inclination is that it should be the pupils, for it is an unconvincing introduction to independent learning if pupils are not allowed the independence to choose their own learning partners. The argument that a teacher's selection will be objective and well-informed, leading to balanced groups in terms of temperament, ability and gender, makes sweeping assumptions about the teacher's knowledge of the pupils. If pupils are cognizant of the importance of the formation and constitution of collaborative groups and aware of a range of criteria that may be applied, observation suggests that they are capable of making their own choices. Questionnaire 2 shows that in only 10.06 per cent of cases were teachers solely responsible for selecting groups, and on these occasions pupils resented the method of selection.

However, no matter how much time is spent in preparation, analysis of Questionnaire 2 suggests that the greater number of pupils will choose to work with their friends for their *first* independent learning project (61.62%). There is evidence that in consequent projects friendship is less likely to be used as a criterion. The apparent advantage of working in a friendship group is that a reasonably homogeneous group is created that offers security to its members. The real disadvantage of using friendship as the sole criterion for collaborative group formation is that it invariably leads to groups of the same sex, interests and ability. A mixed-ability class may set itself into a typical pattern which, without too much tongue in cheek, will look something like this:

Groups 1 and 2: bright, high-achieving, middle-class girls
Group 3: bright, high-achieving, middle-class boys
Group 4: quiet, hard-working girls
Groups 5 and 6: loud, not-very-hard-working boys
Group 7: resentful, verbally belligerent, out-of-their-depth girls
Group 8: bewildered, apathetic, out-of-their-depth boys

It is probably unavoidable that pupils initially move into friendship groups (teachers inevitably did on the residential in-service training courses I directed) but a partial check can be to combine friendship with another criterion. Responses to Questionnaire 2 reveal that pupils created the following friendship-related hybrid criteria: friendship plus subject, friendship plus work ethic, friendship plus expertise and friendship plus teacher-aided choice.

Another method that may be used is pupil-guided choice, in which pupils choose their own groups within certain parameters laid down by the teacher – for instance number and gender mix. However, this can lead to the gender polarisation referred to earlier. Groups were observed forming in this way in many schools and often, during the process of forming groups, pupils teamed up with a friend to form a pair, almost inevitably splitting the class into boy pairs and girl pairs. To form a collaborative group (3–5 members, mixed gender), each boy pair joined with a girl pair. This can be just an illusion of mixed groupwork; the reality is single-sex pair work. Nevertheless, if the teacher is vigilant, pupil-guided choice can offer a basis for the development of mixed gender collaborative groupwork.

In secondary schools in Greenshire classes tend to be setted by ability to a greater degree in each year of Keystages 3 and 4. In 1992–93, 84 per cent of Year 7 English classes were mixed-ability, 52 per cent of Year 8 classes, 39 per cent of Year 9 and 22 per cent of Years 10 and 11. Using pupil-guided choice to group a setted class is problematic. In a 'top' set the gender imbalance will almost certainly mean a higher proportion of girls, often to the extent that there are just enough boys to be shared around, one to each group. A Year 9 English set at Cord undertaking an independent learning project contained 24 pupils, 6 boys and 18 girls. A guided choice that specified a mixed gender group of 3–5 pupils could only resolve itself with the formation of six groups of 4 pupils or three groups of 5 pupils and three groups of 3 pupils, each group comprising one boy and two, three or four girls. In practice, neither boys nor girls seemed to object to this rather clumsy social engineering. Teenage boys seemed quite willing to spend lessontime working collaboratively with their female peers. As Questionnaires 1 and 2 show, girls place more importance upon group dynamics and thus boys are generally welcomed into a supportive learning environment. However, this selection system is much more discomfiting for the handful of girls in a 'lower' set where the gender imbalance is the other way around and they may have to work singly with a group of product-oriented boys who are less concerned with creating an embracing and positive working atmosphere.

Questionnaire 2 shows that when given freedom of choice, the majority of pupils used friendship as the sole criterion for forming collaborative groups and that this resulted in just over half the population working in single gender groups. However, during the Keystage 3 and 4 tracking, boys and girls hardly ever sat together, let alone worked together, so it can be concluded that independent learning is more conducive to boys and girls collaborating, with, on a first independent learning project, 48.5 per cent of pupils choosing to work in mixed gender groups.

A more sensitive way of influencing the group-forming criteria that pupils might apply is to use pupil-negotiated parameters. Here the pupils themselves suggest limits for the formation of groups and these suggestions are refined in class discussion. Generally, the parameters of number and gender are offered by pupils but, often, in not so precise a way as when stipulated by a teacher: 'You could work with someone you haven't worked with before.' (Year 7 girl, Poltewan); 'You wouldn't want too many in a group.' (Year 9 boy, Budleigh); 'Two people isn't really a group is it?' (Year 10 girl, Carnmore). Forming the groups in this slightly less rigidly defined way does give the opportunity for shifts and changes as, somehow, the emphasis is upon the division of the co-operative group into workable units rather than the creation of autonomous collaborative groups. Pupils are often astute at evaluating the contribution others can make to their collaborative group: 'We'll have Denzil because his dad's got a video shop.' (Year 9 girl, Carnmore); 'Mary's good at organising things out.' (Year 10 boy, Gardenmoor).

The techniques of pupil-guided choice or pupil-negotiated parameters are useful in widening the range of group-forming criteria. Other criteria that may be considered are subject and expertise.

If subject is to be used as a criterion, the co-operative group may suggest about eight to a dozen subjects that collaborative groups might take as a focus for their work. The pupils then make their choices and groups form. This is similar to the Carnmore modules system, which worked effectively in dividing a year-group into subject-choice classes. As a means of dividing a class into collaborative groups, however, the criterion of subject was observed to be less effective. I think that this may have been because the Carnmore modules were class-size and, therefore, allowed friendship groups to choose together, whereas the collaborative groups were small. Given the choice between staying in a collaborative friendship group and joining a collaborative subject group, observation revealed that most pupils stayed with their friends. Therefore, what may appear to be subject groups are more often friendship groups which have chosen, as an already formed group, to study a particular subject. Nevertheless, a combination of friendship and subject as criteria was quite common and served to focus the initial, undirected enthusiasm of a friendship group. In Questionnaire 2 choice of subject was identified as very important to the harmony of group dynamics and the quality of the outcomes, but was favoured, in preference to friendship as the sole criterion, by only 7.55 per cent of pupils (although a further 5.34% of pupils used a combination of subject plus friendship as criteria and 3.46% used subject plus teacher-aided choice). It is interesting that no matter how attractive a subject is, when it comes to choosing groups a pupil's first priority is invariably to work with at least one friend. How independent can one become under such circumstances? An important part of the teacher's role in independent learning is progressively to loosen the bonds of friendship as inviolable criteria of group formation.

The criterion of expertise can be used but teachers and pupils should be aware that its use may lead to the establishment of efficient, functional, product-dominated groups whose members are likely to allocate tasks and thereafter may work in isolated individuality. Within the co-operative group there will almost certainly be a range of expertise in the skills needed by each collaborative group: confidence in speaking in public, the discipline needed for research, familiarity with a computer keyboard or media technology, writing skills and so on.

Collaborative groups could be formed by ensuring a fair distribution of such expertise throughout the groups. If the collaborative groups are prepared to share the tasks, this system can work very well indeed as each 'expert' helps the other members of the group. In practice, however, groups often found it simpler (because a range of expertise was usually twinned with a range of preference) to allocate, rather than share, tasks. Thus pupils did not have the opportunity of a broad and balanced curriculum – instead they consolidated a limited proficiency. If this is allowed to happen, as it often is in classes, it can be difficult for the 'expert' to break out of her role or for the novice to gain experience in a new part of the curriculum. This problem was often observed with mixed-gender groups that were following the five outcomes of an independent learning project: the boys monopolised the technology and the girls concentrated on compiling the magazine. These difficulties can be obviated to some extent by making it clear that the process skills of the project also demonstrate expertise and including them in the expertise profile of a collaborative group.

A teacher at Sir James Redbourne, whose lesson was being observed, when asked what criteria had been used, and by whom, for the formation of the hard-working and happy groups, replied: 'I just pull names out of a hat' and pointed to an old top hat on a filing-cabinet. 'The kids love it. Great fun!' Ironically, this random method seemed to work at least as well as some of the more socially engineered ways, perhaps because pupils saw that there was a fairness (or a universally equal unfairness) about this lottery method and, as there was really no choice of whom one would work with, there was not the resentment or disappointment of having been offered a choice of partners but not getting the ones most wanted. Admittedly, Liz only used this method for short tasks, perhaps lasting for one lesson, and not for the formation of collaborative groups for a project lasting a term. As an ice-breaking exercise for use in preparatory sessions, it was a quick and exciting way of getting pupils to work with others, often across the gender divide, for short periods of time. Hopefully, it illustrated that cutting the umbilical cord of friendship is a necessary and painless procedure that prepares the way for future autonomy.

My research as an advisory teacher was rich in opportunities to work in many different schools, but it was my experience as Head of English at Carnmore that allowed some longitudinal study of collaborative groupwork amongst the same population of pupils. Pupils quickly became adept at making sophisticated choices of collaborative partners – choices which were not based on the simple application of single criteria such as friendship, subject or expertise. Combinations of criteria were used and different criteria were applied to different members of a collaborative group. This flexibility became more apparent when the purpose of collaborative groupwork was clearly explained, when different ways of choosing were made explicit and when time was allowed for experimentation. Where little time or thought was given to the formation of collaborative groups by teachers or pupils, pupils continued to work in friendship groups, marooned on the plateau of success for both process and product that was achieved in the first project.

Whatever system is used, once collaborative groups have formed it is worth spending some time in reflection to see if the co-operative group has organised its human resources in the best way. A method used at Carnmore, inspired by the early democratic practice of citizen-juries in the Greek city states, was for the co-operative group of the class, sitting in their collaborative groups, to comment on each other's groups. This might sound a horrendously insensitive and public manner of doing things but it has the valuable effect of emphasising to pupils that they have a responsibility not just to themselves or their own collaborative group but also to the co-operative group of the whole class and that they have a right, as a member of the co-operative group, to state any reservations that they may have about the constitution of the collaborative groups. Comments such as 'It's stupid to have Simon and Alex together because they'll just muck about' (Year 9 girl, Carnmore), aired and shared, led to a smiling rather than a begrudging acceptance of this point by Alex and Simon, who might then plead their case and be allowed to remain together on the condition that they behaved responsibly. In instances such as this the influence of the peer group tended to carry more weight than the insistence of the teacher.

Pupils' advice: organisation of collaborative groups

Of the pupils who advise that groupwork needs planning and organisation, 31 per cent are boys and 69 per cent are girls. Careful thought is advocated before decisions are made and actions taken. 'Think about it alot' advised a Year 7 boy at Cord. 'Prepare everything in advance' and 'Plan it out well' suggested a Year 8 boy and a Year 9 girl also from Cord. '*PLAN*!!!' emphasised her classmate. 'PLAN what you are going to do before starting filming else you will end up in a right mess!' urged a Year 8 girl from Saltair. A Year 7 boy at Dore warned about the danger of over-elaborate planning: 'Plan but not too much plan'. A Year 8 girl at Dore, however, felt that pupils should 'Plan each day from the start'. A Year 9 girl at Stonall advised: 'Plan the project very carefully and stick to that plan'.

Some pupils gave helpful advice of a more specific nature. A Year 9 girl from Dore was clear about what planning should entail: 'Plan who does what and when they're to do it', a view shared by the Year 10 Stonall girl who wrote: 'Plan the project well and make sure everyone knows exactly what their doing.' A Year 9 boy at Ashfordton suggested tackling the different outcomes chronologically. His advice was 'To get on with the magazine and Presentation before the video', a view echoed by a girl classmate, but with a different order of priority: 'Do the video 1st then do your paperwork'. A Year 9 girl at Stonall explained why planning was so important: 'You should plan very carefully because you could go wrong and ruin everything', an opinion endorsed by the Year 7 girl at Dore who wrote: 'Be aware of problems even little problems can be hard to fix'. A Year 9 girl at Coppersand warned that plans should be clear and practical: 'Make sure you understand what you are doing'. Whilst most of the pupils who mentioned planning advised that a plan must be made before any work was started, a Year 10 girl at Poltrice advocated that pupils 'don't waste any time planning – start working straight away'. A Year 10 girl at Stonall wanted the best of both worlds: 'Start working right away and plan thoroughly'. Eighteen pupils stressed the importance of making a good start.

The references to group organisation tended to be shorter and rather more cryptic: 'getting organised' (Year 8 boy, Castlefort), 'be organised' (Year 8 boy, Cord), 'get organised' (Year 8 girl, Saltair), 'be orginised from the beginning' (Year 9 girl, Dore), 'organise your work and good luck' (Year 10 girl, Ashfordton), 'get organised' (Year 10 boy, Stonall), 'work hard and get organised' (Year 9 girl, Ashbridge), 'get organised' (Year 7 boy, Poltrice), 'organisation' (Year 8 girl, Carnmore), 'organisation is the key' (Year 8 boy, Coppersand).

Organisation may well be the key but clues to what constitutes 'being organised' are hard to find in the questionnaire responses, possibly because the state of 'being organised' is self-evident to pupils. Profiles of the 40 pupils who referred to 'team plus organise' suggest that the concept of organisation is seen as a fusion of good planning and then the orderly execution of the plans. This execution is dependent upon careful time management and an equal sharing of the workload within the collaborative group.

Pupils' advice: choice of collaborative groups

The second strand of advice offered by pupils concerns the formation of groups. The first principle is epitomised by this Year 7 boy at Ashfordton: 'Choose your own groups'. Given that right, the most common advice concerned working relationships within the groups. 'Try to get on with your people in your group' wrote a Year 8 boy from Cord. A Year 8 girl at Carnmore advised: 'Act sensible about the whole project. Also don't row, and try to communicate with people. And if you don't like something just go along with it'. Pupils are more likely to get on if they 'choose people you like' or 'people you can work with' or 'people you trust'. These working relationships are not necessarily the same as out-of-project friendships. 'Never work with you best friend' advised a Year 8 girl from Poltrice.

Pupils' advice: conduct of groups

The third strand of advice concerns the conduct of groups. Having made an appropriate choice of members and planned the group's schedule of work, pupils should begin work quickly and continue to work at pace. 'Get started on solid work soon, don't talk for ages about what to do' warned a Year 9 girl from Ashfordton. 'I haven't got much advice', wrote a Year 7 girl from Cord, 'but I would tell them to get things done quickly. 'Work fast' counselled a Year 9 boy from Coppersand. 'Don't take your time!' was the tip from a Year 8 boy at Saltair. Arguments are to be avoided: 'Don't argue with your group as it gets you nowhere' (Year 8 girl, Castlefort). Messing around is also admonished: 'Do not mess around or you will not finnish in the short time'. (Year 8 boy, Saltair). Pupils should 'work hard and work together' (Year 8 boy, Carnmore) or, as his classmate put it, 'put your brain in go and put as much efert in as you can in your plan. comunicate with yure grupe'. As the project develops it is important that all members of the group should make an equal contribution: 'ORGANISE – EACH PUPIL TO HAVE A TASK' (Year 9 girl, Ashbridge); 'Don't leave to late and get a good plan worked out for each person' (Year 9 girl, Cord). Members should 'help each other' (Year 8 boy, Dore), 'learn to work in a group and try to cooperate well' (Year 8 girl, Coppersand) and, if necessary, 'BE PATIENT' (Year 7 girl, Cord). They may need to 'stay calm if something goes wrong' (Year 7 boy, Cord).

FACTOR 2: CO-OPERATIVE GROUPWORK

Co-operative groupwork describes the interaction between collaborative groups, the action of the collaborative groups when working in unison or the responsibility that the various collaborative groups have to the larger group, the co-operative group, to which they all belong.

The kind of interaction that might take place within the co-operative group of the class could be showing someone in another collaborative group how to use software (a word-processor or computer graphics programme) or hardware (video-camera, microphone, 4-track recorder), swapping video-footage, sharing an interview with a visitor or swapping techniques or tasks: 'I'll show you how to audio-dub your soundtrack if one of your group does our titles on computer' (Year 9 boy, Cord); 'Could you read this through to see if it makes sense if I check yours for spelling?' (Year 10 girl, Poltrice).

The activities of the co-operative group when working in unison might be a presentation of the work of the collaborative groups to an audience, a class excursion, acting as an audience for a visiting speaker or discussing the constitution of the collaborative groups and formulating a code of conduct for the project. Such a code may contain agreements about public behaviour, meeting deadlines if using a video-camera off-site and returning in time so that another group can go out, and acting in such a way around the school or off campus that will not jeopardise other groups. What will characterise these exchanges, actions and agreements will be a spirit of co-operation rather than competition.

The co-operative group usually comprises the class undertaking an in-dependent learning project and any other people contributing to the project, such as teachers, ancillaries, parents, visitors. However, the boundaries of the co-operative group are more fluid than that of the collaborative groups. If more than one class in a school is involved in an independent learning project, it may be considered that the co-operative group comprises both or all of them. 'Centennial' was a cross-curricular and cross-phase independent learning project that culminated with 800 pupils from four secondary and six primary schools giving a presentation to an audience of 2500 at a public theatre. In this instance the co-operative group comprised the pupils from all ten schools, their teachers, other classroom helpers, transport providers and, arguably, the audience itself.

It is important that membership of the co-operative group extends beyond the pupils to include, as people of equal status, all involved. This sometimes appeared to be the most difficult conceptual step to take for teachers and pupils new to independent learning. If the teacher does not regard herself as a member of the co-operative group, which will require abrogating some of her decision-making power of class control, it becomes difficult for the collaborative groups to feel any sense of autonomy. The project can become an illusion of in-dependent learning practised upon the pupils for, in reality, invested power still resides in its traditional bastion: the hands of adult experts and controllers.

Conversely, if pupils do not recognise teachers and other adults as members of the co-operative group, they are also being excluded from parity of status and the pupils are practising discrimination. This is an example of how the simple transfer of invested power can corrupt the new holders. As such exclusivity is antipathetic to the concept of global citizenship, it is detrimental to the independent learning practice of the collaborative groups, a practice intended to develop the skills and attributes of global citizenship. If pupils do not extend the franchise of the co-operative group to include teachers and other adults, they deny themselves the opportunity to practise equal interaction with holders of greater responsibility. What is required is a transformation to divested power (see Chapter Seven).

Several headteachers in Greenshire argued that independent learning must always be something of a well-intentioned confidence trick, for there are certain responsibilities that a teacher cannot cede (her responsibilities in loco parentis) and others that pupils cannot legally assume (the full responsibility for her education, that is whether or not to attend school), and so there cannot be equality of status within a co-operative group and there cannot be autonomy for collaborative groups.

This argument only holds true within a conceptual framework of invested power where responsibility is seen as synonymous with power and used as a criterion of status. Educational citizenship does not require all members of the co-operative group to share the same responsibilities but does demand that all are offered equal status based upon the criteria of global citizenship suggested earlier. The autonomy of the collaborative groups is informed by the definition of the global citizen that is central to educational citizenship. In this definition the citizen is described as 'autonomous in her critical disposition…but her actions tempered by a concern for social justice…with a sense of civic duty'. The autonomy of a collaborative group is restricted by the outcomes of the project, the factors of independent learning and the co-operative code. Specifically, the autonomy of collaborative groups enables them to determine their area of study, plan their own tasks, manage their own time, control the assessment process and place their own constraints on behaviour. This is not the personal autonomy of Summerhill, Steutel's (1991) sense of animal freedom or the amoral and self-centred decision making that Harre (1983) depicts, for the boundaries of collaborative autonomy are *voluntarily* prescribed by the collaborative groups when formulating their co-operative code.

Research for this book indicates that teachers need have no fear that their authority will be challenged during an independent learning project, particularly if the concept and nature of collaborative and co-operative group-work are made explicit to pupils and time is invested in the formation of collaborative groups and the code of conduct of the co-operative group. As in all societies, transgressors of the civic code are liable to have their activities curtailed. Thus there exists the sanction of withdrawing from the project any pupil who cannot abide by either the co-operative code or the collaborative code of her group. In five years of independent learning projects with pupils across the full ability range and the 4–19 age range, it was never found necessary for the co-operative group to institute this sanction.

Teachers may be reassured that the conceivable anarchy of an independent learning project is not a reality and that a metaphor of their role as a figure of responsibility within the co-operative group of the independent learning community is more likely to be that of village elder than weaponless wild west marshal.

FACTOR 3: INDIVIDUAL RESPONSIBILITY

Within an independent learning project the individual has a responsibility to adhere to the public code of the co-operative group and to the more private code of her own collaborative group. The collaborative code will be informed by the co-operative code and is likely to be based on agreements concerning the process and the product of the project.

Classroom observation, the findings of the questionnaires, an analysis of pupils' project diaries and the comments contained in pupils' written and oral end-of-project evaluations indicate that there are two recurrent reasons why individuals do not honour the groups' codes: first, process problems of task planning, time management and personal organisation within the collaborative group that lead to arguments, resentments, frustrations, forgetfulness, apathy and alienation and second, product problems with equipment failure or un-availability, lack of skills from literacy to video editing and difficulties with completing outcomes when pupils have chosen for themselves, or been allocated by the group, a task that is too difficult or too easy.

Experience during the intervention phase of the fieldwork research has shown that if a co-operative group of thirty pupils contains seven or eight collaborative groups, there need only be four individuals wrongly placed, each in a different collaborative group, to seriously undermine the co-operative venture. With just one discontented member, a collaborative group is weakened; with half of the collaborative groups affected, there is the possibility of a general malaise of disillusionment or even a serious transgression of the co-operative code (fight, public incident, damage to equipment), so that the whole project can become a miserable experience for all involved. Thus the symbiotic relationship between the first three factors of independent learning (collaborative groupwork, co-operative groupwork and individual responsibility) is critical to the success of an independent learning project. This relationship is also a microcosmic reflection of the interactions of collaborative and co-operative groups, and the individuals within them, in the universal model of post-modern democratic citizenship described by Giddens (1994) when he writes that:

> Enhanced solidarity in a detraditionalizing society depends upon what might be termed *active trust*, coupled with a renewal of personal and social responsibility for others. Active trust is trust that has to be won, rather than coming from the tenure of pre-established social positions or gender roles. Active trust presumes autonomy rather than standing counter to it and it is a powerful source of social solidarity, since compliance is freely given rather than enforced by traditional constraints. (p.14)

FACTOR 4: PUPIL-DESIGNED TASKS

A task is a section of work, executed by a pupil or pupils, that contributes to the completion of one of the project outcomes. It is helpful if the range of tasks can encompass the differing interests, abilities and forms of expression likely to be found within the co-operative and collaborative groups. This is the main reason why each extended independent learning project (of termly or annual duration) had four predetermined shared outcomes: the making of a video, the compilation of a magazine, the performance of a live presentation and the creation of a bibliography. (The fifth outcome, the keeping of a personal project diary, was not a collaborative task). Tasks for the video making included story-boarding, scripting, filming, organising transport to film on location, creating a soundtrack, creating titles and credits and editing. Tasks for the magazine outcome were writing, drawing, editing, word-processing, desktop publishing and photo-copying. Some of the live presentation tasks were scripting, rehearsing, wardrobe, lighting, make-up, sound effects, direction and production. Research tasks, necessary for all the outcomes, included the search for, and retrieval of, texts from libraries, databases and other sources, telephone contacts, meetings, interviews and surveys, and the interrogation, sorting and summarising of data.

It could be argued that the predetermined outcomes are an imposition upon pupils, constraining their freedom, and that such an imposition contradicts the philosophy of educational citizenship. The clearest practical refutation of this argument is made by the overwhelming majority of pupils involved in in-dependent learning projects who regarded the outcomes not as an imposition but as a novel and exciting liberation from the confines of their usual curr-iculum. The outcomes were intended to give a framework for pupils and teachers new to independent learning to aid both the execution and the monitoring of the project. Whilst the outcomes facilitated the development of independent learning by requiring a shift away from a conventional curriculum and its presentation, in which opportunities for independent learning were scarce, there is no need to be rigid in their application. If independent learning projects required collaborative groups to produce a video, a magazine and a live presentation at the end of every project *ad nauseam*, such projects, as a means of stimulating educational citizenship, would become self-defeating. As pupils' and teachers' knowledge of independent learning grows, so the outcomes could be changed, expanded or reduced. Sandy, an Ashfordton teacher, suggested that the four outcomes could be spread over a year, with different groups working to different outcomes in termly projects. Don, from Carnmore, believed that there was no need to stipulate any range of outcomes, although it was useful to specify the kind of outcomes that pupils might aim for. John Truddock, Coppersand, advocated that outcomes could be jettisoned 'like stages from a rocket' during the development of a project, with different collaborative groups concentrating on one outcome after initial research and experimentation. Paul, Ashfordton, felt that the co-operative group should decide on one outcome at the beginning of a project and each collaborative group should aim for it. Nick, Sir James Redbourne, considered the range of presentation encompassed by the three outcomes to be all-inclusive and that there were no alternatives.

Co-operative and collaborative outcomes

A distinction can be drawn between co-operative and collaborative project outcomes. Co-operative outcomes can be classified by theme alone or product and theme.

The value of a thematic co-operative outcome is that the various coll-aborative groups work on self-selected facets of a co-operative theme that can unite the project and enhance the sense of the co-operative group. Examples of co-operative themes within English are concepts (Winter, Loneliness, Out-siders), texts (story, poem, play, film, TV programme), scenarios ('The Island', 'Lost', 'School Under Siege'), social issues (Fox-hunting, Travellers, Sexism), local events, places (local town, quarry, mine, farm). Two Year 7 classes at Stonall combined to take the co-operative theme of 'Our Town' with each collaborative group researching a different facet, such as tourism, leisure facilities, shopping, education. A Year 10 class at Venturers took the theme of alienation, inspired by the poem *Breakfast* by Jacques Prevert, with each group responding to the poem in different ways. A co-operative group comprising every class at Jamestow primary school took the local marsh as the theme for a year's work, with classes making visits to the marsh to record the changing seasons. This theme stimulated curricular work in every National Curriculum subject. A Year 7 class at Churchtown used an audio-recording of the shipping forecast as the stimulus to an investigation into the effect of the sea on life in the locality. The whole class met and interviewed people whose lives were connected with the sea, such as the harbour-master at Budleigh, a deep-sea fisherman, a member of the local lifeboat crew, a meteorologist from an RNAS station, the manager of a steamboat company and a lighthouse keeper. A thematic co-operative outcome gives cohesion to the co-operative group for there is a clearly identifiable connection to all the activities of the collaborative groups, yet as long as the theme is appropriate for the class there is opportunity for each collaborative group to exercise freedom of choice and action.

With a product-based co-operative outcome, the various collaborative groups work to a shared outcome, such as a play, a video programme, a presentation, a publication, an audio-recording or an expedition. The coll-aborative groups in a Year 9 class at Woodcoombe each created, and took on the persona, of a rock band. The product-based co-operative outcome was a combined video and audio album. Pupils from Cedric Harvey secondary and Buttwood primary schools formed a co-operative group to write and illustrate stories for infants and their stories were published, in book form, by a national print-house. Year 9 pupils at Woodcoombe, after a reading of *Walkabout*, planned and undertook an overnight expedition on moorland – designed to give them a simulated experience of a nomadic, subsistence lifestyle. Minorities, Centennial and Europeans are examples of cross-curricular co-operative themes with product-based outcomes – the Minorities open day, the Centennial evening presentation, the Europeans travelling exhibition.

A product-based co-operative outcome gives a structure to the work, with group responsibilities and an agreed end-of-project form of presentation. It is an effective way of directing a group's energies for their working parameters are closely defined. However, the emphasis on a product-based co-operative outcome that is to be publicly displayed in some way can present anomalies to the spirit of educational citizenship and the intention of independent learning: it pressurises groups to conform, it does not give them the opportunity to 'fail' and it can become competitive as, with a similar style of outcome being demanded from each group, people may make partisan and superficial comp-arisons of worth. 'Brilliant – much enjoyed, and Shearpool were certainly among the best'. 'Felt our school was super – one of the best' (comments about the theatre presentation of Centennial by a Shearpool parent and teacher). The effect of any, or all, of these anomalies can be to detract from the process of the project and to give exaggerated importance to its product.

A public presentation to an uninformed audience, say of parents or governors, has many pitfalls. Normally, the 'pupils' work' that is exhibited to the public bears the heavy imprint of teacher control: editorial revisions to articles in the school magazine, the selection, production and direction of school plays, the training of pupils for public speaking competitions or Christmas assemblies, the correction of written work on classroom walls, the rehearsing of infants for nativity plays. It has become a paradoxical ritual of headteachers to introduce such displays by thanking the teachers for their heroic efforts whilst implicitly denying their contribution by simultaneously praising the pupils for 'what you are about to see is all their own work'.

This background to the public viewing of pupils' work raises certain hazards. First, the product of an independent learning project will almost certainly look a little ragged compared to the general run of schools' sanitised public presentations. Second, most pupils do not perform well in front of their parents, particularly vulnerable and self-conscious teenagers. Third, virtually no parents of present pupils had the opportunity to work with sophisticated media equipment when they were at school so do not have a normative frame of reference to evaluate the quality of what they are viewing. Thus a three-minute documentary about the rain forests, made by a group of 12-year-olds at Cord, may be unfairly compared to a similar treatment on Panorama and a 15-year-old Rynsey girl who has written and recorded her own song has her performance compared to the quality of dad's new CD player belting out Cher's greatest hits. Fourth, from a parental audience there can be a puzzlement rising towards antagonism about identifying this kind of work within a statutory subject curriculum. (Carnmore mother after watching her daughter's class present a 'pedagogical entertainment' entitled *Do The Education*: 'How's this going to help with her English? All she did last term was some play or other she wrote').

Who should choose a co-operative theme? It may be that the teacher has to because she is bound by a content-laden syllabus, either that of the National Curriculum or a public examinations board. If such constraints do not apply, the co-operative group can be involved in the decision-making process. This can provide an opportunity for pre-project planning and preparation. If a theme is suggested by the class, the teacher may legitimately question its viability. This was an approach used by Kate, at Dore, with a Year 9 class which wanted to be involved in the Centennial project and requested that its decade of study should be the 1970s. After an initial discussion in which pupils had expressed their enthusiasm, Kate took the following position: 'OK, you want to to do a project about the seventies. So convince me you can get the materials and the ideas together and we'll do it'. This is a good way of preparing for a project and a sense of excitement builds as firms, charities and other agencies reply to letters, often enclosing useful research materials or colourful posters for display; as pupils, parents and teachers video-record TV programmes that might be of use; as a local register of people willing to be interviewed is compiled (and carefully checked); as pupils, perhaps having an extra-curricular planning meeting once a week, begin to firm-up their ideas, maybe even so far as scripting and checking locations for later filming.

Sometimes a co-operative theme will emerge from a discussion of the intentions of each collaborative group. Within a Year 9 class at Cord collaborative groups freely chose the following subjects without any teacher-direction or adherence to a predetermined co-operative theme: the Gulf war (2 groups), whaling, shoplifting, deforestation and its effect on Amerindian tribespeople and an exploration of the poem *The Naming Of Parts*. A case could be made that these apparently disparate subjects were linked by a co-operative theme based upon ethical considerations of freedoms and constraints, liberty and authority, the moral versus the expedient.

There is no need for there to be a co-operative outcome. An independent learning project can be characterised by collaborative outcomes alone. Schools such as Cord, Saltair, Dore, Ashfordton and Poltrice, each undertaking an independent learning project for the first time, saw no benefit in having a co-operative outcome, believing that the common outcomes and the factors of independent learning were sufficient to unify the work of the collaborative groups. One of the advantages of this way of working is that it concentrates attention on the process aspect of the project, which is common to all groups. The absence of any clear shared theme forces pupils and teachers to be clearer, to themselves and others, about why they are working in this way. This tends to have the effect of raising discussion about the process of independent learning.

FACTOR 5: PUPIL-NEGOTIATED ASSESSMENT

Assessment may have several purposes: to give information about pupils' performance or about the quality of a scheme of work or the content of a curriculum, to encourage a pupil to further learning, to reward 'success' or recognise 'failure', as a stimulus to learning or as an aid to planning. When a pupil's school career, self-esteem and future prospects are dependent upon the assessment of others, and the assessor's opinion is inviolable, assessment can also be considered to perpetuate the mystique and control of an invested power system.

Assessment is the most significant icon of the educational structure of invested power. Allowing pupils to choose their work partners, their subject of study, and to organise the execution of tasks becomes meaningless as a representation of educational citizenship if the responsibility for the assessment of the project outcomes is retained exclusively by the teacher. A parallel can be seen between teachers' control of pupils' assessment and the introduction of schools' assessment by the government. The clear message is that those who control the assessment procedure have control over the curriculum, its con-comitant pedagogy and the destiny of those engaged in it.

Considerable progress was made during the 1980s to broaden the assessment franchise to include the pupil in her assessment (initiatives such as profiling, records of achievement, pupil-negotiated statements, subject counselling, peer assessment). However, these initiatives were invariably restricted to the formative process of a pupil's educational experience or, if part of the summative school-leaving document, they concerned personal and social development and not academic achievement. Nevertheless, until 1992 pupils did have the possibility of negotiating their education throughout its statutory period. This opportunity was taken from pupils and teachers with the im-position of national Keystage Tests, beginning in 1991 for Keystage 1 pupils and culminating with the government-imposed abolition of 100 per cent coursework for 1994 GCSE examinations (Keystage 4 pupils).

The original purpose of the tests was claimed to be to give teachers the chance to moderate their own internal assessments against a normative refer-ence. The first tests were intended to be integrated within the pupils' normal lesson experience – they were known as SATs, the acronym for Standard Assessment Tasks. Their format and purpose soon altered. Short, sharp, 'pencil and paper' examinations were introduced and the nomenclature was changed to 'tests'. The results of the tests are used to formulate an annual national league table of the performance of schools, based on the test results as the sole criterion of success.

Whilst it is apparent how crude and distorted such tables must be, the publicity that they gain undoubtedly affects schools throughout the country and, as the tests are based upon the National Curriculum, they exert powerful influences on every state school's curriculum and its presentation to pupils. The two most pronounced influences are that teachers appear to feel that in order to fulfil their professional commitment to pupils to provide them with the best opportunity for public examination success (particularly at the age of 16, but also at 7, 11 and 14), they must not deviate from the confines of the various National Curriculum syllabi and, second, that the most effective method in inculcating pupils with a mass of subject-based knowledge and preparing them for examinations that are essentially tests of memory is to resort to a didactic presentation and to check its effectiveness by instituting departmental tests as a training for the national tests. Further pressure for schools to prioritise achievement in academic examinations as an educational aim is brought to bear by a system of per capita funding:

> for local authority funded schools funding is dependent upon the total number of pupils, so in order to receive the grant schools have to attract more students; and to attract more, they have to succeed in the examinations game and perform well in the published league tables of academic success. (Hutton 1995, p.215)

Secondary headteachers, in resisting the unfairness of the Tests but accepting that they are unlikely to be abolished by either a Conservative or a Labour government (a point confirmed in 1993 by Jack Straw when Shadow Education Minister), have lobbied for a change in the league tables to reflect what is called additionality, a 'value-added' factor, some measurement of a pupil's progress during her school career based upon an assessment of the difference between her performance at the ages of 11 and 16. This would avoid the present situation in which an inner-city comprehensive school with a high proportion of pupils with English as a second language is directly compared with an all-girls selective direct-grant school. The value-added factor is, according to National Association for the Teaching of English (NATE) sources, seen by some government advisers, including Chief Inspector Chris Woodhead, as a bid by headteachers to regain control of the assessment procedure (and, therefore, the curriculum and its presentation) by dictating the form of reference upon which the assessment is based.

The present model of schools' assessment by government is undoubtedly, as heads and other teachers claim, an unfair system. Ironically, it is also a facsimile of the microcosmic invested power structure of schools themselves. In the same way as government controls the schools' curriculum, heavily influences its presentation and uses an unfair normative reference of assessment, so schools, when they did have the freedom to do differently, visited the same constraints upon pupils. Moreover, headteachers who subscribe to the notion of value-added criteria of assessment are asking for an ipsative reference of assessment, a system that they have, until the introduction of school-leavers' records of achievement, rarely advocated as a significant part of the summative assessment of their own pupils' school experience.

Three points from this commentary are directly relevant to independent learning: that assessment should be curriculum-led, that is that the curriculum should determine the assessment rather than the assessment dictate the curriculum; that if pupils are to be given control over their choice of curriculum, they should be given control over its assessment; and that the ipsative reference is the most equitable reference to be used in assessment for it disposes power and reflexivity to the learner.

If assessment is determined by the curriculum, what might be assessed in the work of an independent learning project? It would be possible, although not necessarily desirable, to assess all five of the outcomes: video, magazine, live presentation, bibliography and diary. In projects in which I was involved it was a clause of the co-operative contract that the pupils' diaries need not be shown to anyone else but should be kept as a personal record of the project, lesson by lesson, a dialogue with the self, between pupil and person. This is not to say that the pupil will not make her own assessment of the diary or show it to someone else for peer or shared assessment, but it enshrines the principle that pupils should decide which examples of their work are available for assessment. Some assessment of the bibliography could be made, taking into account the number and range of texts and their appropriacy to the chosen subject. The bibliography itself may be used as an assessment tool to gauge the amount of research undertaken and the commitment and organisation of a collaborative group. Assessment of the other outcomes will certainly be made by all pupils because they will have some opinion about them, which, in itself, is a form of assessment. An assessment is, therefore, unavoidable. It is important that pupils are informed of the various references that they might use, and the criteria that underpin them – particularly as some research indicates (Griffith 1999) that pupils may undervalue their own efforts.

It is difficult to evaluate the video outcome using normative-referenced assessment for, as yet, there is no accepted norm for a 'good', 'average' or 'bad' video produced by pupils in different years across the 5–16 age range. This also makes it problematic to compare such genres as an animated cartoon, a social documentary, a play, a pop video, and an illustrated poem (all produced by a Year 9 class at Ashfordton in 1992). Within a particular co-operative group it might be possible to use a numerical or alphabetical 1–10 or A–G scale to place work in some sort of rank order (essentially a localised normative reference) based upon peer assessment. Although the assessments might appear to be subjective, they must be informed by some criteria. A shared analysis of why, for instance, one live presentation was given a B rating and another a D might make the implicit criteria that pupils are using clearer to them. This might lead to a more informed application of criterion-referenced assessment with the co-operative group drawing up their own criteria for the outcomes.

An ipsative reference, in which present is compared with previous performance to see if there is a discernible improvement, is the reference that pupils naturally used during independent learning projects. However, an ipsative reference requires explicit criteria, not necessarily to determine whether a pupil has improved but to analyse the improvement that has taken place. An ipsative comparison of two examples of a pupil's work, one completed in September and the other the following March, may show progress but a criterion-referenced analysis will show why.

For this reason it may be that the best assessment system is one that combines criterion and ipsative references, so that a group of pupils can evaluate whether progress has been made and decide in what areas further improvement is necessary, like this pupil captured on video during a collaborative discussion in which the group is reflecting on a term in which they undertook two half-termly independent learning projects:

> yes, we are doing better, because, because if you look at what we did last time…and then this time, then it's better…it is better. And if we get these, uh, these other things more sorted out, if we could just work more as a group and get things agreed when we'd said and who would do them then we'll be better again next term. (Year 9 boy at Poltewan, 1990.)

All of the above deals with group assessment. Many people (year tutors, parents, the pupils themselves) will also want an individual assessment. This can easily be accomplished, arising from the group assessment. Each member of the collaborative group lists what she or he did for each outcome, has the list approved by their group and then uses the co-operative criteria to assess their own contribution. Perhaps the teacher will be asked to validate that assessment, or other members of the group, someone else, or maybe a combination. It might be that the group is in the best position to evaluate the pupil's contribution to the video but that the teacher is chosen to validate the comment the pupil has attached to her contributions to the magazine and bibliography, whilst a member of the audience is chosen to validate the pupil's contribution to the live presentation and the pupil chooses not to include her diary in the assessment process. As long as everyone involved uses the co-operative criteria and there is honest discussion, this system is rewarding and consistent.

If it was felt useful, the criteria could be mapped onto a series of levels, alphabetical or numerical, perhaps for reporting purposes or to get a general feeling of the co-operative group's strengths and weaknesses. If there was a class trend that the video outcome was generally given a lower grading than the others, that could alert the co-operative group to making changes for the future. A collaborative group could use the results as a norm-reference to see if their work on any particular outcome was out of kilter with the general class trend.

It is a short step from using a criterion-based system to a graded-criterion system as in GCSE. This was the system used in the Carnmore modules, with pupils coming to their chosen teacher to validate the grade that they had given themselves, perhaps in discussion with parent or peer, based on a copy of the Southern Examining Group criteria that each pupil had in their coursework folder. Where the teacher's assessment did not coincide with the pupil's, negotiation took place. If no agreement was reached, the pupil could ask another teacher for a second opinion. If any grading remained unresolved after this, the pupil had the choice of either withdrawing the essay from her folder, including it without teacher validation, or including it with the teacher's grade and a note asking for the moderator's reconsideration.

A pupil's profile booklet that combines ipsative and criterion references may be used. Profiling is not just another system of assessment, it is a policy of learning that enfranchises the learner and releases the teacher from feeling that she bears the sole responsibility for progress. Teachers become supporters of the educational process rather than controllers of it. Profiling, in which pupils are given a greater sense of ownership of their own education, is almost certain to mean, in practice, a movement towards independent learning with pupils negotiating their own tasks and, therefore, a movement away from classwork in which the pace, content, style and format of the lessons is decided by the teacher. Independent learning project diaries are a form of profiling that informs ipsative-referenced assessment.

When should assessment take place? Assessment benefits from being moved to within the curriculum so that teachers and pupils can deliberate upon the formative process of a task rather than pass sentence on the finished product. This type of assessment and response, often oral rather than written, is dynamic. It can change things for the better. The collaborative group should be assessing its progress constantly so that work can be continued or changed and improved. Such assessment is an integral part of the organisation of a collaborative group. More formal assessments may be made once a term or at the agreed end of a project, which might be two or even three times a term.

It might be considered useful to hold less formal assessments at certain stages throughout the term – interim reviews for the various groups to report progress and discuss problems, although the common but time-consuming practice of drawing all the collaborative groups together at the end of each lesson for a 'sharing' session was resisted during independent learning projects. A simple profiling sheet, like the one used at Tavyford, was helpful to pupils in keeping their group on task (Appendix 9). The sheet was used at the beginning of lessons every third week during a term's project with Year 9 and 10 pupils. This single-sided A4 sheet was used by the pupils as a record of achievement and self-assessment, a planning aid, a job organiser so that tasks were shared equally, a homework planner/recorder and an incentive device. It was used by the teacher as a record of the aims and objectives set for the project by the group, an insight into the progress of the project and a method of motivating, stimulating and encouraging. After completing the sheet, each collaborative group came to the teacher for a discussion and if everything seemed all right they were given an extension of a week or a fortnight to continue their work without further teacher intervention. If there were problems, collaborative groups attempted to resolve them.

Year 7 pupils at Cedric Harvey school in the autumn term of 1989 were encouraged to select for themselves three pieces of work for assessment, to format their own assessment sheets and to choose whoever they wished, as well as themselves, to be involved in the assessment process (Appendix 10).

All the comments above have been about assessment of the product generated by an independent learning project and not about its process. It may not be practicable or possible that the attributes of global citizenship, and the complex personal and social skills embedded within its definition, can be reduced to a convenient hierarchy of sub-skills that can be progressively assessed. Nor might it serve the development of these attributes to have short-term assessment points. Experience at Poltewan, in which an attempt was made to gather some evidence about the development of the process skills within a project, left the teachers and researchers involved very wary of allowing, over the span of an independent learning project, a sort of insidious sub-text to develop that the pupils learn off by heart and give back to the teacher because they know it is the response she wants and they wish to please her:

'We learnt to get on with one another'. (Year 9 boy)

'We learnt not to be too hasty in judging others'. (Year 7 girl)

'We learnt how to get on and manage for ourselves'. (Year 9 girl)

'Sometimes we had arguments but we managed to sort them out because we wanted to get the work done'. (Year 7 girl)

'I learnt not to be forgetful because people are relying on you and you mustn't let them down'. (Year 9 boy)

'I think the best thing was we learnt how to find out things for ourselves. Before this I'd never really talked to old people'. (Year 7 boy)

These comments were all made by Year 7 and 9 pupils at Poltewan school after a one-term project in the autumn of 1990. Each group had recorded a video profile at the end of the project, from which the quotes are taken. It may well be that these comments are sincere but their public expression seems too evangelical, pupils publicly proclaiming themselves born-again independent learners. It may be that such comments are insincere but reflect a desire on the part of pupils to thank a teacher that they have grown to like for a pleasant classroom experience. A more structured evaluation of a pupil's full contribution to an independent learning project may be made by using the 12 factors of independent learning as a tool of assessment and asking a pupil to provide evidence of her contribution to, or participation in, each factor. This was the approach taken with the case study of the Carnmore collaborative group, MOB (Griffith 1991).

FACTOR 6: PUPIL-NEGOTIATED DEADLINES

Of the 4112 responses to the eight questions of Questionnaire 2, most referred to four aspects: group dynamics, video making, other project outcomes and time management. The questionnaire findings suggest that apart from resolving or avoiding arguments within the collaborative group, the group's planning of a sensible schedule of work is the key to its success. The main constituent of time management that pupils felt that teachers could help with was to 'allow pupils more time' to complete the project.

However, it is not the length of time of a project but how pupils divide the time up and then use it that is important. Questionnaire 2 distinguishes between perceived problems caused by the length of a project and those caused by the poor management of time within a project. Although a number of pupils would like to spend more time on a project, it was the planning of the work of the project to a series of staged deadlines that pupils identified as critical to harmonious collaborative relationships and the completion of outcomes.

An independent learning project at Saltair school lasted for a term and a half (8 January to 7 May), during which time a class of Year 8 pupils, an upper ability set, worked with both their English and their Music teacher in all their lessons and homework. In addition, the school, using TVEI funds, had bought £3000-worth of video equipment, including a Panasonic editing suite, to which pupils had access during and after school hours. Yet the work produced was not of as high a quality, nor were as many outcomes completed, as by a mixed-ability class of Year 8 pupils at Cord who spent two 50-minute lessons a week for one term (the same spring term as the Saltair class) and had access to video equipment during only six of those lessons. The total lesson time devoted to the project was 18.3 hours at Cord and 62.5 hours at Saltair.

Because classes are used to working in very short sections of time in their normal timetable, with work in one lesson often unrelated to work in the next, when given the opportunity to spend an extended length of time completing certain specific outcomes, many pupils experienced difficulty. Pupils seemed to react in two ways: either they were simply incapable of time planning, even though they tried; or no attempt was made at planning, so the first half of the project time was typified by complacency, the second half by panic.

Planning deadlines properly inevitably means making decisions about what the group is going to do and who is going to do what, so the whole future of the group is involved in these early decisions about subject choice and the distribution of tasks to complete the project outcomes. It is worth spending time to check the group's subject choice and that appropriate tasks have been chosen both by the group as a whole and individual members of the group.

The teacher can offer some kind of temporal framework, perhaps issuing a planning sheet to each collaborative group, listing the dates of the lessons and adding a few handrails like the schedule for a Carnmore project *Breaking Down the Barriers* (Appendix 11). With two classes working together at Axton on a project called *Other People*, a help-sheet was given to each collaborative group (Appendix 12). Both of these projects had a short time-span, about three or four weeks, so that in itself lent a sense of purpose, even urgency, to the work. Good time planning reduced panic.

Sometimes, particularly if one or two collaborative groups are obviously having problems, a planning tool with an even shorter time-scale can be used to kick-start some action, like the Tavyford profile. The schedule for *Friends With The Earth* (Appendix 13) took a great deal of the time-planning responsibilities from the pupils and yet, despite its paramilitary tone, still gave many opportunities for independent learning.

Planning has to allow flexibility. It is easy for a group to lull itself into a false sense of security when they complete their time plan for a whole term's work. Work has been shared or allocated within the group and these responsibilities have been written on to a time-planner. Equipment has been booked on a series of dates: one week a video camera to film an interview, the next the editing suite, the week after the audio suite to overdub music and commentary and so on. People have been contacted who will give information or interviews. Parental drivers have been prevailed upon to provide transport for location filming or community research. But the group has overlooked the French exchange when three members of the group are in Brittany for a fortnight, that every Thursday Brian misses the last twenty minutes of English for his violin lesson, that every other Tuesday pupils in the school hockey and football teams leave 15 minutes early to travel to away games, that three of the lessons will be cancelled for the school cross-country event, the carol service and for the combined forces band that is coming to play at an extended assembly. These were all foreseeable disruptions that could have been identified by checking the school calendar. But added to these disruptions will be others that can occur but cannot be mapped onto a time plan. Over a term there will almost certainly be absences owing to illness within the group. There will be problems with the video equipment: batteries will run down, external microphones will be used to conduct a filmed interview on location and when the tape is played back at school it will be discovered that the mike has been switched off. A trip to film location scenes for a documentary or play has to be cancelled because it is pouring with rain. The person to be interviewed for an article has gone on holiday, is ill, has changed her mind, had never been asked in the first place. The drama studio is not available for the rehearsal of the live presentation. The school photo-copier is being serviced on the day a group intended to duplicate its magazine.

One of the major influences upon time planning is the choice of subject that the collaborative group makes. Questionnaire 2 reveals that pupils' experience leads to this advice for a collaborative group: choose a subject with which it already has some familiarity and a shared interest, that is clearly focused and for which it will be easy to gather information and conduct research.

Giving pupils the responsibility for planning their collaborative work to self-imposed deadlines is essential to the integrity of an independent learning project, for if the teacher were to assume the onus of time management for a group, she would also have to subsume from the group the decision making about subject choice, task distribution and other aspects of group dynamics. To assume this responsibility for one collaborative group would imply a similar commitment to all the other groups, and this would be an impossible task for the teacher to fulfil. There are clearly identifiable steps that lead to successful time management for collaborative groups: to accept that the outcomes can be completed within the time limit of the project, to check planning against the school calendar, to prepare fallbacks for unforeseen problems, to ensure that the choice of subject is compatible with the time limit of the project, to have a scheme of deadlines that is flexible, to commit members to short-term deadlines that develop the project from lesson to lesson, to include some statements about time management in the group contract and to consult the teacher, particularly at the outset of the project.

FACTOR 7: PUPIL-INITIATED RESEARCH

Participant observation of primary and secondary school lessons and critical action research between 1988 and 1993 suggests that pupils very rarely undertake their own research.

What passes for pupil-initiated research are comprehension exercises, note making, science or maths investigations and topic work. In the secondary sector there is much use of comprehension exercises in all subjects, in which the 'research' field is determined by the teacher or an exam syllabus. The research is limited to a short text selected by the teacher, the research questions are predetermined and contained within the exercise that accompanies the text, and the pupil researcher knows that all the answers she is required to find will be located within a single text. The rightness or wrongness of her answers and any conclusions she may draw from the data are generally prescribed by a marking scheme. This applies to maths and science investigations and note making in English and the humanities. In many primary schools, and a very few secondary departments, an integrated-topic approach is taken, which appears to offer a pupil-research-based education. However, particularly since the introduction of the National Curriculum, the field of research is not open to choice but is dictated by the various subject syllabi. The 'research' may consist of pupils doing little more than copying from published texts without questioning or understanding their often complicated sentence structure and inaccessible vocabulary.

Comprehension exercises, note making, investigations with a predetermined focus, methodology and outcome, and the lowest common denominator of topic work cannot be regarded as pupil-initiated research. Nor can such practices be justified as a training, so that pupils may undertake their own research at a later stage, for they contain none of the features of research. Research requires engaging with a topic, clarifying a research question, planning an investigation, recruiting and organising the research team, testing the research method for reliability, validity and comparability, undertaking fieldwork and interrogating findings, placing the research in a wider context by a search of the field literature, drawing conclusions that are justified by the findings and deciding upon an appropriate form of presentation. Contemporary research is often dependent upon the use of computer technology for the interrogation of both quantitative and qualitative data and a wider awareness of the meaning of text is expected. A literature search, or fieldwork, may take into account electronic texts, journalistic and moving image texts, audio texts, cultural texts (fiction, poetry, drama) and unpublished texts that may be discovered or created during the fieldwork: orthographies, interviews, transcripts, letters, photograph albums.

Research is dynamic, demanding the development of an intellectual curiosity and a critical disposition, an understanding of the bias of all media forms, an ability to plan and execute sequential tasks and the placing of the research within a peopled context. Such research can foster the attributes of global citizenship. Conversely, comprehension exercises and much topic work *et al.* suppress the development of these attributes. Research is restricted to the reading of a limited range of printed texts, the provenance of which is accepted without question. The impulse of the pupil's enquiry is generally factual rather than sociological, even when the research field may lend itself to sociological or political discussion and at a time when the laws of science and social systems (and the acts of cultural faith embedded within them) are increasingly regarded as only partial constructions of empirical truth. Knowledge is seen as powerful but neutral, to be assimilated but not questioned, yet many of the texts offered to pupils contain insidious cultural messages. Humankind is often referred to by the generic use of the word 'Man', emotively pejorative terms such as 'backward', 'primitive' or 'unsophisticated' are used to describe non- technological communities, war is depicted as a series of acts of heroic individuality, other planetary animals are categorised as 'dumb friends' or 'savage predators' and the British class system is presented as a positive symbol of stability and continuity. The status of the pupil-researcher is low: she reports on the findings of adult experts, her own voice is not heard, she has no opportunity to locate her work in any research paradigm, there is little sense in which what she is doing is really is 'her work' at all. The quasi-research of comprehension exercises and topic work serves to inculcate pupils within an ontology of scientific certaintude and social servitude that does not portray the reality of historical or contemporary human existence.

Independent learning projects offer the real opportunity for each collaborative group to become a research team. Whatever subject is chosen, no matter how anodyne, research skills can be developed. However, given a free choice of subject, most pupils (73%) choose to research a social or ethical issue. By examining a list of the videos made by independent learning project pupils between January 1990 and June 1992, various genres of subject choice can be distinguished: 39.6 per cent of the videos (and therefore the magazines and live performances) concerned local social issues, 33.4 per cent global social issues, 15.8 per cent sports and hobbies, 6.4 per cent had a literary basis and 4.8 per cent could not be categorised in this way. Often, a video made connections between local and global issues – the local issue providing a focus for active research within a wider context. Two Year 8 Special Needs pupils at Benallick made a film about pollution on Ladrum beach that carried a message about all pollution but was made more effective by its 'in our own backyard' approach. A mixed group of Year 10 pupils from Stonall made a video about sewage using pupils' own footage filmed at a sewage works and from a coastal flight. This footage was edited with stills from books and shots recorded from TV. A voice-over script was added with *Salt Water* by Julian Lennon as background music. A group of boys and girls, aged from 10 to 13, from four different schools collaborated during the *Minorities* project on a video about an evening spent at

Rowlands Fair during its annual visit to Westwood. The programme included interviews with the fair owner and young fairground workers. This video illuminated attitudes that went far beyond the contemporary locality, particularly when viewed with a video made by primary pupils of an interview with a local Romany and another tape of filmed slides and stills culled from books with pupils' commentary. A mixed Year 9 group from Stonall took an animal welfare theme. Their video included TV footage and the pupils' own filmed interviews with members of the local hunt and the owner of a horse and donkey sanctuary. The twelve schools (6 primary and 6 secondary) involved in the *Europeans* project all made video programmes about their local community which were sent to partner schools in every country in the European Union.

If the choice of contemporary social issues typified the subjects chosen for the pupil-initiated research, the selection and organisation of the personnel in the collaborative groups constituted the establishment of a research team. The distribution of tasks, whether by task allocation or task sharing, and the planning of project deadlines clarified research methodology. Most groups undertook fieldwork in the local community and environment. The literature search was an important part of the research but, unlike with comprehension and copied topic work, did not constitute the whole of the research.

The literature search was much wider than the consultation of printed texts from the school library. Pupils accessed public utility databases, either from the school resource centre or the public library, televisual databases like Ceefax and Oracle, telephonic systems like Prestel or stand-alone computer systems like microfiche. A Year 10 Poltrice girl used the school modem to access the computer at the county reference library and get a print-out of addresses pertinent to her group's project. A Year 10 Stonall group phoned the Unilever public relations office to quiz them on the obfuscations concerning animal testing in the text of the literature Unilever had sent to the group. They audio- and video-recorded the conversation – and told the Unilever representative that they were doing so. During a *Europeans* open evening at Penmouth, messages of support constantly arrived, via Campus 2000, from pupils in schools throughout Europe.

As part of any independent learning project, pupils were encouraged to enrol at the local library and were given the opportunity to visit during school times. Many towns have other library systems that may be used by the public: newspaper offices, courts, councils, museums, colleges, universities. Libraries, even small rural ones, offer an impressive range of services. The Citizens' Charters have led to more information being released into the public domain and pupils should be aware that although a polite insistence may be needed, they have a legal right to access public utilities and private companies for information. It was quite proper for a Year 10 girl at Poltrice, during a telephone conversation with someone at the Department for Education, to make the point that if the government wanted to use her GCSE results for political purposes, she claimed the right to demand an answer to her question.

Research offers the full range of letter-writing skills: letters of request, for information, sponsorship, help, money; letters of invitation to guests, speakers, experts, audiences; letters of thanks; letters of organisation outlining arrangements, meeting-places, travel, schedules, payments, responsibilities; long-term correspondences with people in other places. There is a literacy about reading letters – reading between the lines. Responses to pupils' letters give opportunities for this kind of learning:

> Dear Emily and Sean,
>
> H——- D———, the Right Honourable Member of Parliament for —— thanks you sincerely for your invitation to him to visit your class to discuss local pollution problems, particularly those of sewage disposal, but unfortunately he regrets that at this time he is unable… (Venturers, 1989)

Pupils' research will often involve interviews with representatives from the school community, the local, national and international communities. Interviews can be conducted by letter, by phone and in person and can be recorded in notes or questionnaire forms, by audio- or video-recorder, or onto lap-top word processing or database systems. Pupils should be encouraged to be audacious. International directory inquiries will give Yeltsin's number. The White House is patient, Conservative Central Office, polite but stonewalling.

The conducting of surveys and questionnaires as part of a research programme can offer an opportunity for task sharing within the collaborative group as there are several different strands, all involving different skills: the construction of the questionnaire, its format and wording; the production and duplication of the questionnaire, perhaps using a word-processor and photocopier; the public use of the questionnaire and the confidence and oral skills required to engage with the community; the recording of the answers, requiring listening and writing skills or the technical expertise to use recording equipment; the tabulation of the results, perhaps requiring poster presentation skills or the ability to use a database; the interpretation of the results, involving group discussion; and the recording (in writing or other means) of the group's conclusions.

By going through this process, pupils can come to understand the fallibility of statistical information: how certain questions can be worded in such a way as to prompt a desired answer, how quotations can be used out of context to gain a particular effect, how figures can be manipulated to present a certain impression, how percentages carry a spurious credibility even if the number of people questioned is very small, how different forms of presentation (bar graph, scatter graph, pie chart, lists) can give different effects, how different subcultural groups respond to the same questions.

FACTOR 8: PUPIL-USE OF LANGUAGE TECHNOLOGY

Human society has always used the technology available to make a lasting record of its texts. Cave-painters employed the technology of the time to set the paradigm for all that has followed. These early writers created texts that were aesthetic and transactional, at the same time a story, a poem, an art-form, a social document that recorded hierarchy, behavioural codes, power-structures and gender-roles, as well as being a functional manual for passing on scientific skills: hunting, shelter building, fire making. Little has changed, in terms of textual purpose or the use of language technology, since then. Papyrus, hieroglyphics, the quill, Caxton's press, slates, blackboards, ink-pens, biros, typewriters, word-processors, spreadsheets, databases, audio-recorders and video-recorders are just further steps along the technological-textual continuum in which each successive society uses the technology available to create and store its texts.

Information technology encompasses much more than the computer, the calculator and the word-processor. Digital watches, telephone answering and facsimile machines, microfiche, video-recorders, audio-recorders, video, film and still cameras, microwave ovens, musical synthesisers and sequencers are all examples of information technology.

The use of information technology in schools can be divided into two distinct but overlapping areas: audio-visual IT and micro-computer IT. Unfortunately, these areas often do not overlap enough – or sometimes even at all – and pupils' education in information technology can be sporadic and incomplete. There seem to be at least five reasons for this.

First, departmental insularity, epitomised in practical terms by an unwillingness to make links across subjects so that equipment can be shared. The synthesisers and four-track recorders are only for use by music pupils, the computer database is the property of the maths department, the video-camera is only available to GCSE media studies pupils, and at lunchtime the English department locks the room that houses the departmental word-processor. Used imaginatively, this equipment could provide the technological resources for a cross-curricular study. A simple survey, as outlined above, could utilise all this equipment. Used piecemeal, its potential as a learning aid is limited.

Second, the notion of subject curricula is identified with the use of different items of information technology. The introduction of the National Curriculum, with statutory curricula for the ten core and foundation subjects, has tended to delineate boundaries between subjects so that teachers become more concerned about the 'Englishness' or the 'Historyness' of a project rather than its obvious general educational value. Is a survey that uses a database Maths or is it English? Is writing a poem English but using a synthesiser to write a lyric Music? Can a project on pollution that requires the use of computer spreadsheets and calculators be undertaken in English lessons or is pollution the preserve of Environmental Studies? Is the use of video technology Media Education and not English?

Third, departmental funding – language technology equipment is not cheap. At current prices it would cost a minimum of £5000 to buy the equipment needed for a simple but very effective audio/video editing suite. For most departments, this would require phased spending over two or three years and, as 'new' money would be unlikely to be available, this expenditure would mean diverting funds from hardy perennials like sets of readers, exercise books, language course books.

Fourth, the need for departmental retraining – no department is going to make that kind of financial outlay if its staff do not have the skills to use the equipment when it arrives, and some teachers seem to have a terror of technology.

Fifth, there is an intellectual snobbishness that manifests itself in a denigration of media and electronic texts as inferior to the canon of published literary text. Clear evidence of this has been the downgrading of the media education strand of English in the National Curriculum and the reinforcement of the cultural heritage attitude to certain texts, as exemplified by the insistence that all pupils study Shakespeare and other pre-twentieth-century writers. (Some educational observers, including members of NATE and the ill-fated Language in the National Curriculum (LINC) project, maintain that the political prejudice against language technology and media education is not just based on snobbishness but upon a desire to maintain an electorate that is illiterate in the reading of media texts, upon which most people now rely for their reading of the world and their place in it).

The cumulative result of these five different reasons for a resistance to language technology is that pupils are not generally encouraged to use contemporary technology to record their texts. Instead, they use fifteenth- century technology – pen and ink. However, as readers, they are bombarded by twentieth-century technological texts: photographs, film, radio, television, video, compact disc, computer games, newsprint, published print, databases. There is a dichotomy between pupils' prescribed writing of texts and their voluntary reading of texts. A great deal of curricular time, particularly in English lessons but also in the humanities, is devoted to encouraging pupils to create their own texts in the style of published authors in the poetic, dramatic, fictional, discursive and factual genres. Why? Only a small percentage of ex-pupils write regularly for pleasure or work purposes and fewer still make a living from writing. The reason for the insistence on pupils creating different kinds of text is presumably aimed at equipping pupils with the skills of cultural analysis, impelled by the belief that by practising as writers themselves, pupils are better able to understand the texts of other writers. If this is so, it must surely be an inarguable proposition that language teachers have a responsibility to develop pupils' ability to read contemporary texts by giving them the opportunity to write them – and that requires the pupils' use of language technology so that pupils can create the kind of late twentieth-century texts that they most read.

By doing so, pupils may develop a literacy in their reading of films, CDs, TV, radio, advertisements, newspaper editorials, party political broadcasts, the speeches of bosses or union representatives, their own school's aims as published in the school handbook and the government's claims about their school's and their own performances as published in national league tables.

FACTOR 9: COMMUNITY INVOLVEMENT AND THE USE OF THE ENVIRONMENT

Participant observation, interviews with pupils and the data provided by pupils' evaluations reveals that one of the most exciting and satisfying aspects, for many pupils, of an independent learning project is the chance to move outside the classroom.

The use of the local environment as a location for pupil-initiated research, and the involvement of the community as participants in the research, offer the chance to pupils to carry their work away from the confines of the classroom and the time limits of the school day, move into the local environment and community and work there unsupervised. The curriculum is not socially and morally isolated. Learning is promoted as a part of the everyday living of the citizen, in which she interacts with multi-environments and multi-communities, rather than a decontextualised exercise of the pupil.

The use of the local environment as a location for pupil-initiated research, and the involvement of the community as participants in the research, has been exemplified in Chapter Five. The community and the environment also offer many possibilities for the presentation of pupils' work: poetry posters in the local shops, poetry roadshows, story-tellings, drama productions, displays, presentations on social issues, booklets and magazines, articles in the local press, interviews on local radio, features on regional television programmes.

Old people's groups, parenting groups, the unwaged, playgroups, nursery and primary schools, pupils' parents, holiday-makers, charity organisations and fêtes can all offer audiences for pupils' work. They can also provide a stimulus for that work or become a part of the project so that, for instance, local groups or individuals give assistance in the form of information, resources, facilities, funds, time and transport. It may well be that the presentation of a project becomes a joint effort, involving the community and the pupils.

When organising school trips or inviting speakers in, pupils can be involved in the planning, the letter-writing, the telephoning, the catering arrangements, the transport details, the budget.

Literature, whether presented through media or literary text, offers a vicarious experience for pupils and plays an important part in preparing them, at a safe distance, for the real experiences of their own adolescent and adult lives. Meeting and talking with people in their own community can enhance this process. Pupils can learn much and be comforted by the reflections of others on how they have come through times of fear, challenge, threat and insecurity.

The chance to talk with, and to learn about, other sub-cultures within one's own community is important for it allows pupils to challenge their own prejudices and, thus, to recognise the malevolent power of language to stereotype groups of people. This, in turn, can move them towards an in-dependence of viewpoint, an emerging ability to make their own judgments, rather than accept, without reservation or question, the pronouncements of others.

Examples of pupils' perception of the local environment and community as a symbol of the global environment and community to which we all belong have been given. By engaging with their own local community, pupils are offered the opportunity to gain a real understanding of the concept of community and the inter-relatedness of the global community for by examining their own community they can better understand all communities. The same is true of the environment: by coming to care for and value the local environment, so pupils develop a concern – and a sense of responsibility – for the global environment. This liberation from a parochial viewpoint is a crucial characteristic of global citizenship and was the basis of the cross-curricular and cross-phase in-dependent learning projects *Minorities, Centennial* and *Europeans.*

FACTOR 10: A SENSE OF AUDIENCE

The potential dangers of a large-scale presentation of the work of the co-operative group have been detailed earlier. These pitfalls do not usually apply to the work of individual collaborative groups who have chosen their own audience. Presenting work to a real audience that the group has chosen itself gives added purpose to the work, clarifies the style of the work (a presentation to infants will require a different style than a presentation to a group of well-informed adults) and develops critical awareness on the part of the group.

FACTOR 11: PRESENTATION IN VARIOUS FORMS

Presentation in various forms (word-processed, dramatic, oral, visual display, audio-recorded, video-recorded, others) means that all pupils, not just those more adept at producing mechanically accurate and neatly handwritten pieces, can make their own personal and powerful contributions to project outcomes. The promotion of standard English, spoken in a particular dialect (based upon class rather than region), of technical accuracy rather than contextual message in writing, and the demotion or exclusion of other forms of presentation have the effect of disempowering and silencing many young people as pupils, people and citizens.

FACTOR 12: REFLEXIVITY

Independent learning encourages reflexivity by giving pupils a personal stake in their education – it is pupils, in self-selected groups, who choose the subject of, plan and execute an independent learning project. There should be opportunities throughout an independent learning project for both the collaborative and co-operative groups to reflect upon their experiences. The writing of the diary entries provides an ongoing time for self-critical reflection. Collaborative groups will need to reflect on their achievements and perceived failures as a project develops and changes are made, perhaps to task distribution or to time management. At the end of a project it is useful for the co-operative groups to reflect, in talk and in writing, on how the project went and what could be improved upon in the future. Assessment of any kind requires reflexivity. The subject choices made by pupils will often bring pupils to reflect upon ideas and attitudes that they have held, as will meeting members of different social or cultural groups during a project. The choice of a social or moral issue as a subject for study is likely to involve pupils in reflexive considerations. Reflexivity is expedient for the success of a project. It is also an attribute of the post-modern citizen, as identified in Giddens' phrase 'the reflexive project of the self'.

IMPLICATIONS FOR INDEPENDENT LEARNING IN THE FUTURE

The present 12 factors have been shown to facilitate the transformation from invested to divested power in the classrooms of some 11–16-year-old pupils in the UK. But that is only a starting-point. It is important that the practices of independent learning do change, evolve, find new directions. Nothing could be more antithetical to the development of educational citizenship than a monotonous succession of projects, each with the same preordained and inflexible outcomes, each with a prescribed learning style that must not deviate from 12 immutable factors. Independent learners must not become dependent on the existing factors of independent learning any more than emergent global citizens should depend upon current ideals of global citizenship.

Looking to the future, it is possible to make some predictions concerning the development of independent learning after a successful introduction based upon the 12 factors. As the criteria for the formation of collaborative groups develop and the nature of outcomes changes, so the delicate balance between collaborative and co-operative groupwork and individual responsibility will evolve. There is likely to be less rigid adherence to both the factor of collaborative groupwork and the precept of predetermined outcomes so that, at any time, some pupils may be working in groups, some in pairs, some individually, all on subjects of their own choosing, with different time-spans. Over a school year, all the factors of independent learning would operate, apart from, possibly, collaborative groupwork. It might be that a few pupils would work individually for the whole year, although this is regarded as unlikely and it is considered a responsibility of the teacher to ensure that no pupils are denied the full possibilities of educational citizenship by always working in isolation.

With different collaborative groups working to different time limits, the idea of a co-operative theme or product will dissipate – which, hopefully, will alter any perceptions of independent learning as an endless series of discrete projects. This may well benefit the development of independent learning – the independent learning projects in the study LEA were not intended to be isolated experiments that were dependent upon the support of external personnel but introductory pilots to a new pedagogy that was applicable to the mainstream curriculum of a school in its daily practice.

An advantage of these likely developments will be that individual pupils will have an even greater control over the time, direction, pace, subject and style of their own learning. A disadvantage might be that without the cohesion of a co-operative tension, the integrity of the co-operative group may be diminished through a lack of joint purpose. With skilful teaching support, however, the co-operative group's purpose can be strengthened through pupils' understanding of the importance of concepts such as trust, commitment to a shared ideal of education and citizenship and an appreciation of the worth of others' efforts and opinions, no matter how different they are from one's own – a celebration of the cultural diversity of the independent learning community as a microcosm of a planetary community of global citizens.

It is also possible to envisage independent learning programmes being distorted so that far from contributing to a transformation to divested power, they are used to consolidate the existing invested power systems of some educational institutions. As a persuasive part of the process of introducing educational citizenship into the school timetable and curriculum, it was expedient to reassure adults and pupils that independent learning was an effective pedagogy for the presentation of the National Curriculum. Both involved pupils and teachers have commented that pupils worked more industriously and often to a higher standard during independent learning projects than in their normal lessons. There may, then, be a danger that aspects of independent learning may be adapted solely as an efficient way of improving examination performance in NC examinations and that the ideals of educational citizenship become relegated to the rhetoric of the school prospectus – a return to the Drudges and Frogs versus Princesses and Princes image that introduced this discussion.

CHAPTER SEVEN

State Education in the UK and Educational Citizenship

THE RHETORIC OF EMPOWERMENT

The rhetoric of empowered citizenship via education – effectively, educational citizenship – abounds. Examples are the ratification of the UN Convention on the Rights of The Child (1991), the Speaker's Commission on Citizenship (1990), the Education Reform Act (1988) statement that education should promote the spiritual, moral, cultural, mental and physical development of pupils, the Council of Europe Recommendation on education (1985) and the text of LEA and individual school prospectuses. At international level, some progress, however patronising, has been made – for example the Children's Hearings at the UN Conference of the Environment held at Rio de Janeiro in 1992. More than lip-service has been paid to the involvement of children in the Norwegian Voice of the Children project and the 1992 International Conference on the Rights of The Child at Exeter University. However, the work of such researchers as Hart (1992) and Franklin (1992) indicates that there is still a gulf between the international and national rhetoric and the reality of practice in educational institutions at regional levels.

The Princesses and Princes image, that all pupils in a late-twentieth-century liberal democracy do have a full entitlement to a free state education intended to empower them as adult citizens, is ostensibly accepted without question. Yet in the United Kingdom the extension of a universal educational franchise is a continuing and uncompleted process rather than a concluded series of historical events. For many pupils, personal empowerment via educational citizenship has always been, and continues to be, unrealised rhetoric.

Only a generation ago, until CSE examinations were introduced in 1965, around 60–80 per cent of pupils were disenfranchised, from the age of 11, from any form of terminal 16+ examinations and thus the opportunity of a higher education. It was seven years (1972) before the Raising of the School Leaving Age Act ensured that all pupils would stay at school until they had had the chance to take public examinations at 16. It was not until 1975 that gender distinction in pupils' choice of post-14 CSE and GCE courses was made illegal. It was merely nine years ago (1988) that the odious class distinction between

CSE and GCE was resolved with the introduction of the GCSE. It is only during the present decade of the 1990s that the integration of pupils with a handicap into mainstream education has really developed.

There is evidence to suggest that these legislative changes may have had a formal, rather than a substantive, effect upon providing empowering educational opportunities for all pupils. In 1994 the government connived to defeat its own parliamentary bill originally intended to equalise the opportunities of the handicapped, significant clauses of which concerned educational entitlement. Under the budgetary arrangements of LMS (Local Management of Schools), some of the cost of providing facilities for pupils with a physical or emotional and behavioural handicap is devolved to individual schools which, in some cases, have been unable to finance the changes needed so that all pupils in the catchment have an equal entitlement to attend their local school. Many ethnic minority pupils are still disadvantaged by a monolinguistic state examination system that insists that, in England and Northern Ireland, all lessons other than Modern Languages must be taught in English and that all examination papers must be written and answered in English. In 1995 the ideal of a comprehensive state educational system – equal educational opportunities to create a more equal society – is far from realised. Nearly a third of the local education authorities in England and Wales have retained grammar and secondary modern schools; private schools for the children of fee-paying parents allow a privileged section of society to circumvent the National Curriculum; via grant-maintained status, some state schools are effectively moving into the independent sector and operating their own selection processes for 11-year-old pupils, which may disadvantage Individual Needs pupils. The tiered system of examination entry for GCSE English, Mathematics and Science restricts pupils to pre-imposed bands of achievement (in effect, the segregated system of the old GCE and CSE exams). A recent survey (Corrigan 1990) showed that the statistical probability of C3 working-class boys moving through the educational system to take up A1 professional qualifications had decreased since the 1970s. There is a growing body of research (Whyld 1983; Riddell 1992; Measor and Sykes 1992; Herbert 1992; AGIT 1994) that reveals that girls in many schools do not enjoy equality of opportunity with boys, nor do they feel parity of status, even though their academic achievement may be higher.

There seems to be no shared agenda that members of the existing adult citizenship have for the education of those who will be the citizens of the future. The attempt to hold in a sensible balance the past of their own education, the present of their citizenship and the future of a citizenship of those over whom they currently make the educational decisions leads to confusions between the expectations citizens have for their children's education and a curriculum (and its form of presentation to pupils) that is unlikely to fulfil these expectations.

Because there are differing views of citizenship, so there are differing views about the kind of education most suited to develop the kind of citizens that a particular society wants at a particular time. Should the child be given an education that prepares her to enter comfortably and acceptingly the existing society (an autarchic model of citizenship) or should she be educated to question the tenets of the *status quo* so she may contribute to the change and development of the existing society (a critically reflective model of citizenship)? This uncertainty of purpose is exacerbated in the United Kingdom by the polarisation of two-party Government over the last 50 years, one generally supporting an autarchic, the other an autonomous model.

Research in the study LEA demonstrates that parents want their children to use new technology, be involved in active learning and develop the social skills that collaborative and co-operative working encourages. Government claims that it wants to create an adaptable workforce, capable of working in teams, solving problems, negotiating between groups, flexible enough to retrain and retool as circumstances change. Industry clamours for confident, articulate managers, creators and planners, literate in reading electronic text and in the use of information technology. Society as a whole sees a new need for its citizens to celebrate cultural diversity, at the same time expressing a sincere feeling of responsibility for the commonweal of humankind and a concern for its shared global environment. The educational system itself rings with metalinguistic catch-phrases such as entitlement, empowerment, enfranchisement. In short, society sees a need for the Princesses and Princes image of *school-leavers*: reflexive, adaptable, resourceful pupils about to claim their place as participants, the decision takers and policy makers, in the era and culture of high modernity. Autonomous but morally aware, these young people will be the citizens of the next century.

And yet, by and large, the shared perception of all these factions as to what constitutes a good teacher (and hence an effective pedagogy) has hardly shifted from the 1950s archetype of a fair but formal Miss or Sir, authoritative, didactic and certain. Similarly, the shared perception of what constitutes a good education is to do with a knowledge-based rather than a social-skills-based (citizenship) curriculum. The Joseph Priestley-driven view (1778) that education should be knowledge-based rather than experiential has, during 125 years of state education in the UK since the Foster Act of 1870, developed and consolidated its own concomitant pedagogy: a didactic class presentation of factual information that should be committed to memory.

It is this content-based notion of education, with its most economic style of presentation (the passive class lesson) and its simplistic forms of assessment (written tests of memory), that underpins the National Curriculum and thus dominates state education in the UK. The National Curriculum itself is little more than ten long but fairly arbitrary lists of things for pupils to learn off by heart. Its assessment procedures reinforce this: short, sharp tests, timed essays, the distrust and consequent reduction of coursework, national tests to be taken by all pupils repeatedly between the ages of 7 and 16. What few opportunities there are for pupils to express an opinion are sullied by a concern for the proprieties of Standard English and Received Pronunciation and a view of literacy that is obsessed with the mechanics of handwriting and spelling. In short, society sees a need for the Drudges and Frogs image of school pupils: neatly and uniformly dressed pupils sitting attentively in orderly rows, listening obediently to the didactic presentation of a clearly defined area of factual knowledge, given by an authoritarian, albeit benign, teacher.

Such an educational system offers virtually no opportunity for educational citizenship.

There appears to be an illogical dichotomy between what British society wants for its children and about how it wants that to happen. These two desires are incompatible if not irreconcilable. It seems that what people are either actively seeking, or passively accepting, is a brace of educational opposites: first, a knowledge-based curriculum which is at odds with the type of education that parents want their children to have and that the rhetoric claims pupils are getting – educational citizenship – and, second, a didactic pupil-management system at odds with the way parents want their children to learn that curriculum – independent learning.

To reiterate the point made in Chapter Two, there is a belief that a Drudges and Frogs education will produce Princesses and Princes citizens. But the social alchemy required to turn Drudges into Princesses and Frogs into Princes requires a fairy-tale formula. These things don't happen in real life. There is an atmosphere of confusion that pervades educational planning as the close of the century approaches. In the UK the principal agencies responsible for the education of young people do not have a clear and shared view of what constitutes an education appropriate for the era of high modernity, nor of the most suitable style of classroom presentation of its curriculum. The expectations held for the outcomes of the 5–16 educational system are dissonant with its curriculum and its pedagogy.

In the study LEA teachers and parents often expressed the commonly held view that, increasingly during the last decade, the two agencies most directly responsible for the education of the young – parents and teachers – have been asked to take ever more responsibility with ever less support. These changes have taken place in a growing atmosphere of culpability: centralised support is withdrawn but when schools are then perceived to be failing, blame is apportioned at the local level. Social workers and educational advisory staff are ridiculed in the populist press ('Why Are Our Schools Still Run By Cranks?', *Daily Mail* headline, 26.06.91). Local education authority funding is decreased, diverted or strings are attached. Individual schools are isolated by the dis-solution of the LEAs, the advisory services and HMI. School departments feel threatened by new 'hard-line' inspections and the planned publication of the raw results of pupils' subject performance in national tests. Teachers are made to feel inadequate and insecure by the introduction of appraisal, the possibility (or covert reality) of payment by results and a relentless media campaign that depicts them as bumbling comic caricatures ('Many teachers today cannot spell and often have a worse command of English than their pupils. We want you – parents and kids – to tell us about howlers made by teachers or education officials. Send it to TEACHERS, The Sun, 1 Virginia Street, LONDON E1 9XP', *The Sun*, 28.11.94). The workload on headteachers and deputies is increased with the devolution of delegated budgets, on departments with the imposition of subject syllabuses under the National Curriculum and on teachers with the vastly increased administration required by national testing and inspection.

Many teachers in the study LEA, in primary, secondary and tertiary phases, feel that there has also been a sustained campaign by the Conservative government and press to create distrust between the two agencies of teachers and parents and to erode the sense of a mutually-respected partnership. Former Education Minister John Patten's endorsement of licensed and articled teachers, and the proposed recruitment of a 'Mum's Army' to teach reading, devalued the professional skills of teaching. The Parents' Charter, National Testing and the recruitment of inspection teams, including 'at least one person not working in education – to give an outside view' (DES 1991) contributed to a feeling that parents needed to be constantly checking on wayward teachers. This contrived schism was vigorously promoted in the populist press:

> An army of mums teaching the under-10s the Three Rs. Sounds a good idea to us. The experience they've gained from bringing up their own children would be invaluable. We hope Education Secretary John Patten isn't put off the plan by the bleats of the teachers' union. Mum knows best! (*The Sun*, editorial, 18.08.91)

> Three-quarters of seven-year-olds cannot spell words like earth, honey and paint. These revelations will not surprise parents. They will welcome the plans by Education Secretary John Patten to hold tests in schools. If the kids fail, we shall know who to blame. The teachers who failed them should be made to put on the dunce's cap. (*The Sun*, editorial, 12.10.92)

> Education is too important to be left to teachers. It's what parents want that counts: And that means results. Our children's futures are at stake. (*The Sun*, editorial, 07.04.93)

> PARENT POWER: Your Guide to Choosing The Best of Education in Britain (*Sunday Times Supplement*, 29.08.93)

Having undermined public confidence in the general status and capability of teachers, a consistent and vituperative harangue from press and politicians concentrated criticism on specific, widely-accepted areas of curriculum content and pedagogical practice that were suddenly deemed unsound. Integrated topic work, groupwork, 'real' books and investigative approaches to maths and science were all denounced as responsible for a decline in academic standards (for which no authoritative figures have ever been produced). Moreover, such practices were linked with a decline in moral and social values. In the 'The Sun Speaks Its Mind' editorial about the death whilst on duty of PC Patrick Dunne, the leader writer appeared to proclaim that teachers are a greater threat to society than thieves, muggers, rapists and murderers:

> We have watched without protest as society degenerates. We have failed to teach our children the basis of morality. It is never too late to stand up and cry: Halt. We must crack down on those who rob, maim, rape or kill. But in the name of Patrick Dunne we must do more. We should renounce the trendy, liberal creeds of the sixties which have bedevilled our schools and our social policies. PC Dunne was a teacher before he became a copper. He will have seen the void in our children's education. *We don't teach them the difference between right and wrong.* They don't learn respect for authority. Worse, they don't learn respect for other people. We have to pull back from the edge of this moral precipice. (*The Sun*, editorial, 22.10.93)

Teachers may take some solace that such criticism is not new. Just as contemporary politicians and tabloid editorials fulminate against teachers as being responsible for the moral decline of society, so, in 1769, this broadside from Thomas Sheridan thundered out:

> British Education: Or, The Source of Disorders of Great Britain. Being An Essay Towards Proving, that the Immorality, Ignorance, and False Taste, which so Generally Prevail, Are the Natural and Necessary Consequences of the Present Defective System of Education.

The solution to allegedly declining academic, social and moral standards was to be a Back to Basics approach, with an emphasis on the didactic presentation ('more chalk and talk') of a restricted knowledge-based curriculum ('the importance of the 3 R's') by authoritarian teachers who would exemplify the traditional virtues of conservatism (rather than 'trendies whose basic purpose is to instil in the minds of impressionable youngsters the self-evident virtues of socialist levelling down' (Honeyford 1991)).

The right wing, whilst clamouring for moral rearmament, campaigned against teachers' attempts to raise the moral and social awareness of pupils by relating schoolwork to a contemporary social context. There was what amounted to a frenzied suspicion that any attempt to deal with topical issues, to socialise the curriculum, was part of some totalitarian indoctrination and that pupils should be protected by isolating their education from real life. Professor Ronald Carter, Chair of the government-funded Language in the National Curriculum project (LINC) wrote that:

> Language should be studied in its own right, as a rich and fascinating example of human behaviour. It should be explored in real, purposeful situations, not analysed out of context. Language reveals and conceals much about human relationships. There are intimate connections, for example, between language and social power, language and culture, and language and gender. (Introduction to the LINC units, 1991, unpublished)

It might have been thought that such self-evident and common-sense views would have been uncontroversial. The response of the then Minister of State for Education, Tim Eggar, was to suppress the publication of the LINC materials (after a two-year project costing £21 million and involving 150 personnel) with comments that made it clear that the Conservative government viewed its National Curriculum as an academic curriculum with an instructional pedagogy not just unrelated to, but deliberately separated from, the real world. Carter's vision of a socially-contextualised language study was dismissed as: 'a distraction from the main task of teaching children to write, spell and punctuate correctly. Of course language is a living force, but our central concern must be the business of teaching children how to use their language correctly' (Eggar in *The Times Educational Supplement,* 26.06.91)

Eggar's dismissal was mild compared to the continuing press coverage that sought to caricature the teaching profession as riven between two camps: either sensible and conscientious practising teachers or irresponsible, 'trendy so-called experts' whose theorising was motivated by a clandestine politically-motivated agenda rather than any working knowledge of schools and a concern for children. Examples of the no-nonsense approach to teaching generally came from the right wing of the profession:

> I have considerable sympathy for Mr Eggar's decision. There has been far too much lengthy, over-elaborate advice from so-called curriculum experts who've never taught 3C on a wet Thursday afternoon. (Peter Smith, General Secretary of the Assistant Masters and Mistresses Association, quoted in *The Daily Mail,* 15.06.91)

> Even then [NATE] were becoming a pressure group, rather than a society of people interested in the teaching of English. The teaching of reading, spelling, punctuation and grammar was decried. They seemed to be more dedicated in those days to the Left-wing indoctrination of children, of implanting their political ideology, than actual teaching. Formal and traditional methods were pushed aside with a certain amount of contempt. They were even advocating that the traditional classroom, with desks and a blackboard, should disappear altogether. (Peter Bullock, former Head of English at King Edward VI Grammar School, Stratford-upon-Avon and a member of the National Association for the Teaching of English in the 1960s, *Mail on Sunday,* 31.01.93)

Attacks on LEA educational advisers and advisory teachers, professional bodies such as the National Association for the Teaching of English, university professors and prominent members of the government's own committees, such as Brian Cox of Manchester University (Chair of English 5–16 Working Group) or Ron Carter of Nottingham University (National Co-ordinator of the LINC project) all portrayed educationalists as either ridiculous or dangerous:

> If [the LINC Report] were widely available for public discussion, its smarmy modernism, its desolating banality of thought and phrase, and its sub-scientific jargon…would invite widespread ridicule… There is every reason to believe that the report reflects the ineradicable prejudice of large swathes of the teaching profession… In the wake of this fiasco there must be a new look at the

institutes of education who produce this sort of thing by the yard. Who staffs them? How much do they cost? What purpose do they serve? The time may well have come to deconstruct them altogether. (*Daily Telegraph*, editorial, 28.06.91)

Mr Eggar said the way in which the Government's straight-forward idea to improve grammar teaching had been 'captured' by the trendies, turning it into an 'abstract argument between educational theorists' was a salutary lesson. 'It ends up with the basics not being taught to children and with under-expectation of what children can achieve.' (*Daily Mail*, 26.06.91)

The Government must halt the continued march of trendy self-interested ideologues and sundry experts. Indeed, it should support those who believe that education is about the pursuit of excellence in all things. Schools are for educating children. They are not for using children in insidious ideological experiments aimed at creating a new socialist nirvana. (Ray Honeyford, ex-headteacher, author of 'Why are our schools still run by cranks?', *Daily Mail*, 26.06.91)

Enlightened ideas of educational empowerment were depicted as subversive:

I am reliably informed that of the 25 members of this committee [the LINC project], no fewer than 21 belong to an ideological pressure group [NATE] bent on destroying the concept of correctness in language and literature. An independent expert has been quoted as saying: 'A lot of them believe teaching children standard English and grammar is an oppression of the working class. They aim to reshape English on multi-cultural, anti-racist, and anti-sexist lines.' (*Daily Mail*, 26.06.91)

Thus, despite an official rhetoric of educational citizenship during the period of research for this book (1988–93), the reality was quite different. Legislation imposed a knowledge-based curriculum at odds with educational citizenship. Secretaries of State for Education, particularly Kenneth Clarke, took further measures to quarantine the National Curriculum from contemporary society (the History syllabus was to end in 1945; the Music syllabus was to concentrate on the appreciation of classical scores rather than the creation of tunes in contemporary idioms). Government campaigns and the reports of carefully-selected placemen (Woodhead, Rose and Robin 1992) insistently promulgated didactic teaching styles. Media manipulation created a parental atmosphere of suspicion of the teaching profession. Suggestions of educational change consistent with a concept of educational citizenship were either ridiculed as the numskull brainstorms of madcap boffins in educational ivory towers (*The Sun* approach) or exposed as anarchist plots to destabilise society hatched by devious moles, sleepers and agents-in-place who had infiltrated the educational service in a conspiracy spanning three decades (*The Daily Mail* approach). The cumulative effect of this onslaught was to disempower and silence teachers, a direct consequence of which was the disempowerment and silencing of their pupils. There is no climate of empowerment and voicing (other than for the traditional stakeholders of power) when the 'aim to reshape English on multi-cultural, anti-racist, and anti-sexist lines' is seen as a subversive threat and ridiculed by the Prime Minister in her speech to the Conservative Party Conference.

During my fieldwork research data were gathered not only in one UK local educational authority but during attendance at five national annual educational conferences and nineteen regional meetings (South-West of England). These data provide evidence that suggests that since the late 1980s the three factors of dependent learning (indoctrination via the suppression of a critical disposition, the social and moral isolation of the curriculum, and the denial to pupils of the opportunity to practise the rights and responsibilities of global citizenship) have become more firmly entrenched in the state-maintained schools of the United Kingdom as a direct result of government education policies, despite the misgivings and resistance of many teachers.

THE REALITY OF DISEMPOWERMENT

During the five years of fieldwork research schools became more publicly accountable. The 1988 Educational Reform Act required schools to publish a range of information, including examination results, levels of pupil attendance, the allocation of scale points for teachers' salaries, the number of post-16 pupils located in jobs or further education, and also to hold an annual meeting at which members of the public could question school policy. Since 1992 league tables of LEA and individual school performance have been published in the national press, and there have been plans to publish the examination results of individual departments. The previously confidential reports of the Inspectorate on particular schools, and departments within them, entered the public domain. In a more generous political climate these could have been regarded as progressive changes intended to integrate the school more fully with the community, to have an open-door policy and to provide, rightfully, a fuller range of information to parents and the general public.

However, in the climate of distrust of the teaching profession promulgated by some politicians and journalists, the information put out by schools almost immediately became used for comparative purposes. With devolved funding directly linked to the number on the school roll and government exhortations to parents to shop around for the best school for their children, and at a time when public services were being subjected to scrutiny based upon criteria for industrial success (via the various Citizens' Charters and the government drive for performance-related pay in the nationalised caring services such as health and education), comparison inevitably became competitive. Schools were encouraged by government to became more business-modelled, aware of public image and 'product marketing'. In 1988, of the 31 secondary schools in the study LEA, only two offered scale posts for Press Officers. By 1994, all did. School prospectuses became glossy brochures. Some secondary schools in the study LEA developed travelling roadshows, slick with audio-visual aids, which toured local primary schools in an attempt to persuade prospective parents and pupils to choose them. Public areas of secondary schools were given a more glamorous façade and parental tours, guided by members of the senior management team, were designed to show the school to best advantage.

A closer study of these changes reveals a perpetuation of the well- intentioned rhetoric referred to above at international level, mirrored at regional level. In a survey of the study LEA's 31 secondary school prospectuses (in 1993), inconsistencies between rhetoric and reality are evident. All of them made claims consistent with the Princesses and Princes image of the ends of secondary schooling with mission statements or school aims such as the following three examples taken at random from the 31 prospectuses:

> Pupils have the opportunity to develop and display their own individual personality.

> Pupils are encouraged to think for themselves and work independently, as well as to work collaboratively with others as part of a team.

> To ensure that pupils develop their individual intellectual skills to the highest level of which they are capable, by providing a lively and enthusiastic atmosphere in which a love of learning and a questioning approach to life may be stimulated.

Yet all the prospectuses, to varying degrees, also promoted a Drudges and Frogs view of the means of achieving these aims. Every prospectus, despite its claims to nourish individuality, had a section dealing with the obligatory uniformity of a school dress code. The intended audience for each prospectus was invariably the prospective parent, not one prospectus was written to the prospective pupil. There were also many inconsistencies between a promise to promote a faculty for critical reflection on society and a commitment to assimilation into the existing order. The following quotes come from the same three prospectuses as the quotes above:

> It is our aim to encourage all pupils to appreciate the values society respects and to develop a sound character.

> The school sees it as a principal duty to ensure that pupils achieve the maximum possible success in public examinations. This is achieved within a framework of firm discipline and an ordered working environment in which we insist on the highest standards of work and behaviour.

> The behaviour of pupils in uniform but out of school reflects directly on the School as much as the pupils themselves. The staff take a serious view of any pupil bringing the name of the School into disrepute.

> Earrings and jewellery are unsuitable for school wear and must not be worn. We ask parents to cooperate by discouraging their children from wearing these items.

Thus a tortuous balancing act between a Princesses and Princes vision of the citizen-pupil and a Drudges and Frogs vision of the serf-pupil institutional climate intended to achieve this development. No phrase can capture this sense of conspiratorial entrapment more devastatingly than: 'We ask parents to cooperate by discouraging their children...'

A further tectonic friction between the grinding plates of rhetoric and reality was seen in the public and private areas of all the schools visited. The following cosmetic touches, intended for the adult visitor, were noted: new school logos, visitors' parking spaces, a carpeted reception area, soft chairs and furnishings in waiting areas, potted plants, coffee percolators in reception areas for the use of the adult public, attractive display stands featuring photographs of pupils' excursions and activities (theatre trips, school camps, cultural exchanges, all depicting happy pupils collaborating in active harmony), the executive suite of secretarial staff and headteacher's office, the power-dressed headteacher, the body-contact of handshakes. This can be contrasted with a pupil-eye view: uniform, a register of attendance taken every 50 minutes throughout the day, pupils locked out of classrooms apart from lesson times, no-go areas during break times, different entrances and exits for pupils and members of the public. There were also examples of how teachers are victims of the institutional pecking-order: teachers locked out of the photocopying room, better classroom facilities for heads of department than other teachers, the headteacher's use of first names but staff referring to her by title or surname, the insistence on ties for male teachers and the stipulation that female teachers should not wear trousers, named car parking spaces for senior staff. The hierarchy of school-workers other than pupils was also plain: different staff rooms for teachers and catering and caretaking employees, cleaning staff referred to by first names but responding by surnames to teaching staff, only teachers included in group photographs of the staff or invited to end-of-term cheese and wine parties.

To see more clearly what lay beneath the adult rhetoric of educational entitlement as evidenced in international declarations, government publications, LEA policy documents, school prospectuses and carefully controlled school tours for prospective parents, lessons were observed in 31 (100%) of the secondary schools and 45 (20%) of the primary schools between April 1990 and April 1993. The purpose of these observations, conducted in each of the four Keystages of the National Curriculum, was to gather evidence as to how and to what extent the Princesses and Princes aims of a school, as promoted in its prospectus, were explicitly pursued through the curriculum. What was the rhetoric, what was the reality?

Research to date has shown that in the secondary sector, whatever the well-intentioned aims expressed in the school prospectus, the predominant teaching style was a didactic presentation of factual information. There was very little collaborative groupwork and what there was was poorly structured. There was little or no active research. 'Discussion' was invariably teacher-led question-and-answer on a right or wrong basis. Pupils did not design their own tasks and were not involved in the assessment of their own work. Lesson content was hardly ever related to the experience or interests of the class, to the wider social world or to knowledge in other subjects. It existed without external relevance. There was little or no community interaction or movement from the classroom to the surrounding environment. The purpose of pupils' work was never intrinsic but only preparation for public examination. To this end, the audience for all work was always negatively critical: teacher or examiner as marker.

The tracking of pupils during a curricular week corroborated earlier findings that practices likely to develop the characteristics of both education and citizenship are not common in the secondary sector. During the 3000 minutes of tracking time which were observed at Keystages 3 and 4, only 6 per cent of the time involved collaborative groupwork. For 68 per cent of lessontime pupils worked individually on comprehension exercises or note making. Only during 2 per cent of lessontime were pupils asked to conduct their own research. Lesson structures appeared to discriminate against the equal involvement of girls in discussion, with boys three times more likely to speak voluntarily or be asked to speak by the teacher. (In one lesson, the most extreme example, boys spoke 67 times, girls 4 times). Discussion was exclusively limited to information verification rather than social or moral debate. In 274 minutes of 'class discussion', one of the tracked pupils (a girl) contributed for only five seconds. Continuity between lessons, either of the same or different subjects, was not evident. After note making, the largest body of time was spent moving from one lesson to the next – 22 per cent of curriculum time. There was no evidence that any of the aims of the schools, as advertised in their prospectuses, were planned into lessons.

When asked, not one teacher or pupil could quote any of the school aims.

Starkey's belief that 'The school is no longer the information-rich action-poor isolated institution that Torsten Husen described' (1991, p.16) is not borne out by the research to date. The visited schools were not social microcosms of liberal democracy. They were structured as totalitarian regimes and Havel's comment on such regimes is directly pertinent: 'Between the aims of the system and the aims of life is a yawning abyss: while life, in its essence, moves towards plurality, diversity, independent self-constitution and self-organisation, in short towards the fulfilment of its own freedom, the system demands conformity, uniformity and discipline' (1986, pp.43–44).

It was concluded that the factors regarded as most detrimental to the development of a school committed to educational citizenship were the factors most typical of the LEA's secondary schools:

1. The notion of learning based on content knowledge rather than the promotion of critical faculties which results in the division of the curriculum into discrete subjects and, therefore, the division of the daily timetable into short, uniform periods. This compartmentalisation effectively prevents any possibility of an holistic education.

2.   A view of the pupil population as a number of individuals that are best isolated from each other by grouping systems, by a hierarchical view of knowledge appropriate to different groupings, by the attempt to impose silence during lessons, by the denigration of collaborative groupwork as either an easy option or a form of cheating, by a system that frequently imposes timed, individual examinations and by a sense of individual competition rather than group co-operation.

3.   By a pedagogy that has a lesson content unrelated to the communities and environments of the real world, a reliance on teacher-disseminated texts (blackboard notes, videos, books, worksheets, software) as the source of authority of knowledge rather than pupil research, no sense of audience for the work and an almost exclusive reliance on traditional manuscripts as the sole means of presentation.

The findings of the illuminative evaluation fieldwork research suggest that the conventional curriculum and timetable offer few, if any, opportunities for personal empowerment – despite the claims of schools, in their stated aims, that attributes of empowerment are encouraged. The isolation of the pupil from her peers, aggrandised by her institutional powerlessness, is detrimental to the development either of social relationships or any sense of a holistic learning experience. The system casts the individual into a void where making fulfilling connections with other people or between various aspects of the curriculum is almost impossible. It is a Kafkaesque climate, not of education but of alienation.

The normal classroom style that was observed was characterised by pupils working individually on short micro-activities that were specified by the teacher. This teaching and learning style was not universally approved by teachers but was commonly adopted as it was regarded as an expedient means of presenting the National Curriculum. A high majority of the teachers inter- viewed over the five years of the study expressed strong ideological and pragmatic reservations about the contemporary constitution of a liberal ed- ucation. Indeed, teachers were keen to experiment and libertarian classroom projects were undertaken in all of the 31 secondary schools between 1989 and 1993. Each of these projects lasted between 6 and 12 weeks, during which time pupils worked in small collaborative groups of their own choice to research a topic of the group's choosing. The research was active and pupils spent much time outside the classroom, often moving into the local environment and community. A range of computer and audio-visual technology was used by the pupils and live presentations of groups' work were made to community audiences. Pupils decided whether any assessment should be made of their work, who should make an assessment and upon what criteria assessment should be based. Essentially, pupils aged 11–16 were encouraged to take the responsibility to study whatever they wanted, however they wanted, with whoever they wanted, for periods of up to a whole term, within particular subjects or lessons. These independent learning projects were overtly intended to promote a learning atmosphere and environment in which individual children could empower themselves along the lines suggested by the definition of the global citizen.

The first of the five principal findings of the five years of action research (46 half- or full-term projects in all the 31 secondary schools in the study LEA) is unsurprising:

1. Independent learning projects (despite the rhetoric of international, national, local and parochial publications which suggest that the style of independent learning is the pedagogical norm) were a great novelty to staff and pupils.

What was less predictable were the other four principal findings:

2. The standard of work improved.

3. Both staff and pupils responded enthusiastically and enjoyed working in this way.

4. They found the projects fulfilling because they were demanding.

5. They would like to repeat the experience.

Data were collected in a variety of ways from a variety of sources within the research partnership. The vast majority of those involved in independent learning projects, and those who observed them, found them to be stimulating and educationally effective in the domains of cognitive and affective development. The opportunities enjoyed by pupils for the development of a critical disposition, for personal autonomy within a vision of community, for the opportunity to discuss their own involvement in topical social and moral issues and to advance the reflexive project of the self indicate that independent learning is a convincing pedagogy for the promotion of personal empowerment and preparation for citizenship in the third millennium.

Much data on each of the 12 factors were gathered. Some dominant themes are the difficulties and rewards of collaborative groupwork, problems of time management, the personal engagement that pupils felt with the topic they chose to study, the technological literacy, dexterity and creativity pupils displayed in presenting their work via video, audio and computer technology and the ingenuity that pupils showed in active research within the environment and working with members of the community (a group of 14-year-olds at one school arranged for their class to be flown around the coastline in an RAF aeroplane so that they could video-record sewage outflows before a tour of a local sewage works and a meeting with the Chair of the District Council and representatives of the regional water company). One of the most impressive findings was that, given a free choice of topic, the majority of collaborative groups (73%) chose to investigate a social issue.

Analysis of the pupils' end-of-project evaluations and responses to open-ended questionnaires clearly shows that they felt that they had developed qualities of global citizenship. Teachers too expressed enthusiasm for independent learning as a means of cultivating personal and social skills but some had reservations as to the amount of mandatory syllabus content that could be covered in this way. A large majority of pupils felt that they had worked more industriously than in other lessons and that the work had been demanding and stimulating. This was a view shared by most teachers. Many commented that the quality of the work produced by pupils was of a higher standard than usual.

Common to successful independent learning projects was an appropriate level of support for teachers and pupils after they had accepted the responsibility in undertaking a project. By the end of the control phase of the intervention research it was clear that the greatest support to teachers and pupils was an understanding of the purpose of the 12 factors of independent learning in relation to personal empowerment and global citizenship. This support was considerably strengthened when that understanding was shared with, and approved by, a school's senior management team, parents, governors and LEA officials. Independent learning projects offered an agreed framework for the negotiation of changes to the normal power structure of the classroom so that during the transition from an authoritarian to a libertarian style of learning, both teachers and pupils felt supported, confident and proactive. In effect, the projects acted to bridge the divide between an invested and a divested system of power.

TRANSFORMING POWER RELATIONSHIPS

The nature of invested power

An invested power system is hierarchical, linear and competitive. All traditional Western institutions conform to this model – from the forces, to commerce and industry, to economic trading and banking, to education, to the processes of Parliamentary government itself. It is a system that rewards individual success, the rewards being social prestige and economic status. Examples of social prestige are type of job and promotion within its structure, membership of certain clubs and forms of public recognition such as the honours system. Economic status is evinced in salary, bonuses, share options and the attendant conspicuous consumption associated with large amounts of personal money: type and number of cars, clothing, holidays, houses owned, private education and health care. These two markers are not distinct – for instance a partnership, a directorship or becoming a shareholder all suggest both social prestige and economic status.

The membership processes of invested power are steeped in ritual: initiation ceremonies, arcane rules, curious dress codes, terms of address. This is true of the child's first day of school, her confirmation within a range of world religions, her becoming a teenager, entering university, taking a position in a firm.

It is a membership process that believes in apprenticeship: it seeks to absorb the next generation into its monolithic structure from an early age. Examples of this apprenticeship aspect of invested power are often seen in operation in schools: School Councils, Head Girls and Head Boys, Team Captains, prefects, monitors of various kinds, pupil librarians, pupils helping in the tuck shop. An extension of invested power is offered to the selected neophytes of the next generation who are considered most likely to consolidate the *status quo*. Essentially, schools with an invested power structure have an autarchic view of the socialisation role of education (Steutel 1991).

Invested power has a form of language of its own, a language that obscures processes, that sanitises, that depersonalises: citizens are not killed, there is collateral damage; lies are not told, there is economy of the truth; people's jobs are not sacrificed to a political ideology of privatisation but are subject to the exciting challenge of market forces. Children are referred to as the point-of-delivery consumer in the educational process. It is a language of suave intimidation impelled by a determination to protect its power. To this end, it denigrates the language of others and seeks to deny them their own voice by insisting on monolinguism, by promoting Standard English and Received Pronunciation as the spoken code of power, by deriding accent as a class indicator or a source of belittling ethnic or regional humour, by simply not allowing people such as pupils to talk at all. In these ways the silenced are prevented from finding their own forms of voicing.

The holders of invested power are loathe to experiment in the transfer of power for the way in which these stakeholders define the success of their selves is inextricably bound up with the amount of invested power that they maintain. To share is to diminish the power. The attraction of invested power, and its main characteristic, is that it is exclusive to an élite minority. Invested power obeys the law of centripetal force, it draws to the centre.

Even when there is an undeniable and successful transfer of power (change of government via national elections, the appointment of a new headteacher, the rites of passage of the maturational process that progressively bestows increased responsibilities upon the child as she metamorphosises to young adult), it is only the balance rather than the nature of invested power itself that is changed – there may sometimes be new holders of the old power but the system of invested power is not compromised, in fact it is protected and perpetuated.

The stakeholders of invested power in the UK are conservative government, the right wing establishment and the white upper and middle classes.

The nature of divested power

Divested power is characterised by being corporate and distributive in that it diffuses and gives to the periphery with an organic, regenerative and dynamic view of society that regards change as constant and celebrates diversity. It is the form of power that fits most closely with the definition of the global citizen, with educational citizenship and the actual practice shown in successful independent learning projects.

Divested power is predicated upon an ethical rather than an economic democracy, it is non-hierarchical and believes in equality of status based upon participation in citizenship. Its citizens envisage society as changing, adapting, growing and transforming and are excited, not threatened, by this flux. Its membership processes are wide and open and show no discrimination, encouraging the expression of an individual's multi-faceted personality. Society is pictured as an infinite number of interdependent and interactive collaborative and co-operative communities.

The language of divested power is human rather than technocratic. Emphasising a shared and supported responsibility, it is non-adversarial – conversation and discussion rather than point-scoring and argument. It has no tone of culpability, it strives to understand the other person's point of view. It is the language of arbitration and negotiation rather than that of command and certainty. Its register is that of the ethical dialectic of relativism rather than the moral absolutism of right and wrong, good and bad, and questions, caution and doubt are regarded as strengths not weaknesses. It is a language rich in the expression and promotion of its dialects and accents. It is the language of voicing.

The stakeholders of divested power are every citizen, including the holders of invested power, for the transformation, rather than the transfer, of power frees them as much as anybody else. The transformation of power changes the nature, not just the balance, of power. The nature of the power is transformed from invested to divested power but the old holders of invested power are not disenfranchised: they are sharers in divested power. A topical example of this is the situation in South Africa. President Mandela wanted not merely a transfer of the invested power of the National Party but a transformation of that power so that no sociopolitical faction, including the white minority, would feel dispossessed. When the final election results showed that the ANC had taken 62.7 per cent of the vote, Mandela expressed his gladness that he had *not* won the extra 4 per cent that would have given his party the power to rewrite the Constitution alone. Now all the other parties must be involved. Mandela clearly wanted not merely a transfer of the National Party's invested power but a transformation of the nature of that power to the harmony of divested power. This transformation can be compared with the first-past-the-post electoral system of the UK in which, for most of this century, the two principal political parties have simply transferred, temporarily, the invested power between them rather than consider the possibilities of transformation that proportional voting and coalition might afford.

The transfer and the transformation of power in educational establishments

As the development of global citizenship will require a change from an invested power system to a divested power system, so independent learning projects, intended as microcosms of the macrocosm, necessitated a change from the invested power system of the typical classroom to the divested power system of collaborative and co-operative working. This change was not a crude matter of 'letting the kids do whatever they wanted'. This would have meant a direct transfer of invested power from teacher to pupils – the simple libertarianism of Summerhill or the ill-fated free schools of the 1960s and 1970s. Early and unsophisticated attempts at independent learning during the circumspection phase of the research spiral, and an analysis during the literature search of the reasons for the failure of libertarian experiments in the free and state schools, led to certain tentative conclusions about such a transfer of invested power.

First, it is virtually impossible for a teacher within the UK state system to transfer her invested power to a class and then support the pupils as they adapt to the change. The whole style and structure of state education precludes this. But even if it were attempted, it seems unlikely that it could be achieved because the nature of invested power is based upon a hierarchy in which the many obey a singular representative of invested authority. The chain of command may be long (a constitutional monarchy in which, theoretically, every member of the state is ultimately subject to royal decree) or direct (class to teacher) but the principle of the singular authority of invested power invariably applies. Therefore, the teacher, in simply abandoning her power, is attempting to distribute among the many something that is indivisible. For an effective transfer of invested power it would need one pupil to take on the teacher's role, but research observation suggested that in practical terms this does not happen for the hierarchical essence of invested power is no longer in place: the pupil does not have the singular authority, reinforced by an institutional hinterland, that is necessary to impose an invested power system upon her peers. Classroom observation revealed a common tendency, when a teacher attempted a transfer of invested power from herself to her class, for each pupil to become the leader of a community of one – herself. It was concluded that the attempted transfer of invested power from a hierarchy to a group of peers is likely to lead to anarchy (a point recognised and regarded positively by teachers and pupils involved in libertarian educational experiments in the 1970s (Shotton 1993)).

Second, the apparent transfer of invested power is often an illusion. Observation of the dynamics of collaborative groups of pupils showed that some groups organised themselves as microcosmic invested power hierarchies with group leaders reporting to the teacher if group members were not fulfilling their tasks. All that had happened in such cases was that some pupils (the 'collaborative' group leaders) had been subsumed into a lower level of the existing class-teacher chain of command. The result for the invested power base is a strengthening of the *status quo*.

Third, there may be a limited and temporary transfer of power to groups of pupils but without the support they need to succeed. The group 'fails', their dependence upon the teacher is re-established and once again the invested power of the familiar class-teacher relationship is reinforced.

The final conclusion was that the transfer of invested power was not a relevant issue to independent learning projects because the nature of invested power is antagonistic to the development of global citizenship. What is needed to enable pupils to empower themselves is not a transfer of invested power but for a transformation of power to a form of divested power.

Independent learning as a mechanism for the transformation of power

If a state educational system is structured as a model of invested power, the opportunities for pupils to use the resource of their education to empower themselves are likely to be few. The fieldwork research showed that educational institutions of invested power are unlikely to structure the curriculum and the timetable to make provision for the collaborative and co-operative practices associated with the divested power of independent learning projects. However, when school managers have attempted to break from the predominant invested power system of state education they have been vilified (Wright 1989; Shotton 1993). If attempts to introduce libertarian practices failed in the liberal climate of the 1960s and 1970s, what chance is there in the 1990s?

Whilst many would agree with Shotton (1993) that Conservative government has sought to strengthen its centralised power over state schools, it can be argued that its approach has been inconsistent (seven different Ministers for Education since 1979 have all brought different emphases to the job) and some of its measures have had unintended effects so that it is also possible to sketch a scenario in which individual schools are in a stronger position than ever before to develop as empowering institutions. The clumsy consumerism of the Parents' Charter does offer the opportunity for parents to be more engaged in, and more critical of, educational opportunities at a local level and to feel they have a decision-making role to play in the neighbourhood school. Local management of schools and the erosion of the stature of local educational authorities has placed more responsibility, but also greater freedom, in the hands of head-teachers and heads of department. Changes in the legal responsibilities of governing bodies and different procedures for their election and constitution have meant that the role of governor is no longer a comfortable sinecure for the traditional holders of invested power.

All of these changes, generally believed by left-wing commentators to have been intended to make schools directly accountable to the local community and so to check any libertarian degeneration, have actually led to the greater autonomy of schools and their communities to institute libertarian policies of educational citizenship, transform their management structures to a model of divested power and unite with similar communities in articulate campaigns to protect or extend their independence. Examples that this is increasingly happening were the nation-wide campaigns against National Curriculum Tests at 14 in 1993, for universal nursery education in 1994 and against proposed cuts in government funding in 1995. (This is particularly interesting in view of Shotton's belief that many of the embryonic libertarian state schools succumbed to external pressures because they were isolated and could not draw upon any support network).

Analysis suggests that condemnation of state and free schools that attempted to introduce a system of divested power in the 1960s and 1970s was not based upon ideological grounds (for most state schools continue to embrace the *rhetoric* of personal empowerment and educational citizenship) but upon practical perceptions of an appropriate libertarian pedagogy. It is the practice, not the philosophy, of libertarianism that has been the stumbling block, a point made by the only free school teacher to write a book about free schooling: 'If the free schools preliminary pronouncements have little indication of what free schools were actually going to do when they got started, description of what happened once they were established showed that they were floundering – in some cases badly' (Wright 1989, p.107).

Thus it may be that the route to developing schools as empowering institutions of educational citizenship is via practice that is effective in implementing libertarian aims but is also acceptable to a conservative audience of parents, media and educational officialdom.

The series of independent learning projects that are described in this book took place in a conservative, rural shire county in the south-west of the United Kingdom between 1989–1992, a period during which the 'chalk and talk, back to basics' lobby was particularly vociferous. The findings of the fieldwork research in the study LEA demonstrate that independent learning, as an effective pedagogy of libertarian education, was well-regarded by pupils, teachers, parents and other observers, including LEA advisers and inspectors. The independent learning projects that were perceived by participants and observers as successful were those that achieved a transformation of power, alienating neither the teachers nor the pupils, so that the teachers felt they had a valuable role to play within the co-operative group and the pupils were supported as they explored their new responsibilities.

Before independent learning projects were launched in schools, meetings were held with pupils, teachers, senior management teams, governors and parents. At these meetings the factors of independent learning were clearly and directly related to the rhetoric of educational citizenship as promulgated in the schools' prospectuses and in DFE documentation. For instance, the text of English in the National Curriculum was trawled for the following phrases, all of which have a connection with one or more of the factors of independent learning: 'group activity, informal, continuous and incidental assessment, arguing and persuading, supporting of others, working in groups of different sizes, beyond the confines of the school, activity related to the local community, work with adults, undertake real transactions, planned outcomes, presentations, collaborate on assignments, problem-solving, communicate' (Stock 1990, p.3).

In effect, a platform of adult support for an independent learning project was established by 'legitimating' the concept of educational citizenship and the pedagogy of independent learning via references to school-produced and DFE texts as well as other literature. Whilst such an approach may be considered to lack the crusading idealism of the founders of the Free School movement, experience in the study LEA has shown that this pragmatic introduction has been expedient in not alienating the stakeholders of invested power before the commencement of an independent learning project clearly intended to bring about, even if only temporarily, a transformation to divested power.

A clear understanding of the 12 factors of independent learning by all who might be involved in an independent learning project, as participants or observers, was essential to this strategy.

Closing the gap between intention and execution

As has been stated, it was during the late 1980s and early 1990s that independent learning projects took place, successfully and publicly, throughout a conservative, rural shire county. The success of these libertarian initiatives in a transformation to a divested power system was based upon three critical features:

- creating or strengthening a non-hierarchial partnership between parents, pupils and teachers
- exploiting the published rhetoric of empowerment and citizenship
- instituting an effective pedagogy (of independent learning) to realise that rhetoric.

Schools and other educational institutions must be honest in examining their actual practices and policies in the light of the philosophic rhetoric promulgated in their aims. A school's aims must be apparent in its activities if it is to claim that it is fulfilling them. Too often, enlightened aims disappear under the exigencies of day-to-day expediency. I have sought to argue that the disparity between intention and execution – between rhetoric and reality – is caused primarily by a state educational system of invested power that has a content-laden, rather than a child-centred, view of education, a view exemplified by the National Curriculum. Such a view leads to a didactic presentation of the curriculum that precludes the development of the qualities of citizenship that empower not just the individual but the collaborative and co-operative groups to which every individual belongs.

Typical features of the didactic presentation of a content-laden curriculum are: subject specialism requiring discrete lessons in different rooms, the division of the timetable into short, unconnected lessons, the grouping of pupils in such a way that alienates them from peer contact and support and a lesson structure that discourages groupwork, talk, research and activity in favour of silent, individual short tasks usually associated with a worksheet distributed by the teacher. No matter how well-intentioned are the school managers, the underlying ethos of such schools – as experienced by the pupils – is competitive, untrusting and dictatorial.

The findings of an extended fieldwork study suggest that there are ways of stimulating global citizenship even within the strictures of the National Curriculum. The 12 factors of independent learning were identified to contribute to such development. Without undertaking a longitudinal study of daunting complexity, it is not possible to show that pupils educated as global citizens become more active citizens in their adult life. What it is believed that the research does illustrate, however, is that a pedagogy of independent learning, impelled by the definition of global citizenship, is more likely to promote a learning ethos of educational citizenship (Princesses and Princes) than the typical practice in schools of the didactic presentation of a content-laden curriculum (Drudges and Frogs).

There is an undeniable rhetoric of educational empowerment and global citizenship that can be capitalised upon to transform schools to divested systems of power and so to provide a climate of opportunity for pupils to empower themselves as the citizens of a global future. Those involved in education may consider moving forward to greet these new ideas rather than remaining imprisoned in the institutional bunker of invested power, and moving forwards with arms extended in welcome rather than raised in surrender. Goethe wrote – and his observation applies to international, national, local and school government – that 'That government is best that teaches us to govern ourselves'. Such government, at whatever level, requires the transformation of power relationships and the emergence of new understandings of the nature and purpose of power appropriate to the global citizenry of the third millennium:

> We declare our firm belief in the principles enunciated in the Universal Declaration of Human Rights that everyone has the right to education; that education shall be directed to the full development of human personality and to the strengthening of respect for human rights and fundamental freedoms. It shall promote understanding, tolerance and friendship among the nations, racial or religious groups and shall further the activities for the maintenance of peace. (Mandela 1986, p.38)

Photocopy and printed copy of Natalie's open evaluation

Cesspit Siege A Personal View

It was two weeks into the new term. The date was the 24th September 1991. Our video projects were just beginning. Groups had been sorted out.

In my group were Sophie, Sarah, Tamsyn and I. We decided to do our project on sewage.

One week before the 24th, Rhys Griffiths and Peter Zaleck had given us an insight on what we had to produce. We were also shown how to edit and mix. It looked quite hard.

On the 1st October our groups did some still photographs. We merged one picture into another but these were not used for the end product. We also went out and used the video camera so we got used to it.

We chose our backing music on the 2nd October. We decided on the "Love Theme from Twin Peaks." It is a slow and sad but serious song.

Tuesday 15th October Sarah, Tamsyn and I went down to the Cober valley to film. We filmed a little pipe running into the river and the tranquil scenery trying to show the comparison. Unfortunately, these pictures weren't used either.

Mrs Jones, who is a counciller came in on the 30th October to talk about sewage. Sarah recorded her speaking. We used up a whole tape!

On the 5th and 6th of November we watched an Equinox video on Human waste. Some parts were disgusting but all the same it was interesting to watch. I learnt quite a lot.

We wrote to some companies on the 12th

241

November requesting information on sewage and the treatment of sewage. We got some replies on the 19th. We used the information to do some work for our magazine.

The 21st November was a very exciting day for most of the English group, The reason for this being that we were going flying. We were ferried to Culdrose gate where we were met by a bus. We were taken to 860 squadron where we met the pilots and were given a briefing. There were two groups. The first group were up for approximately 45 minutes. I was in group two. We went up and flew around the coast. We got some good shots. It was really good.

Our magazine was shaping up nicely towards the last days of November. In the beginning of December we started to plan our live presentation. Our magazine was just about complete. All our replies to the companies were sent off. All that was left to do was the video!

We were a bit worried that the video was not going to be ready.

Sarah and I did the computer graphics on the computer and did the credits as well but These were lost as somebody took the disk!

The end of term came too quickly. The live presentation was ready but the video wa not ready.

At the beginning of Spring Term '92 we made our video. It was a bit rushed but it was completed.

We did our live presentation and showed our video. It was all finished.

I learned a lot from making the video. My thoughts before were that it would be easy. Now completed, I think that it is very hard to make a video, without full concentration and dedication.

Cesspit Siege: A Personal View

It was two weeks into the new term. The date was the 24th September 1991. Our video [sic] projects were just beginning. Groups had been sorted out. (*HOW?*)

In my group were Sophie, Sarah, Tamsyn and I. We decided to do our project on sewage. (*WHY?*)

One week before the 24th, Rhys Griffiths and Tony Stone had given us insight on what we had to produce. (*WHAT INSIGHT?*) We were also shown how to edit and mix. It looked quite hard. (*WHY?*)

On the 1st October our group did some still photographs. We merged one picture into another but these were not used for the end product. (*WHY NOT?*) We also went out and used the video camera so we got used to it. (*WHERE TO?*)

We chose our backing music on the 2nd October. (*HOW?*) We decided on the 'Love Theme for Twin Peaks'. It is a slow and sad but serious song.

Tuesday 15th October Sarah, Tamsyn and I went down to the Timor Valley to film. We filmed a little pipe running into the river and the tranquil scenery trying to show the comparison. Unfortunatly, these pictures were'nt used either. (*WHY?*)

Mrs Yanes, who is a councillor came in on the 30th October to talk about sewage. (*WHO INVITED HER?*) Sarah recorded her speaking. We used up a whole tape!

On the 5th and 6th of November we watched an Equinox video on Human waste. (*CHOSEN BY?*) Some parts were disgusting but all the same it was interesting to watch. I learnt quite a lot. (*SUCH AS?*)

We wrote to some companies (*WHICH?*) on the 12th November requesting information on sewage and the treatment of sewage. We got some replies on the 19th. We used the information to do some work for our magazine. (*WHAT WORK?*)

The 21st November was a big day for most of the English group, the reason for this being that we were going flying. (*WHO ARRANGED THIS?*) We were ferried to the RNAS gate where we were met by a bus. We were taken to 850 squadron where we met the pilots and were given a briefing. There were two groups. The first group were up for approximately 45 minutes. I was in group two. We went up and flew around the coast. We got some good shots. It was really good. (*IN WHAT WAY?*)

Our magazine was shaping up nicely towards the last days of November. (*DETAILS?*) In the beginning of December we started to plan our live presentation. (*DETAILS?*) Our magazine was just about complete. All our replies to the companies were sent off. All that was left to do was the video!

We were a bit worried that the video was not going to be ready.

Sarah and I did the computer graphics on the computer and did the credits as well. These were lost as somebody took the disc! (*WHO?*)

The end of time term came too quickly. The live presentation was ready but the video was not ready.

At the beginning of Spring Term '92 we made our video. It was a bit rushed but it was completed.

We did our live presentation and showed our video. It was all finished.

I learned a lot from making the video. My thoughts before were that it would be easy. Now completed, I think that it is very hard to make a video, without full concentration and dedication.

Photocopy and printed copy of
Joanne's open evaluation

"Murder Or Mercy?"
By 'The Black Ferries"

At the beggining of the term, we were set a project to do. It involved using various mixers, video cameras, computers, electric organs, microphones and televisions. We had to get into groups and choose a subject to do a project on. The end result had to be a video, a Magazine, a live presentation, an individual Diary or log produced by each one member of the group and a literary review.

Cheryl Skeggs, Antony Reed, Emma Thornton, Emma Bolitho and I formed our group which is called "The Black Ferries", I don't know why we called it that name, It's original I suppose! First of all, we were going to do our project on Aids, but we decided that it was too strong a subject and that it would take too long to finish it. We wanted to do some-thing serious, so we decided to study animal cruelty.

In the first lesson we were given journals so that we could write down any notes and information which we needed. To start off with, everybody in the group wrote a diary in every English lesson about what they did but as time went on, most of us forgot about writing it up.

On Tuesdays, Rhys Griffiths and Peter Zallick came; Rhys came one week and Peter came the next. They helped us with the video work and they supplied all of the equipment we needed for the video. Mr Sykes also came into the lesson sometimes. In the first lesson with Peter and Rhys, mr Sykes showed our group how to use the school video camera and Rhys Griffiths showed us how to print titles which go onto the video and how to use PC Paintbrush, but most of us had a fair idea of how to use it because of our computer lessons.

Emma Bolitho and I sorted out what order we were going to put the magazine in and it was all worked out, but in about

Colloquial exp. three weeks, Emma had written up a load of information and put it into the magazine in whatever order, so I left it in the end! Antony wrote out half a page to in the magazine, Cheryl wrote a page, I wrote a page and I don't know if Emma Thornton did anything.

exp. I asked around to people on my school bus some questions on animal testing and I wrote it as a survey for the magazine. I also designed the cover for the magazine which we called 'murder or mercy'—that is also what we called our video. Cheryl Skeggs was absent from school for about a week or two because she went on holiday to Spain.

Emma Bolitho, Antony Read and Cheryl Skeggs went to the RSPCA for a loot around and did some filming there and we got a few pictures from the edited video from it. So Emma Thornton and I went to mr Sykes and we put the moving pictures onto the video, after I had worked out how long Emma Thornton's voice over would will take to say and I wrote it

down. We put about four moving pictures into the video. After mr Sykes put the last moving picture on the video; he thought he was being dramatic, so he just left the screen bright red for blood. So when Emma Thornton and I put the still pictures on afterwards, there was a flicker of red behind the pictures! Emma Bolitho did not want to come with Emma and me to do the still pictures because she wanted to see her boyfriend. After Emma

Thornton came out, the two Emma's had an argument because Emma Bolitho said to Emma Thornton that she had done it wrong, so we didn't all work in peace and harmony!

First of all, we were going to have "Falling" from Twinpeaks as our backing music on our video, then Emma Thornton suggested "Bohemian Rhapsody", but in the end we all thought "Crazy" by Seal was more appropriate as it had more appropriate lyrics.

Emma Bolitho phoned two companies (cosmetics) to ask them some questions on animal testing because we got two inadequate replies when we wrote to them. Emma was filmed by Antony, and Emma Thornton and I were in the next room listening to the phone calls on the other telephone with a dictaphone recording it. The first company said that there was nobody who would talk about it and the next company said that they would write to her and they would not talk about it on the telephone.

Rhys Griffiths gave us the idea of putting somebody onto the video saying what happened on the 'phone call' and then show her phoning so it was like 'That's Life' First of all, Cheryl was supposed to do it, but I filmed her and she said her lines too soon, so some of it was missed out. Antony filmed her twice and exactly the same thing happened. We were going to film her again, but she went somewhere and was absent again. Antony filmed me doing what Cheryl was supposed to do, but the start of it was missing again, so we gave up in the end and did not do it at all.

This term, I have learnt a lot by doing this project from research and now I am against animal testing and I now buy my cosmetics from The Body Shop.

An excellent account of your personal involvement
& how the project developed.

'Murder Or Mercy?' By 'The Black Ferries'

At the begging of the term, we were set a project to do. It invoved using various mixers, video cameras, computers, electric organs, microphones and televisions. We had to get into groups and choose a subject to do a project on. The end result had to a video, a magazine, a live presentation, an individual diary or log produced by each member of the group and a literary review.

Cheryl, Antony, Emma T., Emma B. and I formed our group which is called 'The Black Ferries', I don't know why we called it that name, it's original I suppose! First of all, we were going to do our project on AIDS, but we decided that it was too strong a subject and that it would take too long to finish it. We wanted to do something serious, so we decided to study animal cruelty.

In the first lesson we were given journals so that we could write down any notes and information which we needed. To start off with, everybody in the group wrote a diary in every English lesson about what they did but as the time went on, most of us forgot about writing it up.

On Tuesdays, Rhys Griffiths and Tony Stone came: Rhys came one week and Tony came the next. They helped us with the video work and they supplied all of the equipment we needed for the video. Mr Jacques [the school audio-visual assistant; RG] also came into the lesson sometimes. In the first lesson with Tony and Rhys, Mr Jacques showed our group how to use the school video camera and Rhys showed us how to print titles which go onto the video and how to use PC Paintbrush, but most of us had a fair idea of how to use it because of our computer lessons.

Emma B. and I sorted out what order we were going to put the magazine in and it was all worked out, but in about three weeks, Emma had written up a load of information and put it into the magazine in whatever order, so I left it in the end! Antony wrote out half a page to go in the magazine, Cheryl wrote a page, I wrote a page and I don't know if Emma, T. did anything. I asked around to people on my school bus some questions on animal testing and I wrote it as a survey for the magazine. I also designed the cover for the magazine which we called 'Murder Or Mercy' – that is also what we called our video. Cheryl was absent from school for about a week or two because she went on holiday to Spain.

Emma B., Antony and Cheryl went to the R.S.P.C.A. for a look around and did some filming there and we got a few pictures for the edited video from it. So Emma T. and I went to Mr Jacques and we put the moving pictures onto the video, after I had worked out how long Emma T's. voice over will take to say and I wrote it down. We put about four moving pictures into the video. After Mr Jacques put the last moving picture on the video, he thought he was being dramatic, so he just left the screen bright red for blood. So when Emma T. and I put the still pictures on afterwards, there was a flicker of red behind the pictures! Emma B. did not want to come with Emma and I to do the still pictures because she wanted to see her boyfriend. After Emma T. came out, the two Emma's had an argument because Emma B. said to Emma T. that she had done it wrong, so we didn't all work in peace and harmony!

First of all we were going to have 'Falling' from Twinpeaks as our backing music on our video, then Emma T. suggested 'Bohemian Rhapsody', but in the end we all thought 'Crazy' by Seal was more appropriate as it had more appropriate lyrics.

Emma B. phoned two companies (cosmetics) to ask them some questions on animal testing because we got two inadequate replys when we wrote to them. Emma was filmed by Antony, and Emma T. and I were in the next room listening to the phone calls on the other telephone with a dictaphone recording it. The first company said that there were nobody who would talk about it and the next company said that they would write to her and they would not talk about it on the telephone.

Rhys gave us the idea of putting somebody onto the video saying what happened on the 'phone call and then show her phoning so it was like 'That's Life'. First of all, Cheryl was supposed to do it, but we I filmed her and she said her lines too soon, so some of it was missed out. Antony filmed her twice and exactly the same thing happened. We were going to film her again, but she went somewhere and was absent again. Antony filmed me doing what Cheryl was going to do, but the start of it was missing again, so we gave up in the end and did not do it at all.

This term, I have learnt a lot by doing this project from research and now I am against animal testing and I now buy my cosmetics from 'The Body Shop.'

Printed copy of Vanessa's open evaluation

Sources of electrical energy

1. General Impressions

The general impressions I had after finishing this project were of some regret and resentment aswell as feeling relieved, quite pleased and satisfied at the work we produced.

I think this regret was mostly about the last minute panic to finish the magazine and complete other work where this work could have been done under much less pressure, more relaxed to perhaps a higher standard.

In our group we went on many visits, met many interesting people and discovered alot about researching for information. In the class our groups seemed to have taken totally different approaches to the work than our group did. I enjoyed this term in English ~~as this~~ though project was something I had never imagined to work like it did.

2. Good things about the project

The good things about the project were working in small groups, being able to take the respondisibilty of organizing our time for ourselves, being able to choose a topic we were interested in, working at our own pace, using computer equipment, the video editing suite, having a whole term left for us to specifically work on the project and visiting places eg. Hinkley point, Delabole windfarm, Truro library, ~~etc~~

I enjoyed researching the subject of energy sources instead of having information thrown at us on printed notes and told to inwardly digest it. I think I have learnt alot of information without conciously trying at I have been interested in the subject ~~asand~~ an so naturally I have learnt alot of material I would have previously shut my mind to because ~~I hadn't~~ wouldnt have researched the topic myself, I would have had no active involvement and that information would pass without ~~me understanding it~~ th processing, selecting, reading etc that took place in our ~~in our~~ project

3. Bad things about the project

The bad things about the project were mainly about the group. My position in the group seemed to change every week. ~~and was often not sure of what place In~~ At first our group seemed simple and quite natural but as time went on things became more complex and confused.

I think everyone could have made ~~th~~ everything much easier and simple for everyone else if t we had discussed how we personally felt ~~regulally.~~ regularly

Other bad things ~~was were the xxxx xx xxxxxxx xxx~~ were how we were expected to do this project in one of our GCSE years. The time we were allow was long enough if we had organised and planned the term better.

4. How things could have been better

As I have said more guidance from teachers should have been given to the time management knowledge ~~involved~~ we needed. I think having mixed groups was okay but there were many drawbacks suchas ego conflicts, ~~domiance domience~~ dominunce power, not confronting real emotions, not wanting to express inner feelings, resentment and competitiveness between the sexes and each other.

If we had undertaken this project in Year 9 it would have been 50% easier. I think we all coped quite well and maybe it has given us all an idea of how we can cope, restrain, opt out, thrive or ~~the give in~~ have a total nervous breakdown under ~~xxxxxx~~ pressure and the threat of deadlines.

5. What I learnt

I learnt alot about wind power to a great depth and to a lesser extent about other sources of electrical energy. I've learnt some skills in communicating opinions and relating to other people.

I've carried out an interview with the owner of the wind farm at Delabole, Mr Edwards which has now given me a bit of confidence for the future if I happen to be put in similar situation.

I've learnt about researching and investigating a subject through the use of people, libraries, museums, etc.

6. Advice for other people working like this

Don't. Seriously if you were to undertake a project similar to this I would give the following advice concluded from the mistakes I and our group made.

1) Organisation – organise everything really well so you can enjoy the project right to the end instead of panicking.

2) Separate workload equally and make each person of the group responsible for his/her allocated part.

3) Help and support each other. You are all in the same group so work together. Help other groups if you can.

4) Keep an open mind. If your project dosent turn our exactly like you imagined in the first place then it is probably for the best. Try out and discuss all possible ideas.

5) Enthusiasium is really important. Be interested in the subject you choose and think positively.

+ The Best of Luck.

7. Our Group

The subject we chose was ~~soucre~~ sources of Electrical Energy. In our group there was Alastair Lee, Darren Wilcock, Matthew Evans, Juliet Burnard and myself.

Our group sometimes merged as one, sometimes separated as the bond cracked. At the start of project our group was quite a unusual mixture An Interesting combinations of personalities which seemed on a superficial level to work. About a month into the project underflowing emotions rose and disagreements happened. There was arguing, shouting and screaming, especially between Juliet and myself, until we both started to calm down and restrain ourselves from throttling each other.

Towards the end of the project our group worked really well all together. We achieved ~~all the xxx~~ all we had ~~ami~~ aimed to achieve ~~and a bit extra I think~~. What we achieved was good considering all the things that went wrong.

8. Would you like to do something similar again? If so, why?

Yes I would because I think I have learnt much more from this project than I realise at the moment. This project ~~xxxxx xxxxxxx~~ created alot of oppertunities and chances to experience new and ~~xxx~~ interesting activities which might not happened ~~xxxx~~ if we didn't ~~do~~ participate in project. eg visiting a Nuclear Power station, Delabole wind farm, using video equipment, computers and word processors etc etc.

Teachers gave us exactly the right amount of support, encouragement and interest in what we were doing ~~xxxx xxxxxx~~ throughout the project. Parents and libirarians were equally helpful and so were many friends.

I enjoyed this term in English and think the project ~~xxxxx~~ has had many benefits. ~~My~~ I would like to do a project ~~similiar~~ similar to this in the future because next ~~th~~ time it would be better ~~th~~ now we ~~had~~ have completed this project. and have gained experience.

APPENDIX 4

Photocopy and printed copy of
Shaun's open evaluation

COURSE REVIEW

GENDER	M ✓	F	SCHOOL: Poltice School	DATE: 8,4,92 CLASS: 8¹⁰

HOW TO USE:

1. Spend 15 minutes answering on your own.
2. Spend 5-10 minutes discussing your responses with a companion. Make changes if you want to.
3. Spend 10-15 minutes discussing your responses with the rest of your group for this project. Make changes if you want to.
4. Spend 5 minutes re-reading your own review. Make any changes you want to.

1. **General Impressions**

i wanted licke to be a nurse q throut the hospatoll proejacr was der yintresmg and wee learnt a lot abot hospatil

2. **Good things about the Project**

i enjoyed me vrdo weysrd crrncs we bclk to the nurs and patien

3.   **Bad things about the Project**

i dinked ~~like~~ not takeing the video
camera to the hospatyl.

4.   **How things could have been better**   ve should have

wate plays

5.   **What I learnt**   i lernwt where the
                    Old ladyes   were and
                    the old man   cartg
                    lor about the hospatyll

6.   **Advice for other pupils working like this**   worting in plays
                                                        doing a
                                                        job

6.   **Our Group**   i enjoyed worttng vn
                    greps

7.   Would you like to do something similar again?   If so, why?   *shows*

plays

Printed copy of Shaun's open evaluation

1. General impressions
I wanted like to be a nurse a throght the hospatill proegact was very intresing and we learnt alot abot hospatll

2. Good things about the project
I enjoyeb the vido
we used carmes
we taklk to the nursand patien

3. Bad things about the project?
i dinted like not taking the vido camera tothe hospatll

4. How things could have been better
we should have had plays

5. What I learnt
i learnt where the old lades were and the old man i learnt a lot about the hospatpll

6. Advice for other pupils working like this
working in playes
doing a show

7. Our Group
i enjoyed working in groups

8. Would you like to do something similar again? If so, what?
shows plays

Independent learning project: review and reflection file

THANK YOU FOR AGREEING TO FILL IN THIS FILE – I KNOW IT WILL TAKE YOU SOME TIME AND I REALLY APPRECIATE YOUR HELP.

YOU MIGHT FIND IT ENOYABLE TO DO THIS WITH A FRIEND WHO IS ALSO FILLING IN HER OR HIS FILE, OR WITH MEMBERS OF THE GROUP IN WHICH YOU WORKED. ANY WAY YOU CHOOSE IS FINE, AS LONG AS YOU PUT YOUR OWN ANSWERS IN YOUR FILE.

THE IMPORTANT THING IS TO MAKE ONE OF THE FOLLOWING DECISIONS:

EITHER TO TAKE THE TIME IT NEEDS AND TO FILL IN THE FILE AS BEST YOU CAN

OR TO EXERCISE YOUR PERFECT RIGHT NOT TO FILL IT IN AT ALL.

✦

ABOUT 400 PUPILS WERE INVOLVED IN YOUR PHASE OF THE INDEPENDENT LEARNING PROJECT. THERE WERE PUPILS AGED 11–16 FROM CASTLEFORT, CORD, DORE AND SALTAIR SCHOOLS. ALL OF THEM ARE BEING ASKED TO FILL IN THIS FILE.

THE PURPOSE OF THIS FILE IS THREEFOLD:

    1)   TO TRY AND SEE WHAT HAS BEEN LEARNT;

    2)   TO TRY AND SEE IN WHAT WAY THINGS HAVE BEEN LEARNT;

    3)   TO TRY AND SEE HOW WE CAN IMPROVE THINGS FOR ANOTHER 400 PUPILS WHO WILL BE INVOLVED IN THE NEXT STAGE OF THE PROJECT, STARTING IN SEPTEMBER 1991.

ALL FILES ARE ANONYMOUS.

YOUR RESPONSES TO THE QUESTIONS IN THIS FILE WILL BE PUT ONTO A DATABASE. ALL PUPILS WHO HAVE BEEN INVOLVED IN THE PROJECT ARE WELCOME TO A COPY OF THE DATABASE INFORMATION AND CONCLUSIONS.

THANK YOUR FOR YOUR HELP.

RHYS GRIFFITH
SENIOR ADVISORY TEACHER (ENGLISH)

HOW TO FILL IN SECTION 1 OF THIS FILE
SECTION 1 OF THIS FILE CONTAINS 8 QUESTIONS.
EACH QUESTION STARTS 'HOW DID YOU LEARN…'
FOR INSTANCE:

QUESTION 1: 'HOW DID YOU LEARN TO USE AN EXTERNAL MICROPHONE?'

THERE ARE UP TO 8 POSSIBLE RESPONSES TO EACH QUESTION.
THESE ARE

- A –   KNEW ALREADY
- B –   TOLD/SHOWN BY TEACHER
- C –   TOLD/SHOWN BY A MEMBER OF MY GROUP
- D –   TOLD/SHOWN BY A MEMBER OF ANOTHER GROUP
- E –   TOLD/SHOWN BY SOMEONE ELSE
- F –   WORKED IT OUT MYSELF
- G –   WORKED IT OUT WITH SOMEONE ELSE
- H –   TOLD/SHOWED SOMEONE ELSE HOW TO DO IT

YOU ARE ALMOST CERTAIN TO HAVE LEARNED THROUGH MORE THAN ONE OF THESE WAYS.
FOR INSTANCE, YOUR ANSWER TO QUESTION 1 'HOW DID YOU LEARN TO USE AN EXTERNAL MICROPHONE?' MIGHT BE A BIT OF A, SOME OF B, A BIT OF F AND QUITE A LOT OF G.
THEREFORE, FOR EACH OF THE ANSWERS, A–H WE NEED A SCALE LIKE THIS:

- 1 –   NOT AT ALL
- 2 –   A BIT
- 3 –   SOME
- 4 –   QUITE A LOT
- 5 –   MOSTLY

ON YOUR ANSWER SHEET, YOUR ANSWER TO QUESTION 1 WOULD LOOK LIKE THIS:

A	B	C	D	E	F	G	H
(1)	1	1	1	1	1	1	1
2	2	2	2	2	(2)	2	2
3	(3)	3	3	3	3	3	3
4	4	4	4	4	4	(4)	4
5	5	5	5	5	5	5	5

IN THREE OF THE ANSWERS IT WOULD BE USEFUL TO KNOW WHO YOUR ANSWER REFERS TO, SO I HAVE ADDED A SPACE FOR THAT ON THE ANSWER SHEET.
FOR EXAMPLE:

A	B	C	D	E	F	G	H
(1)	1	1	1	1	1	1	1
2	2	2	2	2	(2)	2	2
3	(3)	3	3	3	3	3	3
4	4	4	4	4	4	(4)	4
5	5	5	5	5	5	5	5
				WHO		WHO	WHO

Jane – she is in my group

I'D ALSO LIKE TO KNOW HOW MUCH YOU THINK YOU'VE LEARNT, COMPARED TO WHAT YOU KNEW BEFORE THE PROJECT. SO I'VE ADDED ONE LAST COLUMN ON THE ANSWER SHEET, HEADED BY THE LETTER 'I'. THIS COLUMN STANDS FOR THIS QUESTION:
AT THE END OF THE PROJECT HAD YOUR EXPERIENCE IN THIS AREA

- V –   GOT WORSE THAN IT WAS BEFORE
- W –   STAYED THE SAME
- X –   IMPROVED A BIT
- Y –   IMPROVED SOME
- Z –   IMPROVED A LOT

TO ANSWER THE 'I' COLUMN, YOU SIMPLY RING THE ONE RESPONSE CLOSEST TO YOUR OWN FEELINGS. FOR EXAMPLE:

A	B	C	D	E	F	G	H	
(1)	1	1	1	1	1	1	1	V
2	2	2	2	2	(2)	2	2	W
3	(3)	3	3	3	3	3	3	X
4	4	4	4	4	4	(4)	4	(Y)
5	5	5	5	5	5	5	5	Z
				WHO		WHO	WHO	

Jane – she is in my group

YOU MIGHT FIND IT MAKES MORE SENSE TO ANSWER ALL THE A TO H RESPONSES FIRST FOR ALL 8 QUESTIONS AND THEN COME BACK AND QUICKLY ANSWER ALL 8 'I' QUESTIONS.
LASTLY, REGARD TONY AND ME AS TEACHERS, WHEN RESPONDING TO THE QUESTIONS.

INDEPENDENT LEARNING PROJECT QUESTIONNAIRE
SECTION 1

QUESTION 1: HOW DID YOU LEARN TO USE AN EXTERNAL MICROPHONE?

A	B	C	D	E	F	G	H	
1	1	1	1	1	1	1	1	V
2	2	2	2	2	2	2	2	W
3	3	3	3	3	3	3	3	X
4	4	4	4	4	4	4	4	Y
5	5	5	5	5	5	5	5	Z
				W		W	W	
				H		H	H	
				O		O	O	

QUESTION 2: HOW DID YOU LEARN TO PLAN YOUR VIDEO?

A	B	C	D	E	F	G	H	
1	1	1	1	1	1	1	1	V
2	2	2	2	2	2	2	2	W
3	3	3	3	3	3	3	3	X
4	4	4	4	4	4	4	4	Y
5	5	5	5	5	5	5	5	Z
				W		W	W	
				H		H	H	
				O		O	O	

QUESTION 3: WHO DID YOU LEARN TO FIND LOCATIONS WHERE YOU WOULD FILM?

A	B	C	D	E	F	G	H	
1	1	1	1	1	1	1	1	V
2	2	2	2	2	2	2	2	W
3	3	3	3	3	3	3	3	X
4	4	4	4	4	4	4	4	Y
5	5	5	5	5	5	5	5	Z
				W		W	W	
				H		H	H	
				O		O	O	

QUESTION 4: HOW DID YOU LEARN TO INVOLVE MEMBERS OF THE COMMUNITY IN YOUR WORK (PARENTS COUNT)?

A	B	C	D	E	F	G	H	
1	1	1	1	1	1	1	1	V
2	2	2	2	2	2	2	2	W
3	3	3	3	3	3	3	3	X
4	4	4	4	4	4	4	4	Y
5	5	5	5	5	5	5	5	Z
				WHO		WHO	WHO	

QUESTION 5: HOW DID YOU LEARN TO MAKE THE NECESSARY ARRANGEMENTS IF YOU WERE GOING OUT OF SCHOOL AS PART OF YOUR PROJECT?

A	B	C	D	E	F	G	H	
1	1	1	1	1	1	1	1	V
2	2	2	2	2	2	2	2	W
3	3	3	3	3	3	3	3	X
4	4	4	4	4	4	4	4	Y
5	5	5	5	5	5	5	5	Z
				WHO		WHO	WHO	

QUESTION 6: HOW DID YOU LEARN TO GET JOBS DONE ON TIME?

A	B	C	D	E	F	G	H	
1	1	1	1	1	1	1	1	V
2	2	2	2	2	2	2	2	W
3	3	3	3	3	3	3	3	X
4	4	4	4	4	4	4	4	Y
5	5	5	5	5	5	5	5	Z
				WHO		WHO	WHO	

QUESTION 7: HOW DID YOU LEARN TO DO RESEARCH FOR YOUR PROJECT?

A	B	C	D	E	F	G	H	
1	1	1	1	1	1	1	1	V
2	2	2	2	2	2	2	2	W
3	3	3	3	3	3	3	3	X
4	4	4	4	4	4	4	4	Y
5	5	5	5	5	5	5	5	Z
				W		W	W	
				H		H	H	
				O		O	O	

QUESTION 8: HOW DID YOU LEARN TO GET ON WITH OTHERS IN YOUR GROUP?

A	B	C	D	E	F	G	H	
1	1	1	1	1	1	1	1	V
2	2	2	2	2	2	2	2	W
3	3	3	3	3	3	3	3	X
4	4	4	4	4	4	4	4	Y
5	5	5	5	5	5	5	5	Z
				W		W	W	
				H		H	H	
				O		O	O	

SECTION 2: YOUR THOUGHTS

1. WHAT WAS THE HARDEST THING YOU HAD TO LEARN?

2. WHAT WAS THE MOST IMPORTANT YOU LEARNT?

3. WHAT DID YOU MOST ENJOY ABOUT THE PROJECT?

4. WHAT DID YOU LEAST ENJOY ABOUT THE PROJECT?

5. WHAT WOULD YOU DO DIFFERENTLY IF YOU WERE DOING THE PROJECT AGAIN?

6. WHY?

7. WHAT COULD THE TEACHERS INVOLVED (INCLUDING ME AND TONY) DO TO IMPROVE THE PROJECT?

8. WHAT ADVICE HAVE YOU FOR OTHERS STARTING THE PROJECT?

ANY FINAL COMMENTS, OPINIONS, SUGGESTIONS, THOUGHTS? PLEASE WRITE SOMETHING HERE.

SECTION 3
RING OR FILL IN AS APPROPRIATE
SCHOOL YEAR   7   8   9
BOY
GIRL
SCHOOL
MIXED ABILITY
SETTED (PLEASE SAY WHICH ONE)

Questionnaire 1: Response 010

SECTION TWO

YOUR THOUGHTS

1. **WHAT WAS THE HARDEST THING YOU HAD TO LEARN?**
   To work without a teacher.

2. **WHAT WAS THE MOST IMPORTANT YOU LEARNT?**
   to co-operate with people and work.

3. **WHAT DID YOU MOST ENJOY ABOUT THE PROJECT?**
   Doing the computer titles

4. **WHAT DID YOU LEAST ENJOY ABOUT THE PROJECT?**
   filming and re-filming until we got it right.

5. **WHAT WOULD YOU DO DIFFERENTLY IF YOU WERE DOING THE PROJECT AGAIN?**
   Choose a better poem

6. **WHY?** Because our poem was a bit too short.

7. **WHAT COULD THE TEACHERS INVOLVED (INCLUDING PETE AND ME) DO TO IMPROVE THE PROJECT?** provide the equipment in school all the time

8. **WHAT ADVICE HAVE YOU FOR OTHER PUPILS STARTING THE PROJECT?** Choose people you can work with and don't mute around.

ANY FINAL COMMENTS, OPINIONS, SUGGESTIONS, THOUGHTS. PLEASE WRITE SOMETHING HERE.

This project was enjoyable and educational. I would like to do this project again

SECTION THREE

RING OR FILL IN AS APPROPRIATE

SCHOOL YEAR   7   (8)   9   10   11
BOY
GIRL
SCHOOL
MIXED ABILITY GROUP
SET (PLEASE SAY WHICH ONE) Mixed ability

	Q / A	B	C	D	E	F	G	H	I
1	1 2 (3) 4 5	1 2 (3) 4 5	(1) 2 3 4 5	1 2 3 4 5	1 2 3 4 5 WHO	1 2 3 4 5	1 2 3 4 5 WHO	1 2 3 4 5 WHO	V W (X) Y Z
2	1 (2) 3 4 5	1 2 3 4 (5)	1 2 3 4 5	1 2 (3) 4 5	1 2 3 (4) 5 WHO [illegible]	1 2 3 4 5	1 2 3 4 5 WHO	1 2 3 4 5 WHO	V W (X) Y Z
3	1 2 (3) 4 5	1 2 3 (4) 5	1 2 3 4 5	1 2 3 4 5	1 2 3 (4) 5 WHO Mrs Banks	1 2 3 4 5	1 2 3 4 5 WHO	1 2 3 4 5 WHO	V W X (Y) Z
4	1 2 3 4 5	1 2 3 (4) 5	1 2 3 4 5	1 2 3 4 5	1 2 3 4 5 WHO	1 2 3 4 5	1 (2) 3 4 5 WHO Darron	1 2 3 4 5 WHO	V (W) X Y Z
5	1 (2) 3 4 5	1 2 (3) 4 5	1 2 3 4 5	1 2 3 4 5	1 2 (3) 4 5 WHO Mrs Banks	1 2 3 4 5	1 2 3 4 5 WHO	1 2 3 4 5 WHO	V W X (Y) Z
6	1 2 (3) 4 5	1 (2) 3 4 5	1 2 3 4 5	1 2 3 4 5	1 2 (3) 4 5 WHO Mrs Banks	1 2 3 4 5	1 2 3 4 5 WHO	1 2 3 4 5 WHO	V W (X) Y Z
7	1 2 3 4 (5)	1 2 3 4 5	1 2 3 4 5	1 2 3 4 5	1 2 3 4 5 WHO	1 2 3 4 5	1 2 3 4 5 WHO	1 2 (3) 4 5 WHO Jason [illegible]	V W X Y (Z)
8	1 2 3 (4) 5	1 2 3 4 5	1 2 3 4 5	1 2 3 4 5	1 2 3 4 5 WHO	1 2 3 (4) 5	1 2 3 4 5 WHO	1 2 3 4 5 WHO	V W (X) Y Z

Questionnaire 1: Response 141

SECTION TWO

YOUR THOUGHTS

1. WHAT WAS THE HARDEST THING YOU HAD TO LEARN?
   To work with X and X

2. WHAT WAS THE MOST IMPORTANT YOU LEARNT?
   Not to get the video camera insides wet

3. WHAT DID YOU MOST ENJOY ABOUT THE PROJECT?
   working in a group.

4. WHAT DID YOU LEAST ENJOY ABOUT THE PROJECT?
   The graphics went wrong

5. WHAT WOULD YOU DO DIFFERENTLY IF YOU WERE DOING THE PROJECT AGAIN?
   I chose a different group of friends.

6. WHY? Because we had a few difficulties last time.

7. WHAT COULD THE TEACHERS INVOLVED (INCLUDING PETE AND ME) DO TO IMPROVE THE PROJECT? Help a little more although u were very helpful.

8. WHAT ADVICE HAVE YOU FOR OTHER PUPILS STARTING THE PROJECT? To work carefully. because One mistake. Costs a lot.

ANY FINAL COMMENTS, OPINIONS SUGGESTIONS, THOUGHTS. PLEASE WRITE SOMETHING HERE.

I enjoyed the project Very much, but sometimes my friend and i had to shout at the boys because they were mucking around.

SECTION THREE

RING OR FILL IN AS APPROPRIATE

SCHOOL YEAR (7) 8 9 10 11
~~BOY~~
GIRL ✓
SCHOOL Comprehensive.
(MIXED ABILITY GROUP)
SET (PLEASE SAY WHICH ONE) _____

Grid 5

	I	V	W	X	Y	Z
H	1	2	3	4	5	WHO
G	1	2	3	4	5	WHO
F	1	2	3	4	5	
E	1	2	3	4	5	WHO
D	1	2	3	4	5	
C	1	2	3	4	5	
B	1	2	3	4	5	
A	1	2	3	4	5	

(O/2 noted in left margin) — **5**

Grid 6

	I	V	W	X	(Y)	Z
H	1	2	3	4	5	WHO
(G)		2	3	(4)	5	WHO
F	1	2	3	4	5	
E	1	2	3	4	5	WHO
D	1	2	3	4	5	
C	1	2	3	4	5	
B	1	2	3	4	5	
(A)	1	(2)	3	4	5	

6

Grid 7

	I	V	W	X	(Y)	Z
H	1	2	3	4	5	WHO
G	1	2	3	4	5	WHO
F	1	2	3	4	5	
E	1	2	3	4	5	WHO
D	1	2	3	4	5	
C	1	2	3	4	5	
B	1	2	3	4	5	
(A)	1	2	3	(4)	5	

7

Grid 8

	I	V	W	X	(Y)	Z
H	1	2	3	4	5	WHO
G	1	2	3	4	5	WHO
F	1	2	3	4	5	
E	1	2	3	4	5	WHO
D	1	2	3	4	5	
C	1	2	3	4	5	
(B)	1	(2)	3	4	5	
(A)	1	2	3	(4)	5	

8

Grid 1

	I	V	W	X	Y	(Z)
H	1	2	3	4	5	WHO
(G)		2	3	4	(5)	WHO
F	1	2	3	4	5	
E	1	2	3	4	5	WHO
D	1	2	3	4	5	
C	1	2	3	4	5	
B	1	2	3	4	5	
A	1	2	3	4	5	

1

Grid 2

	I	V	W	X	(Y)	Z
H	1	2	3	4	5	WHO
G	1	2	3	4	5	WHO
F	1	2	3	4	5	
E	1	2	3	4	5	WHO
D	1	2	3	4	5	
C	1	2	3	4	5	
(B)	1	2	3	4	(5)	
(A)	1	(2)	3	4	5	

2

Grid 3

	I	V	W	X	Y	Z
H	1	2	3	4	5	WHO
G	1	2	3	4	5	WHO
F	1	2	3	4	5	
E	1	2	3	4	5	WHO
D	1	2	3	4	5	
C	1	2	3	4	5	
B	1	2	3	4	5	
A	1	2	3	4	5	

(O/2 noted in left margin) — **3**

Grid 4

	I	V	W	X	Y	Z
H	1	2	3	4	5	WHO
G	1	2	3	4	5	WHO
(F)	1	(2)	3	4	5	
E	1	2	3	4	5	WHO
D	1	2	3	4	5	
C	1	2	3	4	5	
B	1	2	3	4	5	
(A)	1	2	3	4	(5)	

4

Questionnaire 2

NATIONAL CURRICULUM ENGLISH PROJECT QUESTIONNAIRE

During this school year, you have been involved in a one term project which involved working in a small group and planning and taking decisions for yourselves so that your group aimed towards one or more of the following outcomes: producing a magazine, a live presentation, a video, a bibliography and a personal diary.

Please could you answer the following questions?

YOU MIGHT FIND IT ENJOYABLE TO DO THIS WITH A FRIEND WHO IS ALSO FILLING IN HIS OR HER QUESTIONNAIRE OR WITH MEMBERS OF THE GROUP IN WHICH YOU WORKED. ANY WAY YOU CHOOSE IS FINE, AS LONG AS YOU PUT YOUR OWN ANSWERS IN YOUR QUESTIONNAIRE.

ïE IMPORTANT THING IS TO MAKE ONE OF THE FOLLOWING DECISIONS:

EITHER TO TAKE THE TIME IT NEEDS AND TO FILL IN THE QUESTIONNAIRE AS BEST YOU CAN.

OR TO EXERCISE YOUR PERFECT RIGHT NOT TO FILL IT IN AT ALL.

THE PURPOSE OF THIS QUESTIONNAIRE IS THREEFOLD:

1) TO TRY AND SEE WHAT HAS BEEN LEARNT;

2) TO TRY AND SEE IN WHAT WAY THINGS HAVE BEEN LEARNT;

3) TO TRY AND SEE HOW WE CAN IMPROVE THINGS FOR OTHER PUPILS WHO WILL BE INVOLVED IN THE NEXT STAGE OF THE PROJECT.

ALL QUESTIONNAIRES ARE ANONYMOUS.

YOUR RESPONSES TO THE QUESTIONS WILL BE PUT ONTO A DATABASE.

ALL PUPILS WHO HAVE BEEN INVOLVED IN THE PROJECT ARE WELCOME TO A COPY OF THE DATABASE INFORMATION AND CONCLUSIONS.

THANK YOU FOR YOUR HELP.

RHYS GRIFFITH
SENIOR ENGLISH ADVISORY TEACHER (SECONDARY)

1.   GIRL   BOY   (Tick as appropriate)

2.   NAME OF SCHOOL ....

3.   NATIONAL CURRICULUM YEAR 7,   8,   9,   10 (Ring as appropriate)

4.   MY CLASS IS MIXED ABILITY/SETTED   (Ring as appropriate)

5.   THERE WERE 2 3 4 5 6 PUPILS IN MY COLLABORATIVE GROUPS.
     (Ring as appropriate)

6.   OUR GROUP WAS ALL BOYS / ALL GIRLS / MIXED (Ring as
     appropriate)

7.   WHAT SYSTEM WAS USED FOR FORMING YOUR COLLABORATIVE GROUP?

     _____

8.   WHAT WAS THE HARDEST THING YOU HAD TO LEARN?

     _____

     WHAT WAS THE MOST IMPORTANT THING YOU HAD TO LEARN?

     _____

10. WHAT DID YOU MOST ENJOY ABOUT THE PROJECT?

     _____

11. WHAT DID YOU LEAST ENJOY ABOUT THE PROJECT?

     _____

12. WHAT WOULD YOU DO DIFFERENTLY IF YOU WERE DOING THE PROJECT
     AGAIN?

     _____

13. WHY?

     _____

14. WHAT COULD THE TEACHERS INVOLVED (INCLUDING ME) DO TO IMPROVE
     THE PROJECT?

     _____

15. WHAT ADVICE HAVE YOU FOR OTHER PUPILS STARTING THE PROJECT?

     _____

16. ANY FINAL COMMENTS, OPINIONS, SUGGESTIONS, THOUGHTS. PLEASE
     WRITE SOMETHING HERE

     _____

     _____

     _____

     _____

     _____

Tavyford Profiling Form

TAVYFORD PROFILING SHEET   SPRING 1990
INDEPENDENT LEARNING PROJECT

YEAR				

NAME OF GROUP	

NAMES OF GROUP MEMBERS	1	
	2	
	3	
	4	
	5	

PROJECT TITLE

AREA OF STUDY (state briefly what your project is about)

PROGRESS SO FAR (state briefly what you have done so far)

WORK IN HAND (state briefly what you intend to do)

TODAY	

NEXT WEEK	

WEEK AFTER	

EXTENSION GRANTED (Tutor to initial)	NONE	ONE WEEK	TWO WEEKS

Cedric Harvey Assessment Sheet

Assessment Sheet

Carla Fletcher 1H2

My comment: I thought my piece of work was quite good probably because I was writing about my favourite pet but I could of [have] described her better.

Parents comment:

A very truthful piece of work You could have mentioned how your hamster gets on with the other animals in this household in order to add some humour to the essay.

Much care and thought has been taken on this theme Attention to detail and a good working knowledge on pet care has been considered.

Teachers Comment:

Well-organised and carefully thought out. Some useful advice. I agree that you don't really convey your hamster's personality. Recalling some humorous incidents would have achieved this.

'Breaking Down the Barriers' Schedule

BREAKING DOWN THE BARRIERS

This project is designed to break down some of the barriers that exist between and within groups of people.

THE TASKS:

1) Working in a mixed group of 3 - 5 members, research a topic for presentation to an audience of your choice. The presentation must include a literary and an oral component.

2) Working in pairs - although you may take the group's advice - make a liaison within the community.

3) Working individually, undertake an activity that is new to you.

4) Keep a written record of your group, pair and individual work.

ALL TASKS MUST BE PRESENTED IN WRITING TO YOUR TEACHER FOR APPROVAL BEFORE YOU BEGIN WORK.

DEADLINES:

COMPLETION: THURSDAY, OCTOBER 20TH, 1988.
PRESENTATION: TUESDAY, WEDNESDAY AND THURSDAY, NOVEMBER 1ST - 3RD, 1988.

'Other People' Help Sheet

<u>TODAY'S LESSON: SOME THOUGHTS</u>

I would like you, as a group, to do the following things:

1) Come to terms with working with each other. There will be problems: some people in your group will not want to do what you want to do, or what you want them to do. Some people will be lazy. You must sort yourselves out.

2) As a group, try and find solutions to your problems by talking amongst yourselves. If other groups seem to be getting on better that you, ask their advice. Ask any of the three teachers to sit in with you.

3) Keep clearly in the front of your minds that this kind of learning gives you a lot of freedom to do what you want. *That freedom requires you to act responsibly and show that you can get on without teachers telling you what to do and how to behave.*

<u>THINGS THAT NEED TO BE DONE TODAY:</u>

1) Each group must focus attention on some aspect of the project "Other Peple" and decide what they are going to do. You could carry on with the work you started last week; or you could choose one of the other tasks on offer last week; or you can come up with your own ideas. DON'T WAFFLE ON ENDLESSLY! IF YOU ARE NOT GETTING ANYWHERE, ASK FOR ADVICE.

2) Each group must agree what each member of that group is going to do to help the project along. THEN GET ON WITH IT.

3) Be thinking about what you are going to do when you go into the primary school of your choice. You will have 10-15 minutes to work with a class or group, on the subject of "Other People". What will you do? How will you make it interesting? What resources will you need? What age-group are you going to work with? How are you going to get in touch with the primary school?

4) Everybody must keep a diary of these lessons. In your diary, write down truthfully what you feel about these lessons, your own contribution, and how you feel about the people in the rest of your group. Ten minutes will be given over to writing your diary at the end of each lesson, but you can add to it later if you want to.

'Friends With the Earth' Schedule

<u>MONDAY</u>

1000H   FIRST JOURNAL ENTRY

1230H   SECOND JOURNAL ENTRY

1430H   GROUP EQUIPMENT LIST

1530H   GROUP MENUS

<u>TUESDAY</u>

0900H   THIRD & FOURTH JOURNAL ENTRIES

1100H   MAP-READING TUITION

1100H   FIRST-AID TUITION

1200H   GROUP PROVISIONS LIST

1300H   FIFTH & SIXTH JOURNAL ENTRIES

1400H   FIRST-AID TEST

1400H   COMPLETION OF MAP-READING COURSE

1430H   GROUP INFORMATION SHEETS COMPLETED

1530H   SEVENTH JOURNAL ENTRY

<u>WEDNESDAY</u>

0900H   GROUP EQUIPMENT CHECK

0915H   GROUP PROVISIONS CHECK

0930H   INDIVIDUAL SURVIVAL KIT SPOT-CHECK

0945H   EIGHTH & NINTH JOURNAL ENTRIES

1000H   EXPEDITION LEAVES.

FRIENDS WITH THE EARTH
PLANNING ACTIVITIES

THIS LIST IS DIVIDED INTO TWO SECTIONS.

SECTION ONE: OBLIGATORY

YOUR GROUP MUST COMPLETE ALL THE ACTIVITIES IN SECTION ONE TO THE SATISFACTION OF THE EXPEDITION LEADERS.

SHOULD YOUR GROUP FAIL IN ANY OF THESE ACTIVITIES YOU WILL NOT BE ELLIGIBLE TO TAKE PART IN THE THREE-DAY EXPEDITION.

SECTION TWO: NEGOTIABLE

YOUR GROUP SHOULD SELECT THE ACTIVITIES IN SECTION TWO THAT YOU THINK MOST APPROPRIATE TO YOUR NEEDS.

****

SECTION ONE

1) EACH GROUP MEMBER IS TO KEEP A JOURNAL TO BE UP-DATED AT THE FOLLOWING TIMES: AT THE START OF THE DAY, AT MID-DAY, EVENING, END OF THE DAY.

The journal should record your thoughts on what has happened, is happening and will happen. The journal is for your use only and no-one else should read it. To confirm that you are keeping a journal, the expedition leaders will ask you to hold open your written entries at a distance from them of five paces.
DEADLINE: spot-checks by the expedition leaders at any of the times specified above throughout the five days.

2) FORM YOUR GROUP, USING THE GIVEN PARAMETERS. NAME YOUR GROUP. CHOOSE A SLOGAN FOR YOUR GROUP. INVENT A CHANT OR SONG FOR YOUR GROUP. DRAW UP A CODE OF CONDUCT FOR YOUR GROUP. DRAW UP A CODE OF CONDUCT FOR YOUR RELATIONSHIP WITH THE OTHER GROUPS. DECIDE RESPONSIBILITIES WITHIN THE GROUP.

All of this information needs to be put in writing, with one copy for each group member, one copy for the expedition leaders, and one copy for each of the other groups.
DEADLINE: 1430h Tuesday.

3) DRAW UP AN EQUIPMENT LIST FOR THE GROUP AND GATHER TOGETHER THE EQUIPMENT.

Two copies of this list are required: one for your group, one for the expedition leaders.
DEADLINE for equipment list: 1430h Monday.
DEADLINE for equipment check: 0900h Wednesday.

4) DRAW UP A MENU FOR THE GROUP AND PROVISION IT. EACH GROUP WILL BE GIVEN £10 FOR THIS ACTIVITY.

Two copies of the menu and provision list are required: one for the group, one for the expedition leaders. In addition, the expedition leaders will spot-check the provision store.
DEADLINE for menus: 1530h Monday.
DEADLINE for provisions' list: 1200h Tuesday.
DEADLINE for provisions' store: 0915h Wednesday.

5) MAP-READING COURSE: EACH GROUP MUST SUCCESSFULLY UNDERTAKE A LOCAL ROUTE USING MAP REFERENCES GIVEN BY THE EXPEDITION LEADERS.

Tuition will be given, if requested, by Rhys.
DEADLINE for tuition: 1100h Tuesday.
DEADLINE for completing course: 1400h Tuesday.

6) BASIC FIRST-AID: EACH GROUP SHOULD BE PRACTICALLY COMPETENT IN THE FOLLOWING PROCEDURES: CASUALTY IN SHOCK, CASUALTY IN EXPOSURE, CASUALTY WITH LIMB FRACTURE, SNAKE-BITE, SUN-STROKE.

Tuition will be given, if requested, by Pat.
DEADLINE for tuition: 1100h Tuesday.
DEADLINE for group test: 1400h Tuesday.

7) SURVIVAL KIT: EACH GROUP MEMBER MUST EQUIP A PERSONAL SURVIVAL KIT AS PER HANDOUT.

Should any group member not have a satisfactory survival kit, then the whole group will be disqualified.
DEADLINE: 0930h Wednesday.

8) ENTERTAINMENT: EACH GROUP WILL PREPARE A FIVE-MINUTE ENTERTAINMENT FOR PRESENTATION AROUND THE CAMP-FIRE ON THURSDAY EVENING.

This entertainment can be developed during the week, but if props, costume or effects are required, then these have to be gathered by our departure time of 1000h Wednesday morning. All members of the group must be involved in the entertainment.

SECTION TWO

1) SHELTER-BUILDING

All groups will have the opportunity to practise shelter-building techniques with equipment provided by the expedition leaders during the first two days.

2) FIRE-LIGHTING

All groups will have the opportunity to practise fire-lighting, under supervision, on the school-grounds, during the first two days.

3) LIBRARY RESEARCH

All groups will have the opportunity to research all aspects of expedition-making at the School and St. Just libraries, during the first two days.

4) VIDEO RESEARCH

All groups will have the opportunity to view a range of video-programmes about expedition-making. Videos will be watched by single groups and groups will be encouraged to present a synopsis to a gathering of all the groups, using the FF control, with links and explanations made by members of the presenting group.

5) PROBLEM-SOLVING

All groups will have the opportunity to undertake a series of practical problem-solving activities, designed to develop teamwork, lateral thinking and physical abilities.

FINALLY

SOME WORDS OF ADVICE

You might think that we are asking too much of you; and you, as an individual, would be right. You cannot complete these tasks alone.

But you can complete them, safely and enjoyably, if you work as a team. You can do this in two ways:

BY WORKING COLLABORATIVELY: this means working with other members of your group.

BY WORKING COOPERATIVELY: this means your group working with other groups.

TODAY'S LESSON: SOME THOUGHTS

I would like you, as a group, to do the following things:

1) Come to terms with working with each other. There will be problems: some people in your group will not want to do what you want to do, or what you want them to do. Some people will be lazy. You must sort yourselves out.

2) As a group, try and find solutions to your problems by talking amongst yourselves. If other groups seem to be getting on better that you, ask their advice. Ask any of the three teachers to sit in with you.

3) Keep clearly in the front of your minds that this kind of learning gives you a lot of freedom to do what you want. *That freedom requires you to act responsibly and show that you can get on without teachers telling you what to do and how to behave.*

THINGS THAT NEED TO BE DONE TODAY:

1) Each group must focus attention on some aspect of the project "Other Peple" and decide what they are going to do. You could carry on with the work you started last week; or you could choose one of the other tasks on offer last week; or you can come up with your own ideas. DON'T WAFFLE ON ENDLESSLY! IF YOU ARE NOT GETTING ANYWHERE, ASK FOR ADVICE.

2) Each group must agree what each member of that group is going to do to help the project along. THEN GET ON WITH IT.

3) Be thinking about what you are going to do when you go into the primary school of your choice. You will have 10-15 minutes to work with a class or group, on the subject of "Other People". What will you do? How will you make it interesting? What resources will you need? What age-group are you going to work with? How are you going to get in touch with the primary school?

4) Everybody must keep a diary of these lessons. In your diary, write down truthfully what you feel about these lessons, your own contribution, and how you feel about the people in the rest of your group. Ten minutes will be given over to writing your diary at the end of each lesson, but you can add to it later if you want to.

References

Abdallah-Pretceille, M. (1991) 'Human rights in the nursery school.' In H. Starkey (ed) *The Challenge of Human Rights Education*. London: Cassell.

AGIT (1994) *Equal Opportunities in School: Sexuality, Race, Gender and SEN*. London: Longman.

Allen, D. (1988) *English, Whose English?* Sheffield: NATE.

Amnesty International (1983) *Teaching and Learning about Human Rights*. London: Amnesty.

Andrews, G. (1991) 'Universal principles.' In G. Andrews (ed) *Citizenship*. London: Lawrence and Wishart.

Arblaster, A. (1994) *Democracy: Second Edition*. Buckingham: Open University Press.

Ashdown, P. (1989) *Citizen's Britain*. London: Fourth Estate.

Bacon, F. (1975) *The Advancement of Learning (1605) Book 1*. London: The Athlone Press.

Bannister, D. (1981) 'Personal construct theory and research method.' In P. Reason and J. Rowan (eds) *Human Enquiry: A Sourcebook of New Paradigm Research*. Chichester: Wiley.

Bannister, P., Burman, E., Parker, I., Taylor, M. and Tindall, C. (1994) *Qualitative Methods in Psychology: A Research Guide*. Buckingham: Open University Press.

Barrow, R. and Woods, R. (1982) *An Introduction to Philosophy of Education*. London: Methuen.

Beehler, R. (1985) 'The schools and indoctrination.' *Journal of Philosophy of Education 19*, 261–72.

Benton, S. (1991) 'Gender, sexuality and citizenship.' In G. Andrews (ed) *Citizenship*. London: Lawrence and Wishart.

Best, F. (1991) 'Human rights education and teacher training.' In H. Starkey (ed) *The Challenge of Human Rights Education*. London: Cassell.

Branson, M. (1991) 'From the Bill of Rights (1791) to the Universal Declaration: The American Tradition of Education for Democracy.' In H. Starkey (ed) *The Challenges of Human Rights Education*. London: Cassell.

Brockman, J. (1977) (ed) *About Bateson*. New York: Dutton.

Bruner, J. (1990) *Acts of Meaning*. Cambridge, MA: Harvard University Press.

Bryman, A. (1988) *Quantity and Quality in Social Research*. London: Unwin Hyman.

Callan, E. (1988) *Autonomy and Schooling*. Kingston and Montreal: McGill-Queen's University Press.

Campbell, D. (1969) *Reforms as Experiments; American Psychologist 24*, 409–429.

Carr, W. (1991) 'Education for democracy? A philosophical analysis of the national curriculum.' *Journal of Philosophy of Education 25*, 2, 183–190.

Claycomb, C. (1989) *Multicultural Education in a Primary School*. York: University of York.

Cohen, L. and Manion, L. (1980) *Research Methods in Education*. London: Croom Helm.

Corrigan, P. (1990) *Social Forms / Human Capacities: Essays in Authority and Difference*. London: Routledge.

Council of Europe (1985) *Recommendation No R (85) 7 of the Committee of Ministers, Appendix 3.2*. Strasbourg: Council of Europe.

Cox, C.B. chair (1989) *National Curriculum Working Group (English) Report to the Department of Education and Science and the Welsh Office. English for Ages 5 to 16: Proposals of the Secretary of State for Education and Science and the Secretary of State for Wales*. HMSO.

Cunningham, J. (1991) 'The human rights secondary school.' In H. Starkey (ed) *The Challenges of Human Rights Education*. London: Cassell.

Darling, J. (1994) *Child-centred Education and its Critics*. London: Chapman.

Davie, R. (1989) 'The National Children's Bureau: evidence to the Elton committee.' In N. Jones (ed) *School Management and Pupil Behaviour*. Lewes: Falmer Press.

Davie, R. (1993) 'Listen to the child: a time for change.' *The Psychologist*, June.

Davies, B. (1984) 'Children through their own eyes.' *Oxford Review of Education* 10, 3.

Davison, A. (1987) *The Best Days of Our Lives*. Newcastle: Northern Micromedia.

Denzin, N.K. (1983) 'Interpretative interaction.' In G. Morgan (ed) *Beyond Method: Strategies for Social Research*. Beverly Hills, CA: Sage.

Department of Education and Science (1991) *Your Child and the National Curriculum: A Parent's Guide to What's Taught in Schools*. London: DES.

Department of Education and Science and the Welsh Office (1990) *English in the National Curriculum*. HMSO.

DES and the Welsh Office (1989) *English in the National Curriculum*. London: HMSO.

Dewey, J. (1897) 'My pedagogic creed.' In R.D. Archambault (ed) *John Dewey on Education (1974)*. Chicago: University Press.

Dewey, J. (1900) *The School and Society*. Chicago: University Press.

Dewey, J. (1916) *Democracy and Education*. New York: Macmillan.

Diesing, P. (1972) *Patterns of Discovery in the Social Sciences*. London: Routledge and Kegan Paul.

Dobbert, M.L. (1982) *Ethnographic Research: Theory and Application for Modern Schools and Societies*. New York: Praeger.

Donnelly, J. (1984) 'Cultural Relatives and Universal Human Rights'. *Human Rights Quarterly 1*, 4, pp.400–419.

Duczek, S. (1984) *The Peace Studies Project: A Case Study*. York: University of York.

Dye, P. (1991) 'Active learning for human rights in intermediate and high schools.' In H. Starkey (ed) *The Challenges of Human Rights Education*. London: Cassell.

Dyson, J. (1986) *Developmental Education for the 14–16 Age Group*. York: University of York.

Education Reform Act (1988) London: HMSO.

Edwards, J. (1993) *Cross-Curricular Theme Pack*. Cambridge: Pearson Publishing.

Edwards, J. and Fogelman, K. (1993) *Developing Citizenship in the Curriculum*. London: Fulton.

Elliot, J. (1991) *Action Research for Educational Change*. Milton Keynes: Open University Press.

Ely, M. (1991) *Doing Qualitative Research: Circles Within Circles*. London: Falmer.

Elyot, T. (1962) *The Book Named The Governor (1531)*. London: Everyman's Library.

Emler, N. and Reicher, S. (1986) 'Managing reputations in adolescence; the pursuit of delinquent and non-delinquent identities.' In H. Beloff (ed) *Getting into Life*. London: Methuen.

English Centre, The (1985a) *The English Curriculum: Gender: Material for Discussion*. London: The English Centre.

English Centre, The (1985b) *The English Curriculum: Race: Material for Discussion*. London: The English Centre.

Feinberg, W. (1983) *Understanding Education*. Cambridge: Cambridge University Press.

Finch, J. (1993) 'It's great to have someone to talk to.' In M. Hammersley (ed) *Social Research: Philosophy, Politics and Practice*. London: Sage.

Flanders, N. (1970) *Analysing Teaching Behaviour*. Reading, MA: Addison-Wesley.

Fogelman, K. (1991) *Citizenship in Schools*. London: Fulton.

Fordyce, D. (1757) *Dialogues Concerning Education Vol 1, 3rd edition.* London: E. Dilly.

Franklin, B. (1986) *The Right of Children.* Oxford: Blackwells.

Franklin, B. (1992) 'Children and decision making: developing empowering institutions.' In M.D. Fortuyen and M. de Langen (eds) *Towards the Realizations of Human Rights of Children; Lectures given at the Second International Conference on Children's Ombudswork.* Amsterdam: Children's Ombudswork Foundation and Defence for Children International-Netherlands.

Freeman, M.D.A. (1987) 'Taking children's rights seriously.' *Children and Society 1*, 4.

Freeman, M.D.A. (1992) 'Taking children's rights more seriously.' *International Journal of Law and the Family 6.*

Freire, P. (1976) *Education: the Practice of Freedom.* London: Writers' and Readers' Publishing Cooperative.

Fukuyama, F. (1992) *The End of History and the Last Man.* London: Hamish Hamilton.

Geldof, R. (1986) *Is That It?* London: Sidgwick and Jackson.

Giddens, A. (1991) *Modernity and Self Identity: Self and Society in the Late Modern Age.* Oxford: Oxford University Press.

Giddens, A. (1994) *Beyond Left and Right: The Future of Radical Politics.* Cambridge: Polity.

Gilligan, C., Ward, J.V. and Taylor J.M. with Bardige, B. (eds) (1988) *Mapping the Moral Domain.* Cambridge, MA: Harvard University Press.

Giroux, H.A. (1991) *Postmodernism, Feminism and Cultural Politics: Redrawing Educational Boundaries.* Albany, NY: State University of New York Press.

Glaser, B.G. and Strauss, A.L. (1967) *The Discovery of Grounded Theory.* Chicago: Aldine.

Goetz, J.P. and LeCompte, M.D. (1984) *Ethnography and Qualitative Design in Educational Research.* Orlando, Florida: Academic Press.

Golby, M. (1994) *Case Study as Educational Research.* Exeter University: Monograph.

Gray, J. (1983) *Mill on Liberty: A Defence.* London: Routledge and Kegan Paul.

Green, T.F. (1971) *The Activities of Teaching.* New York: McGraw-Hill.

Green, T.F. (1972) 'Indoctrination and beliefs.' In I.A. Snook (ed) *Concepts of Indoctrination.* London: Routledge and Kegan Paul.

Griffith, R. (1991) *The MOB diaries and tapes: a case study of an unstructured independent learning project.* Unpublished.

Griffith, R. (1999) *National Curriculum: National Disaster.* London: Falmer Press.

Guba, E.G. and Lincoln, Y.S. (1981) *Effective Evaluation: Improving the Usefulness of Evaluation Results through Responsive and Naturalistic Approaches.* San Francisco: Jossey-Bass.

Guba, E.G. and Lincoln. Y.S. (1982) 'Epistemological and methodological bases of naturalistic inquiry.' *Educational Communication and Technology Journal, 30.*

Gutmann, A. (1990) *Democracy and Democratic Education.* Paper presented at the International Network of Philosophy of Education Conference, London.

Habermas, J. (1971) *Knowledge and Human Interests.* Boston, MA: Beacon.

Hall, C. and Hall, E. (1988) *Human Relations in Education.* London: Routledge.

Hare, R.M. (1972) 'Adolescents into adults.' In Hare (ed) *Applications of Moral Philosophy.* London: Macmillan.

Harre, R. (1983) *Personal Being.* Oxford: Blackwell.

Hart, R.A. (1992) *Children's Participation: From Tokenism to Citizenship; Innocenti Essays No 4.* Florence: UNICEF International Child Development Centre.

Havel, V. (1986) *Living in Truth.* London: Faber.

Heater, D. (1991) 'The curriculum jigsaw and human rights education.' In H. Starkey (ed) *The Challenges of Human Rights Education.* London: Cassell.

Held, D. (1991) 'Between state and civil society: citizenship.' In G. Andrews (ed) *Citizenship*. London: Lawrence and Wishart.

Henwood, K.L. and Pidgeon, N.F. (1993) 'Qualitative research and psychological theorizing.' In M. Hammersley (ed) *Social Research: Philosophy, Politics and Practice*. London: Sage.

Herbert, C. (1992) *Sexual Harrassment in Schools*. London: Fulton.

Heron, J. (1981a) 'Philosophical basis for a new paradigm.' In P. Reason and J. Rowan (eds) *Human Enquiry: A Sourcebook of New Paradigm Research*. Chichester: Wiley.

Heron, J. (1981b) 'Experiential research methodology.' In P. Reason and J. Rowan (eds) *Human Enquiry: A Sourcebook of New Paradigm Research*. Chichester: Wiley.

Holt, J. (1975) *Escape from Childhood*. Harmondsworth: Penguin.

Honeyford, R. (1991) 'Why Are Our Schools Still Run by Cranks?' Daily Mail, 26.06.

Hopson, B. and Scally, M. (1981) *Lifeskills Teaching*. London: McGraw-Hill.

Horvath, A. (1991) 'The practice of theory.' In B. Spiecker and R. Straughan (eds) *Freedom and Indoctrination in Education: International Perspectives*. London: Cassell.

Howe, S. (1991) 'Citizenship in the new Europe: a last chance for the enlightenment?' In G. Andrews (ed) *Citizenship*. London: Lawrence and Wishart.

Hughes, J. (1976) *Sociological Analysis: Methods of Discovery*. London: Hodder and Stoughton.

Hurd, D. (1987 and 1988) *Conservative Party Conference speeches on Active Citizenship*. London: Conservative Central Office Research Library.

Hutton, W. (1995) *The State We're In*. London: Jonathan Cape.

Jeffs, T. (1995) 'Children's educational rights in a new era.' In B. Franklin (ed) *The Handbook of Children's Rights: Comparative Policy and Practice*. London: Routledge.

John, M. (1993a) *Children With Special Needs as the Casualties of a Free Market Culture; International Journal of Children's Rights 1*. Netherlands: Kluwer Academic.

John, M. (1993b) 'Children's rights and new forms of democracy.' In M.D. Fortuyen and M. de Langen (eds) *Towards the Realizations of Human Rights of Children; Lectures given at the Second International Conference on Children's Ombudswork*. Amsterdam: Children's Ombudswork Foundation and Defence for Children International-Netherlands.

Jones, N. (1990) 'Reader, writer, text; knowledge about language and the curriculum.' In R. Carter (ed) *The LINC Reader*. London: Hodder and Stoughton.

Kandel, I.L. (1949) 'Education and human rights.' In *UNESCO Human Rights: Comments and Interpretations*. London: Wingate.

Kazepides, T. (1991) 'Religious indoctrination and freedom.' In B. Spiecker and R. Straughan (eds) *Freedom and Indoctrination in Education: International Perspectives*. London: Cassell.

Kelly, G.A. (1955) *The Psychology of Personal Constructs*. New York: Norton.

Kilpatrick, W.H. (1918) *The Project Method*. Teachers College Record No 19.

Kincheloe, J. (1991) *Teachers as Researchers: Qualitative Enquiry as a Path to Empowerment*. London: Falmer.

Kirk, J. and Miller, M.L. (1986) *Reliability and Validity in Qualitative Research*. London: Sage.

Kohlberg, L. (1971) 'Stages of moral development as a basis for moral education.' In C. Beck, B. Crittenden and E. Sullivan (eds) *Moral Education*. Toronto: University of Toronto.

Kohlberg, L. (1985) 'Resolving moral conflicts within the just community.' In C.G. Harding (ed) *Moral Dilemmas*. Chicago: Precedent.

Kohlberg, L. and Gilligan, C. (1971) *The Adolescent as a Philospher. The Discovery of the Self in a Post-conventional World*. Boston, MA: Dedalus.

Kolb, D.A. (1984) *Experiential Learning: Experience as the Source of Learning and Development*. Englewood Cliffs, NJ: Prentice Hall.

Kundera, M. (1984) 'A kidnapped west or culture bows out.' *Granta* No 11.

Langford, G. (1985) *Education, Persons and Society: A Philosophical Enquiry*. London: Macmillan.

Latour, B. (1987) *Science in Action*. Milton Keynes: Open University Press.

Lewin, K. (1947) 'Group decision and social change.' In T.M. Newcomb and E.L. Hartley (eds) *Readings in Social Psychology*. New York: Holt, Rinehart and Winston.

Lincoln, Y.S. (1993) 'I and Thou: Method, Voice and Roles in Research with the Silenced'. in *Naming Silenced Lives*. D. Mclaughlin, W.G. Tierney. London: Routledge.

Lister, I. (1990) *The Exclusive Society: Citizenship and the Poor*. London: Child Poverty Action Group.

Lister, I. (1991) 'The challenge of human rights for education.' In H. Starkey (ed) *The Challenges of Human Rights Education*. London: Cassell.

Lyeseight-Jones, P. (1991) 'Human rights in primary education.' In H. Starkey (ed) *The Challenges of Human Rights Education*. London: Cassell.

Lynch, J. (1992) *Education for Citizenship in a Multicultural Society*. London: Cassell.

Mandela, N. (1986) *The Struggle Is My Life*. London: International Defence and Aid Fund for Southern Africa.

Marie, J.-B. (1985) *Human Rights or A Way of Life in a Democracy*. Strasbourg: Council of Europe.

Maruyama, M. (1981) 'Endogenous research: rationale.' In P. Reason and J. Rowan (eds) *Human Enquiry: A Sourcebook of New Paradigm Research*. Chichester: Wiley.

McCluhan, M. (1968) *The Medium Is The Message*. Harmsworth: Penguin.

McLeod, K. (1991) 'Human rights and multiculturalism in Canadian schools.' In H. Starkey (ed) *The Challenges of Human Rights Education*. London: Cassell.

Measor, L. and Sykes, P. (1992) *Gender and Schools*. London: Cassell.

Meighan, R. (1993) *Theory and Practice of Regressive Education*. Nottingham: Educational Heretics Press.

Meighan, R. (1995) *The Freethinkers' Pocket Directory to the Educational Universe*. Nottingham: Educational Heretics Press.

Mill, J.S. (1965) 'On genius (1832).' In J. Scheewing (ed) *J.S. Mill, Essays on Literature and Society*. New York and London: Collier-Macmillan.

Mulgan, G. (1991) 'Citizens and responsibilities.' In G. Andrews (ed) *Citizenship*. London: Lawrence and Wishart.

National Curriculum Council (1990a) *Curriculum Guidance 3: The Whole Curriculum*. York: NCC.

National Curriculum Council (1990b) *Curriculum Guidance 8: Education For Citizenship*. York: NCC.

Neill, A.S. (1960) *Summerhill: A Radical Approach to Child Rearing (1926)*. New York: Hart Publishing Company.

Oelkers, J. (1991) 'Freedom and learning: some thoughts on liberal and progressive education in freedom and indoctrination.' In B. Spiecker and R. Straughan (eds) *Education: International Perspectives*. London: Cassell.

Osler, A. (1988) *Do It Justice: Resources and Activities for Introducing Education in Human Rights*. Birmingham: Development Education Centre.

Parekh, B. (1991) 'British citizenship and cultural difference.' In G. Andrews (ed) *Citizenship*. London: Lawrence and Wishart.

Parlett, M. (1981) 'Illuminative evaluation.' In P. Reason and J. Rowan (eds) *Human Enquiry: A Sourcebook of New Paradigm Research*. Chichester: Wiley.

Pateman, C. (1988) *The Sexual Contract*. Cambridge: Polity.

Peters, R.S. (1979) 'Democratic values and educational aims.' *Teachers College Record 8*, 3, 463–481.

Phillips, A. (1991) 'Citizenship and feminist politics.' In G. Andrews (ed) *Citizenship*. London: Lawrence and Wishart.

Plant, R. (1991) 'Social rights and the reconstruction of welfare.' In G. Andrews (ed) *Citizenship*. London: Lawrence and Wishart.

Pollis, A. (1982) 'Liberal, socialist and Third World persepctives of human rights' in P. Schrub and A. Pollis (eds.) *Towards a Human Rights Framework*. New York: Praeger.

Priestley, J. (1778) *Miscellaneous Observations Relating to Education. Most Especially as it Respects the Conduct of the Mind. To Which is Added, An Essay on a Course of Liberal Education for Civil and Active Life*. Bath: R. Cruttwell.

Prince's Trust (1994) *Annual Report and Accounts*. London: Prince's Trust.

Prince's Trust (1995) *Trust: Inspiring Young People; summer*. London: Prince's Trust.

Programme Directing Committee (1986) *Education 10–14 in Scotland*. Dundee: Dundee College of Education.

Raz, J. (1986) *The Morality of Freedom*. Oxford: The Clarendon Press.

Reason, P. and Rowan, J. (1981) *Human Enquiry: A Sourcebook of New Paradigm Research*. Chichester: John Wiley.

Rendel, M. (1991) 'Challenging patriarchy and hierarchy: the contribution of human rights education to the achievement of equality for women.' In H. Starkey (ed) *The Challenges of Human Rights Education*. London: Cassell.

Rey, M. (1991) 'Human rights and intercultural education.' In H. Starkey (ed) *The Challenges of Human Rights Education*. London: Cassell.

Riddell, S. (1992) *Gender and the Politics of the Curriculum*. London: Routledge.

Roaf, C. (1991) 'The challenge of human rights to the education of children with special needs.' In H. Starkey (ed) *The Challenges of Human Rights Education*. London: Cassell.

Rogers, C.R. (1983) *Freedom To Learn For The Eighties*. Columbus, OH: Merrill.

Rousseau, J.-J. (1762) *Emile* trans. Foxley B (1911). London: Dent.

Ruskin, M. (1991) 'Whose rights of citizenship?' In G. Andrews (ed) *Citizenship*. London: Lawrence and Wishart.

Sanford, N. (1981) 'Action research.' In P. Reason and J. Rowan (eds) *Human Enquiry: A Sourcebook of New Paradigm Research*. Chichester: Wiley.

Scetlander (1986) *Carrigan Street*. Glasgow: Scetlander.

Scetlander (1986) *Project Space*. Glasgow: Scetlander.

Schofield, J.W. (1993) 'Increasing the generalizability of qualitative research.' In M. Hammersley (ed) *Social Research: Philosophy, Politics and Practice*. London: Sage.

Schwab, P. 1981. 'Rethinking Human Rights in Ethiopia.' *Transitional Perspectives 8*, 2, pp. 6–9.

Schwartz, P. and Ogilvy, J. (1979) *The Emergent Paradigm; Changing Patterns of Thought and Belief*. Menlo Park, CA: SRI International.

Scriven, M. (1967) 'The methodology of evaluation' in R.W. Tyler (ed) *Perpectives of Critical Evaluation*. Chicago: Rand McNally.

Shaftesbury, A.A.C. (1978) *Characteristicks of Men, Manners, Opinions, Times, in Three Volumes (London 1711)*. Hildesheim and New York: Geor Olms.

Shakespeare W. (c1598–1602) *The Tragedy of Hamlet, Prince of Denmark*. eds P. Abrahams, and A. Body. London: Minster Classics (1968).

Sharron, H. (1987) *Changing Children's Minds*. London: Souvenir Press.

Sheridan, T. (1769) *British Education: Or, The Source of Disorders of Great Britain. Being an Essay Towards Proving that the Immorality, Ignorance and False Taste, which So Generally Prevail, Are the Natural and Necessary Consequences of the Present Defective System of Education. A New Edition, revised by the author, with additions and alterations.* London: E. and C. Dilly.

Shiman, D. (1991) 'Teaching human rights: classroom activities for a global age.' In H. Starkey (ed) *The Challenges of Human Rights Education.* London: Cassell.

Shotter, J. (1984) *Social Accountability and Selfhood.* Oxford: Blackwell.

Shotton, J. (1993) *No Master High or Low: Libertarian Education and Schooling 1890 – 1990.* Bristol: Libertarian Education.

Siegel, H. (1991) 'Indoctrination and education.' In B. Spiecker and R. Straughan (eds) *Freedom and Indoctrination in Education: International Perspectives.* London: Cassell.

Sieyes (1789) 'Reconnaissance et Exposition Raisonée des Droits de l'Homme et du Citoyen: address to Constitutional Committee.' In H. Starkey (ed) *The Challenges of Human Rights Education.* London: Cassell.

Silverman, D. (1985) *Quantitative Methodology and Sociology.* Aldershot: Gower.

Spiecker, (1991) 'Indoctrination: the suppression of critical dispositions; in freedom and indoctrination.' In B. Spiecker and R. Straughan (eds) *Education: International Perspectives.* London: Cassell.

Stake, R.E. (1978) 'The case study in social inquiry.' *Educational Researcher 7.*

Starkey, H. (1991) (ed) *The Challenges of Human Rights Education.* London: Cassell.

Steedman, C. (1982) *The Tidy House: Little Girls Writing.* London: Virago.

Steutel, J.W. (1991) 'Discipline, internalisation and freedom: a conceptual analysis.' In B. Spiecker and R. Straughan (eds) *Freedom and Indoctrination in Education: International Perspectives.* London: Cassell.

Steward. F. (1991) 'Citizens of Planet Earth.' In G. Andrews (ed) *Citizenship.* London: Lawrence and Wishart.

Stobbart, M. (1991) 'Foreword to the challenge of human rights education.' In H. Starkey (ed) *The Challenges of Human Rights Education.* London: Cassell.

Stock, J. (1991) *Case Studies in English.* Manchester: Trafford.

Stradling, R. (1984) *Teaching Controversial Issues.* London: Arnold.

Szucs, J. (1988) 'Three historical regions of Europe.' In J. Keane (ed) *Civil Society and the State.* London: Verso.

TESS (Times Educational Supplement, Scotland) (1988) *Curriculum Policy Rift Grows.* Article, p.1, 24.06.88.

Torbert, W.R. (1981a) 'Why educational research has been so uneducational: the case for a new model of social science based on collaborative enquiry.' In P. Reason and J. Rowan (eds) *Human Enquiry: A Sourcebook of New Paradigm Research.* Chichester: Wiley.

Torbert, W.R. (1981b) 'A collaborative enquiry into voluntary metropolitan desegregation.' In P. Reason and J. Rowan (eds) *Human Enquiry: A Sourcebook of New Paradigm Research.* Chichester: Wiley.

Torney-Purta, J. and Hahn, C. (1988) 'Values education in the Western European tradition.' In W.K. Cummings, S. Gopinathan and Y. Tomoda (eds) *The Revival of Values Education in Asia and the West.* Oxford: Pergamon.

Tyack, D.B. (1967) (ed) *Turning Points in American Educational History.* Waltham, MA: Blaisdell.

United Nations General Assembly Official Records, Resolution 217, 3rd Session, Part 1 (1948) *The Universal Declaration of Human Rights.* New York: UN.

United Nations General Assembly Official Records, Resolution 25, 44th Session (1989) *The United Nations Convention on the Rights of the Child.* New York: UN.

US Department of State, Bureau of Public Affairs (1988) *Current Policy No. 1091*. An address by Paula Dobriansky, Deputy Assistant Secretary for Human Rights and Humanitarian Affairs, 03.06.88.

Vajda, M. (1988) 'East-central European perspectives.' In J. Keane (ed) *Civil Society and the State*. London: Verso.

Watney, S. (1991) 'Citizenship in the age of AIDS.' In G. Andrews (ed) *Citizenship*. London: Lawrence and Wishart.

Weil, S.W. and McGill, I. (1989) (eds) *Making Sense of Experiential Learning*. Oxford: OUP.

Weiss, L. (1988) (ed) *Class, Race and Gender in American Education*. Albany, NY: State University of New York Press.

White, J. (1991) 'The justification of autonomy as an educational aim; in freedom and indoctrination.' In B. Spiecker and R. Straughan (eds) *Education: International Perspectives*. London: Cassell.

White, J.P. (1972) 'Indoctrination and intentions, and indoctrination without doctrines?' In I.A. Snook (ed) *Concepts of Indoctrination: Philosophical Essays*. London: Routledge and Kegan Paul.

Whyld, J. (1983) (ed) *Sexism in the Secondary School Curriculum*. London: Harper and Row.

Wigley, D. (1995) *A Democratic Wales in a United Europe*. Cardiff: Plaid Cymru.

Wilson, J. (1972) 'Indoctrination and reality.' In I. Snook (ed) *Concepts of Indoctrination*. London: Routledge and Kegan Paul.

Wilson, J. (1991) 'Religious (Moral, Political, Etc) Commitment, Education and Indoctrination.' In B. Spiecker and R. Straughan (eds) *Freedom and Indoctrination in Education: International Perspectives*. London: Cassell.

Wolcott, H.F. (1973) *The Man in the Principal's Office: an Ethnography*. New York: Holt, Rinehart and Winston.

Woodhead, C., Rose, J. and Robin, M. (1992) *Curriculum Organisation and Classroom Practice in Primary Schools: A Discussion Paper*. London: HMSO.

Wright, N. (1989) *Assessing Radical Education*. Milton Keynes: Open University Press.

Yin, R.K. (1989) *Case Study Research: Design and Method*. New York: Sage.

Youniss, J. (1980) *Parents and Peers in Social Development*. Chicago: University of Chicago Press.

Youniss, J. (1981) 'Piaget and the self constituted through relations.' In W.F. Overton (ed) *The Relationship Between Social and Cognitive Development*. Hillsdale, NJ: Erlbaum.

Index

action 40, 197
A Level 18
affective 49, 74
  aspects 37
  development 48, 129, 179,
    181, 231
  domain 44, 48, 136
Africa 41
African Charter on Human and
  People's Rights
America 29, 42, 59
American Bill of Rights 28
Amnesty International 38, 43
anarchy 194, 235
  anarchist 225
Another Day in Paradise
  144–146
art 36
  Art and Design 117, 122,
    124, 126
  plastic arts 36
assessment (see also independent
  learning factor 5) 19, 20,
    22, 77, 78, 114,
    199–205, 220
  and response 15
  criterion reference 202
  crude methods of 9
  ipsative reference 201, 202
  normative reference 15, 200,
    201, 202
  oral assessment 21
  peer-assessment 20, 200, 202
  practical assessment 21
  self-assessment 20, 183
Association for Curriculum
  Development 37
Athens 42
Australasia 42
authority 56, 141, 194, 223,
    230, 235
  didactic 13, 220
  hierarchical 74, 130
  institutional 20, 35, 49
  moral 40
  symbolic 42
    authoritarian 23, 26, 59,
      60, 82, 128, 129, 169,
      221, 222, 232
    authoritarianism 42, 129
autocracy 46

autonomy 45–46, 51, 59, 78,
  'R81, 182, 189, 193, 194,
    195, 231, 237
autonomous 21, 26, 40, 44,
    169, 188, 220

back-to-basics 26, 223, 237
bibliography 80, 195, 201–202
biology 37
Business Studies 133, 134,
    138, 139

capability 26, 81, 222
Carnmore 14, 18, 24, 104,
    151, 188, 189, 190, 198,
    203
Centennial 138, 150, 152,
    167, 193, 198
Central Europe 30, 31, 42
Centre for Citizenship Studies
  in Education 33
Centre for the Study of
  Comprehensive Schools
    75
CSE 15, 18, 116, 218, 219
Charter 88 30
cheating 15, 141, 230
China 42, 54, 136, 138
choice 20, 21, 54, 197
  allowing pupils to choose 22
  and control of the curriculum
    48
  of partners 79, 191
  of reading texts 19
  of subject 20, 93, 174, 209
citizen(s) (see also global) 19, 23,
    58, 76, 115, 219, 220
  active 25, 39
  Citizen's Charters 27, 30,
    210, 226
  critically reflective 9
  of the classroom 183
  of tomorrow 9, 11
  of the third millennium 39
citizenship (see also global) 21,
    25, 26–62, 152, 220
  active 9, 32, 33, 39
  and education 9
  as a cross-curricular theme
    36, 49
  as a discrete subject 36
  attributes of 9, 25, 27, 105,
    142
  concept of 10, 28, 42
  critically reflective model of
    220
  democratic 195
  for education 45
  of the third millennium 37,
    231

traditional criteria of 10
citizenry, educated 9
Civis Romanus 27
cognitive 49, 74
  aspects 37
  development 48, 129, 179,
    181, 231
  domain 44, 48, 136
collaboration 15, 100, 104,
    134, 141
  collaborative groups (see also
    independent learning
    factor 1) 93, 94, 96,
      105, 144, 152, 156,
      159, 168, 171, 180,
      192, 195, 229
  choice of 191
  conduct of 191–192
  criteria for the formation of
    185–190
  organisation of 190–191
  outcomes of 196–199
collaborative outcomes
  196–199
collaborative research 21, 22
collaborative work 47, 75,
    122, 220, 228, 231
collaborative writing 19
collectivism 38, 158
community (see also independent
  learning factor 9) 20, 23,
    28, 32, 33, 38, 50, 58,
    60, 61, 63, 70, 77, 82,
    93, 125, 130, 136, 141,
    144, 151, 152, 153, 172,
    180, 210, 226, 228, 230,
    231
communism 27, 42
comprehension exercises 117,
    208, 229
competition 26, 32, 192, 230
co-operation 26, 47, 50, 58,
    192, 230
  co-operative groups (see also
    independent learning
    factor 2) 156, 159, 180,
      188, 190, 195
  co-operative outcomes 174,
    196–199
Conservative Party 30, 226
Council of Europe 36, 48, 218
County Multi-cultural
  Education Advisory
    Teacher 81, 121
County Senior Advisory
  Teacher for Secondary
    English 24, 116
coursework 21, 22, 221
Cox Report 24

critical disposition 21, 44, 48,
    51, 54, 55, 56, 57, 74,
    78, 129, 140, 141, 183,
    208, 226, 231
    faculties 21, 136, 227, 229
    friend 88, 109, 112
    paradigm 10, 63, 68, 69, 85,
        105–109, 112
culture
    autarchic 27, 220
    cultural diversity 29, 35, 220
    cultural pluralism 34
curriculum 15, 20, 22, 23, 26,
    30, 33, 36, 45, 48, 57,
    58, 63, 6'17, 77, 117,
    125, 126, 128, 129, 130,
    138, 140, 152, 174, 181,
    182, 200, 217
    artificial divisions in 17
    content-based 117, 119,
        238–239
    cross-curricular connections
        140
        dimensions 135–136
        elements 135–138
        involvement 152
        skills 125, 126, 133, 137
        studies 24, 125, 126
        themes 36, 125, 126, 137
    English 16, 18
    extra-curricular activities 36
    knowledge-based 56, 220,
        221, 223
    National Curriculum 9,
        10,11,12, 26, 36, 44,
        48, 57, 60, 66, 68, 81,
        110, 113, 115, 117,
        135, 142, 167, 168,
        198, 200, 212, 217,
        219, 220, 222, 224,
        228, 230, 238
    presentation of 16, 238–239
    social and moral isolation of
        50, 129, 130, 140, 226
    socially and ethically located
        23
    socially oriented 24
    statutory 11

dance 36
*Declaration of the Rights of Man
    and the Citizen* 28, 39
decontextualised exercises 18,
    19
democracy 11, 42, 48, 49
    classroom democracy 23
    democratic citizenship 27,
        29, 76, 195
    democratic classroom 20

democratic culture 49
democratic schooling 24
democratic teaching and
    learning styles 9, 169
democratisation of state
    schooling 13, 84
    liberal 27, 52, 218
    post-modern democratic
        society 9
dependent learning 10, 50–62,
    84, 113–142, 226
    at Keystage 3 127–128
    at Keystage 4 140
DFE 74, 114
diary 80, 170, 175, 195,
    201–202
dignity 40, 44, 48, 78
discipline 26
discrimination 34, 193
discussion with teachers 114
disempowered, the 10, 21, 29,
    63, 140, 141
    disempowerment 125, 140,
        225, 226–232
documentation 114
drafting 15, 123
drama 17, 18, 135, 138, 139
Drudges and Frogs 26, 51,
    217, 221, 227, 239

Eastern Europe 29, 31, 42
economy 28
educated person
    concept of the 9
    educated person, the 9, 10,
        25, 59, 76
education 11, 20, 25, 26, 220
    about citizenship 36, 49
    Centre for Global 38
    child-centred 32, 33, 55, 57,
        238
    content-based 220, 238
    for citizenship 26, 31, 32,
        34, 36, 49, 81, 137
    further 18
    in citizenship 36, 49
    in human rights 36
    in Human Rights Network
        38
    intercultural 36–37
    liberal 31, 55–57, 61, 74,
        230
    personal and social 36
    Political 81
    progressive 55, 57–58, 60,
        74
    state 30, 43, 218–239
    utilitarian view of 18

educational citizenship 10, 11,
    12, 13, 14, 18, 19, 20,
    21, 22, 23, 24, 54, 64,
    66, 74, 76, 79, 82, 111,
    112, 113, 115, 117, 129,
    140, 142, 180, 182, 183,
    193, 196, 217, 218–239
    concept of 43–48
    definition of 48–49
    implications of 49–50
    practices that may suppress
        50–62
Education Reform Act 26, 30,
    218, 226
educational system 48
    national 31, 32
    state educational system 10,
        31, 236, 238
    state educational system of
        the UK 11
    state-maintained educational
        system 43, 51, 59
    state-maintained educational
        system of the UK 10
    state-maintained liberal 9
Elton Report 45
Emily Jay 116, 130–141
empowerment 9, 19, 26, 28,
    42, 84, 218, 220, 225,
    230, 231, 232, 237, 238
enfranchisement 26, 220
England 27
England and Wales 26
English 36, 68, 128, 133, 136,
    139
    Advisory Support Teachers
        81
    Advisory Team 81, 96
    department 21, 22, 23
    GCSE 20, 21
    Head of 14, 116
    Heads of 116
    in the National Curriculum
        122, 123, 124, 237
    lesson(s) 14, 17, 120, 124,
        125, 126, 138
    outdoor education club 23
    reports 23
    second-in-department 14
    secondary 15
    teachers of 15
    textbooks 16
enterprise 32
entitlement 26, 28, 29, 30,
    218, 219, 220
environment (*see also*
    independent learning
    factor) 9) 20, 23, 33, 38,
    58, 61, 67, 75, 77, 82,

109, 125, 130, 141, 172, 180, 183, 210, 220, 228, 230
Equal Opportunities 121, 137
equality 34, 36, 38, 48, 219
ethics of global citizenship 39, 41
  ethical attributes of citizenship 59
  collectivism 38
  concern 22, 39, 40, 43, 44, 50, 78, 79
  criteria 62
  data-collection 84
  duty 85
  grounds 82
  imprimatur 40
  problem 81
  rights 51
  ethically informed 49
  located 23
eudemonic test 18
Europe 59
European Community 155–156
European Convention for the Protection of Human Rights 43
European Social Charter 41
European Union 43
Europeans 138, 150, 152–168, 210
Eurovision Song Contest 43
Exeter University 24, 180, 218

feminism 29
FIAC 75
freedom 28, 29, 34, 36, 38, 39, 48, 57, 59, 60, 129, 149, 172, 187, 195, 197, 229
French 123, 126
Froebel 58

GCE 15, 18, 219
GCSE 20, 21, 85, 113, 116, 200, 203, 211, 219
gender 98, 105, 121, 136, 137, 139, 170, 171, 175, 186–187, 218
geography 36, 120, 123, 124–125, 126
German 124, 126, 130, 133, 134, 135, 138, 139
global citizen 183, 217
  picture of 40
  qualities of 10, 11, 21, 22, 43, 50, 51, 54, 59, 76
  definition of 79, 194, 231
global citizenship 49, 50, 51, 57, 76, 78, 82, 129, 130,

185, 193, 209, 216, 226, 231, 232, 235, 236, 239
  construct of 10, 37–43, 62
governors 17, 63, 182, 198, 232, 236
government 26, 41, 62, 199, 219, 220, 226, 239
  Conservative 32, 222, 224, 233
  democratic 31, 32
  Labour 32
  local 32
  national 43
  totalitarian 31
Green Party 38
Greenpeace 38, 43
Greenshire 10, 11, 13, 15, 114, 187, 193
group dynamics 92, 93, 170, 171, 172, 185, 205
groupwork 117, 128, 130, 134, 135, 172, 222
Gulf War 43

history 36, 122, 133, 134, 136, 138, 139
Hong Kong 28
humanities, the 54

ILEA 75
immigration 28
independent learning 10, 11, 13, 14, 20, 24, 50, 67, 76, 88, 90, 93, 104, 112, 113, 115, 142, 143–217, 221
  as a mechanism for the transformation of power 236–238
  as fun 175–178
  at Keystage 3 127
  at Keystage 4 139
  12 factors of 10, 11, 23, 62, 66, 74–79, 86, 90–91 93, 94, 108, 109, 111, 129, 142, 153, 182, 232
  Factor 1: collaborative groupwork 76, 78, 90, 91, 127, 139, 154–155, 159, 183– 192
  Factor 2: cooperative groupwork 76, 78, 90, 127, 139, 155–158, 159, 192–194
  Factor 3: individual responsibility 76, 78, 91, 127, 139, 155, 158–159, 194–195

Factor 4: pupil-designed tasks 77, 78, 91, 127, 139, 149, 155, 159, 195–199
Factor 5: pupil-negotiated assessment 77, 78, 91, 127, 139, 155, 159–160, 199–205
Factor 6: pupil-negotiated deadlines 77, 78, 91, 127, 139, 156, 160, 205–207
Factor 7: pupil-initiated research 77, 78, 91, 92, 127, 139, 155, 159, 160–161, 208–211
Factor 8: pupil-use of a range of language technology 77, 78, 91, 127, 139, 155, 161, 212–214
Factor 9: community involvement and the use of the environment 77, 78, 91, 92, 127, 140, 155, 161–164, 214–215
Factor 10: a sense of audience 77, 78, 92, 127, 140, 155, 159, 164–165, 215
Factor 11: presentation in different forms 77, 78, 91, 92, 127, 140, 155, 159, 165, 215
Factor 12: reflexivity 78, 79, 91, 92, 127, "140, 155, 166, 216
Project, the 81
projects 10, 11, 68, 79–81, 85, 86, 88, 92, 96, 98, 111, 116, 230
  cross-curricular, cross-phase 68, 149–168, 179
  implications for the future 216–217
  in English lessons 143–151, 168–178
  secondary phase 68
  observers' opinions of 181–182
  process of 170, 181, 183–184, 204
  product of 170, 181, 183–184
  pupils' opinions of 168–178
  teachers' opinions of 179–181
  questionnaires 80–81
Questionnaire 1 93, 97–103, 112

Questionnaire 2 91, 93, 103–105, 112
India 42
individual needs pupils 20, 93, 96, 153, 219
individual responsibility (see independent learning factor 3)
individuality 28, 32, 38, 48, 57, 58, 125, 127, 129, 188, 226
indoctrination 32, 50, 51–57, 74, 87, 129, 136, 140, 223, 224
International Conference o"n the Rights of the Child 218
investigation 26, 208

Japan 31
Joanne 91–92
Josie Leigh 116, 117–130
justice 40, 44, 47, 48, 68, 78, 183

Keystage Four 36, 83, 110, 111, 115, 130–142, 168, 200, 229
cross-curricular elements 135–137
conclusions 140–142
curricular disorientation 138
grouping systems 139
lesson times 138
option choices 139
other lesson activities 135
reading 134
seating 135
talk 130–134
tracking 115, 130–140
writing 134
Keystage One 200
Keystage Three 83, 110, 111, 115, 168, 229
conclusions 140–142
curricular disorientation 125
didacticism and subject specialism 126
knowledge-based approach 124
other lesson activities 124
reading 122–123
seating 124
skills-based approach 125
talk 119–122
tracking 115, 117–130
writing 123–9–124
Keystage Two 126

knowledge 49, 57, 100–101, 122, 126, 130, 136, 140, 141, 209
and Virtue 56
-based approach to Keystage 3 124–125
-centred 55
decontextualised, 'factual' 9, 26
didactic presentation of 26, 200, 220, 221, 222, 228
didactic transmission of 9, 44, 56, 141
foundation of 98, 100, 169, 170
hierarchical view of 229

Labour Party 28, 30
language 19, 36
and literature 14, 15, 36
body 19, 144
development 18, 125
different forms of 15
meta- 20, 220
modes of the pupils 20
of divested power 234
of invested power 233
of institutional authority 20
or literature 16
technology 23, 77
LEA 9, 61, 63, 70, 74, 114, 219, 221
learning 31
about citizenship 33–34
active 32, 33, 57, 58, 220
child-centred 44, 58
experience 20, 23, 75, 84, 105, 126, 230
experiential 48, 58, 100, 220
in citizenship 34–35
partner 24
partnership 23
place 24
pupil-centred approach to 20, 125
socially placed 9
Liberal Democrats 30
Liberal Party 30
LINC 24, 213, 223–225
literature 19, 20
Literature, GCSE 20, 21
live presentation 80, 146, 170, 175, 184, 190, 195, 201–202
Lord of the Flies 30, 134, 136

magazine 20, 80, 93, 170, 175, 184, 190, 195, 201–202
Mansfield 15, 16
marking 15

mathematics 37, 53, 117, 121, 122, 124, 126, 130, 133, 135, 139
media
artifacts 77
education 18, 20, 21, 24, 212
texts 20, 123, 213
Mini-Enterprise in Schools Project 75
Minorities 150–152, 166–167, 209
mixed-ability 21, 96, 128, 186
MOB 94, 95, 110, 205
modernity
high 26, 37, 46, 220, 221
post 43, 195
modules 20, 21, 22, 23, 36
monarchy 28
morality 34, 46–47, 130
moral action 40
authority 40
autonomy 44, 47
awareness 74, 129
code 40
component 46
conceptions 47
concern 47, 51
context 180
development 30–31, 46, 47
dimension 48
duty 85
isolation of the curriculum 57–59, 84, 129
issues 21, 130, 231
precipice 223
pressure 40
principles 38
rearmament 223
relevance 58
values 223
morally aware 26, 220
autonomous 47
music 36, 121, 126

NAAE 75
NATE 201, 213, 224–225
NCC 114
Natalie 90–91, 95
National Children's Bureau 45
nationality 28
negotiation (see also independent learning factors 5 and 6) 20, 21, 24, 160, 220, 232
Northern Ireland 27
note making 117, 123, 130, 134, 135, 208, 229

OFSTED 114
Open University 17

oracy 18
Outdoor Education Team 81

parents 11, 17, 61, 63, 182,
    220, 221, 226, 227, 232,
    237, 238
    Parents Charter 26, 222, 236
participation 28, 33, 35, 38,
    44, 45, 46, 51, 63, 83,
    98, 99
Peace Studies 81
pedagogy 20, 23, 44, 47–48,
    49, 55, 62, 66, 76, 113,
    129, 130, 136 139, 142,
    153, 180, 200, 217, 220,
    224, 230, 231, 237
    didactic 9, 22, 23, 26, 56,
    75, 100, 130, 168, 169,
    220, 221
P.E. 117, 126, 138, 139
Penmouth 104, 116–142
Performing Arts Advisory Team
    81
Personal and Social Education
    117, 125, 137, 139
Pestalozzi 58
philosophy of education 139,
    140, 141
    coherent 18
    knowledge-based 141
    liberal 10, 55–57
    libertarian 10, 59–62, 68
    progressive 10, 55, 57
physics 37
Plaid Cymru 28
playgroups 64, 83
power 61
    discourse 129
    divested 11, 193, 233–234,
    235, 237
    divesting of 19, 21
    divesting to pupils 21
    hierarchy of 15, 141
    in schools 49
    institutional 21
    invested 11, 35, 193, 199,
    201, 217, 232–233,
    235
    invested holders of 21
    nature of 11
    structure 128, 232
    transfer of 11, 235–236
    transformation of 11, 19, 50,
    216, 232–239
personhood 29, 39
Preparation for Life in a
    Multicultural Society
    135–136

presentation in different forms
    (see also independent
    learning factor 11) 23
press 17, 222, 226
primary liaison 24
'Princesses and Princes' 26, 51,
    217, 218, 220, 221, 227,
    228, 239
project work 16, 17, 18
public examinations 15, '821,
    141, 200, 228

RSA Education for Capability
    Award 75
reading 15
    at Keystage 3 122–123
    at Keystage 4 134
    personal choice 17, 18, 122
reciprocity 47, 50, 74, 129
reflexivity (see also independent
    learning factor 12) 27, 51,
    78, 79, 91, 92, 108, 109,
    111, 136, 201, 231
research (see also independent
    learning factor 7) 21, 24,
    50, 77, 87, 93, 144, 172,
    189, 195, 220, 228
    action research 9, 64, 66, 68,
    69, 81, 83, 84, 113,
    151, 159, 183, 208
    case studies 115–142
    detailed description 117
    multi-site studies 117
    typicality 116, 142
    circumspection phase 66, 68,
    74, 76, 103, 108, 111,
    114
    control phase 66, 68, 108,
    111, 114, 232
    data contamination 95, 111
    evaluations, guided 84,
    92–94
    evaluations, open 84, 88,
    90–92 93–94
    evaluations, written 84, 88,
    153, 194
    experimenter bias 95, 111
    fieldwork research 9, 10, 63,
    106, 180, 226
    generalisability 106,
    109–110, 115
    grounded theory 69, 86,
    104, 105, 109
    illuminative evaluation 67,
    69, 76, 82, 107, 108,
    111, 230
    intentional interaction
    67–68, 69, 76, 82, 107,
    108

intervention 10, 64, 66,
    67–68, 69, 76, 82, 86,
    108, 109, 111
interviews 70, 88, 95, 104,
    211
multi-faceted data 69, 70–74,
    88–105, 107
multi-perspective data 70–74,
    88, 107, 179
non-intervention 10, 64, 66,
    67, 83, 108, 109, 111
observation, classroom 9, 74,
    98, 194
observation, lesson 70, 99,
    113, 136, 208, 228
partnership 10, 63, 66, 68,
    70, 81–84, 87, 107,
    108, 109, 112, 145, 231
pre-emption phase 66, 68,
    76, 103, 108, 111, 114
profiles 102–103, 104, 191,
    203–204
project diaries 70, 84 94–95,
    104, 194, 203
qualitative analysis 98
qualitative data 69–70, 102,
    105, 112, 136
quantitative data 69–70, 105,
    112, 136
questionnaires 77, 84, 90,
    96–97, 111, 194, 211
questionnaires, guided 70
questionnaires, multi-choice
    70, 97, 103
reliability 111
representativeness 88, 90, 92,
    95, 111
researcher bias 104
respondent bias 96, 111
triangulation 69, 84, 107,
    109, 112
validity 69, 88, 90, 92, 95,
    105–111, 115–116,
    130, 179
video profiles 70, 84, 88, 96
rhetoric 9 ,11, 23, 27, 33, 141,
    217, 218–226, 227, 228,
    231, 237, 238, 239
Rideout, Ronald 16, 17
rights 23, 39, 42, 48
    and responsibilities 28, 32,
    33, 39, 50, 59–62, 129,
    130, 180, 226
    children's 29, 45
    citizens' 76
    civil 28–30
    cultural 28
    economic 28–30
    equal 50

ethical 28
for young people 44
human 33, 34, 37
inalienable 30
individual 27, 28, 29
lesbian and gay 29
national 28
of global citizenship 140
of pupils 47
political 28–30
social 28–30
rigour 26

Saltair 13, 14, 16, 17, 18, 97,
    105
SCAA 114
School Curriculum Industry
    Partnership 75
schools
    British state 13, 60
    comprehensive 76, 79, 96,
        110, 116, 117, 142
    free 60–62, 237
    grammar 219
    independent 60
    inspectors 26
    managers 27
    primary 10, 11, 64, 67, 68,
        180, 226, 228
    private 58, 60, 61
    programmes 17
    secondary 9, 10, 11, 13, 64,
        67, 68, 96, 110, 111,
        115, 116, 173, 180,
        226, 228
    secondary modern 18, 219
    state 10, 11, 32
    tertiary 10, 83, 180
science 36, 53, 54, 120, 124,
    125, 126, 133, 134, 135,
    138, 139
Scotland 27
Scottish National Party 28
SEAC 114
sense of audience (see also
    independent learning
    factor 10) 19, 23, 230
Shaun 93
silenced, the 19, 20, 21,
    84–88, 94, 112, 225
    teachers as the silenced 87
    silencing of the
        disempowered 140
    silencing of the researcher
        87–88
Sir James Redbourne 116–142
Social Democratic Party 30
Sources of Electrical Energy
    146–149

South Africa 42, 234
South America 42
Soviet Union 42
Speaker's Commission on
    Citizenship 218
standards 26
Star Trek 43
study LEA, the 11, 64, 67, 68,
    79, 81, 87, 96, 110, 111,
    114, 116, 142, 153, 173,
    217, 220, 221, 222, 226
Swann Report 32, 75
syllabi, content-laden 9, 141
synthesis of education and
    citizenship 10, 44–50

talk 19, 75, 117, 119–122,
    128, 130–134
    pupil-to-pupil 130, 132, 134
    teacher-led 117, 119, 120,
        121, 122, 124, 130,
        132, 133, 134, 135, 137
task allocation 92, 210
task sharing 92, 210
technology (see also independent
    learning factor 8) 18, 24,
    81, 122, 124, 170, 220
tests 26, 48, 200, 220, 221,
    222, 237
texts 19, 20, 56, 75, 86, 117,
    123, 134, 136, 180, 195,
    220, 230
Thatcherism 30
Theatre Arts 20, 21
theory-in-the-literature 21, 25,
    49, 111, 112
third millennium 9, 25, 27, 49,
    62, 105, 142
time management (see also
    independent learning
    factor 6) 23, 93, 114,
    170, 172, 191, 194,
    205–207, 231
timetable 27, 36, 61, 63, 67,
    79, 81, 110, 116, 117,
    125, 126, 129, 139, 140,
    173
totalitarianism 29, 42, 223,
    229
traditions 26
trust 19, 195
tutor 21
TVEI 24, 75, 121

Ulster Unionists 28
Unesco Convention Against
    Discrimination in
    Education 43
United Kingdom 9, 10, 11, 27,
    28, 30, 36, 57, 62, 110,

114, 142, 218, 220, 221,
    226, 233
United Nations Conference on
    the Environment 218
United Nations Convention on
    the Rights of the Child
    41, 42, 218
Universal Declaration of Human
    Rights 41
USSR 54

video (see also independent
    learning factor 8) 17, 80,
    84, 93, 104, 144–146,
    173, 175, 184, 190, 195,
    201–202, 205
    camera 100, 101, 169
    hire libraries 16
    lesson(s) 17, 18
    recorder 16
    recordings 20, 70, 74, 108,
        153
    watching 123, 130, 135
Vanessa 93
voicing 19, 20, 21, 84–87, 88,
    104, 105, 112, 141, 225
Voice of the Child Project
    218
voice of the pupil 20, 85,
    141
volleyball 130, 135, 138

Wales 27
Welsh National Party 28
Western Europe 29
Woodhead, Chris 143, 201
worksheet(s) 16, 117, 123,
    134, 239
World Cup 43
World Environmental
    Conference 43
writing 14
    at Keystage 3 123–124
    at Keystage 4 134

youth unemployment 18
youth training schemes 18